MAUD CUNEY HARE

NEGRO MUSICIANS AND THEIR MUSIC

AFRICAN-AMERICAN WOMEN WRITERS, 1910–1940

HENRY LOUIS GATES, JR. *GENERAL EDITOR*

Jennifer Burton *Associate Editor*

MAUD CUNEY HARE

NEGRO MUSICIANS
AND THEIR MUSIC

Introduction by
JOSEPHINE HARRELD LOVE

G. K. HALL & CO.
An Imprint of Simon & Schuster Macmillan
New York

Prentice Hall International
London Mexico City New Delhi Singapore Sydney Toronto

G. K. Hall & Co.
An Imprint of Simon & Schuster Macmillan
1633 Broadway
New York, NY 10019

Library of Congress Catalog Card Number: 96-17696

Printed in the United States of America

Printing Number
1 2 3 4 5 6 7 8 9 10

Library of Congress Cataloging-in-Publication Data

Cuney-Hare, Maud, 1874-1936.
  Negro musicians and their music / Maud Cuney-Hare ; introduction
  by Josephine Harreld Love.
    Includes bibliographical references.
    ISBN 0-7838-1417-8 (alk. paper)
    1. Afro-American musicians. 2. Afro-Americans—Music—History and
criticism. 3. Music—United States—History and criticism.
4. Music—Africa—History and criticism.   I. Love, Josephine
Harreld.   II. Title III. Series.
  ML3556.H32   1994
  780' .89'96—dc20   96-17696
                                                                   CIP
                                                                   MN

This paper meets the requirements of ANSI/NISO Z39.48.1992 (Permanence of Paper).

CONTENTS

GENERAL EDITORS' PREFACE

The past decade of our literary history might be thought of as the era of African-American women writers. Culminating in the awarding of the Pulitzer Prize to Toni Morrison and Rita Dove and the Nobel Prize for Literature to Toni Morrison in 1993 and characterized by the presence of several writers—Toni Morrison, Alice Walker, Maya Angelou, and the Delaney Sisters, among others—on the *New York Times* Best Seller List, the shape of the most recent period in our literary history has been determined in large part by the writings of black women.

This, of course, has not always been the case. African-American women authors have been publishing their thoughts and feelings at least since 1773, when Phillis Wheatley published her book of poems in London, thereby bringing poetry directly to bear upon the philosophical discourse over the African's "place in nature" and his or her place in the great chain of being. The scores of words published by black women in America in the nineteenth century—most of which were published in extremely limited editions and never reprinted—have been republished in new critical editions in the forty-volume *Schomburg Library of Nineteenth-Century Black Women Writers*. The critical response to that series has led to requests from scholars and students alike for a similar series, one geared to the work by black women published between 1910 and the beginning of World War Two.

African-American Women Writers, 1910–1940 is designed to bring back into print many writers who otherwise would be unknown to contemporary readers, and to increase the availability of lesser-known texts by established writers who originally published during this critical period in African-American letters. This series implicitly acts as a chronological sequel to the Schomburg series, which focused on the origins of the black female literary tradition in America.

In less than a decade, the study of African-American women's writings has grown from its promising beginnings into a firmly established field in departments of English, American Studies, and African-American Studies. A comparison of the form and function of the original series and this sequel illustrates this dramatic shift. The *Schomburg Library* was published at the cusp of focused academic investigation into the interplay between race and gender. It covered the extensive period from the publication of Phillis Wheatley's *Poems on Various Subjects, Religious and Moral* in 1773 through the "Black Women's Era" of 1890–1910, and was designed to be an inclusive series of the major early texts by black women writers. The Schomburg Library provided a historical backdrop for black women's writings of the 1970s and 1980s, including the works of writers such as Toni Morrison, Alice Walker, Maya Angelou, and Rita Dove.

African-American Women Writers, 1910–1940 continues our effort to provide a new generation of readers access to texts—historical, sociological, and literary—that have been largely "unread" for most of this century. The series bypasses works that are important both to the period and the tradition, but that are readily available, such as Zora Neale Hurston's *Their Eyes Were Watching God*, Jessie Fauset's *Plum Bun* and *There Is Confusion*, and Nella Larsen's *Quicksand* and *Passing*. Our goal is to provide access to a wide variety of rare texts. The series includes Fauset's two other novels, *The Chinaberry Tree: A Novel of American Life* and *Comedy: American Style*, and Hurston's short play *Color Struck*, since these are not yet widely available. It also features works by virtually unknown writers, such as *A Tiny Spark*, Christina Moody's slim volume of poetry self-published in 1910, and *Reminiscences of School Life, and Hints on Teaching*, written by Fanny Jackson Coppin in the last year of her life (1913), a multi-genre work combining an autobiographical sketch and reflections on trips to England and South Africa, complete with pedagogical advice.

Cultural studies' investment in diverse resources allows the historic scope of the *African-American Women Writers* series to be more focused than the *Schomburg Library* series, which covered works written over a 137-year period. With few exceptions, the authors included in the *African-American Women Writers* series wrote their major works between 1910 and 1940. The texts reprinted include all the works by each particular author that are not otherwise readily obtainable. As a result, two volumes contain works originally published after 1940. The Charlotte Hawkins Brown volume includes her book of etiquette published in 1941, *The Correct Thing To Do—To Say—To Wear*. One of the poetry volumes contains Maggie Pogue Johnson's *Fallen Blossoms*, published in 1951, a compilation of all her previously published and unpublished poems.

Excavational work by scholars during the past decade has been crucial to the development of *African-American Women Writers, 1910–1940*. Germinal bibliographical sources such as Ann Allen Shockley's *Afro-American Women Writers 1746–1933* and Maryemma Graham's *Database of African-American Women Writers* made the initial identification of texts possible. Other works were brought to our attention by scholars who wrote letters sharing their research. Additional texts by selected authors were then added, so that many volumes contain the complete oeuvres of particular writers. Pieces by authors without enough published work to fill an entire volume were grouped with other pieces by genre.

The two types of collections, those organized by author and those organized by genre, bring out different characteristics of black women's writings of the period. The collected works of the literary writers illustrate that many of them were experimenting with a variety of forms. Mercedes Gilbert's volume, for example, contains her 1931 collection *Selected Gems of Poetry, Comedy, and Drama, Etc.*, as well as her 1938 novel *Aunt Sarah's Wooden God*. Georgia Douglas Johnson's volume contains her plays and short stories in addition to her poetry. Sarah Lee Brown Fleming's volume combines her 1918 novel *Hope's Highway* with her 1920 collection of poetry, *Clouds and Sunshine*.

The generic volumes both bring out the formal and thematic similarities among many of the writings and highlight the striking individuality of particular writers. Most of the plays in the volume of one-acts are social dramas whose tragic endings can be clearly attributed to miscegenation and racism. Within the context of these other plays, Marita Bonner's surrealistic theatrical vision becomes all the more striking.

The volumes of *African-American Women Writers, 1910–1940* contain reproductions of more than one hundred previously published texts, including twenty-nine plays, seventeen poetry collections, twelve novels, six autobiographies, five collections of short biographical sketches, three biographies, three histories of organizations, three black histories, two anthologies, two sociological studies, a diary, and a book of etiquette. Each volume features an introduction by a contemporary scholar that provides crucial biographical data on each author and the historical and critical context of her work. In some cases, little information on the authors was available outside of the fragments of biographical data contained in the original introduction or in the text itself. In these instances, editors have documented the libraries and research centers where they tried to find information, in the hope that subsequent scholars will continue the necessary search to find the "lost" clues to the women's stories in the rich stores of papers, letters, photographs, and other primary materials scattered throughout the country that have yet to be fully catalogued.

Many of the thrilling moments that occurred during the development of this series were the result of previously fragmented pieces of these women's histories suddenly coming together, such as Adele Alexander's uncovering of an old family photograph picturing her own aunt with Addie Hunton, the author Alexander was researching. Claudia Tate's examination of Georgia Douglas Johnson's papers in the Moorland-Spingarn Research Center of Howard University resulted in the discovery of a wealth of previously unpublished work.

The slippery quality of race itself emerged during the construction of the series. One of the short novels originally intended for inclusion in the series had to be cut when the family of the author protested that the writer was not of African descent. Another case involved Louise Kennedy's sociological study *The Negro Peasant Turns Inward*. The fact that none of the available biographical material on Kennedy specifically mentioned race, combined with some coded criticism in a review in the *Crisis*, convinced editor Sheila Smith McKoy that Kennedy was probably white.

These women, taken together, began to chart the true vitality, and complexity, of the literary tradition that African-American women have generated, using a wide variety of forms. They testify to the fact that the monumental works of Hurston, Larsen, and Fauset, for example, emerged out of a larger cultural context; they were not exceptions or aberrations. Indeed, their contributions to American literature and culture, as this series makes clear, were fundamental not only to the shaping of the African-American tradition but to the American tradition as well.

Henry Louis Gates, Jr.
Jennifer Burton

PUBLISHER'S NOTE

In the *African-American Women Writers, 1910–1940* series, G. K. Hall not only is making available previously neglected works that in many cases have been long out of print, we are also, whenever possible, publishing these works in facsimiles reprinted from their original editions including, when available, reproductions of original title pages, copyright pages, and photographs.

When it was not possible for us to reproduce a complete facsimile edition of a particular work (for example, if the original exists only as a handwritten draft or is too fragile to be reproduced), we have attempted to preserve the essence of the original by resetting the work exactly as it originally appeared. Therefore, any typographical errors, strikeouts, or other anomalies reflect our efforts to give the reader a true sense of the original work.

We trust that these facsimile and reprint editions, together with the new introductory essays, will be both useful and historically enlightening to scholars and students alike.

INTRODUCTION

BY JOSEPHINE HARRELD LOVE

Almost sixty years have passed since the 1936 publication of Maud Cuney Hare's *Negro Musicians and Their Music*, close to two-thirds of a century of profound change and development in the field of historical research and writing on music created by the people of Africa or those of African ancestry living in other parts of the world. The music has itself undergone developments brought about naturally during the course of aesthetic evolution and revolution. Use of the terms *musicology* and *ethnomusicology* has become far more readily acceptable within academic disciplines. Scholars have moved into these areas and are producing increasing numbers of thoughtful, thoroughly researched studies. Popular acceptance of black performers has changed considerably on the concert and dance stage, in opera houses, and in venues of chamber and orchestral music, to say nothing of numerous varied musical expressions created purely and primarily for popular entertainment—in the theatre, dancehall, nightclub, and electronic media. Nevertheless, Maud Cuney Hare's unique contribution continues as a priceless legacy of accomplished documentation of contributions within the field of music made by black peoples of the world through the 1920s and into the mid-1930s, the time of her death, and is valuable for meticulous, sensitive scholarship, discernment, and devotion.

Only one such consolidated effort preceded hers. James Monroe Trotter, interestingly enough also a resident of Boston, wrote a general history, *Music and Some Highly Musical People*, published in 1878, that prefigured any other attempt by an

American writer of any race to produce a general history of music in the United States. It has been described by music historian Eileen Southern, author of *The Music of Black Americans*, as a "landmark in the field of writings about black American music."[1] It was unique for its time, the period to the date of its publication, and for its contents. James Trotter, incidentally, was not a music scholar but a Civil War lieutenant, a prominent Democrat, one of the first black officers in the Boston Post Office, and later, Recorder of Deeds for the District of Columbia, a post that had been held by Frederick Douglass. Louis Frederick Rutter's 1883 volume, *Music in America*, was an earnest but pallid effort to write a general history of music in the United States. Trotter's book preceded it by five years and remains valuable, readable, and usable by reason of the quality of his writing and painstaking information-gathering.

Maud Cuney Hare's *Negro Musicians and Their Music* was copyrighted and published in 1936 by Associated Publishers, Inc. of Washington. In the preface Mrs. Hare wrote, "The Negro, a musical force through his own distinct racial characteristics, has made an artistic contribution which is racial but not yet national. Rather has the influence of musical stylistic traits termed Negro, spread over many nations wherever the colonies of the New World have become homes of Negro people." Read today, sixty years later, the words seem prophetic. Mrs. Hare continued with an observation that melodic and rhythmic expressions of Negro music were a compelling force in American music that influenced thoughtful musicians throughout the world. One becomes even more appreciative of the writer's prescience and her ability to cast a long shadow into comprehension of the world of music today and the debt owed to musicians of African descent and origin.

The preface, written from "Sunnyside," in Squantum on Massachusetts's North Shore, is signed and dated January 30, 1936, exactly two weeks to the day before her death on February 13. She was in her sixty-second year. Completion of writing had been undertaken over a period of prolonged poor health following a surgical procedure from which she never fully recovered. However, the quality of her research and writing seems in no way to have been affected by her condition.

Republication of *Negro Musicians and Their Music* is long overdue, and a much-to-be-welcomed event in the documentation of music history. At the time of initial publication, it made available rare information about African music and its tributary musics in the western hemisphere. As such, it was of inestimable value, all the more to be appreciated when one considers the circumstances surrounding Mrs. Hare's efforts. In contrast to the financial resources music scholars today often have at their disposal, her efforts would have been undertaken out of pocket: the trips to libraries, archives, and depositories of papers, correspondence, reproduction, and all of the incidental costs leading to publication. I am certain also that Associated Publishers, who issued the book, would have been in no position to offer more than a modest fee for her effort. This is in contrast to rates of compensation for today's scholarly output, small as they may seem sometimes to those involved in producing treatises in various fields.

I have been increasingly fascinated during the course of preparation for this assignment, the writing of an introduction for republication of *Negro Musicians*. It would have been a textbook used alongside others available for "Music of Black Americans," a course I have offered from time to time in three of Michigan's state universities: Oakland, the University of Michigan, Ann Arbor, and Wayne State over the past twenty-five years but was not in print and had to be placed on reference shelves for these courses, for lectures and seminars given elsewhere, and for various writings. It was my good fortune to inherit the book as part of the musical legacy from my father, Kemper Harreld, who had over the years assembled a remarkable music library. The book was purchased by him, I am sure, shortly after the first printing in 1936. I do not recall a time during earlier years of my life when the name of Maud Cuney Hare was not referred to, although I have no memory of having seen or met her in person. I am sure that my father knew her and I may yet discover additional correspondence from her among his papers, which I explore on a periodic basis, hoping for the time and ability to investigate them more thoroughly, and to sort and assign them to appropriate repositories. In my possession are a few documents she sent to him and one program sent by a friend living in the Virgin Islands.

Mrs. Hare does mention the name Harreld in complimentary terms in the book, referring to his contributions in the field of music, intercollegiate orchestral concerts presented in Atlanta, Georgia, and the role he played over the years in the founding and development of the National Association of Negro Musicians. She also writes about his Morehouse College quartet's appearances at the White House during Franklin Roosevelt's presidency, large festival choruses he recruited citywide and conducted on various occasions in Atlanta, his violin recitals, and his college and studio teaching of music.

As I leaf through the book I encounter names and faces that are familiar—musicians of my parents' generation, visitors in our house during my early and middle childhood, whose artistic ambitions were encouraged by a circle of responsible, knowledgeable music patrons recruited by my parents, their friends, and faculty colleagues at Atlanta's colleges, and by those at greater distances. Many of the artists were close family friends. They shared various platforms within a somewhat closed—by custom and social code— racially divided concert circuit. Beyond that are musicians and other persons known only by name from reading and reference. They represent fascinating linkages within a historic past.

One might describe Maud Cuney Hare as a musical archaeologist who unearthed treasures of an Africa-based musical Pompeii and Herculaneum that had rarely been explored. As far as one can determine, she worked on her own and was well equipped for the undertaking. An earlier book, published in 1913, the biography of her father, is as meticulously researched in the sphere of Southern politics.[2] She had lived between the Deep South and Massachusetts, with the exception of a short time spent in Chicago. During almost four decades spent in New England, she would have enjoyed visiting libraries close at hand that were well stocked with valuable resource materials. Many are listed in an impressive bibliography—books, periodicals, manuscripts, musical scores, papers of one sort and another, photographs, and a variety of documents. She was able also to visit libraries at a distance—in New York, Washington, and cities outside the United States. Folk-song research took her to areas of Creole culture, especially those around her hometown of Galveston, Texas, and the New Orleans, Louisiana, vicinity.

Her connection with various periodicals offered further advantages. She contributed articles to *Musical America*, the *Musical Observer*, *Christian Science Monitor*, and to listings of events important to music and art reported in columns of *Crisis* magazine. An essay written by her appeared in Nancy Cunard's *Negro*, published in 1934 by Wishart and Company.

The story of her life is an exceptional one. She was born on February 16, 1874, in Galveston, and was the daughter of Norris Wright and Adelina Dowdy Cuney. Her father, of Indian, African, and Swiss-American extraction, had married the youngest of the five "handsome Dowdy girls" of Woodville, Mississippi. By the time of their daughter's birth he was well established among Texas politicians, a distinction he would enjoy up to the time of his death in 1897. Both parents were products of mixed-race alliances between slave parents and slave-master fathers who were able and willing to offer their offspring exceptional advantages for personal development. The elder Cuneys loved music. Both sang, and Adelina played the piano. Wright, as he was usually addressed, favored Irish songs, martial tunes, and Italian opera airs.

His marriage to Adelina Dowdy took place on July 5, 1871. Family history and the employment and pastimes of members of her family undoubtedly are significant clues to understanding the development of Maud Cuney Hare's interests and eventual undertakings. Life in the Cuney home was infused with love of natural and man-made beauty. Despite some physical frailty, the mother was a devoted gardener. She cultivated a variety of rosebushes and other flowering plants and planted orange, plum, pomegranate, purple fig, and mulberry trees on whose branches her children often sat and read. At Eastertime they assisted her in stripping the garden for bouquets of flowers that were sent to Galveston hospitals.

Wright's three older brothers lived close by. Their children helped form a cadre of Cuney playmates in play areas, at the beach, and wherever they assembled for family outings and celebrations. Traditional New Year's Eve gatherings of the children were followed on New Year's Day by more sedate receptions for grownups. Among the books given at Christmas were examples of literature produced in New England such as Edward Everett Hale and his sister's *A Family Flight Around Home*. Older cousins Richard and Wright Cuney read and rehearsed scenes from the plays of Shakespeare, while siblings Nisi, Philip, and Daisy and cousins Lloyd and Maud formed a devoted audience. Theatre at another level was experienced during family trips to Boston. As a matter of principle the Cuneys never crossed the threshold of the segregated theatre houses in the South. Family visits were made also to San Antonio, followed by overnight trips to Mexico's lovely gardens and the foothills of the Sierra Madre mountains.

Norris Wright Cuney would later be described by his daughter as "my worshipping and worshipped father." Home life was tranquil and family gatherings filled with the joyful companionship of children and adults. On the outside conditions were far less agreeable, characterized by political unrest, mounting violence, and accelerating mob action such as news of lynchings in nearby Ford Bend County and threats to possible victims, who were nevertheless given asylum in the Cuney home.

Following graduation from Galveston's Central High School, Maud was sent, in 1890, to visit family and friends in Newport, Rhode Island, and in the fall she moved to Boston to enroll at the New England Conservatory of Music. As a piano major, she studied this discipline with Franz Liszt's student Edwin Klahre and theory under Martin Roeder, followed by lessons with Edwin Ludwig, a pupil, during earlier years, of Anton Rubenstein.

Assigned to the Conservatory's boarding residence, Maud shared a room with another African-American student. Shortly afterward, conservatory officials, with obvious insensitivity and lack of principle, suggested off-campus housing for both young ladies in panicked response to protests on the part of a handful of white student residents. Wright Cuney, responding to his daughter's bewilderment, wrote directly to the Conservatory's director in defiant protest. At the same time he tactfully suggested to Maud that she sit out the controversy—and she did. One can only hope that the prejudices of her schoolmates subsided to the extent at least of not adding to any further discomfort on her part. In all likelihood, however, her strongest defense was the innate sense of security and self-confidence that appears to have been characteristic of an outlook on life in general cultivated from early childhood.

Details of her life during the years spent in Boston from 1891 to about 1896 or '97 are not abundantly available. She is mentioned in David Levering Lewis's *W. E. B. Du Bois: Biography of a Race* (1994) as having moved within an elite circle of black Bostonians accustomed to gathering in the home of Mrs. Josephine St. Pierre Ruffin for social, literary, and musical evenings. William Edward Burghardt Du Bois, candidate for a graduate degree in social science at Harvard University, was among the regular visitors. Du Bois apparently fell almost immediately and deeply in love with Maud. In his autobiography he described her as a "tall, imperious brunette, with golden bronze skin, brilliant eyes and coils of black hair."[3] She referred to him affectionately as "Du" and frequently was escorted by him to social affairs on and off the Harvard campus. They went boating on the Charles River and visited friends on other New England college campuses. One of these trips was to the 1892 graduation from Amherst College of mutual friends. In his autobiography Du Bois states that they were engaged. He wrote, "That he would also be leaving Maud Cuney behind, if the fund recognized his claim, was the bittersweet price of destiny."[4] The engagement was broken but the friendship lasted more than forty years. Comments made by him at the time of her death are deeply affecting.

Maud was visited by her father in 1892, following his involvement in that year's Republican convention, held during June. They traveled home by boat, leaving July 9 onboard the S.S. *Concho* of the Mallory Line. The captain was one of Cuney's wide circle of friends. In *Sketch Made at Sea*, an account of the voyage, Edwin Markham, a fellow traveler, wrote, "We stand the latest, and if we fail, probably the last, experiment of self-government by the people. Hon. Wright Cuney, the head of the Republican Party in Texas and Collector of the Port of Galveston, is one of the men to make the experiment successful. He is among our passengers, returning with his daughter to their home and post." Wright Cuney lived until his fifty-second year. He died in 1898. Maud Cuney had by that time returned to Texas.

In 1897 Maud was appointed director of music at the Texas Deaf, Dumb and Blind Institute in Austin. During the following year, 1898, she married Dr. J. Frank McKinley, a local physician.

The marriage lasted only a few years. Shortly after their wedding the couple moved to Chicago. Dr. McKinley had established a successful medical practice in the South among African-American people but found this to be less profitable than expected. He decided, apparently with considerable forethought, to abandon a black clientele and discard any pretext of social or professional attachment among persons of his own race. He demanded that his and Maud's daughter, born in 1900, be kept ignorant of her parents' racial identity and asked Maud to subscribe to the racial designation *Spanish-American* and to abandon all relationships on a social level with members of their own race. During the years 1900 to 1901, however, she was employed in the settlement program of the Institutional Baptist Church on Chicago's South Side, a neighborhood rapidly becoming characterized by its steady influx of African Americans directly from the South.

In 1892 she left McKinley, and stated publicly her intention not to abandon her racial identity and connections. She returned to Texas, found employment at the newly established State Industrial College for Negroes in Prairie View. Two years later her husband successfully sued for divorce and for the care of their daughter. Maud was not present to enter a protest but when notified of the divorce, she returned to Chicago where she was able to effect a mild compromise in arrangements for the child that awarded her custody three months each year. This ruling was overturned, however, in 1904 when she married Boston's William Parker Hare and returned to live in that city. Massachusetts would be her home for the rest of her life. Two years later Dr. McKinley remarried and obtained total responsibility for the daughter. Following her marriage to Hare, Maud had refused to honor the previous agreement. The child died in 1908, following a prolonged illness.

In Boston Maud Cuney McKinley Hare became increasingly involved in music, as a private studio teacher of piano, a performer, and, frequently, as an accompanist. In 1910 W. E. B. Du Bois was appointed editor of the NAACP's *Crisis* magazine, and within a short time Maud Hare became music and art correspondent for the magazine, contributing items of interest within the world of fine arts to a music and art column. She applied her considerable energies also to writing and research. Her first major efforts as a writer resulted in an impressively well-documented and researched nonmusic volume, a biography of her father, entitled *Norris Wright Cuney*. Published by the Crisis Publishing Company in 1913, it remains on some library shelves these eighty-odd years later and is a fascinating chronicle of an extraordinary life and career.

The author's bent toward meticulous research methods is evident throughout the volume. She writes as one who understands perfectly the "ins and outs" of the American political system, with the ability to express thoughts and opinions openly and with ease. Her career as a writer was underway.

A second, more ambitious undertaking was an anthology of poetry, *Message of the Trees*, published in 1918. The foreword was written by Boston's eminent black poet, literary journalist, critic, commentator, and anthologist William Stanley Braithwaite. The book's general appearance is most attractive, with a simulated bark book cover and leaf woodprint-decorated endpapers. The subtitle reads "an anthology of leaves and branches" and the dedication is

TO MY LITTLE DAUGHTER
VERA
1900–1908

Here are the budding boughs again,
   But where the budding child,
That from greener slopes to green shores
   Last April was beguiled?

O little life, with all thy buds
   Close-folded-laid in death;
Would they had oped in bloom and fruit
   About thy mother's path

The verses were written by Ethelwynn Wetherald, whose poems appear among those in the collection. Acknowledgments are made to publishing houses and magazines, and to individual poets or members of their families who gave permission for publication of the poems and passages of prose in the anthology. Charming headings separate the groupings—*The Leafy World, Message of the Trees, From Brown Boughs Breaking, Talking Branches* and *Whispering Leaves, Bare Ruined Choirs,* and *Comforts and Consolations* are among those used. Sources are widespread—American, European, and Middle and Far Eastern. A number of Mrs. Hare's selections represent a cadre of emerging poets of the early twentieth century. Efforts of small publishing houses are represented.

During this period she was also responsible for numerous musical programs. In 1912 distinguished Afro-British composer Samuel Coleridge-Taylor died. A memorial tribute presented on January 13 of the following year at Jordan Hall in Boston undoubtedly was organized by Maud Cuney Hare and a memorial address was delivered by W. E. B. Du Bois. The program's roster of distinguished musicians included Roland Hayes, tenor; Harry T. Burleigh, baritone; Melville Charlton, organist; William Richardson, baritone; Jacques Hoffman, violinist, and Ludwig Nast, cellist, of the Boston Symphony Orchestra, and organist Frederic White. Earlier, on October 16, 1912, a "Concert of Colored Composers" was presented at Boston's Columbus Avenue AME Zion Church that Mrs. Hare had assisted in organizing. Listed on the program were works of well-known composers Coleridge-Taylor, J. Rosamund Johnson, Clarence Cameron White, and a group of musicians practically unheard of today who were prominent at the time, among them J. Shelton Pollen, a Washington pianist, whose *Fantasie Stücke* for violin was being premiered; songwriter Henry Williams of Washington; Hartley Benson; M. Hamilton Hodges, who is mentioned on the program as having studios in Boston *and* in Wellington, New Zealand; DeKoven Thompson, a Chicago organist and songwriter, whose songs had apparently been included in the concert repertoire of Mme. Ernestine Schumann-Heink. Maud Hare is listed as pianist, program director, annotator, and accompanist of baritone William H. Richardson. Over the period of more than twenty years that would follow, Richardson was a close friend and collaborator. The duo toured much of the United States and the Virgin Islands, making frequent appearances in and around Boston. The *Negro Musicians and Their Music* dedication reads:

TO
WILLIAM HOWARD RICHARDSON
BARITONE
IN REMEMBRANCE OF
TWENTY HAPPY YEARS OF
MUSICAL PARTNERSHIP

Richardson, born in 1869, was a native of Liverpool, Nova Scotia, whose family had moved to Boston during his childhood. He received there the major portion of his training as a concert singer. He appeared often as soloist in performances of oratorio and opera and was a successful studio voice instructor. Philip Hale, Boston's veteran music critic, spoke of his "virile, rich, and beautiful voice. He not only sang artistically, he gave significance to the music as the expression of the verse."

Hare and Richardson recitals assumed a unique format—the programming of conventional fare: works of world-famous composers of the seventeenth to the twentieth centuries—Scarlatti, Handel, Leoncavallo, Gabriel Fauré, Rachmaninoff, Elgar, Schubert, Massanet, Liszt, Chabrier, Verdi, Hahn, Cyril Scott, and Schoenberg. They also performed compositions of the less well-known British and American composers Granville Bantock, Frank LaForge, Edward Kilyeni, Warren Storey Smith, Kurt Schindler, Charles Gilbert Spago, Carrie Jacobs Bond, and Arthur Foote, as well as a fascinating array of black American, British, and West Indian musicians: Coleridge-Taylor, Montagu Ring, Edward Margetson, Alton Adams, Edmund Dédé, and Gottschalk. Included also on the programs was music of Egypt, Morocco, Persia, Mexico, and the Middle East. Of singular value were Maud's collecting and performing of French and Spanish Creole folk music that she had gathered over the span of many years, a pioneering effort.[5] Mrs. Hare's songs were assembled and recorded many years before similar, more widely distributed efforts such as that made by Howard University faculty member and native of

New Orleans Camille Nickerson, published in 1942 by the Boston Music Company, and collections by Gilles Salla, Rene Beaux, and Henry Wehrmann distributed by New Orleans's Philip Welein in 1946, and the compilation from Paris Editions Vianelly in 1950, the last-named obviously inspired by appearances in concerts given by a group of young Creole women.

Programs from Hare and Richardson recitals include groups labeled "Songs from the Orient and Tropics," "Afro-American and Creole Folk Music," and "Educational Recitals." The two musicians often appeared in costume. Occasional collaborating performers were well-known concert artists—Hartford, Connecticut, pianist R. Augustus Lawson, Clarence Cameron White, composer/violinist, and composer/pianist Carl Diton. A program presented at Boston's Jordan Hall on January 30, 1919, contains the name of Arthur Fiedler. Remembered today as conductor of widely televised concerts by the Boston Pops Orchestra and recently deceased, he is listed as an accompanist.

Maud Cuney Hare established more than one studio for teaching piano in Boston. The Musical Art Studio is listed at 295 Huntington Avenue, opposite the New England Conservatory, one block from Symphony Hall and from the Boston Opera House and the Allen A. Brown music library housed in Boston's main library. An earlier studio location was 43 Sheridan Steet in Jamaica Plain. Mrs. Hare is listed as teaching piano and theory and offering lecture courses in music history and appreciation, studio musicales, exhibits, class lessons, and library research services. William Richardson gave voice lessons.

In his introduction to the book *Negro Musicians* White mentions Mrs. Hare's sponsorship of the "Little Theatre" movement in the Boston area, an art center connection, and her authorship of an original play, *Antar of Araby*, based on the real life of a seventh-century Arab/Abyssinian slave poet. Mention is made elsewhere of her organization and sponsorship of an Allied Arts Centre, a training school, and a theatre group, the Allied Art Players, referred to as the first "Colored Little Theatre" in Boston. A photograph of actors in their costumes for *Antar* appears in *Crisis* magazine, in an issue from the 1920s. Mentioned in the Boston *Guardian* obituary notice is her connection with a

"Primitive African Art Center." Individuals involved in these groups would, after its discontinuance, move on to other drama organizations and appearances in leading productions on Boston and New York stages,

Maud Cuney Hare's writings of shorter length—*Music and Art* columns in *Crisis* magazine, articles published between 1910 and 1935 in the musical journals *Musical America* and *Musical Observer* and in the *Christian Science Monitor*—demonstrate her wide-ranging knowledge and her sensitive and insightful commentary. Of additional interest are two essays that appeared in an extraordinary publication of 1934 created and edited by Nancy Cunard and titled, simply, *Negro*. Its 855-page contents, gathered from more than eighty of the world's most capable writers, covered a broad spectrum of subjects, all relating to matters affecting members of the black race around the world.

Maud Hare's contributions, titled "Folk Music of the Creoles" and "Negro Music in Puerto Rico," are packed with delightful details and illuminating observations. She defines the term "Creole" as it applies to persons of blended ancestry—French, Spanish, African, Native American—in differing ratios. Both are fascinating accounts of the unique song and dance traditions of people of the French and Spanish West Indies, coastal Louisiana, and neighboring regions short distances across state lines whose splendid linguistic patois reflects their French settler origins.

Her descriptions of various locales associated with Creole people, recital of historic events, definitions of terms, and analyses of characteristic song, dance, movement, and verse reveal the broad range of her scholarly investigations. Coupled with her superior literary and language skills, these resonate well when placed alongside the greatly extended musicological scholarship of today.

A printed announcement dated March 26, 1935, less than a year before Mrs. Hare's death, advertises

The Musical Art History Course
A national study course with complete survey of the contributions of
the Afro-American to the
art of music,

a correspondence course designed to "give a complete and thorough understanding of the various phases of the art with particular attention paid to the part played by colored musicians from the 6th century to the present day. The story of the Negro in music goes side by side with the growth of art, and embraces facts drawn from my personal collection of Early American, Afroamerican and Creole Music." The announcement goes on to propose a plan for the course's adoption and suggests formation of classes of twenty or more students led by a local "counselor" under her direction. She also lists annual contests, quarterly question tests, honors awards, and the eventual possibility of an annual scholarship to be offered for the study of voice and piano in Boston. The costs listed are extraordinary—"90 cents per student per term of 9 months." The two-page document bears her signature and under this, "Chronicler-teacher."

Of additional interest is a lengthy review of one of the Hare-Richardson folk-song lectures in the *New York Age* "In the Realm of Music" column written by Lucien H. White. The program, presented in Brooklyn, New York, during February 1920, opened with African war and coronation songs, sung by William Richardson, and followed by a group of spirituals, love and play songs, and a sea chanty, Spanish-Creole songs, piano compositions written around Creole and West Indian folk themes, and a varied closing group of southern Louisiana folk-song arrangements. Comments were made by Mrs. Hare throughout the program. Of interest is the distinction made between *Creole* and *Place Congo of New Orleans* music.

Maud Cuney Hare died on February 14, 1936. Services were held three days later at Boston's E. L. Morrison's Chapel and at St. Peter's Episcopal Church in Cambridge. An obituary column in *The Guardian*,[6] Boston's African-American weekly newspaper, describes the final rites at great length. A group of players from the little theatre formed by her presided over the morning's memorial service in the funeral home chapel, with music performed by a string trio and readings by former Allied Arts Players. During the early afternoon, services took place in Cambridge. The article concludes with names of close surviving relatives: her husband, William P. Hare, and her brother, Lloyd G. Cuney. It also lists names of donors of floral tributes that are interesting in their revelation of a wide circle of friendships.

The obituary mentions also the fact that at the time of her death Maud Hare was awaiting release of *Negro Musicians and Their Music* and that during the final days of her life she had read proofs from her sickbed. It refers to the critical role she played at the center of the cultural life of Boston.

The reissue of *Negro Musicians and Their Music* offers evidence of an extraordinary early effort to document African-American music and its progenitors. There are fifteen chapter headings, preface, appendix, bibliography, and index. It contains sixteen pages of illustrations. Although the author proofread the book during her final illness, one finds no evidence of diminished power. An introduction was written by her close friend and musical associate Clarence Cameron White, who at the time was living in Boston and performing in England. Footnotes throughout the volume are of great value and supply marvelously detailed information.

Chapters 1 and 2 trace African-American music to continental Africa's early history. Linkages with the West Indies and the southern United States are referred to and musical illustrations presented. Tribal practice is described, dance and song given names, various archaeological dig findings reported. Obviously, she consulted numerous sources of information available at the time and drew parallels between customs and rites of Africa and those of black America. Classics of African research literature—writings of Herskovitz, Junot, Frobenius, and Burton and periodical comment, French and American, had been consulted. She mentions African groups seen and heard in live performance or on the radio.

Chapter 2 presents evidence of the influence of the music of Africa on that of the United States. Mentioned also is Nicholas Ballanta of Sierra Leone, whose visits to St. Helena Island off the coast of South Carolina and findings there had been summarized in a still much-used publication from the 1920s. It is evident that she made every effort to understand and appreciate importation of African music and dance to the United States during the 1920s and '30s. The book contains numerous scholarly "gold pieces"—

bits of information of great value not easily obtainable elsewhere, its author undoubtedly a keen observer of theoretical detail and a listener who understands subtleties of sound—intervallic relationships, rhythmic distinctions, musical embellishments.

In chapter 3 Mrs. Hare enters domains of African-American folk music and early years of American minstrelsy, the use of primitive sound-producing materials—buckets, bones, wooden blocks—and lists names of the earliest "blackface" troupes. She mentions disagreements about the true authorship of various tunes—falsely or unfairly attributed, the misuse of "borrowed" material, the issue of impersonation, the responsibility for this of various publishing houses. Obviously, she had directly consulted sources far and wide that included many standing private and public collections.

Chapter 4 discusses technical details and problems of accurate notation in the recording of folk music on paper. Here Mrs. Hare displays wide knowledge of structural details and familiarity with a variety of musical systems and folklore. She is sympathetically responsive to "differences," and had an astonishingly wide range of reading and reference. I find particularly intriguing the inclusion of South Carolina and Georgia "rowboat" chants. One is reminded of the years Norris Wright Cuney spent on salt- and freshwater sailing vessels and on the docks of Galveston. Like father, like daughter, she appears perfectly comfortable sharing with readers her sensitivity and awareness of the role played by *water* in folk song. Attributions to printed materials—songbook collections, folk and popular song—of earlier publications of the 1800s and 1900s are extensive. She obviously consulted with a wide variety of people—casual acquaintances, persons encountered on the street, children observed at play, hucksters and street vendors seen and heard within home territory *and* at great distances during her visits to Louisiana, the West Indies, Puerto Rico, Cuba, and the Virgin Islands. Gathered also were snippets of local history, names of prominent families, festivals, local custom, migrations, hymnology, local proclamations, a variety of musical forms, cross-cultural trade-off, speech patterns, and references to various linguistic sources. In addition are references to dance form, costumes, and accessories such as canes, sticks, gourds, and calabashes. She draws interesting parallels between ancient and modern patterns of steps and sounds and quotes from a wide variety of authorities—Friedenthal, Carl Van Vechten, the Lomaxes, Raoul Laparra, Lofcadio Hearn, and Henry Cowell. She comments on the issue of racial admixture, African infiltration and importation, and exchange of specific terminology, and shows a quite remarkable ability to record on paper differences in pronunciation and accurately to reproduce in the *written* words the *sounds* of words.

She quotes numerous consultants throughout the book and displays her own general knowledge of history of the United States and other parts of the world. Of further interest are anectodal tidbits, for example, the origins of words written by Julia Ward Howe to an exciting popular army marching song, an old African-American refrain that became "The Battle Hymn of the Republic," according to certain authorities.

She mentions revived interest being shown in folk music of the white race—balladry, "mountain" folk song, the role being taken by composers and music scholars David Guion of Texas and John Powell of Virginia, and language professor George Pullen Jackson of Tennessee, and a musical inheritance from English and Scots-Irish early settlers. She mentions what she refers to as intellectual dishonesty on the part of one self-styled authority, Professor Jackson of Vanderbilt University, whose views are considered controversial even today. She makes trenchant comments about the folk music of France, Spain, Russia, and England and displays an astonishingly broad acquaintance with history, relating various events to her subject matter. Her conversance with items of news is remarkable. One wonders, "Where are the snippets—news clippings—to which she makes reference? The program books from which she quoted? The pamphlet material?"

Chapter 7 moves into the province of "Negro Idiom and Rhythm." She describes various distinctions between "art music" and the less rigid expressions of jazz improvisation, dance music, musical comedy, and ragtime. She deplores the influence of the last-named on young people. She mentions the versatility of members of quadrille orchestras and various band musicians, demonstrating her astonishing familiarity with individuals and groups in various parts of the country. She quotes from letters written by individual musicians to their fellows or to editors of newspapers. One of great interest to me was written in December 1926 to the *New York Times* by Will Marion Cook that deplores the credit given to producer George White of the Broadway *Scandals* as originator of the Charleston and Black Bottom. An inaccurate attribution, Cook states, and directs attention to the dance movements' origins in the South Carolina offshore islands and their adaptation by African-American children and dance comedians. Mrs. Hare shows broad knowledge of various celebrities of the dance world, black and white, and mentions singular events that took place in the world of musical entertainment. She mentions James Reese Europe's fabulous recruitment of black instrumentalists during the early 1900s, his studio in Leipzig, Germany, years of conducting musical comedy, and organization of the Clef Club, which eventually became a body of 150 to 187 orchestra musicians recruited from as far away as South Africa and the Sudan. Europe's explanation of unconventional groupings on stage is quoted—mandolins and banjo players replacing second violins, the use of ten pianos, two clarinets instead of one oboe, baritone instead of French horns. Mrs. Hare includes letters written in disagreement with certain of Europe's statements and mentions his assignment to organize an army band during World War I that resulted in enthusiastic response at war's end overseas and during a tour of leading American cities.

A chapter of general American music history contains information of interest and value often overlooked even by more meticulous scholars. Mrs. Hare presents evidence of the infectious quality of post–World War I popular music created by African-American composers and instrumentalists, and mentions names of persons who rarely are spoken of in historical accounts of the period. Again, one must remark about the astonishing breadth of her source materials and references, her knowledge of people and events, of the music world, the eventual involvement of musicians of recognized stature in the field of jazz composition and performance, and the new coalitions of management personnel.

Radio had, by the early 1920s, entered the picture. She writes about new programs on the air that employed black actors and singers, and makes reference to their use of African-American musical idiom.

Chapter 8 deals with musical comedy, revue, and incidental background music used in drama. She relates fascinating stories throughout this and other chapters of the book that shed light on music history by anecdotal and factual revelations. Many of these make one regret not having been born early enough in the century to have had exposure to a period of exquisite creativity.

She makes it quite evident that many of the 1900s to 1920s musical comedians and producers were of a rare breed—some highly educated and a number exceedingly accomplished. Each story is told in great detail, supplying information often not included in more recent historical accounts, details concerning venues, acts, family backgrounds, degrees of education, and, especially, the wide range of influence shed on the American musical scene. There is amazing accuracy of detail and only an occasional slight error that persons of rare musicohistorical background might stumble upon. She sheds light on details of personal history that one is not likely to find elsewhere and is astonishingly knowledgeable about her subjects' everyday lives. One gains deeper insight into the intensity of effort on the part of a cadre of exceptionally gifted performers, the reaction of the daily press to their efforts, and a broad vision of period. She gives details of casting of plays and films and engages in critical estimates of their quality that are extremely valuable.

Chapter 9 deals with happenings in the world of music, makes insightful comments, and supplies details concerning the efforts of a number of composers in Mexico, Cuba, Peru, Spain, Russia, and France; of the ones to whom she refers, some were of mixed racial heritage. Comments on the use of folk melodies within formal composition reveal the wide range of her knowledge of the subject and keen musical insight. She addresses also the universal employment of African-American folk themes and furnishes musical specimens that support her proposition.

She mentions interviews she conducted with outstanding critics and authorities of the day and shares valuable comments made by them. Details of performances in various locations are given— dates, programs, press comments—minutiae of inestimable value that might otherwise be lost completely. One might predict that wider distribution of the book now possible could result in the renewal of interest in her subject, which over the years has been cast aside and overlooked.

Chapter 10 supplies a marvelous account of the role played by nineteenth-century African-American performers and composers. Her own knowledge of the city of New Orleans enhances the value of the information she presents. She apparently had at her disposal an endless supply of resource material, gathered by reading and by interview: mid-nineteenth-century journals are quoted, among them the *Daily Pennsylvanian*, whose issues of 1854 and 1856 include accounts of performances by prominent black artists of the period. She mentions Thomas Bowers, a Philadelphian born in 1836, called the "American Mario." (According to custom of the day, black musicians often were referred to with such designation as "Black Patti," for Elizabeth Greenfield, an outstanding singer, the black counterpart of the period's leading white soprano, Adelina Patti.) Mrs. Hare mentions conversations with persons who knew her subjects well and were able to supply valuable information concerning them. One gains greater insight into an era that might otherwise remain completely obscure and into the wide range of talent within the black musical community.

History and art commingle. She refers to musicians active in matters of public interest, such as antislavery societies, and to the intervention of well-known public figures serving the interests of members of the music profession. She presents an astonishing array of assorted talent—singers, instrumentalists, musical organizations, performing ensembles—dates of their appearance, comments by critics, response by the public, details concerning their early training—a fascinating compendium of information that might otherwise not ever be brought to light.

Of exceptional value are chapters devoted to prominent musicians of the nineteenth and early twentieth centuries about some of whom little is known today: Frederick Elliott Lewis, born in 1846, an organist, flutist, violinist, and composer; Samuel Jamison (1855–1930), an 1876 graduate of Boston Conservatory; John T. Douglas (1874–c. 1920), first violin teacher of David Mannes. Douglas's name, at least, has not been forgotten totally; the musician chanced to hear an eight-year-old Mannes attempting to play his violin and offered to teach him without charge, realizing that the family was too poor to pay for lessons. Many years later the very prominent and successful Mannes founded a music settlement school in Harlem as an expression of gratitude to his benefactor.

There are intriguing references gathered in the course of the remarkable volume of reading on the author's part. They were drawn from a list of music journals and newspapers on both sides of the Atlantic and from the east to the west coasts of the United States that have long been unavailable outside of library storage areas. Mrs. Hare mentions interviews held with older musicians in different parts of the country and records details of shared recollections and souvenirs.

She forges fascinating chains of association. Margaret Jones was an accomplished Philadelphia singer. Her granddaughter, well-known Boston sculptress Meta Warwick Fuller, had studied in Paris with Rodin. In 1903 singer Theodore Drury formed an opera company whose one-performance-per-year season included a production of *Il Guarany*, written by well-known nineteenth-century Brazilian composer Antonio Carlos Gomes. This work and others of his operas were in the repertories of a number of European opera houses.

Mrs. Hare writes about musical expatriates who left the United States to study and who launched their careers abroad at a time when there were better opportunities for recognition overseas. One, M. Hamilton Hodges (1869–1928), traveled back and forth between studios he had established in Boston and New Zealand.

Another exceptional musician, whom Hare had met in person, was Creole composer Edmund Dédé (1829–1903), who as a young man left New Orleans and traveled to Mexico and England before settling in France. Years later, en route to Louisiana for a visit, his boat was shipwrecked offshore from Galveston. Before continuing his travels he was welcomed into their home by the elder Cuneys. Maud Hare often included Dédé's compositions on her programs. His French West Indian-Creole ancestry, not unlike her own, added a unique flavor to his musical expressions. Certainly Maud

Cuney Hare's volume of research and musical tastes had been strongly influenced by her own matrilineal Creole family background, her mother's origins as a native of Woodville, Mississippi.

She includes information concerning the efforts and achievements of individuals and organizations, prizes awarded for notable accomplishments in composition, and concert appearances that reveal the breadth and scope of her own well-rounded research efforts. One chapter includes information about musicians of the Middle East whose ancestry was partly African. Her drama with music, *Antar*, was developed along these lines and contains references in storyline and music she was uniquely well equipped to provide.

Other "world musicians of color" are listed with balanced evaluation of their contributions to meritorious musical tradition. Some pages are devoted to British composer Samuel Coleridge-Taylor and his son's and daughter's involvement in the music profession. There are paragraphs about the actor and singer Ira Aldridge, an American-born expatriate, who eventually made his home in Great Britain and whose daughters were both gifted musicians.

Chapter 14, entitled "Torch Bearers," singles out contemporary composers of the 1920s and '30s on both sides of the Atlantic. The author alludes to problems of race affecting their careers and supplies fascinating details of family background that underscore the authenticity of stories one has heard repeated many times. The author records comments made by leading music critics of the day and provides lists of compositions seldom furnished in other accounts of their productivity and, often, details of performances presented with dates, chief collaborators, critical notices, and the people involved in advancement of their careers. She goes on to mention awards given in recognition of outstanding achievement and various contests entered and won by these artists.

"Interpretive Musicians" are dealt with in the final chapter, 15. Mentioned are the different routes followed by many performers in the pursuit of their goals. One is happy to learn in greater detail about William Howard Richardson, Maud Hare's longtime friend and musical companion: their partnered performances, his involvement with other outstanding musicians, their tours of foreign countries and coverage given their recitals by music critics.

There is no questioning the absolute faith shown by her in an exceptional artistic collaboration. A number of other musicians whose careers she describes were close friends. Her estimate of their ability and of others less well known is amply supported by what one has learned about them during more recent years. She was, without a doubt, capable of rendering precise and sound evaluations.

A final paragraph is devoted to singer Anne Brown, the original Bess of *Porgy and Bess*. The opera's pre-Broadway opening took place in Boston in September 1936, barely four months before Maud Cuney Hare added her signature to the preface of *Negro Musicians and Their Music*. Anne Brown, now in her early eighties, has lived in Oslo since the mid-1940s and is a revered and active figure in Norway's world of music and drama.

One can only wish that Maud Hare could have been in the audience during *Porgy and Bess*'s Boston tryout featuring the young star Mrs. Hare had so recently applauded, and that it were *she* who could have enjoyed twenty more years of a life that over six decades had been exceptionally rich and productive.

The volume contains two appendixes. The first is devoted to descriptions of African musical instruments that Hare examined in their museum settings in Boston, Washington, and Philadelphia. She furnishes precise and detailed analyses of performance capabilities of each one, scientific data, and their historic, legendary use within African culture.

A second appendix conveys background information on Negro folk song. These supplementary materials offer visual evidence of Mrs. Hare's careful scholarly investigation and use of all possible authoritative sources and references.

If one is to find fault with *Negro Musicians and Their Music*, it would have to do only with shortcomings of presentation and not with any aspect of Mrs. Hare's execution. One could wish for improved photographic reproduction, typesetting, and layout. But one also must recall the publishing scene of the 1930s, the indifference of major publishing houses to the serious output of black writers and the story of black culture. Associated Publishers, founded in 1917 by Dr. Carter Woodson, took on a formidable and admirable assignment when it made available to a multiracial reading public volumes that otherwise would have remained unpublished. It is our good fortune that landmark publications such as this volume will again be available at the other end of the century. Maud Hare's splendid documentation of the achievement of black people of the world within the field of music leaves behind a priceless legacy of meticulous scholarship, discernment, and devotion to music history.

* * *

There obviously are documents to be consulted when a more thorough search can be made. A visit to the most widely publicized repository of Maud Cuney Hare's papers was rewarding *and* disappointing. In 1940 the "Hare papers" were sent to the Atlanta University Library and turned over to the original chief librarian, Charlotte Templeton. I went there to search and found many fascinating items—the manuscripts of Creole folk-song arrangements by Mrs. Hare, priceless early-twentieth-century-published works of turn-of-the-century composers of "popular" music but a disappointing number of clippings, letters, and other documentary materials—far less than expected. Continuing search will undoubtedly produce more wide-ranging "finds." I shall continue.

I would like to acknowledge indebtedness to Mrs. Elaine Williams of the Archives/Special Collections Department of the Woodruff Library of Atlanta University Center, for valuable assistance during the time spent there, and to Mrs. Betty Hillman of Boston.

NOTES

[1]Eileen Southern, *The Music of Black Americans* (New York: Norton, 1971), 59.

[2]*Norris Wright Cuney: A Tribune of the Black People* (New York: Crisis Publishing, 1913).

[3]W. E. B. Du Bois, *The Autobiography of W. E. B. Du Bois: A Soliloquy on Viewing My Life From the Last Decade of Its First Century* (New York: International, 1968), 138–39.

[4]The reference concerns the possibility of an award for study in Europe for which he had applied to the John F. Slater Fund for the Education of

Negroes. It did not materialize and he spent the three years that followed in Germany.

[5]There is one published compilation of Creole folk music gathered by Hare. Other examples of collecting by Hare and others, in manuscript, are among her collected papers. Over the years she traveled the United States extensively assembling folk materials as well as information for *Negro Musicians and Their Music*. Clark Atlanta University's Woodruff Library has in its Hare Collection some items in manuscript as well as her unpublished art songs. One wonders if there is not more waiting to be discovered.

[6]February 22, 1936.

BIBLIOGRAPHY

Cazort, Jean Elder. Entry in *Dictionary of American Negro Biography*. Ed. Rayford Logan. New York: Norton, 1982.

Du Bois, W. E. B. *The Autobiography of W. E. B. Du Bois: A Soliloquy on Viewing My Life from the Last Decade of Its First Century*. New York: International, 1968, 138–39.

Lewis, David Levering. *W. E. B. Du Bois: Biography of a Race. 1868–1919*. New York: Henry Holt, a John McCrae Book, n.d., 105–6, 116.

Locke, Alain. *The Negro and His Music*. Washington, DC: Associates in Negro Folk Education, 1936.

Southern, Eileen. *Biographical Dictionary of Afro-American and African Musicians*. Westport, CT: Greenwood, 1982.

PUBLISHED WRITINGS

Cunard, Nancy, ed. *Negro*. London: Wishart, 1934; New York: Ungar, 1970.

Hare, Maud Cuney. *Norris Wright Cuney: A Tribune of the Black People*. New York: Crisis Publishing, 1913.

———. *Message of the Trees*. Boston: Cornhill, 1918.

NEWSPAPERS AND PERIODICALS

Chicago Defender, 22 October 1907.

Musical Quarterly 14, no. 4 (October 1928): 35–53.

The American Musician

Music Observer

INTRODUCTION

Musical America
Christian Science Monitor

PUBLISHED PLAYS

Antar of Araby. In *Pageants from the Life of the Negro*, ed. Willis
Richardson. Washington, DC: Associated Publishers, 1930.

PUBLISHED MUSICAL SCORES

Six Creole Folksongs. With foreword, original Creole, and translated
English text. New York: Carl Fischer, 1921.

PARTIAL LIST OF ALLIED ARTISTS PLAYERS' PERFORMANCES
DIRECTED BY MAUD CUNEY HARE

Antar of Araby, original play by Maud Cuney Hare. The entr'acte music
includes selections from *Four Moorish Pictures*, described as an
Eastern suite for pianos or for small or large orchestra, composed by
"Montague Ring" (Miss Ira Aldridge of London, daughter of the
famous tragedian), dedicated to Maud Cuney Hare, and from *Syrian
Pictures* and an *Arabian Suite* by the same composer. An overture,
"Antar," was written by Clarence Cameron White.

Forbidden Ground by Armand Boutté

Plumes by Georgia Douglas Johnson

Polly Wakes Up by Alvira Hazzard

The Tents of the Arabs by Lord Dunsany

NEGRO MUSICIANS
AND THEIR MUSIC

By

MAUD CUNEY-HARE

THE ASSOCIATED PUBLISHERS, INC.

WASHINGTON, D. C.

To

WILLIAM HOWARD RICHARDSON
BARITONE
IN REMEMBRANCE OF
TWENTY HAPPY YEARS OF
MUSICAL PARTNERSHIP

NEGRO MUSICIANS AND THEIR MUSIC
BY MAUD CUNEY-HARE

PREFACE

In offering this study of Negro music, I do so with the admission that there is no consistent development as found in national schools of music. The Negro, a musical force, through his own distinct racial characteristics has made an artistic contribution which is racial but not yet national. Rather has the influence of musical stylistic traits termed Negro, spread over many nations wherever the colonies of the New World have become homes of Negro people. These expressions in melody and rhythm have been a compelling force in American music—tragic and joyful in emotion, pathetic and ludicrous in melody, primitive and barbaric in rhythm. The welding of these expressions has brought about a harmonic effect which is now influencing thoughtful musicians throughout the world. At present there is evidenced a new movement far from academic, which plays an important technical part in the music of this and other lands.

The question as to whether there exists a pure Negro art in America is warmly debated. Many Negroes as well as Anglo-Americans admit that the so-called American Negro is no longer an African Negro. Apart from the fusion of blood he has for centuries been moved by the same stimuli which have affected all citizens of the United States. They argue rightly that he is a product of a vital American civilization with all its daring, its progress, its ruthlessness, and unlovely speed. As an integral part of the nation, the Negro is influenced by like social environment and governed by the same political institutions; thus we may expect the ultimate result of his musical endeavors to be an art-music which embodies national characteristics exercised upon by his soul's expression.

In the field of composition, the early sporadic efforts by people of African descent, while not without historic importance, have been succeeded by contributions from a a rising group of talented composers of color who are beginning to find a listening public. The tendency of this music is toward the development of an American symphonic, operatic and ballet school led for the moment by a few lone Negro musicians of vision and high ideals. The story of those working toward this end is herein treated.

Facts for this volume have been obtained from educated African scholars with whom the author sought acquaintanceship and from printed sources found in the Boston Public Library, the New York Public Library and the Music Division of the Library of Congress. The author has also had access to rare collections and private libraries which include her own. Folk material has been gathered in personal travel.

The author is happy to acknowledge her indebtedness to the following: To the Boston Museum of Fine Arts for reproduction of the picture of seventh century musician of East India, to the Metropolitan Museum of Art in New York City for permission to describe African instruments included in the Crosby Brown Collection of Musical Instruments in the Museum, to the *Crisis* for permission to reprint poems from that monthly, and to Clarence Cameron White for assistance in reading the proof.

MAUD CUNEY-HARE.

"Sunnyside"
Squantum, Massachusetts.
January 20, 1936.

CONTENTS

ILLUSTRATIONS

MUSICAL ILLUSTRATIONS

INTRODUCTION

It is with a distinct sense of pleasure and privileged duty that I give the readers of this excellent book a short sketch of the career of Maud Cuney-Hare. One who does not already know of the versatility of this remarkably talented woman will doubtless be amazed at the diversified character of her activities.

Mrs. Hare is a pianist, lecturer and writer whose devotion to the highest ideals of her art has compelled admiration. She is the daughter of the late Norris Wright Cuney of Galveston, Texas, and Adelina Dowdy Cuney of Woodville, Mississippi. She was born in Galveston, Texas, February 16, 1874, and was graduated from the Central High School of that city. Her musical education was received at the New England Conservatory in Boston and later under private instructors among whom were Emil Ludwig, a pupil of Rubenstein, and Edwin Klahre, a pupil of Liszt. Following the completion of her work under these masters, she became director of music at the Deaf, Dumb and Blind Institute, of Texas, and at Prairie View State College in the same State. In 1906 she returned to Boston where she married William P. Hare of an old and well-known Boston family, and has since made her home there. She died there February 13, 1936.

As a concert and lecturer-pianist Mrs. Hare has travelled widely and as a folklorist she has collected songs from far off beaten paths in Mexico, the Virgin Islands, Puerto Rico, and Cuba. She was the first to collect and bring to the attention of the American concert public the beauties of New Orleans Creole Music as attested by her *Creole Songs*, published by Carl Fischer and Company of New York City.

As music historian Mrs. Hare takes high rank. She collected data in this field for more than a generation. She has exhibited her personal collection of Aframerican and Creole music and Early American music which dates chronologically from 120 years ago. As a writer on music subjects she has long been a valued contributor to the *Musical Quarterly,* the *Musical Observer,* the *Christian Science Monitor, Musical America,* and many other newspapers and magazines of the first order. For a number of years she edited the column of music notes for the *Crisis.* As a writer of distinction outside of the field of music she has attracted wide attention with published works of real literary value. In this list may be included a biography of her father and an anthology of poems called *The Message of the Trees.*

During recent years Mrs. Hare found time to establish in Boston the Musical Art Studio. Together with the musical activities of an art centre, she fostered and promoted a "Little Theatre" movement among the Negroes of Boston. Included in the plays produced her original play "Antar," written around the life of the Arabian poet, was staged in Boston under her personal direction. Concurrently with these activities Mrs. Hare has appeared with great success as recitalist, with William Howard Richardson, the baritone, at such educational centers as Wellesley College, Syracuse University, Albany (New York) Historical and Art Association, and elsewhere in costume recitals of music of the Orient and the Tropics.

To do any one of these things well would be a distinct achievement, but to do all of these acceptedly as Mrs. Hare has done is truly amazing. As a crowning achievement she has now given us an authoritative record of *Negro Musicians and Their Music*—a book that is more than an anthology, in fact a source book of great value to musicians, music lovers and all others who wish to be well informed on matters of artistic racial development and progress.

CLARENCE CAMERON WHITE.

Boston, January, 1936.

Chapter I

AFRICA

Earliest Traces of African Music—Dances of Worship—Mystic Dances—Rites of the Priesthood—War Dances—Ceremonial Dances—Festive Customs—Tribal Dances—Dance Forms of African-Negro Influences.

Negro music traced to its source, carries us to the continent of Africa and into the early history of that far off land. We may even journey to one of the chief sections said to hold the music of the past—that of Egypt, for it

HALLELUIAH OF THE COPTS

Al - le - yé yé é yé e yé.....................é

yé yé   yé yé   yé.....................

yé   é yé é yé   yé..................... e

etc.

The Copts are a Christian people, descendants of the Greeks, Nubians and Abyssinians. The Coptic Church is said to have preserved the most ancient and primitive Christian ceremonies.

was the ceremonial music of that land as well as that of Palestine and Greece, which was the foundation of at least one phase of modern musical art. While a continuous recorded history that would so greatly aid in giving knowledge of African art as well as its peculiar type of civilization is not yet complete, we do know that, in spite of the obscurity of the prehistoric period, there existed a great people, as their architectural monuments alone have proved to us.[1]

On the Gold and Slave Coast every god of note has his own individual dance. The Negroes of the Gold Coast believe in an indwelling spirit, the *Kra*, or soul; there are two souls, one of which abides with the body at death while the other departs to the land of the dead. Among the indwelling spirits are those which are believed to inhabit trees. A. B. Ellis gives the following terms used for the gods: Orisha (Yoruban), Bohsum (Tshi-speaking people), Vodŭ and Edrõ (Ewe-speaking people). The term Vodu is derived from võ (to be afraid), or from võ (harmful). Edrõ from drõ (to judge).[2]

Vodu (voodoo or vaudoo) is the term used at the present time in the West Indies and Haiti, but the superstition long remained among the Negroes and Creoles of Louisiana and was introduced in their dance and song. The deity is the python. Festivals held in honor of the accepted god of wisdom were accompanied by singing and voodoo dancing. The crocodile, called Elo or Lo, had neither

[1] Dr. Merlin W. Ennis, archaeologist and anthropologist for the American board for foreign missions, 30 years working in Portuguese West Africa, has been excavating in the heart of the African jungles. Excavating at the Cunene and Kukai rivers, he discovered pyramids indicating a pre-historic civilization. Natives told of a drum in the shape of a hyena, reputed taken from a royal tomb. (1933.)

[2] Ellis, A. B., *The Ewe Speaking Peoples*, p. 29.

priests nor temples; but when canoeing, the canoe men chanted to its praise.

The use of music in healing is very old. In the psychic life of the African, connected with the Bori religion of the Sudan, we find "songs of exorcism" which are performed with various idolatrous methods of healing those whom they believe to be possessed by spirits. In the Nile countries, treatment by tones of the fiddle and the drum continue for seven days when the patient is declared cured. The Goye-player, a fiddler, and in some places a guitarist, plays an important part in these ceremonies. Only outside the Sahara was the drum used.

The player chants the names of the various *alledjenu* (spirits), because each deity has his own particular theme in harmony. The proceeding is likened to a duet or musical dialogue between flute and drum, a combination still in use. The combined treatment of religious observances and music, and sacrifices of rams, ending with dancing, is a part of Shango worship.[3] We hear much today of the therapeutic value of music, spoken of as being in a new, experimental stage, and yet we find uncivilized people practicing the art in the days of long ago.

Dancing clubs representing figures of the god Edju, which is worshipped in North Yoruba, are found made of ivory and of wood. This god dwells at the cross-roads where are placed in his honor small clay cones, around which dances and processions take place at certain annual seasons.

The early religious belief of the Egyptians—that of many gods—has been preserved in their hymns. The exceptional monarch, Akhenaten (or Aknaton), 1450 B. C., father-in-law of Tut-Ank-Ahmen, devoted himself to the worship of one god and believed that god was manifested

[3] Frobenius, *The Voice of Africa*, Vol. II, pp. 524, 562, 567, 570.

IGAMA LOTANDO

[*Bantu Song of Love*]

The expression "he has gone West," referring to the death of a soldier, in the lately ended World War, came from the singing of this folk song by African soldiers.

Sung to the author by Kamba Simango of Portuguese East Africa.

in the rays of the sun. His Hymn to Aten has been published in full by Prof. Breasted, Mrs. A. A. Quibell and other Egyptologists. Of spiritual and lofty thought his poem began:

"Beautiful is thy resplendent appearing on the horizon of heaven,
O living Aten, thou who art the beginning of life. When thou ascendest in the eastern horizon thou fillest every land with thy beauties.
Thou art fair and great, radiant, high above the earth;
Thy beams encompass the lands to the sum of all that thou hast created.
Thou art the Sun; thou catchest them according to their sum;
Thou subduest them with thy love."

The land of Osiris, "the god of the dead," is believed by the Egyptians to be that of the West. The Zulus use the word "west" as the name of this mysterious spirit-land. The word comes from the verb "tshona" to sink or die away, while the complete expression "He went West" —*Zuva lake la vila*—means his sun has set. The expression is common to other African languages. C. Kamba Simango of East Africa gave the author the following Zulu expression of like import: "Zuva rakwe rabira"— "I langa lake li tshonile."

We find that the phrase "He went West" which came to us from the World War, was taken from the African soldiers. Natalie Curtis-Burlin in *Songs and Tales from a Dark Continent* quotes a Zulu love song, a song of grief which Simango also sang to the author of this volume:

"My Darling stayed in the West, Westward faring, he slept in the West. Alas! Alas! Alas!"

Among other songs which Mrs. Burlin recorded through Madikane Cele of South East Africa and Kamba Simango of Portuguese E. Africa, is a song which is supposed to be sung as a farewell by the Familiar Spirit which has entered the *Nyamsolo*, diviner, when treating the sick. The folklorist likens the condition of the diviner to the trance of the spiritualistic medium of modern times.[4]

Many of the African folk songs express implicit faith in the god while a host of their old legends attribute magical power to music. From the ancient races of the Mediterranean to the Kaffir of the South, from Mohammedanism to Shâmânism, through blend of races and influence of religion, Africa presents the greatest vestiges of her past—music and song.

There is unmeasured length from the practised contortions of the voodoo worshippers of heathen tribes, to the rhythmic grace of a Ballet Russe, but the distance is not so great from the ancient dances woven around an incident of pre-historic times to the interpreters of the Scherazade Tales. Alike in spirit, both are indicative of the storyteller's "Once upon a time"—

"When the sun goes down, all Africa dances." Such is the popular saying of the explorer and traveller. The dance is interwoven with every conceivable custom. While the licentiousness of some of the primitive dances have been commented upon by certain spectators, the society dances of the present, tolerated and accepted by the most highly civilized nations, are less than a stepping stone from the gyrations of a heathen people.

The earliest traces of music in native Africa are found in the dances of worship. No matter what form of religious cult was practised, music took an important part in its ritual. Many of the dances are connected with the rites concerning the mythological gods. One of the most interesting of the worship dances is the fire dance, performed at the great seven-day festival accompanied by

---

[4] Curtis-Burlin, Natalie, *Songs and Tales from a Dark Continent*, pp. 24-145.

drum-beating of the *Batta* drummer. A mystic dance practised by the Tshi-speaking people on the Gold Coast, between the Assini river and the Volta, is part of the ceremonies connected with the worship of the tutelary deities.[5] The Dako Boea Dance, to the Great Father, the sacred deity of the Nupe tribe in West Africa, in which the presence of the Great Spirit is invoked, is no longer practised, for the custom has been forbidden by the mis-

[5] Frobenius gives a vivid description of one of the mystic dances in the land of the Muntshi, a pagan people and a freedom-loving nation very much feared by other tribes. Having secured the good will of the people, he was allowed to witness one of the mystic dances.

"Then—what is that peculiar looking ornament shining on that beautiful woman's neck? What a curious, bird-shaped hairpin it is which she is putting into her neighbor's head-dress! What extraordinary bronze spirals decorate the foreheads of the men! How beautifully forged the spear-heads and the iron rings and chains! Just look at that beautifully shaped bronze tobacco pipe; there is no doubt but that we are among a people whose art and industrial development stands high indeed.

"Evening falls . . . A huge wooden signal drum is pushed into the middle of the Square, little field drums as well as flutes and a kakatshi trumpet taken as a war trophy from the Fulbes, are brought along too. The moon goes up. The folks have foregathered in their hundreds from the surrounding villages, laughing and chatting. The first taps of the drum resound: the flutes join in and develop a charming air to which some men dance a measure. All the hundreds assembled begin to move their shoulders and hips. The time gets quicker—the steps get quicker and stronger. More flutes join in until the whole of the vast, old, primeval forest re-echoes with the tunes and the glad shouts of the joyfully excited throngs of the human beings who madly whirl about in circles.

"Separate dancers perform here and there. The melodies are changed. The musical sense tries to obtain fresh combinations and variations of rhythm. The shrieks of the women grow sharper and sharper: the shouts of the men become louder and wilder. A passionate excitement I have never before in all my experience witnessed seizes the crowd. We enjoy the sight till far into the night."
Frobenius, *The Voice of Africa*, vol. I, p. 214.

sionaries.[6] A mystical dance of the Bushmen is called *nagoma* by the Basutos. When a man is ill, this dance is performed around him and is continued throughout the night by men and women who follow each other. The dancers are supposed to have supernatural power.

Among Ewe tribes, dancing is a special branch in the education of both priest and priestess. They must be very proficient in the art, and practise for months in order to acquire the necessary agility. The boy and girl recruits who have studied three years for the priesthood, dance before the King at the Annual Custom. During their novitiate they are taught the dances and chants peculiar to the worship of the gods.; The dances among the Ewe tribes are always performed to the sound of drums. The *addugba* is used for the ceremonies. Another dance

[6] "Formerly, those who took part in the dance were masked and in appearance evidently not unlike the "devils" of the early carnival days in the French West Indies. Two of the masquers, on stilts, many feet high and draped in flowing robes, dance along together. Those who danced around these figures were in their normal dress, except the upper part of the body was unclothed.

"A striking feature of the dance were the devotional songs chanted in rhythm to clapping hands by a group of women who gathered about the tree-trunk. The burden of their prayers to the mighty Dako-Boea was that they might be blessed with motherhood. In front of the singers danced a single figure drawn from the group that danced in ectasy before the symbol of their ancient god.

"It is remarkable how the dances and songs of Africa lead to ethnological facts. Tracing a bit of melody, one finds an old legend and through the myth or folk-tale the prehistoric life of a people is discovered. In 1874, amid the highest mountains of South Africa (the Maluti) and the overhanging rocks that form caves, George Stowe and J. M. Orpen found pictures of dancing figures. Of their mythological significance, Dr. Bleek, a scientist, wrote that it was "an attempt at a truly artistic conception of the ideas which most deeply moved the Bushman mind." Frobenius, *The Voice of Africa*, vol. 1, p. 216-7; Dr. Bleek, *Folk-Lore*, June 30, 1919, p. 155.

connected with the priesthood is that of the Tshi-speaking people of the Gold Coast. When new members were tested for the priesthood in Freetown, the following ceremony took place: The company drums were used, and as the drummers struck up their beat, youths and men raised a song in honor of one of the deities of the company. Just as there is a special hymn for each deity, which is sung to a special beat of the drum, there was also a particular dance for the same; the priest is under the influence of the individuality of a tutelary deity of the company, as soon as he places his hands upon the drum. In honor of this deity, drums give out the rhythm, the singers begin to chant and the priest performs a dance.[7]

The war dances are the finest of the African dances, and perhaps the most important of these is the Dance of the Spears. Usually, when the dances are about to begin, they are heralded by sounds from the fiddle (*goye*) and guitars (*molo*), accompanied by the drums. When the drums are grooved, they are held before the player who scratches them with his nails as they are turned around. There is a spear song and dance that comes from the Thonga of South Africa.

[7] For the benefit of many writers of "African Dances" in art-music, the following description may not be amiss:

"The drummers at once struck up the rhythm. . . . After a few moments the priest stopped (his dance) and putting his head on one side, indicated that the god who now possessed him could not hear the song in his honor—the singing was not loud enough or the particular drum rhythm was not sufficiently marked.—The song and drumming stops; a new start is made. This is repeated until satisfactory; then the priest dances furiously, bounding in air, tossing arms, but keeping perfect time to rhythm of the drum. This must require long practise and great endurance, for the dancer has naked feet and no springy board of floors, but the inelastic earth. Another god enters him and again wild dancing, and then the utterance of oracular sentences." Ellis, A. B., *Tshi-speaking People of the Gold Coast of West Africa*, p. 138.

"Let us stand fast! Let us stand fast!
Do not let your strength go,
It would help the enemy to conquer."[8]

Dances connected with ceremonies of state are attended by elaborate preparations and magnificent display. Of great event are those that are held at the coronation of the kings. In West Africa, after the conclusion of the coronation festivities, a dance is held in the open square in the center of the town. The best singers, clappers and other musicians come to take part, led by the Zobas or "Country Devils," the best dancers of the country. One to three hundred trained women dancers go through many intricate figures.[9]

There are also festival dances. In the territory of Sierra Leone we find what is known as the Hammock Dance,

[8] Henry M. Stanley glowingly described this as a phalanx dance of great volume and color, "The phalanx stood still with spears grounded until at a signal from the drums, Katto's deep voice was heard breaking out with a wild triumphant song or chant, and at once rose a forest of spears high above their heads, and a mighty chorus responded. . . . There was accuracy of cadence of voice and roar of drum." Faces were turned upward, heads bent back; right arms shook clenched fists on high as every soul was thrilled by martial strains. Then heads turned and bowed earthward with thought of the desolation of war-ridden lands and widows' cries. But again heads were tossed backward, "bristling blades flashed and cracked and the feathers streamed and gaily rustled. There was a loud shout of defiance and such an exulting and energising storm of sound that man saw only the glorious colors of victory, and felt only the proud pulse of triumph." Stanley, Henry M., *In Darkest Africa*, vol. I, p. 436.

[9] Bowditch writes of the *Pyrrhic dance* which was performed at a reception given him in the Spring of 1817. He gives a vivid description of barbaric splendor:

"Met by a crowd of 5,000 people, largely warriors, who greeted the party with martial music, they were halted in order that they might witness the Pyrrhic Dance which was performed in a center of a circle of warriors, where flags, English, Dutch and Danish were waved. The Captains held spears in their left hands, while which is one of a number of festive exercises. Another festival dance known in British West Africa is called the *ugowa* and is danced only at the high festivals of the

affixed to a long chain held between the teeth and right wrist, was a scrap of Moorish writing.

"The bands, of which there were more than one hundred, were composed principally of horns and flutes with innumerable drums and metal instruments. Each band had its own peculiar tune for its particular chief. One hundred or more large umbrellas were sprung up and down by the bearers and as the canopies were made of scarlet, yellow and the most brilliant silks and crowned with crescents, pelicans, elephants' ears and swords of gold, all of various shapes, with fantastically scalloped valances, the startling and brilliant effect may easily be conceived.

"The State hammocks were raised in the rear. Large drums, supported on the head of one man and beaten by another, were bound around with the thigh-bones of their enemies and ornamented with their skulls. Kettle drums were scraped with wet fingers. Wrists of the drummers were hung with bells and peculiar shaped pieces of iron. There too, were smaller drums—prolonged flourishes of the horns and ever the deafening beat of drums.

"The dance was witnessed by many native dignitaries who were of the king's escort—the Chamberlain, the Gold Horn-blower, the Captain of the Messengers, the Captain of Royal Executions, the Captain of the Market, the Keeper of the Royal burial-ground and the Master of the Bands."

And then, Bowditch continues, "The royal stool, entirely cased in gold, was displayed under a splendid umbrella, with drums, 'sehukus' (native stringed instruments), horns and various musical instruments cased in gold, about the thickness of cartridge paper. The swell of the bands gradually strengthened on our ears, the peals of the war-like instruments bursting upon the short but sweet responses of the flutes."

Those who wish local color in their pageants, such as has been given in recent years depicting visually the history of Africa, might profitably turn to the vivid pictures of royal settings of the African dance as given years ago by Bowditch.—Bowditch, *Mission from Cape Gold Coast Castle to Ashantee*, pp. 246, 255. 1819.

Occasionally, the King takes a part in the dance. Schweinfurth was privileged to witness in 1870, a performance by Munzo, King of the Monbuttoo. (According to "scientific observations," he

Zanzibar. Thought to be of magical power, the instrument called *kinandi-kinubi* is brought out and borne about the town while the dance is performed to its accompaniment.[10] A dance of the Kafirs which continues from sunset to sunrise is the *ugoma*. It is accompanied by a large kettle-drum which receives its name from the dance. Performed to drums of like name, is the *ukonje* which is danced by the Mpongwe, the Gaboon and the French Congo tribes. The Bushmen are particularly fond of dancing by moonlight. They possess a variety of dances pertaining to social customs, each of which has its appropriate chant. One dance imitates the actions of different animals.[11] Among a variety of dances of West

makes the deduction that the Monbuttoo are of Semitic origin, most thoroughly impressed upon their countenance, to which in particular, the nose very much contributes.) Describing the dance, this traveller writes:

"First of all a couple of horn-blowers stepped forward and proceeded to execute soli upon their instruments. These men were advanced proficients in art, and brought forth sounds of such power, compass, and flexibility that they could be modulated from sounds like the roar of a hungry lion, or the trumpeting of an infuriated elephant, down to the tones which might be compared to the sighing of the breeze or to the lover's whisper. One of them, whose ivory horn was so huge that he could scarcely hold it in a horizontal position, executed rapid passages and shakes with as much neatness and precision as though he were performing on a flute."

Following the professional singers and jesters, the king himself, takes part on the program, making a speech and afterwards assuming the role of a conductor. The baton used was a hollow rattle. After a return visit to Schweinfurth's camp, the king arranged a feast in celebration of a successful raid over the Momvoo. The festival reached its climax mid-day when the king, himself, danced in the presence of his wives and courtiers. It was held in the noble saloon, a royal hall which the explorer calls one of the wonders of the world. George W. Ellis, *Negro Culture in West Africa*, p. 72.

[10] Rose, Algernon, *Internat. Music Soc. Journal*, Priv. Coll. Afr. Instr., p. 60—Nov., 1904.

[11] Theal, *Yellow and Dark Skinned People of South Africa*, p. 47.

Africa is the *ziawa* which is accompanied by song.
Another is the *mazu* in which there is much gesticulat-
ing with the arms. A third, the *timbo*, is the common
native dance. On fine evenings, it is customary for professional strolling singers and dancers to go from house
to house dancing and singing for the amusement of the
wealthy. One of their song-dances is named the *ngere*.
In all civic ceremonies and social institutions pertaining to christening, marriage, death or the political life,
the dance ranks in importance with the feast. It has place
in the training which the youth receive in the societies
of learning in West Africa—the Beri and Sande institutions.[12] At the close of a young man's education in one

[12] Of the dance of the Bondu, the exclusive women's secret society
of Sierra Leone, Newland says:

"As I was permitted to be present at one of these affairs, I
can assure my readers it is almost as artistic and certainly more
quaint than an Alhambra ballet. The tee-tees, or young girls, are
adorned with bracelets of palm leaf fibre encircling the arm and
wrists, their body nets being made of cotton to which are attached small iron plates jingling as their owners dance.

"The dance is sometimes weird and fantastic, especially the
'devil dance,' and is accompanied by the inevitable 'sangboi' or
drum, and a 'sehgura' or kind of guitar made from a hollowed
gourd with seeds threaded on strings to make a sharp, metallic
sound. At the end of the dance, women spectators rushed into
the circle and embraced the dancers."—"Negro Social Life in West
Africa," *Journal of Race Development*, Vol. IV, Oct. 19. H. O.
Newland, *Sierra Leone*, p. 125.

A mask dance of the Ronga and Thonga tribes of South Africa,
is called the "Mayiwayiwane." The mask has its traditional significance. Frobenius found in West Africa that "reverential remembrance" is embodied in a like ceremony of Nupes—"When
Egedi, the founder of the young Empire came into the country
some 475 years ago, the Dako-Boea, a mask of several yards in
height, stood upon his canoe. When Gushi, one of the oldest rulers
of the land died, his corpse vanished and the mask referred to
rose up where it had lain—the associated idea of growth into manhood, the unfolding of masculinity out of the neutrality of childhood."—Frobenius, *The Voice of Africa*, Vol. II, p. 395.

of the societies, classified as these institutions are by age, he is quite likely to meet the girl of his choice, but a long courtship ensues before the marriage takes place. After the season of probation is over, the wedding is solemnized. In the Bantu country, South Africa, a wedding dance is known as the *khana*. The dance consists of leaping and springing up and down with a quivering of the body. The leaps from the ground are made exactly upon the certain note when repeated. This dance extends over the period of the celebration which lasts as long as the bridegroom's relatives provide oxen for slaughter. There are intervals, however, for feasting and for rest. The movement of the men in the dance is different from that of the women. Their mode of dress differs, of course, according to the particular tribe.[13] The native social dance, *bamboula*, is opened with the beating on the tom-tom.[14]

The perfection of the African dance rhythm has produced comment from all those who have been privileged to witness the performances. It is well marked, always

[13] A description, however, of the garb of armed attendants of a chief in southern Africa who took part in the dance, is interesting:

"Their figures are the noblest that my eye ever gazed upon, their movements the most graceful and their attitudes the proudest. Standing like forms of monumental bronze, I was struck with the strong resemblance that a group of Kaffirs bear to the Greek and Etruscan antique remains, except that the savage drapery is more scanty and falls in simpler folds; their mantles, like those seen on the figures of the ancient vases, are generally fastened over the shoulder of the naked arm, while the other is wholly concealed; but they have many ways of wearing the carosse. In the dance, they threw their carosses off and forming a semi-circle, bowed their heads low and bounded upwards with a spring. Our interpreter sung a Kaffir song which was soft and pleasing, for their language is in an uncommon degree musical." Rose, Cowper, *Four Years in Southern Africa*, p. 84.

[14] Pierre Loti, *Le Roman d'un Spahi*, chapter II.

emphasized by the instruments. The time signatures of 2/4 and 4/4 are found oftener than 3/4 or 6/8.

Dancing was the principal part of the songs called "The Songs of Ronga." The dances were performed after harvest. They were taught to the boys and girls, who became proficient in them. Now no longer practised, newer dances having taken their place. The Zulu *mudjatu* and *muthimbo* became popular only in turn to be succeeded by the *shiloyi* in which the performers sit and execute movements in imitation of boat rowers.

It is a significant fact that the youth of the coast are summoned by the chief to take part in the dances, and, while it is not obligatory, it is expected. This causes the conjecture that here perhaps is the beginning of a native ballet![15] A few years ago, Adolph Bolm, the Russian Mime, of the Imperial Ballet School in Petrograd, expressed a desire to stage a Negro ballet with people who had a perfect understanding of that race. He believed that the effect would be thrilling. From the mythological history as expressed through the medium of the African dance, a ballet, replete with the imagery of the people, may yet be evolved under patronage of chiefs and kings.

[15] Junod, Henri A., *Life of a South African Tribe*, pp. 167, 181.

CHAPTER II

AFRICA IN SONG

LEGEND AND FOLK TALE—SINGING IN GENERAL—EXTEM-
PORANEOUS SONG—HARMONY AND RHYTHM—TRIBAL CUS-
TOMS AND SONGS—HARMONY AND FORM—PRESENT-DAY
CHARACTERISTICS—NATIVE AFRICAN MUSICIANS AND OPERA.
1: Drums; 2: Stringed instruments; Harp-type-psaltry,
Lute and Bow-played; 3: Vibrating Sonorous Bodies,
Marimba, Flutes, Trumpets, and Horns; 4: Lesser
instruments.

We have seen how the content or significance of the
African dances may be traced in the legends of that continent. In like manner, many of the songs are found based
on a fable or folk tale, or descriptive of a social custom
of a tribe or nation. Here, through music, we find a related myth that has existed for centuries. Had the ex-
plorers of Africa been musicians as well as archaeologists,
they would have appreciated the mighty ally of song
which was at their hand, and their historical researches
would have been expedited.[1]

[1] René Bassett, noted folklorist, says that certain episodes mentioned in South African stories are to be found in the folklore
of the ancient Greek and Roman, the modern French and Italian,
and in the Scotch and German as well. He gives an explanation
of the phenomenon in which he declares that there may be such a
similarity in the minds of the various races when still in their
primitive phase of development, that they have invented the stories
independently—or that they belong to primitive humanity and all
the races have taken tales with them in their migrations and in
contact between the various races, the tales have spread all over
the world.—*Revue des Traditions Populaires,* "Les Chants et les
Contes des Ba Ronga," June, 1918.

16

THE AFRICAN DANCE

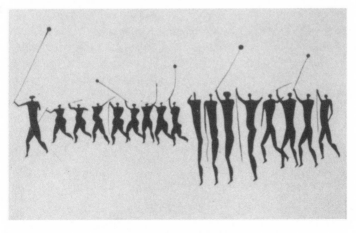

AN AFRICAN PAINTING

We know how the animal stories of Negro-Africa have been assimilated in American literature by Joel Chandler Harris in his *Uncle Remus Stories*. Many episodes of the "Romance of the Hare" alone are found in Bantu folklore. "Brer Rabbit" as the American version of the African hare is an emblem of cunning and wisdom.[2]

Traditions of the Kanuri people are handed down from generation to generation by a school of sages known as "kogolimas" or story-tellers. Grégoire says, "The Negroes have their troubadours, minnesingers and minstrels, named Grals, who attend kings, and praise and lie with wit."

[2] The tales of Africa are very old. A Sudanese proverb reads: "Salt comes from the North, gold comes from the South, but the word of God and wisdom and beautiful tales, they are found only in Timbuctoo." Not only in Jenne, the ancient city which played so important a part in the Sudan centuries ago, but throughout Timbuctoo an entire class of the population was devoted to the study of letters, and here not only talebearers of the old legends are found, but a collection of ancient manuscripts as well. Among the histories found here was one written by Abderrahman Es-Sadi who recorded events before 1656. Of the libraries owned by educated natives, Ahmed Baba declared, "Of all my friends I had the fewest books, and yet when your soldiers despoiled me they took 1,600 volumes."

In the old manuscripts the old writers who also copied books, as material was scarce, were called sheiks—termed "marabuts" by the Sudanese of today. When the marabuts were asked why they did not write more books instead of making records, the explanation closed with this illuminating statement which arouses the sympathy of musicians as well as writers, "Sometimes we are asked to write talismans and to copy books, but that does not give us sufficient to live upon. Many are obliged to devote themselves to commerce and absorbed by the care of not dying of hunger, how can they find time to write?" Du Bois, Felix, *Timbuctoo, the Mysterious*," chap. XIV, p. 319.

The author was told by a learned African, the late Professor Aggrey, that among the Fantis the people resort to the telling of facts and the description of events on wood, not because of ignorance, but because of the prevalence of destructive white ants which causes the people not to attempt the saving of papers.

A peculiar class of professional musicians which may be found nearly everywhere in Africa, make their appearance decked out in the most startling apparel—feathers, roots and bits of wood, with other emblems of magical art. Whenever a listener is discovered, he begins at once to recite details of his travels and experiences, in a chanting recitative. The Arabs have bestowed upon them the name of *hashash* (buffoons). Wandering minstrels, they are held in light esteem by the Niam Niam, who call them *nzangah*.[3]

In the Senegal, minstrels who frequent market-towns, have what is called a song net which is made of a fishing net. On this all manner of things are tied—tobacco pipes, bits of china, bird's heads, feathers, reptiles, skulls and bones, and every object bespeaks a tale. The passer-by selects an object and asks the price for the song. Bargaining ensues; finally a price is agreed upon and the purchaser listens to the song. The saying is that when these singers die, they are put into trees.

The fantastic "song net" reminds one of a home owned by a very aged colored couple in a Tennessee city of the United States. It stands on the outskirts of town, on the road that leads to a well-known college. The trees in front of the house are literally covered with bits of brightly colored glass, glazed crockery, parts of broken earthenware and scraps of gayly flowered china—broken pieces of every known article of a crockery store—and these fastened in the trees! Was it possible that this aged man and woman were the progeny of Senegal minstrels? No one could give me an answer to the riddle.

The principal legend of the Songhay, a nation that dwelt on the Niger, is called the "Originator of the Race." From it is taken the "song of Nana Miriam," composed to celebrate the slaying of the Nile-horse. Miriam, the

---

[3] Schweinfurth, H., *The Heart of Africa*, vol. II, p. 30-31.

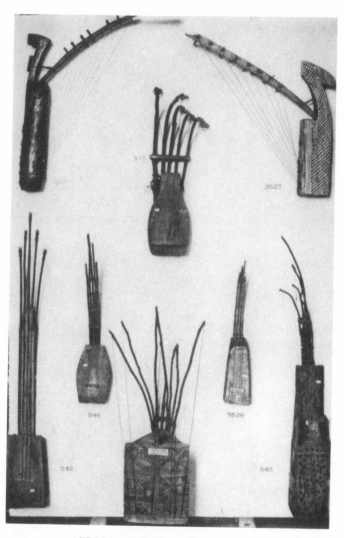

AFRICAN MUSICAL INSTRUMENTS

daughter of Owadia, primal ancestor of all the Sorko tribes, was taught all her father's magic arts. By her incantations, she killed all the river-horses (the hippopotami), that had destroyed the rice fields. Only one she spared because it was a Nile mare in foal. Fara Naka rejoiced, saying, "What a splendid daughter is mine! Nana Miriam I thank thee!" Then he summoned the Kié (Dialli or troubadours) singers. He composed a beautiful song and taught the Kié to sing and play it. All the people in the land, all the singers, all the fishermen, all the Sorko sang the song of Nana Miriam. And since that time whenever anyone makes a charm for hunting the hippopotamus, he always chants over it the name of Nana Miriam.[4]

The songs of the Africans are chiefly a species of recitative or chant with a short chorus. The soloist gives the melody while a chorus sings a refrain, which at times are but ejaculations. The chief singer remains standing while the members of the chorus are seated around him; and as the melody is given out, they turn to one another, each improvising in turn. Their power of invention and improvisation may last for hours. Expert in adapting song to current events, they indulge in mockery, ridicule, and sarcasm, or in flattery or praise of men and happenings.

A song of the bridesmaids offers advice which would occasion great surprise if it were followed. It is from a collection noted by Mrs. Audeoud in Maputju: "Do not go with him." The women friends, upon accompanying the bride to her new home, sing:

"Whither goest thou, mother? Whither goest thou?
They will bring thee the basket full of maize and the
    fan, my mother!

[4] Frobenius, Leo, *The Voice of Africa*. Vol. II, pp. 526-8. Nile here may be confused with some other stream.

When thou hast finished crushing it, they will make thee
    crush it again, my mother!
When thou has plastered the floor, they will make thee
    plaster it again, my mother."[5]

Other songs are sung, not only to the bridegroom and
to the relatives, but to the neighbors, for the marriage is
a community affair. All the songs are in a mocking vein,
rather than in a sentimental one.

The writer to whom we are indebted for the information above also tells of certain rites pertaining to the
festival season which is characteristic of the Bantu. One
of a number of the "first fruit rites" says, "The nkanye
is a beautiful large tree, called by the English the Kafir
plum. It bears a small golden yellow fruit which ripens
in January. The first ripe makanye (plural) are gathered
and the sour liquor, which is made from it, is poured on
the tomb of the dead chiefs in the sacred wood, who are
invoked to bless the New Year and the coming feast which
is about to be celebrated. The new beer is first drunk by
the warriors of the army—it has been medicated to prevent them, by a mysterious spiritual influence, from kill-
ing any of their comrades during the festive weeks. There
are singing and dancing and rejoicing that the men be
spared in battle."

Before the closing day of the carnival which is almost
in the nature of an orgy, the payment of the tax—a large
portion of makanye—must be made to the chief. The
women, as they carry the wine to the town, sing the following chorus: "Hi! Hi! We seek the hawk! Who soars—
In the sky! Hi! Hi! Who is the hawk?—It is Muzila—It
is Muzila!"[6] In this carrier song (there are a number of
them) Muzila, the chief, is compared with the mythical

[5] Junod, Henri A., *The Life of a South African Tribe*, vol. II,
pp. 177-8.

[6] *Ibid.*, vol. I, pp. 373-5 and vol. II, p. 259.

"lightning bird,"—with the hawk that "swoops down from the clouds."

On the Gold Coast, thanks are returned to the gods for having protected the crops. As in other sections, there are apparently two seasons, one in September when the yam crop is ripe; another (Ojirrah) in December when the crop is planted. A minor festival, Affi-nah-dzea-fi, is held in April. The September festival of the Ashanti is commenced by loud beating of drums.[7]

Not only in the agricultural life does the native rejoice in song, but at home as well as abroad, all industrial labor is lightened by music. Much of the travel in Africa is carried on by water-ways. Canoeing or rowing is the favorite manner in which this is done. Wallaschek in quoting Ernst von Weber, says, "The Balatpi reminded Weber of Venetian gondoliers or of the lazzaroni in Naples. One would improvise a strain which others would immediately sing in chorus to a charming melody. Each in turn improvises thus, so that all have an opportunity of exhibiting their talents for poetry and wit."[8]

In Newlands' description of canoeing in Sierra Leone, he writes, "Boat-boys would stand on the bottom of the boat and place one leg upon the seat. Then they lift themselves upon the seat with both legs and while still rowing, each would throw one foot backwards and upwards into the air, balancing on one foot and not relinquishing the oars. At same time they chanted a dirge-like ditty or sang some song, although evidently to them inspiring, had yet to me a melancholy strain of sadness. . . . The boys beat the kettledrums vigorously and the bugle rang out."[9]

[7] Ellis, A. B., *Tshi-Speaking People of the Gold Coast of West Africa*, p. 229.

[8] Wallaschek, *Vier Jahre in Africa*, I, 221.

[9] Newland, H. O., *Canoeing on the Rokelle*, p. 83.

The exclamation *Eji* (*Aië*) found at the close of many African verses is typical of the shield struck by the spear. The war song is stopped at a given signal, immediately the shields are elevated and a hissing *ngu-ngu-ngu* is heard through· the crowd. From this comes the word *ngunquzela*, meaning to stop a war song.

Then there are war dances.[10] The Bantu of South Africa give war-dances (*gila*) at which time medicine is given

SOUTH AFRICAN DANCE SONG[9a]

Uy......   uy za ma-ke - na- ny

Uy- za ma-ng ne Ny-e - za.

the soldiers to make them invulnerable. It follows the war-song. Usually there is but little change of position in the dance, and the movements may consist of simply moving the head and hands with a slow motion of the feet. Always the war-dances are accompanied by old chants, many of which have been noted. One of them, which is the oldest of the Nkuna, dates back to 1820. It was sung before the Zulu invasion before the arrival of Manukosi, in the early XIX century. The dialect is Thonga.[11] In the *gila* a single dancer detaches himself from the circle of

[9a] Noted by M. C. Hare from S. Plaatje of South Africa.

[10] Junod, Henri, *The Life of a South African Tribe*, Vol. II, pp. 436-8.

[11] Junod, Henri, *The Life of a South African Tribe*, Vol. II, pp. 436-8.

warriors and stamps with all his strength on the ground. He beats the earth with one long tread followed by three short ones, all the time brandishing his weapons. His place is taken by a younger man who leaps like an antelope. If the troops are detained in going to battle the young men go dancing to the king to ask permission to go forward.

OLDEST NKUNA WAR SONG

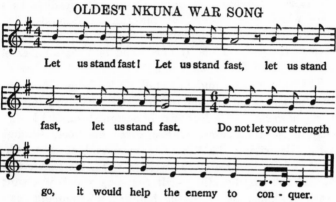

Let us stand fast! Let us stand fast, let us stand

fast, let us stand fast. Do not let your strength

go, it would help the enemy to con - quer.

Henry M. Stanley in *Darkest Africa* describes the Phalanx Dance which was given to celebrate a victory. In the afternoon, one thousand warriors gathered and joined the men, women and children whose voices arose in song high above the drums. The main chorus was that of the Wanyamwezi, called the best singers on the continent, while the Bandussume under Katto, brother of Mazamboni, led the warriors to the Phalanx Dance.

The African boat songs of yesterday may be the origin of our sea-chanty of today. Even in far off Africa the chanty had its use.[12] All these songs help us to trace history.

[12] L'abbé Bouche gives a song by his canoe men when he travelled on the lagoon near Porto Novo.

"You are great, you are strong, Oh Jaledeh! If you choose you could rival Shango (the lightning rod) in power. But to be terrible

It is said that the scientific world was first told of the wonders of the pre-Mohammedan era in Africa by the French, who had carried on early excavations there. The old Arabian explorer, El Bekri, who visited the Hausa in 1050 A. D., told of the red mounds that are still seen in the region of the lower Senegal, as having been ancient royal graves. But the list of the dead kings, then of the second dynasty, is found through the medium of a song which was chanted at the funeral festivals. The singers, so the old "fairy-song of the Nupes" goes, called each of the great chiefs by name, and told the number of years and months of his reign.[13]

The old story as told in detail by Frobenius, fantastic as it is, makes interesting reading. Of particular interest to us, however, is the fact that important historical knowledge of the time before 1275 is given the world through song. Describing the "god-like memory" of those who lived before the time of the written word, the writer tells of the gaffers who still recall the song which was sung when workmen toiled in the building of pyramids, centuries old, and claims that every archaeologist can quote extracts from the natives. While this is true, it is to such scholars as Junod and Frobenius that we are indebted for unparalleled accounts of the musical traditions of the black continent.

Amidst the Tshi-speaking people of West Africa,[14] dancing and singing in honor of the deceased take place at funerals. Decima Moore and Major F. G. Guggisburg in *We Two in West Africa* tell of funeral songs being

and cruel seems to you unworthy of a god, and you prefer to make yourself renowned by the benefits of your protection. We trust in you, oh Jaledeh—be propitious to us." (Chorus repeats) "Jaledeh, good deity, guide us, shield us from harm."

[13] Leo Frobenius, *The Voice of Africa*, vol. II, p. 368.

[14] Ellis, George W., *Negro Culture in West Africa*, p. 24.

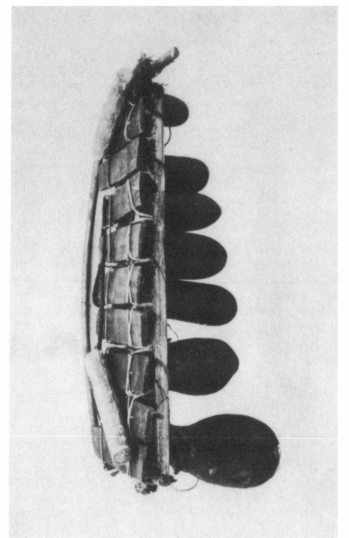

MARIMBA OR XYLOPHONE

heard that were sung by a score of women who went up and down the street dancing a weird measure. They clapped hands in time to their song and circled around and around a man singer, who sang short soli at intervals, the chorus of the dirge being taken up by the women. The song and dance were kept up for days by hired mourners. Always there was the accompaniment of the drum.

George W. Ellis, formerly of Chicago, who was at the town of Bomie when the Vai king died in 1904, stated that, following a death, a large feast is spread and while songs are given, drums announce the festivities of the day. There are many mourning songs descriptive of the loss of a family or tribe. Following the official period of mourning for the dead chief, the African coronation is held, an occasion of great moment. Among many tribes it is a military affair in which the people declare their loyalty to the new chief and he in turn to them. In parts of South Africa the war dance known as the *gila* or *giya*, is followed by the *guba*, which is a solemn chant used interchangeably as a coronation chant, a war song, a funeral dirge or patriotic hymn.

The classical war song of the Tembe and Maputju which inspired Coleridge-Taylor's fine piano transcription "Lo-ko-ku-ti ga" (At the Break of Day), originated at the coronation of Muwai who reigned at the close of the eighteenth century. He was the great, great grandfather of the chief Mabai who was deposed in 1896. Muwai, whose son Makasana reigned from 1800 to 1850, is compared to the rising sun, and the words are thought to recall a coronation at daybreak.[15] Before going to war and during coronation ceremonies the army sings this old coronation song in praise of the royal family. Notice

[15] *Twenty-four Negro Melodies, Transcribed for Piano*, by S. Coleridge-Taylor, Oliver Ditson Co.

is called to the change from minor to major and its return to the major mode.

Sir Richard Burton gives many instances of dancing and singing in connection with the "Grand Customs" about the time of the New Year, 1864. He has many interesting things to say of this very old festival which was founded upon a religious rite, and which included human sacrifice and the slaying of captives. His work would have been more valuable, however, had he not so often descended to flippancy and ridicule. His lack of sympathy with the people of whom he wrote prevented him from discovering the underlying significance of the mystery dances and songs. He tells of sundry dances at which Amazons (women soldiers) chant to a single cymbal, and then to a full band. This was followed by a mock dance of "So," representative of the Thunder god, which he considered buffonery without any mystical meaning. At the king's "So-sin Custom" armed women sang dirges in the minor key, clapped hands and presented arms, after which followed a dance given by six Amazons. These women excelled in the chanting of Nago songs.

It has been long thought that African folk-song has a harmonic background. However, Ballanta, a native of Sierra Leone who has been making musical researches in West Africa under the auspices of the Guggenheim Foundation, wrote in the *Journal of West Africa,* of July 14, 1930, that "there is no perception of harmony as the term is understood in music." He continues:

"What enters into a musical expression by way of tone combination is a highly developed form of polyphony, which may embrace two, or at most three parts. This polyphonic form is the freest from the point of view of concords and discords, and it is preponderantly rhythmic; that is to say, each part preserves its individuality. There appear to be no conditions as to the succession of intervals; and although there are evidences of the use of some intervals rather than others, especially in the cadence, one could not prove the rule.

"The perfect fourth is the basis of harmonic combinations; that is, where two parts sing together tone by tone. Towards the cadence, however, other intervals may be used as the major third and the major second; but the major third is in all cases treated as discordant, whereas, the major second is accepted as a concord.

"Taking the major diatonic scale as a standard, although that scale gives imperfectly the sounds produced, the fourth and seventh of that scale are not fundamental tones in the African perception, but subordinate tones. The principal tone in African perception is that group of tones answering to the second major diatonic scale; the tones next in importance are the fifth and sixth being the fourth below it. The other two tones are subordinate and are used for cadential purposes, or otherwise, to divide the interval of the perfect fourth. This appears to have been the original perception."

Ballanta then concludes, "Each one of these standard tones now has what may be called tones in opposite phases with it. These other tones stand at the distance of about a quarter tone above and below the standard tones and are used for and instead of the standard tones; that is to say, they rarely follow each other, so that the actual intonation of a quarter tone is rare."

Junod says of native South African harmony, that it certainly exists, even if not always easy to detect. "When you hear a chorus of beautiful voices singing in two or three parts, you at once perceive great differences between their system of harmony and ours. These choruses are by no means disagreeable, but are very strange to our European ear. . . . I have succeeded in fixing the two parts of the song of Zili which can be considered typical; I owe it to two girls of Lourenco Marques, who had clear voices and lent themselves willingly and with great patience to the long inquiry. One will notice a curious succession of fourths and sixths quite unusual in our music.

. . . The fourth seems to be more acceptable to the Bantu ear than the third or the fifth.''[16]

The author of this volume has heard a quartette of Bechuanas sing native songs in harmony with half-tone inflections, although the melodies were simple as were the words, after those of a South African proverb. Guided only by the ear, they improvised harmonic parts to the leading voice.

We should note here also present-day characteristics. Ballanta, who travelled about 7,000 miles in research work in his native land and collected over 2,000 specimens of African song, found that the African melodies did not always consist of short melodic phrases of only two or four bars endlessly repeated, but that there existed melodies of from twelve to sixteen measures without the appearance of *one repetition*. This he found true of the Mende (Sierra Leone), Susu (French Guinea), and Munsi (Northern Nigeria) tribes. The most interesting melodies were those of the tribes of the middle region, that had not been influenced by outside culture. Ballanta noted a most interesting example which was a flute solo with vocal chorus which he heard sung by over sixty voices at Makurdi, the town-seat of the Munsi tribe.[17] In describing the dance songs he adds, ''The highest class is the artistic dance of the Yorubas. Cross rhythms in abundance. In these dances one meets with characteristic rhythms; that is to say, rhythms which have meanings ascribed to them in directing the dancer how to proceed; they act as cues, not necessarily with reference to a change of dance steps, but with reference to action, either to retire, or to come forward, or go backward. They are the beginnings of the drum-talking system.''

[16] Junod, Henri A., *Life of a South African Tribe*, vol. II, p. 268.
[17] ''Gathering Folk-tunes in the African Country,'' *Mus. Amer.*, Sept. 25, 1926.

In an essay read at the International Colonial Exhibition of Paris during the International Congress of Ethnography, by M. Félix Eboué, a Negro from French Guiana, graduate student of l'Ecole Coloniale and chief colonial administrator, it was stated that among the Oubanguians who do not know writing, the choruses are sung only in middle range, as the children alone have high voices. According to Eboué-Tell, who had collected thirty-two songs, the minor modes predominate. The measures are in 4/4 or 2/4; the phrases short with ever-changing variations, the longest melodies never over eleven measures while the shortest was that of five.

In the Banda songs from Baubi the language is so musical that they could be written "by means of musical notation as with syllables of our alphabet." The words are reproduced on the *tom-tom lingua* (drum) but they can also be spoken in tune with European musical instruments.[18] Stephen Chauvet in *La Musique Nègre*, (1929) describes the beauty of the music given by characteristic chanting of the porters and voyageurs, with the improvisations which are delicate and subtle, reminders of the song of the troubadours of the Medieval epoch.

Today we find African song creeping from its native heath and arousing curiosity and interest in the concert hall. In London during the music season of 1932, a concert of Bantu songs and rhythms was given by the natives named Montsieloa, Dube and Marimbela. The songs were sung in Zulu, Sesuto, Lizosa, Matebele and other African languages.

Mme. Grall, wife of the doctor-in-chief of the medical Corps of Bambari, who is completing her studies of the African song and speech, makes interesting observations on the connection between African words and instruments.

[18] *Revue du Monde Noir*, April, 1932. Eboué, Félix, *The Banda, Their Music and Language.*

As the D minor triad for a basis, she writes that "the linda (drummer) speaks by striking the linga so as to reproduce exactly the rhythm of his own words and the different tones of his dialect. Even the children understand the messages. . . . Whenever a message is about to be transmitted, the 'broadcasting station' summons those who can hear it by a series of strokes, in which it names those to whom the message is to be given. The beginning phrases may vary among stations, according to the 'mokhoundji linga' or drummer, but all of them mean, 'So and so, listen to me.' "

Certain words are always represented by the same notes and rhythm, and thus Mme. Grall finds it is possible to distinguish a musical vocabulary of the Banda language. It is interesting to note that a South African native, Mark Radabe, conducting research in 1932, with the idea of presenting an opera, the development of the Bantu principles, would portray the Zulus in Basutoland. During the year of 1932, R. C. Nathaniels, a West African composer, gave recitals in Vienna for similar reasons.

Other performances have also invited attention to these characteristics. In July, 1933, a group of African singers, accompanied by dancers and the Royal Ashanti Drum Corps under the direction of Duke Kwesi Kuntu, gave performances at the Century of Progress Exposition at Chicago. Prior to their American visit, Dr. M. J. Herskovits, of Northwestern University, and other anthropologists witnessed their entertainment abroad. According to the American press, the fourteen "well-poised, beautifully molded black men with drums four and one-half feet high . . . gripped, stirred, and thrilled an audience of people from all parts of the world, in most fantastic and rhythmic ceremonial dances."

Kykunkor, "The Witch Woman," a native African opera, the music by Asadata Dafora, a native of Sierra

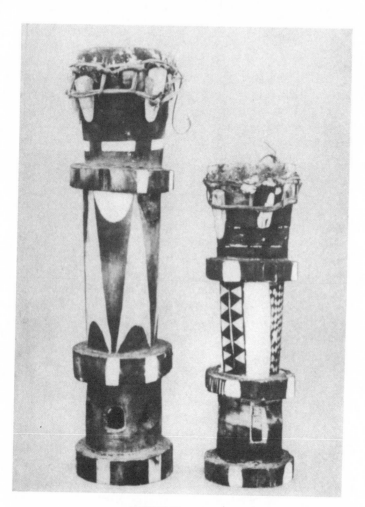

AFRICAN DRUMS

Leone, West Africa, was the artistic sensation of the music world when presented in New York during the season of 1934. The director, Asadata Dafora Horton, who came to New York in 1929, is an African singer and dancer. For some time unrecognized, he struggled to gain a hearing for Negro music that was more than the accepted jazz. Receiving unstinted praise from John Martin, dance critic of the New York *Times,* who heard an early presentation of *Kykunkor* in the Unity Theater Studio, the musician was successful in having the dance opera performed in the Chanin Auditorium, New York, and elsewhere. An act from the opera was broadcast in June, 1934.

The libretto of this African opera is based on a folk legend of love and marriage, and the setting is that of an African village. Effective use is made of traditional chants and dances. Leopold Stokowski, who with Lawrence and other noted musicians have praised *Kykunkor,* is said to have asked that he be taught the intricate African rhythms as exhibited by the drummers. Abdul Assen in the role of the witch doctor, showed remarkable dramatic ability. The opera was given at the Newport Casino, Newport, Rhode Island, during late August, 1934.

Although it is true that dance and song enlivened all sections of Africa, we have long turned to Egypt for first knowledge of music and musical instruments. According to Dr. L. S. B. Leak, who has made a study of conditions in East Africa (1932), recent excavations there give evidence that the history of man goes back to an age greater than in any other section of the world.[19] It is not surprising that many Negro-African instruments show a kinship to many of those found in Egypt, since centuries of commerce and conquest brought into close contact many races of men—Arabian and Moorish, Assyrian and Per-

[19] See Appendix.

sian, Ethiopian and Egyptian. Egypt learned much from
the purely Negro Africa, and the latter from the former.
It is said that stringed instruments owe their origin to
Negro Africa.

The African tom-tom, the drum, although not always
used as a musical instrument, is of unusual importance.
It is claimed that in a hot climate, the older the drum gets
the tauter the string becomes. The method of tuning is
by placing the instrument over a fire to contract the skin
or in water to expand it. The drum has three distinct
and separate usages—by the priests in worship, by the
youth in affairs of love, and by chiefs and rulers in military life. However, there is no custom or ceremony connected with daily life but that the drum has a share
therein. No march is undertaken without the call of the
drum, and it is also used as the hunters prepare for the
leopard hunt. In the Tshi-speaking country, the announcement of all festivals is made by beating of the
large state drum at sunset after which signal, songs and
discharge of fire-arms break out from all quarters of the
town. The harvest festival in September, lasting a fort-
night, is commenced by the beating of the drums. Among
the Kafirs, there are drum-calls for all occasions. Besides the
all-night drumming to scare away wild animals, there is
the summons at day break which is known as the *reveille*.
Much importance is laid upon the morning summons.

The African tom-tom has had parallels abroad. Daniel
Alomia Robles, a Peruvian musician and archaeologist,
has a flute which was found in one of the old tombs in
Peru. Among the old Inca instruments, some of which are
over 3,000 years old, is a 5 string harp. Of the 4 note
instruments, the scale was found to be Re, Fa, Sol, La,
later enlarged by the interval of a third, which is a complete Inca pentatonic scale. Mr. Robles claims this is in
advance of the Greeks. As we know, this Inca music,

later absorbed by the Spanish, was again modified by African influences. In this the "marimba", or xylophone, a native African piano, was an important factor.

In Puerto Rico, as in the Virgin Islands, the *guiro* or *juiro* (pronounced "weero"), is the most popular instrument. It is seen everywhere and is the main instrument of percussion used in that section of orchestras and bands. Here the *juiro* is made of hollowed gourds, cut with many small grooves and decorated with simple motives and two or three cut-outs. The one in the possession of the author is made to resemble a fish. The *juiros*, made of various sizes, are stroked with a steel wire or hair-pin. The author has listened with amazement to the extraordinary playing of a Negro *juiro* performer in the Puerto Rican Municipal Band under the conductor, Tizal, in San Juan. The many and varied rhythmic effects and the rapidity with which he produces syncopated notes, makes him the center of attraction to tourists who listen to the outdoor concerts given in the plaza.

CHAPTER III

AFRICAN INFLUENCES IN AMERICA

NEGRO SONG AND AFRICAN SYSTEMS—COMPARISONS—SONG
IN 1835—NEGRO MINSTRELSY—NEGRO MINSTREL TROUPES—
"JIM CROW" SONG, 1815—STEPHEN FOSTER, 1845—POPU-
LAR BALLADS—SONG WRITERS—PLANTATION SONGS, 1862—
FISK JUBILEE SINGERS—ANTON DVORAK AND THE NEW
WORLD SYMPHONY—LETTER, H. T. BURLEIGH.

During 1913-14, James Barnes the novelist and war explorer, collected a number of folk songs in Central Africa.
The music was recorded by the use of a reproducing phonograph. "It was surprising to me," says Barnes, "to
find how similar African music is to that of the Negroes
in America. That is evident to one who is not a professional musician. As you will see from our films, many of
the dances are like those which our southern Negroes have
made familiar, such as the cake-walk and the shuffle. We
can only approximate the music, of course, for they use
intervals that are strange to our ears."[1] It is quite likely
that the feelings of the Negroes in America were expressed
in the manner of the primitive music of Africa and that
the first generation should unburden their troubled souls,
and voice their homesickness in a medium familiar to
them. Krehbiel remarked that "they contain idioms which
were transplanted hither from Africa, but as songs they
are the product of American institutions."

Within the past few years, a number of native African
youths have come to this country for study. Possessing
intelligence and musical talent, they have been able to give

[1] An interview in *Musical America*, March 6, 1915.

valuable information regarding African music, and at the same time they have made a study of the art of Negro America. Foremost among these are C. Kamba Simango of Portuguese East Africa, a former student at Hampton Institute and Columbia University, who has been heard in African song and playing native instruments. Another was Madikane Cele of Southeast Africa, a product of Hampton Institute, who returned to his country as a minister and later revisited the United States with a group of African musicians who gave performances for the benefit of his missionary work on the East Coast. Still another was Nicholas J. Ballanta of Sierra Leone, who studied at the Institute of Musical Art in New York.

One of Ballanta's compositions was played at a student recital in New York in 1923. Shortly before this, he conducted a number of his works at a Negro pageant given at Symphony Hall, Boston. Just at this time, Kathleen Easmon, a girl of mixed blood, a native of Sierra Leone, a prize-winner in London institutions, brought the message of African music to America; and in Brooklyn, New York, Boston and elsewhere she gave native dances that were surprisingly beautiful in their imagery. This young woman, who returned to Africa as the bride of Simango and assisted him in his educational work for the natives, died in London in August, 1924. Some of her poems were set to music by S. Coleridge-Taylor.

Of this quartette, Nicholas Ballanta was privileged to continue scientific research into the musical conceptions of the people of Africa for comparison with the musical systems of European races, by a grant from the John Simon Guggenheim Memorial Foundation. The scholar states that African music does not survive in its primitive purity when brought into contact with other music systems. Outside influences are shown in different ways. "In the Yorubas in and around Lagos, the effect of this influence is found in the melodic perception, and not in polyphonic or harmonic content. In the Sherbros the influence shows itself in both perceptions; the tribes use major and minor thirds as consistently as American Negroes do.''

Ballanta has concluded that the alteration is seen to be:

"(a) The substitution of the perfect fifth for the perfect fourth as interval or association; (b) the use of the major third instead of the major second as interval of harmonic definition; (c) the exclusion of ternary divisions of the single beat in the rhythmic perception, retaining only the duple divisions, in which, in order to satisfy the craving of ternary divisions, these duple divisions are grouped into three plus three plus two instead of four plus four. It is significant, however, that in those places where the influence is Eastern the African retains his own perception of tone combination.''[2]

This can be accounted for by the strong affiliation between the Oriental and African systems in which the intervallic melodic line and tonal embellishments are alike practised. Examining a number of Negro folk songs, we find that in the majority of them the cadences progress downward and that the phrase ends before the first accent of a measure just as is done in true African song. Negro song in America did not command attention before 1835; however, Sir Grove speaks of melodies ascribed to the American Negro having been printed in London as early as 1782. In June, 1800, the *Boston Review* notes the reprint in the United States of the African song heard by Mungo Park, the explorer, the words of which were adapted by the Countess of Devonshire, and set to music by G. G. Ferrari.

[2] *Negro Year Book*, Chapter XLII, "The Negro in Music," 1931-32. Tuskegee, Ala. From Reprint of article in the *Journal of West Africa*.

This is thought to be the first Negro African song printed in English.

> The winds roared and the rain fell,
> The poor white man, faint and weary
> Came and sat under our tree.
> He has no mother to bring him milk,
>   no wife to grind him corn.

Chorus

> Let us pity the white man, no mother has he,

> The loud wind roared, the rain fell fast,
> The white man yielded to the blast;
> He sat him down, beneath our tree
> For weary, sad, and faint was he;
> And ah, no wife or mother's care
> For him the milk or corn prepare.

Chorus

> The white man shall our pity share,
> Alas, no wife or mother's care
> For him the milk or corn prepare.

> The storm is o'er; the tempest past
> And Mercy's voice has hushed the blast.
> The wind is heard in whispers low;
> The white man far away must go!—
> But ever in his heart will bear
> Remembrance of the Negro's care.

Chorus

> Go, white man, go—but with thee bear
> The Negro's wish, the Negro's prayer;
> Remembrance of the Negro's care.

This song is interesting, mainly, in its expression of the kindly and sympathetic qualities found in African character, and it is not an example of Negro African or Negro American song in its purity.

It is noticeable that before interest was aroused in the inspired and extemporaneous song of the race, Negro minstrelsy was practised by plantation groups of gifted

slaves who were allowed to entertain plantation guests.
As a forerunner of black-face minstrelsy, a troupe of comedians under the direction of Louis Tabary (1791), appeared in New Orleans giving their shows in houses and
tents, and finally in a theater on St. Pierre street between
Royal and Bourbon. Shortly after, white groups were
formed, and with their unique style of entertainment, the
stage setting, a half moon of black faces, an interlocutor
"star," the jocular end men and for music, bones, tam-
bourines and guitars, they gained widespread reputation
here and abroad.

On July 17, 1873, white men with blackened faces and
grotesquely clothed, gave a performance in Cincinnati,
Ohio. This was said to be the first authentic "Negro Minstrel" troupe. But troupes of minstrels were known in
New England some years before this time. Major Dumble-
ton's Ethiopian Serenaders, active in 1844, played in
London in 1848. Jerry Bryant, whose real name was
O'Brien, was of this troupe, but later he led the Bryant's
Minstrels with his two brothers, Dan and Neil, and was
prominent in the North in 1857. Jerry died in 1861, but
the company, said to have been an excellent one, continued
for some years. In 1868, their program included operatic
burlesques.

In 1859, Bryant's Minstrels introduced "Dixie's Land"
which became one of the most popular songs of the nation. It is said to have been written for this troupe by
"Dan Emmett," who published the song in 1860. There
is a controversy as to the authorship. A correspondent
writes in the Boston *Evening Transcript* that he heard
the song in Cincinnati in the early part of 1859, when
it was played by Menter's Military Band. They had been
engaged for a parade in New Orleans and had brought
back this striking air with them. It was said to be of
Negro origin, the sentiment having originated not from

the use of the Mason and Dixon Line but from the currency. In Louisiana, prior to 1860, citizen's notes were printed both in French and English. Among these were popular ten-dollar bills which bore the French term "Dix" and were commonly known as "Dixies."

Eight early versions of the song are found in the Brown University Library (Providence, Rhode Island), under the De Marsan's broadsides. Emmett's "Dixie's Land" was printed on a program of September 12, 1859, and described as "Emmett's Original Plantation Song and Dance." It was also entitled "Dixie's Land, Ethiopian 'Walk 'round'." The first two lines read:

"I wish I was in de land of cotton,
'cimmon seed an' sandy bottom."

As early as March 19, 1860, the song was featured by the Rumsey and Newcomb's Minstrels in New Orleans engagements.[8]

[8] Some few years ago, C. A. Browne, writing "The Story of Dixie" in *The Musician*, stated that when slavery existed in New York, a large plantation on Manhattan Island was owned by a slave-holder named Dixie. As the Abolitionist cause grew in strength, he began to send his slaves south where they found life far more difficult. Their longing for "Dixie's Land" became the burden of their refrain, from which the melody grew. When Daniel Decatur Emmett formed the Virginia Minstrels, together with William Whitlock, Richard Phelan and Frank Brown in 1842, he interspersed "coon songs with jokes." It is said that he wrote "Dixie" on a rainy Sunday, for a Monday performance of Dan Bryant's Company in 1859. Emmett remained with this troupe until 1862. He toured as a minstrel when over eighty years of age.

The Boston *Evening Transcript* printed a copy of the old minstrel song, "I'se Gwine Back to Dixie" under the signature, "L. D. E." The words were found in "Minstrel Songs, Old and New," published by Oliver Ditson & Company, Boston, copyrighted in 1879. The song by C. A. White, was published in 1874.

I'SE GWINE BACK TO DIXIE

By C. A. White

I'se gwine back to Dixie, no more I'se gwine to wander,
My heart's turned back to Dixie, I can't stay here no longer,

Two different stories have been told as to the origin of
the century old song, ''Jim Crow,'' as featured by Thomas
D. Rice (1808-1860), known as ''Dady Rice.'' The Louis-

I miss de old plantation, my home and my relation,
My heart's turned back to Dixie, and I must go.

Chorus:

I'se gwine back to Dixie, I'se gwine back to Dixie,
I'se gwine where the orange blossoms grow,
For I hear the children calling, I see their sad tears falling,
My heart's turned back to Dixie, and I must go.
I've hoed in fields of cotton, I've worked upon the river,
I used to think if I got off, I'd go back there, no, never.
But time has changed the old man, his head is bending low,
His heart's turned back to Dixie, and he must go.

I'm trav'ling back to Dixie, my step is slow and feeble,
I pray the Lord to help me, and lead me from all evil,
And should my strength forsake me, then, kind friends come and
            take me,
My heart's turned back to Dixie, and I must go.

An earlier song may be found in the Evert J. Wendell collection of sheet music of the ''forties.'' A ''Dixie'' song was published in 1860 by Firth, Pond & Co., of New York. It was again
published with the title ''True Dixie for Northern Singers'' pasted
over the original one. The first verse reads:

> ''I'm glad I'm not in de land ob cotton,
>   Good times dar am now forgotten,
> Look away! Look away! Look away! cotton land.
>   In South Carolina dis fuss was born in,
>   Dar Secession had its dawnin','
> Look away! Look away! Look away! cotton land.''

The author has a copy of the 1860 edition of the Dixie song in
five verses, published by Firth, Pond & Company. The cover page
reads—

I wish I was in Dixie's Land
written & composed expressly for
Bryant's Minstrels
by
Dan D. Emmett
Arranged for the Pianoforte by
W. L. Hobbs
Published by Firth, Pond & Co., N. Y., 1860

ville (Kentucky) *Courier Journal*, editorially claims:

"The origin of Jim Crow can be traced directly to Louisville. Tom Rice was playing at one time at the old

The author has other copies of this song from the same house, published in 1856. The minstrel songs are found with guitar accompaniment. And another, "Hark! I hear an Angel Sing," by R. G. Shrival—"As sung by Mr. John Farrenberg of West, Peels & Campbell Minstrels, Piano and guitar. Published by G. A. Oates, Augusta, Georgia, 1856." A third song (in the author's Early American Collection from the music library of Mrs. Henry Holton James—Louise Cushing James, of Boston and Concord) is a queer song of Negro buffoonery, the words of which are enigmatical. This is an unusual example:

Keemo Kimo
Geo. Christy Wood's
Celebrated Banjo Song
Arr. by A. Sedgwick
As sung by P. H. Keenan
Publ. 1854 by Wm. Hall & Son, N. Y.

"In South Car'lina de darkies go
Sing song Kitty can't you ki? me Oh!
   Dat's whar de white folks plant de tow
Sing Song, etc.
   Cover de ground all over wid smoke
Sing Song, etc.
   And up de darkies heads dey poke,
Sing Song, etc.

Cho.

   Keemo Ki mo! Dar! Oh War?
Wid my hi, my lo, & in come Sally singing,
   Sometimes penny winkle, lingtum, nip-cat,
Sing Song Kitty can't you ki? Me Oh.

The following is a song typical of the manner in which the Negro was burlesqued on the black-face minstrel stage. It is found in a Balfe melody printed in the Ethiopian Glee Book "containing songs sung by Christy minstrels—arranged for quartette clubs." "No. 1 and No. 2 by Gumbo Chaff, first banjo player to the King of Congo." The book was published by Elias Howe, Boston, 1848.

I DREAMT THAT I DWELT IN MARBLE HALLS (?)
   I dreamt that I dwelt in Hotel Halls,
   Wid silbery pas at my side, And of all

Louisville Theatre, which stood at Fourth and Green (now Liberty), and behind the theatre there was a livery stable where an amusing old man worked. His name was Jim Crow, and Rice and the other actors had taken to watching him as he went about his work in the stable yard. Laurence Hutton, in his 'Curiosities of the American Stage,' quotes a description of Jim Crow written by one who had seen him:

" 'He was very much deformed, the right shoulder was drawn up high, and the left leg was stiff and crooked at the knee, which gave him a painful, but at the same time ludicrous, limp. He was in the habit of crooning a queer old tune, to which he had applied words of his own. At the end of each verse he gave a peculiar step, 'rockin' de heel' . . . and these were the words of his refrain: 'Wheel about, turn about, do jis so, an' ebery time I wheel about I jump Jim Crow.' "

"Rice watched the unconscious comedy of this performance, and determined to imitate it. One night he persuaded Crow to come and sit in the wings and to lend him his clothes. When Rice appeared on the stage in rags and tatters, crooning the tune and doing his jerky little step, the audience was delighted. The actor, however, had made his performance sure-fire by inventing numerous verses to the Jim Crow melody which dealt with local celebrities and affairs of the day in Louisville, and these little jingles brought down the house.

"The next morning the song of Jim Crow swept over Louisville, and the whole town flocked to the theatre to see Tom Rice do his wonderful act. Soon other cities had a chance to laugh at the antics of the comic Negro, and Rice's fame spread like wildfire, New York greeted him

de buck niggers dat served in dem walls,
Dat I was de pet and de pride.

I had wittles of all kind, boiled and roast
And dishes too many to name,
And I also dreamed, what charmed me most, dat
I lobed Coon, dat I lobed Coon still de same.

The old song "Ginger Blue" is said to have been an earlier Negro minstrel song.—"Walk a chalk, Ginger Blue, git over double trouble, and ole Virginny never tire."

with wild enthusiasm, and thus, it was, that black-face comedy and minstrelsy got their start.''

Another popular version maintains that while playing in Cincinnati in 1830, Thomas Rice heard a Negro stage driver singing a tune, the refrain of which ran, ''Turn about and wheel about an' do jist so, an' every time I turn about, I jump Jim Crow.'' Rice immediately secured the song and used it at an opening performance in Pittsburgh. Joseph Jefferson when quite a young boy had first stage experience in Rice's Minstrel company. Others who later become famous, secured their first practical knowledge of the stage, as did many Negro singing actors on the minstrel boards. Among those thus associated in their early years were J. K. Emmett, Edwin Booth, Edwin Forrest, Nat Goodwin, Fred Stone and Chauncy Olcott.

Edwin F. Christy claimed to be the first to organize a Negro minstrel and has been called the father of minstrelsy. An act which he featured was James Madison Morton's farce given as ''Box and Cox''—''Africanized expressly for George Christy by E. Byron Christy, Esq.''[4]

The Buckleys, James, the father, with his three sons, Richard, George and Frederick, perhaps the first to harmonize Negro tunes, made their appearance with other performers in New York and Boston in 1843. They used their own name until 1844, when having given shows in New Orleans, Louisiana, they changed their name to that of ''The New Orleans Serenaders.'' Philip Hale places the date of the Buckleys' appearance under their new name in the North, as that of November, 1848, at the Bowery Theatre. Meanwhile they had toured Europe.

[4] A copy of Buckley's *Ethiopian Melodies*, copyrighted in 1853 by Philip J. Cozans, is in the possession of David B. Woodbury of South Paris, Maine. *Gentlemen Be Seated, A Parade of the Old-Time Minstrels*, by Dailey Parkman and Sigmund Spaeth. Foreword by Daniel Frohman.

Descriptive names of the black face form of minstrelsy which white performers adapted included those of the Virginia Minstrels followed by Congo Melodists (Boston, 1842), Ethiopian Serenaders, the Sable Harmonizers, and the Nightingale Serenaders. Beginning the 12th of September, 1932, Joseph Weber and Lew Fields celebrated their partnership in minstrelsy by a Golden Jubilee of two weeks' radio performance.

About 1865, the Georgia Minstrels, a Negro troupe, was organized under the leadership of George B. Hicks and later directed by George Callender. The company consisted of twenty-one Negro performers, many of whom were trained musicians, capable of a higher class of work. Outside of the theatre, they entertained in church concerts and private homes. The stage manager, Richard G. Little, possessed a remarkable bass voice of considerable range. John T. Douglass, of New York, and William (Billy) Kersands were members of this troupe when they toured Europe in 1877 and sang before the Queen of England as late as 1883. Members comprising the company in 1877-8, four of whom had been music teachers and three writers of music, were (besides those mentioned above), F. E. Lewis, Samuel Jones, William Elmer Lyle, James Emidy, Peter Devonear, George Cooper, Robert Mack, David Scudder, James Grace, Oct. Moore, R. Emidy, Robert Hight, Charles Anderson, James Fernand, Messrs. Thompson and Gaines, and William W. Morris, interlocutor.

In America they were hailed as "masters of minstrelsy." In the West, according to the Cincinnati *Commercial*, they drew better houses than any white troupe. P. T. Barnum said of them, "They are extraordinary, and the best I ever saw. They fully deserve their large patronage." While in the East, the Boston *Herald* said, "The Georgia Minstrels have burst upon us like an avalanche. All the reserved seats were sold last evening before the performance commenced; and the house was filled by a fashionable audience—one rarely seen at a minstrel entertainment. The troupe have made a decided hit, and their performances last night were received with great enthusiasm. Their songs and choruses are excellent; their puns, jokes, and stories, fresh and laughable; and their special acts new, and of a superior order. The performances of the troupe have happily filled a void which existed in the amusement field." The *Folio,* a musical journal of Boston, said, "As for the whole evening's enjoyment, it may be characterized as novel from the fact that it is native and not imitative, commendable because it is wholly refined, and most pleasant because it is always artistic."

Before the twilight of minstrelsy, the largest Negro company ever known was organized under the name of Callender's Consolidated Spectacular Colored Minstrels, Gustave and Charles Frohman, proprietors (1882). Another well known company was that of Lew Johnson's Plantation Minstrels. Somewhat later, Lew Dockstader's Minstrels, a so-called two-part show, one half white, the other half black, were hailed as the best minstrels of the day. In the Primrose and West Minstrels, 1883, Billy Windom who was a Negro tenor, wrote his own songs, among which was the popular ballad, "She may have seen better days." This troupe was called "The Forty Whites and Thirty Blacks."

At this time popular songs and writers also had their day. The "Jim Crow" Song of Negro minstrelsy days, held the stage between 1815 and 1857, but rumors of its coming were heralded by Negro melodies from Missouri as early as 1810 and 1812. Henry E. Krehbiel mentions a descriptive song of the battle of Plattsburg which he heard sung in Negro dialect in 1815. A song which was printed in the *Negro Singer's Own Book,* 1846, is a Canoe Song typical of the racial songs of canoe and river.

"I got up in the mornin' 'bout brake of day,
I went to de ribber, my canoe gone away,
When I got to de ribber radder wide
I look ober yonder, my canoe on toder side."

It would be difficult, however, to declare that either of these two songs are originally Negro ones. The first was incorporated into a drama while the second is akin to the type of true Negro song that was parodied by white impersonators on the minstrel stage.

The first Negro writer of popular ballads was Samuel Lucas Milady, born August 7, 1848. He wrote "Grandfather's Clock is too tall for the Shelf." When he featured this song in 1878, the Milwaukee *Sentinel* said, "His rendition of 'Grandfather's Clock,' with distant chorus and refrain, was the sweetest music we ever listened to. The audience was breathless; the lowest whisper could be heard distinctly all over the house . . . . As an actor he takes high rank." Lucas died January 10, 1916. One of the Frohmans, who attended the funeral, gave the eulogy. A talented daughter, Marie Lucas, orchestra director, survives him.

"Grandfather's Clock" was published by C. M. Cady of New York as the "most popular song in America," with words and music credited to Henry Clay Work, a Connecticut white man. However, from the time the song became known—in 1876—it was spoken of as Sam Lucas' song. A relative of the comedian's, Bishop Reverdy C. Ransom of the A. M. E. Church, says that Lucas claimed that Work heard the song, lìked it, and bought it from him. He afterwards published it naming himself as author and composer.

As sung by the comedian, it brought the demand of an order of 10,000 copies by Oliver Ditson & Co., from the publisher Cady. A correspondent addressing the Boston *Evening Transcript* a few years ago said, "The song used to be sung by the late Sam Lucas, colored vocalist and actor. He always referred to it as being his own composition. He was always fashionably attired, courteous always, and was in frequent demand when a 'colored aggregation of talent' was given at any of the local theaters. His characterization of Uncle Tom in 'Uncle Tom's Cabin,' was considered his best effort."

The song has been reprinted in various collections such as "Songs the Whole World Sings," "More Heart Throbs," and in "Songs of the Rotary Club."

GRANDFATHER'S CLOCK

My grandfather's clock was too large for the shelf,
  So it stood ninety years on the floor;
It was taller ·by half than the old man himself,
  Though it weighed not a pennyweight more.
It was bought on the morn of the day he was born,
  And was always his treasure and pride;
But it stopped short—never to go again—
  When the old man died.

Chorus:

Ninety years, without slumbering—tick, tick, tick, tick,
  His life-seconds numbering—tick, tick, tick, tick,
It stopped short—never to go again—When the old man
    died.
  In watching its pendulum swinging to and fro,
Many hours had he spent while a boy;
  And in childhood and manhood the clock seemed to
    know
And to share both his grief and his joy;
  For it struck twenty-four when he entered the door,
With a blooming and beautiful bride:
  But it stopped short—never to go again—
When the old man died.

My grandfather said that of those he could hire
  Not a servant so faithful he found,

For it wasted no time and had but one desire—
  At the close of each week to be wound.
It was kept in its place—not a frown on its face,
  And its hands never hung by its side;
But it stopped short—never to go again—
  When the old man died.

It rang an alarm in the dead of the night—
  An alarm that for years had been dumb—
And we knew that his spirit was pluming for flight—
  That his hour of departure had come.
Still the clock kept time, with a soft muffled chime,
  As we silently stood by his side:
But it stopped short—never to go again—
  When the old man died.

The guitar was the favorite instrument used to accompany these old songs. The famous old Mocking Bird song was first published with guitar accompaniment. It evidently appeared before 1854. The lithographed cover of another old song reads—

"What is Home Without a Mother," dedicated to Ann Eliza P. Shuster, by Alice Hawthorne, guitar, piano, and voice, 1854, entered by Winner and Shuster." The cover page gives a list of twenty songs by Alice Hawthorne, author of "My Cottage Home," "Song of the Farmer," "Our Good Old Friends," (et cetera) and "Listen to the Mocking Bird." We learn from this publication that Winner did not at first lay claim to the authorship of the Mocking Bird song, but releases it under the authorship of "Alice Hawthorne," who may have written verses to other songs credited to her son. The Mocking Bird song, with its whistling refrain, for long one of the favorites of the minstrel singers, was a Negro extemporization. An early copy can be seen in the Schomburg collection in the Negro Division of the 135th Street Public Library, New York City.

Among the first singing-comedians whose tunes became

well-known, was Richard (George) Milburn, a barber in Philadelphia. He wrote "Listen to the Mocking-Bird." He spent his leisure in imitating the song of birds and playing the guitar, and was engaged by the Philadelphia Library Company, a Negro literary organization connected with St. Thomas' Episcopal Church, to give exhibitions of his skill. Septimus Winner, a skilled white musician, induced Milburn to whistle to him bird tunes which he wrote down. Milburn, who was also an expert guitarist, is said to have sold his tune, the mocking-bird song, for $5.00, while the publishers realized $100,000 on its sale. In 1855, the song was published with the frontispiece, "Music by Richard Milburn, Words by Alice Hawthorne. Publisher, Septimus Winner." Lee and Walker became later publishers, and the final credit was given to Winner as the creator of the melody. Alice Hawthorne was the mother of Winner.

Other song writers known in Philadelphia wrote a sentimental type of song, well-liked in that day. In 1829, James Hemenway contributed to "Atkinson's Casket" in Philadelphia, and published "That Rest so Sweet like Bliss Above," "The Philadelphia Entree March," and "Hunter and Hope Waltzes." In 1859, A. J. R. Connor's "My Cherished Hope, My Fondest Dreams" was published in the February number of *The Anglo-African Magazine,* a literary publication edited by Thomas Hamilton, a Negro, and printed by the same at 48 Beekman Street, New York. From 1846 to 1857, Connor composed a number of pieces among which were "American Polka Quadrilles" and "New York Polka Waltz," published by music houses of Philadelphia and New York.

Gussie L. Davis of Cincinnati, Ohio, was a well-known writer of ballads many of which were in the favorite waltz rhythm. The best known of his many songs were "Do the Old Folks Miss Me," "My Creole Sue," "The

Light House by the Sea," and "When Nelly Was Raking the Hay." The last-named, dedicated to the tenor, Wallace King,[5] was published in 1884.

One of the most popular songs written about 1875 was James Bland's "Carry Me Back to Ole Virginny." The thousands of Virginians and others who are delighted by this song today ignore the fact that it emerged from the mind of a black man.

One of the principal instruments used by the minstrels was the banjo said to have been derived from the African "bania." A noted banjoist of the period known as the "80's," was Horace Weston, formerly a slave who was said to have "stroked" the strings instead of picking them and who also used a thimble. The white banjoist, Edward C. Dobson, studied Weston's methods and became one of the finest players of his day. These popular ballads together with slave songs, doggerel rhymes, and amusing Negro impersonations may have had but little value as a medium in the development of Negro music in the United States, but they were a type, nationally liked in their time and, in certain of their manifestations, have lived in the rollicking college songs of today.

For some years the melodic line of Negro song had its appeal. In 1845, Stephen Foster entered a competition for a prize offered by a minstrel company for the best Negro song. "Way Down South" was written and liked, but it did not receive the prize. It was followed by "Louisiana Bell" and "O Susannah," after which came songs by which he will be long remembered—"My Old Kentucky Home," "The Old Folks at Home," and "Old

[5] "When Nellie Was Raking the Hay," (dedicated to Mrs. Dora S. King, Portland, Maine), words and music by Gussie L. Davis as sung by Wallace King of Callenders Minstrels, was published by J. C. Greene & Co., Cincinnati, 1884. An autograph copy presented to Mrs. Elizabeth Francis of New York City by Mr. King in 1884 is in the author's collection of Negro-American Music.

Black Joe.'' The latter was written in 1860, and in the first edition, it is described as ''An Ethiopian Melody.'' Stephen Foster's interest in Negro music dates from the time when as a little lad, he was taken by his mother's maid to a Negro church. Hearing the religious melodies sung, he received a lasting impression.

Russell Hanby, another song writer, thus attained fame. The year 1933 marked the centenary anniversary of this writer of ''Darling Nellie Gray,'' one of the well remembered ''heart songs'' of long ago, recently incorporated in a modern composition of old plantation days. The words written as a blackboard singing exercise were first sung by the pupils of the writer at the district school where he taught at Rushville, Ohio. Hanby was born in that town, on July 22, 1833, the son of a minister. He played as a boy in the old yard adjoining the local church which was also used as a school, and he and his playmate Hyde, became interested in a particular grave—that of a runaway slave. A Negro, Joe Selby, who had succeeded in making his escape from Kentucky to Rushville, related, it was said, the story of his disappointed love to a group of sympathetic abolitionists who were gathered at his death-bed.

This slave loved a young girl named Nellie Gray who belonged to a neighboring plantation. After his escape he had striven to earn enough to purchase her freedom, but before he could do so her owner, involved in debt, sold Nellie to a richer plantation farther south. The sad story affected Hanby, who wrote the poem which he long afterwards had copyrighted and then sold for $25. An only living pupil, Mrs. T. M. Adams, learned the song from the composer, and her brother, George E. Kalb, of Rushville, has told the story of Nellie Gray to the American public.

"There's a low green valley on the old Kentucky shore,
Where I've whiled many happy hours away,
A-sitting and a-singing by the little cottage door,
Where lived my poor Nellie Gray.''

The melody of "Way Down upon the Suwanee River''
is said to have been one of pathetic homesickness sung by
a woman slave who was sold from the Suwanee River district in North Central Florida, to Alabama. The song,
which had echoed up the Ohio River, appealed strongly to
Stephen Foster who, taking a voyage down the Tennessee
River to Florence, Alabama, found the original singer and
wrote down the song for publication. The melody is the
same as "Way Down upon the Mobile River.''

The enslaved or newly-freed continued to sing the extemporaneous melodies which for centuries had brought
them comfort and solace. The first authentic picture of
the use of the slave songs, the manner in which they were
sung and their meaning, come to us from the great
Negro statesman, Frederick Douglass, in his autobiography,[6] as they were heard on the Lloyd plantation in
Talbot County, Maryland, during his childhood; this must
have been about 1827. Douglass wrote:

"I did not, when a slave, fully understand the deep
meaning of those rude and apparently incoherent songs.
I was, myself, within the circle, so that I could then
neither hear nor see as those without might see and
hear. They breathed the prayer and complaint of souls
over-flowing with the bitterest anguish . . . The remark
in the olden time was not unfrequently made, that
slaves were the most contented and happy laborers in
the world, and their dancing and singing were referred
to in proof of this alleged fact; but it was a great mis-
take to suppose them happy because they sometimes
made those joyful noises. The songs of the slaves represented their sorrows, rather than their joys.

"Slaves were expected to sing as well as to work.

[6] *Life and Times of Frederick Douglass*, p. 61.

'Make a noise there! Make a noise there!' and 'Bear a hand,' were words usually addressed to slaves when they were silent . . . There was generally more or less singing among the teamsters, at all times. It was a means of telling the overseer, in the distance, where they were and what they were about. But on the allowance days those commissioned to the Great House farm were peculiarly vocal. While on the way they would make the grand old woods for miles around reverberate with their wild and plaintive notes. They were indeed both merry and sad. Child as I was, these wild songs greatly depressed my spirits."

During the anti-slavery activities in the North, song played an important part at the conventions. William Wells Brown, a Negro anti-slavery agent of the Massachusetts Anti-slavery Society, edited *The Anti-Slavery Harp*, a compilation of songs to be used at abolition meetings. These pieces from various sources were published in 1848 and 1849. Sojourner Truth made up her own songs, unique in nature, and religious in mood, and sang them in the reform and abolitionist campaigns throughout the North.[7]

It is now felt that the "Sorrow Songs," as termed by Dr. W. E. B. Du Bois, should be preserved not only for

[7] Mentioning Negro folk-songs, the *Atlantic Monthly* of February, 1862, quoting the poet J. G. Whittier in *Poems At Port Royal, 1861*, said, "It was in 1862 when Miss McKim, later associated with William F. Allen and Charles Pickard Ware in publishing the first and most valuable collection of slave songs, wrote of the plantation hymns in Dwight's *Journal of Music*, that the attention of the public was called to the folk-songs." In September, 1863, E. L. Pierce writing in the *Atlantic Monthly* describes a visit which he made to the St. Helena Islands and to the freedmen at Port Royal. On March 25, on his arrival, he visited a school at which 101 Negro children were receiving instruction. Impressed by their singing, he wrote:

"They sang with much spirit 'My Country 'tis of thee' and also a new Whittier song 'The very oaks are greener clad' . . . The their melodic charm, but because of the fact that they were interwoven with the history of the nation. The cruelty and horror of American slavery had burned deep scars on the hearts and minds of the bondmen, but while passing through their Gethsemane, their pain was embodied in such poignant strains that their heart-breaking song deeply moved the listener by their earnest feeling and deep faith. There were hymns that glowed with religious fervor and constant belief in ultimate victory through the gateway of death, and other melodies that teemed with a joyous pursuit of happiness and the care-

prevalent song, however, and by the wayside, is that of 'John Brown's Body' which very much amused our white soldiers, particularly when the singers roll out—'We'll hang Jeff Davis on a Sour Apple Tree.' The children also sang their own songs, such as

'In de mornin' when I rise (twice)
Tell my Jesus, Huddy Oh!
I wash my hands in de mornin' glory, (twice)
Tell my Jesus, Huddy Oh!
    Pray Tony, pray boy, you got de order, (twice)
Tell my Jesus, Huddy Oh'!"

(Huddy Oh was a contraction for "Howdy do.")

Mr. Pierce was impressed by the manner in which the songs were sung:

"Their shouts are very strange—in truth almost indescribable. The children form a ring and move around in a kind of shuffling dance, singing all the time. Four or five stand apart and sing very energetically, clapping their hands, stamping their feet and rocking their bodies to and fro.

"These are the musicians to whose performances the shouters keep perfect time . . . It is probable that they are the barbarous expression of religion handed down to them from their African ancestors and destined to pass away under the influences of Christian teaching. The people on these islands have no songs. They sing only hymns and most of these are sad."

Following H. G. Spaulding in 1863, Col. Thomas Wentworth Higginson of Boston wrote of the Negro hymns as he heard them sung in South Carolina and called attention to the necessity of preserving them. His appeal in favor of the Slave Songs was heeded.

FISK JUBILEE SINGERS

less abandon of rhythmic dance. Educational institutions have greatly served to perpetuate these improvised songs of a race.[8]

Such interest in this music at Fisk University is a striking example of these efforts. With the idea of raising funds for the enlargement of the institution, a band of students known as "The Fisk Jubilee Singers," under the tutelage and direction of the Rev. George White undertook a concert tour in October, 1871. The troupe left Nashville on the sixth of the month and received their name while breakfasting in Columbus. Those who composed the company were Jennie Jackson and Maggie Porter, soprani; Ella Sheppard, soprano and pianist; Minnie Tate, contralto; Thomas Rutling, tenor; Benjamin M. Holmes, tenor; and I. P. Dickerson with Greene Evans, basses. Later members were Mabel Tate and Hinton Alexander. The songs which soon made an enviable reputation for the Jubilee Singers were the religious folk-songs called "Negro Spirituals."

These musicians relied mainly upon the "songs of their people." "Steal Away" charmed the Council of Congregational Churches at Oberlin as did "Swing Low, Sweet Chariot," when sung for Queen Victoria and the crowned heads in Europe. "No Auction Block for Me" was a favorite song which pleased the Prince of Wales and such patrons as the Earl of Shaftesbury, Gladstone, Whittier, Longfellow, and the daughter of Livingstone. Received everywhere with great favor, these singers raised a fund of $150,000 which built the fine Memorial Hall of Fisk

[8] During the Reconstruction days that followed the emancipation of the slaves, the American Missionary Society of the Congregational Church established the first day school for the freedmen at Fortress Monroe, Virginia, in 1861; and in 1865, a school at Nashville, Tennessee. Minor shcools for colored and Indian had existed since 1620. In 1867, a charter was secured for the school in Nashville now known as Fisk University.

University. Later receipts made possible the building of Livingstone Hall. The history of the Fisk Jubilee Singers—the choice of their song material, the plantation melodies—refutes the statement made in 1932 by George Pullen Jackson, a professor of German at Vanderbilt University, that the Fisk Jubilee Singers depended on the Moody and Sankey type of white revival song, and not on Negro Spirituals.

In July, 1932, the "Fisk Jubilee Singers," for many years the only choral group specializing in the singing of the religious Negro folk-songs, was disbanded by the University. On October 6, 1932, Fisk University and the alumni from every section joined in holding a Jubilee Day celebration in honor of those who constituted the Jubilee Singers of sixty-one years ago. As the old group dispersed others took their place. The tenor, Thomas Rutling, who was with the Jubilee Singers when they were in Hamburg, Germany, in 1878, remained on the continent for further study. After twelve years, he returned to England where he gave lectures illustrated by music. A small volume, *Tom, An Autobiography*, was published in 1907. Lady Astor arranged a special concert by the singers when they were on European tour in 1924 under the direction of James A. Myers. His wife, Mrs. Myers, long devoted to the musical activities of the organization, was voted a yearly pension of $1,000 when the University decided to sponsor no longer this musical aggregation. With these is connected the name of John Wesley Work, who stood out pre-eminently in the history of pure religious song at Fisk University and in the United States at large. His career as teacher, singer, choral conductor and restorer of the Negro Spirituals will be treated in a later chapter.[9]

[9] See pages 348-350.

them. All the great musicians have borrowed from the songs of the common people. Beethoven's most charming scherzo is based upon what might now be considered a skilfully handled Negro melody . . . In the Negro melodies of America I discover all that is needed for a great and noble school of music. They are pathetic, tender, passionate, melancholy, solemn, religious, bold, merry, gay, gracious, or what you will. It is music that suits itself to any mood or purpose.''

In March, 1918, when the piece was played by the Philharmonic Society in New York, this interesting letter from Harry Burleigh appeared in the program book:

"There is a tendency in these days to ignore the Negro elements in the 'New World' symphony, shown by the fact that many of those who were able in 1893 to find traces of Negro musical color all through the symphony, though the workmanship and treatment of the themes was and is Bohemian, now cannot find anything in the whole four movements that suggests any local or Negro influence, though there is no doubt at all that Dvorák was deeply impressed by the old Negro 'spirituals' and also by Foster's songs. It was my privilege to sing repeatedly some of the old plantation songs for him at his house, and one in particular, 'Swing Low, Sweet Chariot,' greatly pleased him, and part of this old 'spiritual' will be found in the second theme of the first movement of the symphony, in G major, first given out by the flute. The similarity is so evident that it doesn't even need to be heard; the eye can see it. Dvorák saturated himself with the spirit of these old tunes and then invented his own themes. There is a subsidiary theme in G minor in the first movement with a flat seventh, and I feel sure the composer caught this peculiarity of most of the slave songs from some that I sang to him; for he used to stop me and ask if that was the way the slaves sang.''

Miss Alice Fletcher claims that she heard the Indians sing the theme of the "Largo," at a time when they had no borrowed music. As the Indians and Negroes inter-married (either with or without sanction of the Church), in both New England and in the South, during the earliest days in America, one may find Indian themes borrowed from the Negro. The Indian folk song is markedly un-melodic.

The deduction of Prof. Leo Weiner of Harvard Col-lege, with respect to the African discovery of America, is of interest to the student of ethnology and may account for the similarity of some of the American Indian melo-dies and the Negro tunes. In 1920, Prof. Weiner con-tended that the civilization of the Indian was profoundly influenced by the Negroes who came to America from the Congo and Guinea before the fifteenth century.

CHAPTER IV

NEGRO FOLK SONGS—RELIGIOUS AND SECULAR

DESIGN—RHYTHMIC PATTERNS—MODE—TEXT—AFRICAN
LANGUAGES—EDUCATION—USE OF SONGS—HISTORY OF
FAMILIAR SONGS—SPIRITUALS—BURYING SONGS—WORK
SONGS—LOVE SONGS—BOAT SONGS AND CHANTEYS—
PLAY SONGS

In a serious study of Negro music it is readily seen that there is a rhythmical relationship and melodic similarity between native African music and that of the Negro American folk song. These two conceptions are an inheritance from a strong root of African ancestry. As the Negro, first brought to the United States with the exploiters of Virginia in 1619, over three hundred years ago,[1] gradually became a product of American institutions in the making, and a new race was developed by a new environment and the fusion of Negro blood with that of the Indian native and white inhabitant, it is obvious that his folk music brought with him from Africa, should have become a particular music absolutely his own.

There is, of course, the universality of certain principles of design which are to be found in all folk music, but the ingenuity shown in the shifting of accent or addition of grace notes and embellishments to give contrast in different repetitions; in the manner of reiteration of the

[1] It is neither African nor Negro Music—it is truly Negro-American. Alexander Haggerty Krappe writing on American folklore says, "There exists no such thing as American folk lore but only European, or African, or, Far Eastern folk lore on the American continent."—Krappe, Alexander Haggerty, *Folk Song*, Chapter on "American Folklore."

same figure or phrase at higher levels; and, in the enhancement of tonal coloring given by intricate rhythmical clapping of hands and patting feet—these qualities produce a folk musical contribution that is unique and apart. We may be reminded that the Irish too repeat their melodic phrases higher and higher, and that the Scotch and Italians employ the jerking figuration of an eighth (1/8) note to a quarter (1/4) note, or a sixteenth (1/16) towards the eighth, but in the entirety the Negro American folk song shows a well-developed sense of form and an original usage of familiar devices. In the working downward to a close, a feeling for tonality is expressed. Of this the song "Roll, Jordan Roll" is an excellent example.

The African Negro was sufficiently advanced to invent musical instruments. As he was stripped of every form of birthright when brought to America, necessity forced him to fashion crude instruments from material at hand —trees, reeds and bones. Added to clapping and patting, one form of rhythm grew from the performers beating an improvised drum in such a manner as to bring the beat and words simultaneously together. The rhythmic patterns, never simple, were made to suit the verbal expression.

Intricacy of rhythm has added to the folklorist's difficulty in notating songs as heard sung. The metre is sometimes changed in the same song such as passing from 4/4 to 2/4 or 4/4 to 3/4. There is a rarity of 3/4 time as explained in another chapter. A frequent change of bar time as practised now by writers of "modern music" is in keeping with a custom followed in Russian and in southern French folk song. To these races the Negro is spiritually akin. Dalcroze in *Eurhythmics, Art and Education*, states that "at present time, owing to Negro and Oriental rhythms, freedom has been restored to rhythmic successions; alternating unequal bars have become natural, and arbitrary accentuations no longer astonish anyone. The old rigidity is dead, and the traditional thematic developments are replaced by variations of tempo and of accent."

The layman speaks of the Negro folk song as being in the minor mode. The fact is that the minor is found to a lesser extent than that of any other key. The songs sound minor because they are in the old "Dorian" (arithmetic) mode—the oldest used in folk songs—one that is based on the dominant of the scale. For example,

C—D—E—F—G—A flat—B flat—C

Here we have the scale of F based on the dominant (fifth tone) C and five whole steps and two half-steps employed. The Hypo-dorian mode C—D—E flat—F—G—A flat—B flat—C is commonly found used in Negro song. Many are in the old North African scale of the Arabians—the "Mixolydian" of which C—D flat—E flat—G flat—A flat—B flat—C. The Negro oftener employs the scale known as pentatonic, which has no minor seconds, but is a whole tone scale best exemplified by playing a scale on all black keys.

Of this "Blin' Man Lyin' at de Pool," as noted in the Calhoun Collection of Plantation Songs, is an excellent example of a melody without a fourth or seventh—the use of a five tone scale. "Drive Satan Away," found in this collection, is in an interesting mode. It is that of the old Syntolydian as founded on C with the F sharp. There are different inflexions used even in the five tone scale which gives an effect of singing in quarter tone intervals. In the author's personal collection there is such a song heard at Sedalia, North Carolina. There in a rural district many quaint old melodies are sung by the students of Palmer Memorial Institute, under the principalship of Charlotte Hawkins Brown. In "Everybody Got to be Tried" they give with pure intonation, and not by an effect of the "glissando," intervals that are between A and A sharp, and G and G sharp. The student group singing quarter tones with the utmost ease, makes a decided and novel impression on the listener.

In the earliest Greek system the musical scale consisted of seven tones that corresponded to the seven planets of Moon, Mercury, Venus, Sun, Mars, Jupiter and Saturn. The seven colors of the rainbow corresponded to the tones of the scale which gives a table for the new exponents of "color" in music. The African had no written musical system but is it not possible that the Yorubans tuned their lyre to their five gods of protection—Hermes (lightning), Shango (thunder), Ifa (prophecy), Helios (sun) and Oshu (moon)? At least it is an amusingly interesting conjecture. The African *kissar* is tuned to a five tone scale.

An imagery of poetic text found in the religious and sentimental songs was born of the Negro's innate gift of oratory and his transcendental reasoning. African folklore abounds with legends and proverbs, and the use of metaphor is very pronounced in the songs of the Negro wherever born. The music is naturally demonstrative and is a true index to a highly emotional nature. Its freedom and lack of restraint mark it apart from that of the pallid and repressed music of the so-called Nordic races. It is noticeable that the words of the songs are grouped in short phrases which are repeated over and over again, the first and third lines usually sung as the verse and the second and fourth as a refrain which is repeated after each stanza. In many songs the verse is varied only by the naming of each family relationship. Outside of the religious songs, the words are often difficult to understand.

It is not surprising that those Africans first brought as captives to America found it difficult to express themselves in the words of a newly-heard language and that the meaning of the words in a number of the oldest songs should be obscure. Language as spoken by their captors had to be acquired as a child learns to formulate words of his parents' tongue, with the exception of those colored persons of later days who enjoyed freedom and education in the North, and the fortunate free people of the South who enjoyed educational advantages.

The African language itself is one of many tongues. The English acquired by the illiterate slave became a mutual means of communication for the early captives from various sections of the African coast.[2] In the Negro dialect as evolved in America all harsh letters such as G, D, T, and R, are softened or eliminated, while as in Latin-America, the V is blurred to B. David Guion, a musician who is interested in Negro song and in his own West Texas cow-boy songs, said in an interview, "Half the beauty of the old, typical Negro music is in the quaint pronunciation of words and their still quainter and more charming mis-pronunciations. If these are altered the value of the song is lowered by half. A proof of this lies in the fact that the Moody-and-Sankey-izing that has been done to much of Negro music has invariably been detrimental."[3]

There are about eight hundred folk songs recorded but the Spirituals, the songs in which the Negro expressed his faith in "a victory that overcometh the world," are the most commonly known of these melodies. Many of

[2] There has lately been awakened an interest in the study of African languages, especially as inaugurated in 1926 by the International Institute of African Languages and Cultures that publishes a journal, *Africa*, and monographs in the orthography of African tongues. The society also issues a series of studies of texts written or taken down by Africans, in their own vernacular with translations.

[3] *Musical America*, September, 1930.

the hymns were known in the early period as "shouts."
These were stirringly sung at camp-meetings and are
still to be heard in rural churches in the South. For
example, in Alabama, the old song, "Redeem, Redeem,"
expressed the thought which could not be spoken—

"Some go to church an' dey put on pretense
    Until de day ob grace is spent.
Ef dey haven' been changed you'll know it well,
    When Gabriel blow', dey will go to hell.
Sunday come' dey'll have Christian faith,
    Monday come' dey will lose deir grace;
De Devil gets in dey will roll up deir sleeve
    Religion come out an' begin to leave."[4]

In this manner, even the religious songs were used as
songs of satire or as "taunts" such as are generously
found in true African song. The hymns or "shouts" also
did duty as rowing songs. The fine old spiritual "Michael,
row the boat ashore" was one of the songs employed interchangeably. John J. Niles' Old Songs Hymnal includes Negro Spirituals characteristic of the highly emotional songs sung at revivals. A reprint in 1929, of the
early collection of Slave Songs of the United States by
William Francis Allen, Charles Pickford Ware, and Lucy
McKim Garrison, who gathered the folk-songs personally
before 1867, places at hand the most valuable historic data
relating to the "shouts" and other forms of folk melodies.

Referring to the singing, the authors give in this book
an illuminating passage to describe the manner in which
the songs were sung at Coffins Point, St. Helena Island,
off the coast of South Carolina. On a neighboring plantation, "The Negroes keep exquisite time in singing and
do not suffer themselves to be daunted by any obstacle
in the words. The most obstinate scripture phrases or
snatches from hymns they will force to do duty with any
tune they please and will dash heroically through tro-

[4] See Plantation Songs, by Calhoun, second edition.

chaic tunes at the head of a column of iambics with wonderful skill."

Of the later day manner of shouting and the use of
shout songs, James Weldon Johnson in his *Book of American Negro Spirituals*, describes the ring shout as that of
a late type which he saw danced in boyhood days in
Florida. He speaks of it as a "survival of an African
ceremony" such as he saw performed in Venezuela and
in Haiti. He rightly adds that educated ministers and
congregations discouraged the shouts. And yet, during
the present year (1935), hysterical and ecstatic shouting
was an excitable feature of "revivals" held in a Negro
church in Boston.

A number of rare old songs in light vein were discovered on the island of St. Helena a few years ago by
Natalie Curtis-Burlin. In these parts, a section least influenced by white civilization, and in not far distant parts,
the odd and peculiar dialect of the *Geechee* people
whom the author sought to hear speak and sing in Georgia, attest the influence of the land of their forbears, that
of Africa. Within recent years, we have a number of
writers investigating and studying the speech and customs of the *Geechees* and *Gullahs* who never came into
close contact with Anglo-Saxons, as their fore-parents
were brought to this country shortly before the emancipation of the slaves. These last cargoes of native Africans
came from the Congo and other sections; hence a difference in dialects.

The plantation songs were used interchangeably—for
revival shouts, for burial songs, for hymns of consolation,
and for signals, or means of communication. In planning
secret meetings or plotting ways by which they might escape to the free North or to Canada, songs that had a
double meaning were used. At St. Michael, Talbot County, Maryland, five young men, Henry and John Harris,

Sandy Jenkins, Henry Bailey and Charles Roberts, plotted with young Frederick Douglass, in 1836, to find means of escaping to free territory. They repeatedly sang "O Canaan, Sweet Canaan, I am bound for the land of Canaan," which meant they were determined to reach the North—their Canaan.

There are now many collections of Negro folk songs available. In the songs herein noted are those that are best known and which might be regarded as "master songs." They are chosen with the hope that the history of each particular one may be of value to serious students. Here are songs of triumphant faith, of solace and comfort, of tribulation, and secular songs pertaining to labor and recreation, love and childhood.

Negro Spirituals

These songs known as Spirituals are the expression of a supreme belief in immortality that transcends mere religious creeds and theoretical dogma. Through them the paganism of African "spirit" songs are reborn and modified by Christian doctrines, and they are the musical expression of spiritual emotion created *by* the race and not *for it*.

"*Swing Low, Sweet Chariot*," an American "Negro Spiritual" in the pentatonic scale, noted in *Fisk Jubilee Songs*, 1871, offers a key to this development. The variants of this song are "Good· Old Chariot," "Swing Low, Sweet Chariot," (Hampton) and "The Danville Chariot." In the first movement of Dvorák's "New World Symphony," in which this theme occurs, it is given out by the flute. The song has been arranged with piano accompaniment by many composers, and transcribed for organ by Carl R. Diton. William Arms Fisher, who has given the melody a setting for solo voice and piano, tells an interesting story about the song, which was told to him by

Bishop Frederick Fisher of Calcutta, India, who had recently returned from Central Africa. He relates:

Zimbabwe

"Bishop Fisher stated that in Rhodesia he had heard the natives sing a melody so closely resembling "Swing Low, Sweet Chariot" that he felt that he had found it in its original form; moreover, the subject was identical. The tribe of natives that inhabit the region near the great Victoria Falls have a custom from which the song arose. When one of their chiefs, in the old days, was about to die, he was placed in a great canoe together with the trappings that marked his rank, and food for his journey. The canoe was set afloat in midstream headed toward the great Falls and the vast column of mist that rises from them. Meanwhile the tribe on the shore would sing its chant of farewell. The legend is that on one occasion the king was seen to rise in his canoe at the very brink of the Falls and enter a chariot that, descending from the mists, bore him aloft. This incident gave rise to the words 'Swing Low, Sweet Chariot,' and the song, brought to America by African slaves long ago, became anglicized and modified by their Christian faith."[5]

In America, it is told that the song arose from an incident which happened to a woman sold from a Mississippi plantation to Tennessee. Rather than be separated from her child, she was about to drown herself and little one in the Cumberland River, when she was prevented by an old Negro woman, who exclaimed, "Wait, let de Chariot of de Lord swing low and let me take de Lord's scroll and read it to you." The heart-broken mother became consoled and was reconciled to the parting. The song became known with the passing on of the story, which seems more legendary than real.[6]

[5] *Seventy Negro Spirituals*, edited by Wm. Arms Fisher, notes on the songs.

[6] A painting of "Swing Low, Sweet Chariot" by Malvin Gray Johnson, N. Y., won the special prize of $250 in an exhibition of Negro artists recently held under auspices of the Harmon Foundation and Commission on Race Relations of the Federal Council of Churches.

Among these songs several others of unusual importance should be noted.[7] "My Lord Delivered Daniel" in major key of G, with a variant from Florida, "O Daniel," and another title of the original in Kentucky. "Wrestling Jacob," with four variants, "My Lord what a Morning," from Southeastern Slave States, "A New Hiding Place" with the same theme, "I Want to be Ready," from Kentucky, with such variants as "Walk Jerusalem Jes Like John," and "Walk Into Jerusalem Jes Like John," and "When I come to Die." Next there was the "Old Ship of Zion," from Maryland and Virginia, with many variants like "Don't You See the Old Ship a Sailing?" and "In the Old Ship Don't You Weep after Me," "Inching Along," "Keep a Inching Along," from Alabama, "Go Down Moses," an interpretation of Hebrew History with variants from Virginia and the Bahamas. As the Lord delivered the Jews so would He the Negroes. We note also "Did not Old Pharaoh Get Lost," "When Moses Smote the Water," and "Turn Back Pharaoh's Army," "When the Lord Called Moses," belonging to this same class.

Of another type was "Nobody Knows the Trouble I've Seen" or "Nobody Knows the Trouble I See," or "Nobody Knows the Trouble I See, Lord," originally from the Sea Islands. "Sometimes I Feel Like a Motherless Child," from Mississippi; "I am Troubled in Mind," "O My Body Racked Wid de Fever," from Georgia, with a version "I'm a Trouble in de Mind," from Port Royal Islands; "Don't Be Weary Traveler," from Virginia, "Let us Cheer the Weary Traveler," from Kentucky; "I Long to See the Day," of major node probably known first in the Bahama Islands; "There's a Meeting Here Tonight," probably noted first from Port Royal Islands; and "My Way is Cloudy," found in several places.

Then there are two distinct types of slave songs, al-

[7] See Appendix for a detailed explanation of these songs.

though there are but few songs using the practice of
slavery as a theme in the text. Some of these are "Many
Thousand Gone," "No More Auction Block for Me," and
"Is Master Going to Sell us Tomorrow?" Then there are
such songs as "O'er the Crossing," from Virginia, with
variants as "My Body Racked wid Fever" from Port
Royal Islands, "O Yonder's My Ole Mother," and "My
God Called Daniel." Next one notes "The Gospel Train"
with variants like "Get On Board," from the Bahamas,
and "From Every Graveyard" and "Git On Board Little
Children," heard in many places. Widely reported, too,
is "Roll Jordan Roll," in E major showing use of the flat
seventh, a variant of the Bahama song, "I Long to See
the Day." Well known also was "Somebody Knocking
at Yo' Do'," with the version, "O Sinner You'd better
Get Ready."

There are striking examples of Burial Hymns developed
from the custom of sitting up and singing over the dead.
Among them are "These Are My Father's Children,"
noted with the variant, "Sooner in de Morning," which
has two other variants, "These Are All My Father's Children," from North Carolina, and "The Trouble of the
World." A fine funeral song is "I know Moon Rise," reported first from Georgia. Impressive also are "Graveyard," and "Lay This Body Down," first noted from
Port Royal.

"I Know Moon-Rise," which is musically illustrated
herewith, is the finest funeral song found in this folk
material. It comes from St. Simon's Island, Georgia.
Writing of this song in the *Atlantic Monthly* of June,
1867, Col. Higginson said, "I was startled when first I
came on such a flower of poetry in that dark soil . . ."
Never since man first lived and suffered was his infinite
longing for peace uttered more plaintively than in that
line "I'll lie in the grave and stretch out my arms."

A possible variant is the melody "Graveyard," which was sung on Capt. John Tripp's plantation and also at Coffin's Point. The variant, "Lay This Body Down," used as a rowing song was noted in 1867 as coming from Port Royal Islands. W. H. Russell of the London *Times* heard this song when on a midnight row from Pocotaligo to the Trescot estate on Barnwell Island. Termed a "barbaric sort of madrigal," it was given by a solo voice then sung by others in chorus. Of the refrain, Lieut. Col. Trowbridge wrote, "It was sung at funerals in the night time —one of the most solemn and characteristic of customs of the Negroes that originated at St. Simon's Island, Georgia."

> Oh, your soul! Oh, my soul!
> I'm going to the churchyard
> To lay this body down;
>
> Oh, my soul! Oh, your soul!
> We're going to the churchyard
> To lay this nigger down.

In the early study of Negro folk song, the Sea Island section receives more notice than that of any other. Miss Elizabeth Putnam, a Boston lady of abolitionist inheritance, wrote of these parts as they were after a battle of the Civil War.

"Some of the plantations and city houses were deserted by their owners, and the slaves came into the Union camps. Then Gov. Butler suggested a name for these refugees; he called them contraband of war. Meantime the Sea Island region had become Union territory, the planters and their families having fled. Mr. Pierce was commissioned to get under way some method of managing the Negroes and starting a cotton crop for 1862. An Educational Commission for Freedmen was organized in Boston, New York, and Philadelphia, and on March 3, 1862, there set sail for Port Royal a party of public-spirited men and women, with salaries of from $25 to $50 per month. With that goodly company of Northern white men and women went Charlotte Forten (afterwards Mrs. Francis Grimké). My friend, H. W., wrote from Port Royal of Miss Forten, who was of partly Negro blood: 'She has one of the sweetest voices I ever heard. The Negroes knew the instant they saw her what she was, but she has been treated by them with universal respect. She is an educated lady'."

"June 1, 1863, came the Emancipation Proclamation. Col. Thomas Wentworth Higginson immediately organized a colored regiment. In June, 1863, Col. Robert G. Shaw led his troops through Pemberton Square to the State House, and they followed the rest out into the South . . ." ·

Col. Higginson proved a sympathetic and willing listener to the singing of the contrabands of war, and the value of his contribution is incalculable—a thrice told story.

When searching for Creole folk songs in Louisiana, the author heard the burial song "Pilgrim's Death" sung by an old woman in New Iberia. The author again came across the melody in West Texas. Some time later, while roaming the country-side of Americus, Georgia, folk song-gathering, the author secured a similar song from a washer woman, heard singing over her tubs in her back yard.[8] After some persuasion, she repeated her hymn.

[8] Three writers, Katherine C. Hutson, Josephine Pinckney and Caroline Pinckney Rutledge, who contribute a chapter on "The Negro Spiritual" in the book *The Carolina Low Country*, give a version called "O Lawd, O Lawd, W'at Shall I Do?" which they found in Bluffton. "Down Een Duh Valley on My Prayin' Knees." (3 times)—"O Lawd, O Lawd, W'at Shall I Do?" (Pp. 318-319.) Published by the Members of the Society for the Preservation of the Spirituals.

O WHAT YOU GOIN' TO DO?

O what... you goin' to do, When death comes steal-in' in your room, O what you goin' to do, When death comes stealin' in your room, O what you goin' to do, When death comes steal-in' at your room, (and 'er) O my Lord, O my Lord, what shall I do?

O what you goin' to do
When Death comes stealin' in your room?
  (three times)
O my Lord, O my Lord,
What shall I do?

I'm goin' to *lay* my *head,*
My head on Jesus' breast, (three times)
O my Lord, O my Lord,
What shall I do?

I'm goin' to breathe
My life out sweetly there, (three times)
O my Lord, O my Lord,
What shall I do?

O I'm so glad,
My soul got a hidin' place, (three times)
O my Lord, O my Lord,
What shall I do?

There were seven verses to the song. As sung in Texas, the added lines were

"We *are*, we *are*,
The true born sons of' Levi.

"We *are*, we *are*,
The root and branch of-er David.

Shining bright-*er*
Than any-er mornin' star.

In Americus, Georgia, the author heard a variant "Go Back Ol' Man," which was sung in the same manner—that of accenting the words that fell on the strong beats of the measures. There was the same striking glissando interpolation—"Welcome travelers, welcome home."

"Go back, ol' man. You dead too late; Ol' Master Jesus locked der door, and carried de key on high."

The song of consolation, burdened by what it does *not* say, "Do Doan' Yer Weep for de Baby," comes from Georgia —the heart of the South.

Two beautiful Spirituals which are Christmas carols are the songs, "De New-Born Baby," and "Go Tell it on the Mountains." These pentatonic melodies have been most fittingly harmonized for solo voice by Harvey B. Gaul. They can be found in *Seventy Negro Spirituals*, edited by William Armes Fisher. The first comes from South Carolina and is sung by the fishermen on the Atlantic seaboard coast. The second was noted in *Religious Folk Songs of the Negro*. It is typical of songs extemporized at Christmas time on the plantations. Three versions of "Mary Had a Baby" are sung on St. Helena Island.[9]

Seldom does one find extant songs of mother-love; of

⁹No. 46-7-8 in Saint Helena Spirituals. Nicholas Ballanta (Taylor).

parting, by death or ruthless fate, an enslaved mother from her helpless child. What words or tones could express her agony?

OTHER SONGS

Children's songs—lullabies, action songs and "rounds" —come from a later period than the Spirituals, and tell a story all their own. "Lil Liza Jane," (taken to France by colored soldiers), and "Crickaney, Crickaney, Craney Crow," sung and played as a game by children as far south as Texas, are types of dance songs found in towns and on plantations. They are familiar to both white and black children.

Memory of childhood days in Texas brings before the writer the picture of a certain little girl in trailing white night-dress, striving to maintain her equilibrium as she stands upright in bed, calling out, "Here I stand, raggety and dirty, if you don't come kiss me, I'll run like a turkey." It was the signal for the morning kiss from an adoring and adored father—a ritual performed without thought that the nonsense words would ever rise to the dignity of being enclosed by quotation marks.

The first of two love songs, of which there are but few, is "Poor Rosy," a lament found in E minor and said to come from Maryland. Variants known as "I'm in hopes to pray my sins away," and "Before I stay in Hell one day," are found in Florida and South Carolina. The song is noted in *Slave Songs of the United States*, 1867, published in 1862 by the authors referred to above. The editors state that a song resembling "Poor Rosy" was heard in 1866 from the boat hands of an Ohio River steamer. "Poor Molly, Poor Gal," was the burden of the refrain. "O Suzanne," in D minor, probably came from the South Eastern States. We find it noted in *Songs of the Slave*, and in an essay in *Lippincott's*, December, 1868.

The custom of slavery with its ruthless breaking of home ties, often caused unhappy separations between lovers, but it evidently did not destroy steadfastness of affection, according to this philosophy of the slave "Strappan," in *Slave Songs of the United States* (page xxxvi):

"Arter you lub, you lub you know, boss. You can't broke lub. Man can't broke lub. Lub stan'—e ain't gwine broke—Man heb to be very smart for broke lub. Lub is a ting stan' just like tar, arter he stick, he stick, he ain't gwine ·move. He can't move less dan you burn him. Hab to kill all two arter he lub fo' you broke lub."

Of secular songs there are but few. The available number has been increased by Mrs. Natalie Curtis Burlin's excellent collection made for Hampton Institute—*"Work and Play-Songs."* Her book contains one "Corn-Shucking Song" that was said to have come from Virginia, although originally sung in Alabama. The American Negro, like the Negro in Africa, found much pleasure and consolation in his music, both while at work and at play. In the fields when cleaning rice, the workers were followed by singers who clapped their hands and stamped their feet as an accompaniment to their song.

One of the oldest work-songs is "Round de Corn, Sally." This song in F minor noted in *Slave Songs of the United States*, 1867, comes to us from Virginia and yet pursues the African custom of bands of singers following the workers as they toiled in the fields, clapping their hands in rhythm to their song, thus through the sway of the tune, inciting the workers to greater labor. The gatherers of the corn swung their arms in rhythm to the song. The words of the song are obscure and their meaning has never been discovered. "Iggle" is "eagle" as expressed in Maryland, Virginia and North Carolina. In Louisiana the song was sung by roustabouts.

The Negro's dance and song tunes and his work songs

were produced just as were his Spirituals, with the same
modes and rhythms; "The Battle of Jericho" could easily
become a ".fox-trot." A fine example of the type of religious hymn that was evolved into a labor song, is one
found in Calhoun's *Plantation Songs* under the title
"Hammering Judgment."

> Don't you hear God talking, hammering, etc.
> He's talking to Moses hammering, etc.
> He's talking through thunder hammering, etc.
> Hammering judgment hammering, etc.
> Hammer keep a ringing hammering, etc.
> God tol' Moses hammering, etc.
> Go down in Egyp', hammering, etc.
> To tell ol' Pharaoh, hammering, etc.
> To loose his people, hammering, etc.
> Ol' Pharaoh had a hard heart, hammering, etc.
> An' would not loose dem, hammering, etc.

The imitative ejaculations of *wham, whum, boum, bam,
hunk,* and *huh* are familiar descriptions given the songs
of the laborers and workers on the railroads and roadways.

"Water Boy" a convict song arranged by Avery Robinson, a white musician, born in Louisville, Kentucky, is
one of the modern secular songs widely known. A version
as sung by a gang of Mississippi laborers reads:

> "Water-boy, water-boy,
> Bring de water roun',
> If yo' don't like yo' job
> Set de bucket down."

The large body of work songs in the making and the
vulgar so-called social songs of the Negro underworld,
now interesting a group of educators and writers, play
little part in the history of Negro music. They are neither
popular songs nor true folk songs of the race at large.

There is found in North Carolina and Texas a slave
song in which the "rabbit sitting on the fence" typifies
fair weather. The song with its lilting refrain became
popular as a campaign song in 1924.

"It ain't a' gwine ter rain,
It ain't a' gwine ter rain,
It ain't a' gwine ter rain no mo';
It rained last night an' de night befo',
Rabbit settin' in de jamb of de fence,
It ain't a' gwine ter rain no mo',
He's settin' there for de lak ob sense
It ain't a' gwine ter rain no mo'.

This old song was sung in the cotton fields and by rural laborers.

"Blow, Boys, Blow" is an example of a slave song that traveled by sea and became widely known. Although listed under the name "Blow the Man Down" in folklore from Nova Scotia, it is not a version of the familiar packet-ship chanty of the Black Ball Line, but is "Blow, Boys, Blow" taken from "A Yankee ship on the Congo River. Her masts they bend and her sails they shiver" which resulted in "Yankee ship coming down the river."[10]

HAUL THE BOWLINE
CHANTEY

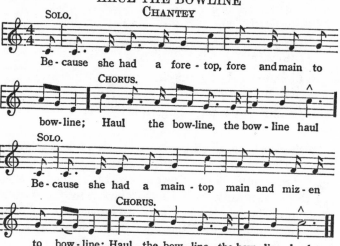

Solo.

Be - cause she had a fore - top, fore and main to

Chorus.

bow-line; Haul the bow-line, the bow - line haul

Solo.

Be - cause she had a main - top main and miz - en

Chorus.

to bow - line; Haul the bow - line, the bow - line haul.

[10] Fauset, Arthur Huff, *Folklore from Nova Scotia*, p. 119; "Roll and Go"—J. Colcord, *op. cit.* p. 7.

The type of folk song known as the chantey is the latest taken up by musicians, and these rollicking old songs have been introduced on the concert stage by soloists looking for novelties, as well as groups of singers such as the *London Singers* who do them so successfully. Many English and American folk songs of the sea are of Negro origin. We find rowing songs in South Carolina where fine old lyrics were used interchangeably as "shouts," chanteys sung on the old clipper ships that sailed to distant seas, and steamboat songs sung in the Southwest. The latter songs were heard from the banks of the Ohio to the Rio Grande and are a part of chantey singing. There, too, are songs that treat of levee life in Cincinnati, songs of the roustabouts, and the slave songs from Kentucky and Virginia that were chanted on the river steamboats.

A popular old melody sung in the roustabout's haunts, ran,

> "Molly was a good gal and a bad gal too,
> O Molly, row gal.

> I'll row dis boat and I'll row no more
> Row, Molly gal.

> Captain on the biler deck a' heavin' of the lead,
> O Molly, row gal.

> Calling to the pilot to give her 'Turn ahead'
> Row, Molly gal."

In singing the song on the Ohio, each verse was repeated twice. The construction of the chantey is akin to that of the "corn songs" of the Negroes, and the method of singing them practically the same as followed by the workers on land. The sailor songs were extemporized at sea by the chanteyman who led the singing, and words and melody partake of the vernacular of the sea-faring man.

The name of *chantey* or *shanty* is said not to have been used before 1869, but the folk song of the sea was known

before that date. *The Sailor's Song Book* was published
in 1842. Since then a number of sailor song anthologies
have appeared. One of the best of these, "Roll and Go"
—*Songs of American Sailormen*—edited by Joanna C.
Colcord in 1924, gives a number of chanteys of the Negro.
Miss Colcord brings forth the interesting supposition of
Sir Richard Runciman Terry, who believes that the term
was taken from the "shanties" of the humbler class
of Negroes—shanties along the waterfront of Mobile from
whence many of the old tunes came. The word "chantey" or "shantey" was thought to have been derived from
the French word *chanter*.

But we rarely think of the French in connection with
sailor songs, while Englishmen, particularly Cecil Sharp,
have made us familiar with these songs. Miss Colcord,
herself born on the sea, a daughter of a master mariner
and skillful chanteyman, writes—that while Englishmen
or Irishmen "were admitted to rank ahead of the white
Americans as chanteymen, they in turn were far out-
stripped by the American Negroes—the best singers that
ever lifted a shanty aboard ship."

Since there is no complete record of life at sea as it
existed during the period of 1812 to 1860, the chantey has
a special value. At one time the ships that were loaded
and unloaded on the wharves at Baltimore, carried what
was called "chequered crews," that is, one half white
and one half colored, and it is thought the white boys
thus learned the Negro chanties.

Sir Walter Runciman who lived some years in the West
Indies, names "Sally Brown" in his collection of chanteys. The musical form is that of a halliard chantey, but
always used for heaving the anchor. "Sally" seems to
be the heroine of all chanteydom, for different versions
appear in various American as well as English collections.
The author's song from New Orleans reads, "Sally Brown

is a Creole lady, Way O, Roll and Go. For seven long years I courted Sally, Way O, Roll and Go.'' But Sally marries a "Negro soldier," and the singer laments the fact that he spent his money on Sally Brown.

From London, Cecil Sharp quotes different verses, while one version which is listed among Windlass and Capstan chanteys, bears these significant words: "Sally lives on the Old Plantation. She belongs to the Wild Goose Nation." The chanteyman who improvised these words probably placed "Sally Brown" as the progeny of the admixture of Negro and Indian blood which was so common in Louisiana as well as in the East. The *Wild Goose Nation* often appears in British chanteys.

The pirate days of the West Indies, the American slave trade, the Irish emigration of the '50s, and the War of 1812 are some of the historic events recorded in the so-called Forecastle Songs, which rang out on the old clipper ships. A Negro chantey, "The Black Ball Line," a halliard chantey, perpetuates the name of the first and most famous line of American packet ships which started their run between New York and Liverpool in 1816. There are a number of versions of this song.[11]

Other popular chanteys of Negro American origin are, "He-Back, She-Back"; "Santa Anna"; "Mudder Dinah"; and "Haul Away, Jo" also called "Sing Sally O." One of the best windlass songs of the Negro, is "Shanadore," of which there are six versions. It is thought that in ignorance, a singer interpreted the name of a river for that of a person.

> "You Shanadore, I long to hear you,
>   Hurrah, you rollin' river,
> You Shanadore, I long to hear you,
>   Oh, Ho, you Shanadore."

[11] A halliard chantey, sung to laborious tasks of pumping ship, hoisting sail, etc. See Joanna Colcord's "Roll and Go" for manner of singing.

As long ago as June 24, 1852, a Boston paper printed in its columns that the "Royal Mail liner *America* sails with full passenger list; the day of clipper packet seems about over" and announces, "the clipper, *Witch of the Wave,* sails around the world voyage in a year." With the final passing of the beautiful old sailing vessels came the end of the making of the gay, oft-times ribald, chantey. The names alone of many of the vessels have a romantic lure. There were the *Sea Witch,* and the famous *Flying Cloud* of 1851. Of the *Flying Cloud* that sailed from the port of Baltimore, the old chantey, evidently from Negro sources, cries:

"The Flying Cloud was a Yankee ship of five hundred
tons or more;
She could outsail any clipper ship hailing out of Baltimore."

When people were tempted to seek their fortune out West, the water route was preferred to the overland route to California. At the time of the gold rush, about 1849, the tune of "De Camp Town Races," a Negro minstrel song, was sung as a capstan chantey. It is in the simple form of stanzas known to these songs.

"Sing and heave, and heave and sing,
To me hoodah! To my hoodah!
Heave and make the handspikes spring,
To me hoodah! To my hoodah!
And it's blow, boys, blow,
For California—o.
For there's plenty of gold,
So I've been told,
On the banks of the Sacramento."[12]

[12] Stanton C. King, official Government chantey-man, says that in his youth, when on a voyage from Philadelphia to Japan and back to New York there was need of a song leader, the Negro stewardess, wife of the cook on the vessel, came out of the galley and led the men in chantey singing.

The Negro of South Carolina and Georgia chanted rowing songs to religious texts, in sentiment quite unlike the rollicking chantey. "J. G. W.,"[13] writing in the *Atlantic Monthly* of May, 1864, on "Life on the Sea Islands," (in which an anonymous colored woman, evidently a teacher on St. Helena Island, describes racial customs), tells thus of the boat songs as he heard them, "As we glided along, the rich tones of the Negro boatmen broke upon the stillness, sweet, strange and solemn:

> "Jesus make de blind to see,
> Jesus make de cripple to walk,
> Jesus make de deaf to hear—
> Walk in, kind Jesus,
> No man can hinder me!"

Col. Higginson in *Army Life in a Black Regiment,* quotes a boat song which he heard in South Carolina that was sung in time to the tug of the oar. It was the Spiritual "I want to go to Canaan," known also as "The Coming Day."

An equally fine boat song was that of "One More River."

> "O, Jordan bank was a great old bank,
> Dere ain't but one more river to cross."

The Negro's custom of singing while rowing came from Africa. The author was told by a native African friend that it is customary for the rowers to join in song after listening a moment to a melody which is extemporized by one of the oarsmen. Each man sings a different part. Charles Pickard Ware explained that the rowing tunes were sung in South Carolina two measures to each stroke,

---

[13] One suspects that the writer, "J. G. W.," is the poet Whittier, for as we know he wrote many articles about the Negro, and was a stanch abolitionist. In November, 1861, he wrote a poem to William Lloyd Garrison that appeared in the Haverhill Gazette, and afterwards gave evidence of interest in Negro gift of song.

the first measure being accented by the beginning of the
stroke, the second by the rattle of the oars in the oar-
locks. The stirring song "Michael Row," was used when
the load was heavy or the tide against them.

Explorer James Barnes in describing the harmony of
African rowing songs, speaks thus of a paddling song which
has similarities to Negro American song, "Some especially
good singer booms out the melody, and it is sung with a
sort of drone accompaniment .... there is a counter tenor
part which maintains an antiphonal repetition of high F,
E, D and C, with an effect almost Wagnerian."[14]

In a story told by Harold Bindloss, the description
given of a French vessel stranded on an African river
bottom and the manner in which a successful effort was
made to get her back into deep water, tallies with the
singing of the work songs in the southern states. Fleming,
the trader, comes to the rescue of the ship and crew that
is stricken with African fever. He calls upon his men,
the Kroo-boys from the river Niger:

"Fetch her home! Sing, oh, confound you, sing! More
steam, Benson, she's moving." The stout hemp cracked
and strained, drawing out to half its size, the tackle
blocks were screaming and link by link the cable came in,
while above the groan of the windlass, the roaring chorus
of a Kroo boy chanty rang out across forest and river!"

An amusing chantey, a "Noah" song, is one given by
Cecil Sharp, which is a version of "A Long Time Ago."
Miss Colcord writes, "I venture to guess that some Ne-
gro shantyman, in a burst of exuberant fancy, sang this
version once, in the hearing of the man who sang it to
Mr. Sharp."

[14] *Musical America.* In this and other places where the author cites
newspapers and magazines without dates the quotations are taken
from clippings, programs, and publications given as such by musicians for her collection.

In 'Frisco Bay there lay three ships. (twice)
And one of those ships was Old Noah's Ark
All covered over with hickory bark.
They filled up the seams with oakum and pitch. (twice)
And Noah of old commanded this Ark. (twice)
They took two animals of every kind. (twice)
The bull and the cow they started a row. (twice)
Then said old Noah with a flick of his whip,
Come stop this row or I'll scuttle the ship.
But the bull put his horns through the side of the Ark,
And the little black dog he started to bark.
So Noah took the dog, put his nose in the hole,
And ever since then the dog's nose has been cold.

The story of Noah as found in Genesis, was a favorite
one with the Negro. It appears in a work-song, and as
a descriptive hymn, "De Ole Ark a Moverin' Along," that
may be found in *Religious Folk Songs of the Negro* as
sung by Hampton Institute. "Who built de A'ak? Norah."
comes from the Carolinas, sung in both major and minor
modes, as noted in *The Carolina Low Country*. Newman
White gives a song which reads:

Who built the ark? Noah built the ark,
Some say Noah was a foolish man,
But I says he's a wise man,
For he built his ark on hard ole ground,
He built his ark of Gopher wood.
All beasts' kind went to his ark,
Noah came riding by,
And they poked a scorning finger at him,
Ole Noah tell the ark to move, move, move.

In Mark Twain's entertaining book, *Life on the Mississippi*, he tells of the romantic old days of steamboating
from New Orleans to St. Louis and on the "upper river"
between St. Louis and Cairo where the Ohio enters. The
departure of the steamers from New Orleans between four
and five o'clock in the afternoon were exciting and bus-
tling moments. "Every windlass connected with every

fore-hatch, from one end of that long array of steamers
to the other, was keeping up a whiz and whir lowering
freight into the hold and the half crew of Negroes that
worked them were roaring such songs as 'De las sack, de
las sack,' inspired to unimaginable exultation by the chaos
of turmoil and racket that was driving every one else mad.''

The same spirit is shown in the following stanza and
chorus of ''Down the Ohio,'' sung by the Negro minstrel
companies in the sixties. It is an admixture of dialect
and English. The song was contributed to the Boston
Evening Transcript, by E. W. F.

Oh, de Massa am proud of the old broad-horn,
For she brings him a plenty of tin;
De crew dey are darkies, de cargo am corn,
And de money comes tumbling in.

Dar is plenty on board for de darkies to eat,
An somethin' to drink an' to smoke;
Dar's de Banjo, de Bones, an' de old Tamborine,
Dar's de clown and de Comic Joke.

Chorus

O the river is up,
And the channel is deep,
And the wind blows steady and strong,
Let the splash of your oars
The measure keep,
As we row the old along
Down the river, down the river,
Down — the — O-hi — O!

This Chantey was sung on the Flat Boats of the Ohio
River.

O, the river is up, the channel is deep,
The wind blows steady and strong,
A' splashing their oars the mariners keep
As they row their boats along.
Down the River
Down the River
Down the O-H-I-O.

"If we could divest ourselves of prejudice," says Haweis in *Music and Morals*, "the songs that float down the Ohio River are one in feeling and character with the songs of the Hebrew captives by the waters of Babylon. We find in them the same tale of bereavement and separation, the same irreparable sorrow, the same simple faith and childish adoration, the same wild tenderness and passionate sweetness like music in the night."

"Oh! Rock Me, Julie," is one of the best known Mississippi River songs, the melody of which is found in the whole-tone scale. This song belongs to the days when old boatmen speak of "back in the thirties" as the period of steamboat races which created great excitement. These words of the second stanza were given to the author by George W. Cable, the author of books on Creole life:

> Oh! rock me, Julie, rock me, Oh! . . . .
> Oh! rock me slow and easy, Oh! . . . .
> Oh! rock me like a baby, Oh! . . . .
> Oh! rock me in de moonshine, Oh! . . . .
> Oh! rock me sweet and weary, Oh! . . . .[15]

Another Texas-Louisiana chantey noted by M. R. Delany, the colored author of *Blake; or The Huts of America* (published in 1859), is a song of the black firemen; which they chanted "when the boat glided steadily upstream, seemingly in unison with the lively though rude and sorrowful song."

> I'm a goin' to Texas, O! O! O! O!—
> I'm goin' to Texas, O! O! O! O!

Slave songs were heard on the river in 1823, and of these laments, Delany wrote, "They were sung to words . . . as if in unison with the restless current of the great

[15] Harry T. Burleigh made an arrangement of the song for solo voice, for Henry E. Krehbiel's excellent study on *Afro-American Folksongs*.

river upon which they were compelled to toil. In the capacity of leader, one poor fellow sang a lament"—

> Way down upon the Mobile River
> Close to Mobile Bay,
> There's where my thoughts is running ever,
> All thro the live long day.
> There I've got a good and fond old mother,
> Tho she is a slave,
> There I've got a sister and a brother,
> Lying in their peaceful grave.
> O, could I somehow a'nother
> Drive these tears away;
> When I think about my poor old mother
> Down upon Mobile Bay.

"In the distance," continues Delany, "on the levee and in the harbor among the steamers, the songs of the boatmen were incessant. Every few hours landing, loading and unloading, the glee of these men of sorrow was touchingly appropriate and impressive . . . . If there is any class of men anywhere to be found whose sentiments of song and words of lament are made to reach the sympathies of others, the black slave-boatmen on the Mississippi River are that class . . . they are seemingly contented by soothing their sorrows with songs apparently cheerful, but in reality wailing lamentations."

This lament, reminiscent of The Swanee River, differs from the Negro capstan chantey, *Mobile Bay:*

> "Was you ever down in Mobile Bay?
> (Cho.) Johnny come tell us and pump away,
> A'screwing cotton by the day?
> Johnny come tell us and pump away;
> Aye, aye, pump away,
> Johnny come tell us and pump away."

Many writers have quoted the jovial, care-free singing of the Negro bondmen as proof of their happy lot and happy-go-lucky spirit. Delany writes of the sad station of the Negro in the later slave days of the Southwest. Similarly a writer discusses the supposed merriment of the enslaved Negro in the West Indies, in a critical review of "Barbadoes." A poem by M. J. Chapman in *Blackwood's Edinburgh Magazine*, October, 1833, shows the same thought.

"Human beings will dance and sing in the midst of many miseries; nor, because they are sometimes seen dancing and singing, are we to conclude that they are contented with their condition. There is much mirth in Newgate. But of that mirth we know the character and the cause—and that it breaks forth in trouble below the shadow of the gallows. Is that the nature of the Negro's merriment? No. It is sincere; it is a part of their being; and proof therefore, of enjoyment. So we are glad to think; but others may attribute it all to wretchedness, and see in it all but an appalling proof of the heart-breaking misery that is the perpetual portion of slaves."

But the Negro from the West Indies and the United States possessed a fortitude and an innate happiness of spirit which enabled them to rise above their degradation, and in common they sang their levee song—

CHANTEY

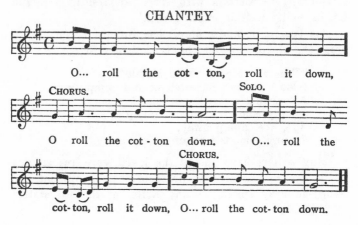

O... roll the cot - ton, roll it down,

CHORUS. O roll the cot - ton down. SOLO. O... roll the

cot - ton, roll it down, O... roll the cot - ton down.

Oh, roll the cotton, roll it down,

I thought I heard our old man say,
  Oh, roll the cotton down;
He'd sail away to Mobile Bay,
  Oh, roll the cotton down.

I heard him say to Mobile Bay,
  Oh, roll the cotton down;
He'd sail away at break of day,
  Oh, roll the cotton down.

Mobile Bay is no place for me,
  Oh, roll the cotton down;
I'll sail away on some other sea,
  Oh, roll the cotton down.

Apart from the groups of self-taught, gifted musicians who were accustomed to play for amusement of the master-class, plantation hands fiddled and danced and sang "Jubilee" songs when-ever there was an opportunity such as the celebration of Christmas holidays—always more of a gala occasion in the South than in the North. There was the chief drummer called "Juba" beater, and from his "Jubilee beating" comes the name of Jubilee Songs.

The dance *Juba* and the tune which accompanies it have been described at length by such reliable writers as Dorothy Scarborough, Thomas W. Talley and Newman I. White. Miss Scarborough was told by Dr. Wyeth, that the tune was that of an old African melody, and that the word Juba meant a ghost.

An improvised "Juba" song known to be over a century old is that of,

"We raise de wheat, dey gib us de corn;
We bake de bread, dey gib us de crust;
We sift de meal, de gib us de huss;
  Walk over, walk over—" etc.

Ballads written by Negro American song writers, in the first song period include: James Hemmenway's "That Rest so Sweet like Bliss Above," published 1829 in a Philadelphia music journal, *Atkinson's Casket;* A. J. R. Connor's "My Cherished Hope, My Fondest Dreams," published in 1859 in *The Anglo-African Magazine,* New York City; Gussie L. Davis's "The Light House by the Sea," "Do the Old Folks Miss Me," "The Fatal Wedding," "Down in Poverty Row," "We Sat Beneath the Maple on the Hill," "The Baggage Coach Ahead," "Send Back the Picture and the Wedding Ring," "When Nelly was Raking the Hay"; Samuel Milady's known as Sam Lucas's "Grandfather's Clock is too Tall for the Shelf," "Carve dat Possum"; James Bland's "Carry Me Back to Old Virginny," "In the Evening by the Moonlight," "In the Morning by the Brightlight," "Oh, dem Golden Slippers."

Writers of popular songs of the theatrical stage and the music hall include Ernest Hogan of "All Coons look alike to Me"; Al Johns of "Go 'Way Back and Sit Down"; Will Accoe of "My Samoan Beauty"; Chris Smith, Sheppard Edmonds, Tim Brymn and Irving Jones of catchy songs of their day; Spencer Williams, Jimmy Johnson, Andy Razaf, Thomas Waller and Maceo Pinkard of the present period. Maceo Pinkard, author of the musical play "Liza" wrote the popular song "Mammy," featured by Al Jolson. Irving Jones composed "You ain't Landlord No More," and "When a Coon Sits in the Presidential Chair." These songs were accepted by Harris, the stage producer. Jones was known as a vaudeville performer.

"Ta-ra-ra-boom-de-ay," made popular in the early '90s by Lottie Collins, was written by Henry J. Sayres, who was said to have heard the song in a St. Louis Negro café. He changed the words, and the song became widely known in England in 1931. Sayres, a white theatrical man, was connected with the farce, "Tuxedo."

A story of Negro music cannot be complete without a
mention of a class of fragmentary tunes which, while not
musically important, are decidedly amusing. These are the
street-cries of the hucksters and vendors who sell both
raw and cooked food on the streets. In Louisiana and in
the West Indies, the cries are not restricted to food, but
to other commodities as well. The most intriguing cries
that the author has heard came from this State and from
South Carolina. An exception are the melodic cries
gathered in Puerto Rico.

"Watermelon Street Cry"
    "Watermillions, goin' by—!
    Mek up your mind, befo' I pass by,
    Mek up your mind, befo' I pass by,
    Watermillions, jes from de vine."

"Chitlins" was recorded shortly after the Civil War by
Wm. Wells Brown.

    "Here's yer chitlins fresh and sweet
        Who'll jine de Union?
    Young hog's chitlins hard to beat.
    Methodist chitlins, jest been biled,
    Right fresh chitlins dey ain't spiled.
    Baptist chitlins by de pound.

    Here's yer chitlins fresh and sweet,
        Who'll jine de Union?"

In New Orleans, children gathered and followed the
chimney sweeps as they trod the streets looking for chim-
neys to clean. There too were the cries of the vendors[16]
who sold the cured Spanish moss for mattress making, and
clothes' props used to support the long rope lines of the
home yard laundry. The old tunes of the Creole onion
seller of a past decade—"Marchand d'Onions"—survives

---

[16] Persons who witnessed the South Carolina play of "Porgy"
remember with pleasure the atmospheric charm produced by the
street cries of the crab man.

in a play song secured from a group of Negro children
in New Orleans.

> "Onions for sale! Sometimes they're high,
>   Sometimes they're low.
> Onions for sale! Sometimes they're cheap,
>   Sometimes they're *good* cheap (a bargain)
> Onions for sale! Onions for sale!"

A child told the author that, making use of this song,
they ofttimes called attention to a "tattler" whom they
would mock as "sometimes cheap." The original Creole
song ran—"Des onions sont a bon marché c'est li ci, c'est
li ca, La commére tournera le dos c'est li ci, c'est li ca."

Educators and writers of the white American class, are
today collecting a large mass of work songs from section-
hands, gang laborers and miners. In the main the songs
are crude, and vulgar and coarse of text. They depict one
form only of Negro life and are not typical of the majority of colored people, many of whom do not know of
their existence. It is to be noted that the "classic" era
of Negro folk song is predominantly the period of the
spiritual, when the soul of the people was mutually tested
and tried. With all people folk music goes out as art
music comes in, and spontaneous expression gives way to
studied and purposeful use of artistic inspiration.

CHAPTER V

FOLK SONG IN THE PROVINCES

THE VIRGIN ISLANDS—FREEDOM, 1848—A FOLK SINGER—
FOLK MUSIC AND DIALECT—PUERTO RICO—RACE AMALGA-
MATION—DANCE AND SONG FORMS—FOLK DANCES.

Of the folk music in the West Indies we have had opportunities to learn much by frequent contacts since our
expansion into that quarter. We know now much more
about the folk music of Cuba, Puerto Rico and the Virgin
Islands than we did forty years ago. A scientific study of
this aspect of culture in all those parts will doubtless reveal interesting music, but we know sufficient today to
indicate the contributions of these transplanted African
people who have had contact with both Europe and the
United States at the same time. Their special contributions will help us to understand those made by the Negroes along the Atlantic.

The Virgin Islands contribute a treasury of Negro folk
music. Within encircled tiers of streets in towns that look
upon the hill-hidden savannahs in the east, is harbored a
romantic and enchanting history, melodically told. The
background is a tragic one. Here are unfamiliar folk
ways due to the great number of racial admixtures—
French, Danish, Dutch, English and Negro. Not long
after the purchase of these islands by the United States
the author visited these new possessions. Wandering about,
one reads with interest and curiosity on monuments the
family names of Andicer, Faisant, Bouge, Mohr, Lassen
and Silvaine, with the Spanish Mirando and the Portu-

guese Corneiro, dating back to 1790 and to subsequent years.

A descendant of Francisco Corneiro maintains today a jewelry store in St. Thomas. One Fermin Corneiro was a flutist of note, and in the early days the Corneiro home was the scene of many musical evenings. Apart from a folk song heritage, St. Thomas lays rightful claim to a musical taste which has been cultivated throughout the years. Sacred festivals were early instituted by the Catholics, and it is said that the beautiful French hymns still sung on the island were brought there by the Corsican Abbé Giorgetti.

Native musicians arose. Barthold Daniel played at the Court of Napoleon III and received praise from the Emperor and Empress. A nephew, Cyril E. Daniel, is a consul at St. Thomas. Walter Stubbs, composer of a Grand Mass dedicated to Canta Teresa de Jesus, won praise from the Archbishop of the Cathedral of Lima, Peru. In his home, chamber music was practised and encouraged.

Many beautiful old hymns were brought over by the French comers, but the "Chachas," an un-mixed, unprogressive French group in the West End of St. Thomas, do not seem to be given to song. In contrast, are the majority of the inhabitants of the island today, who are of mixed breed, with French, Danish, or Dutch, and Negro blood, and an un-mixed element of blacks. The Negro was first brought to the island from Africa by the Danes and the Dutch Company. After St. Croix was purchased from France by King Christian of Denmark, about 1733, slaves continued to work there on the sugar plantations and became servants on the estates of all the islands. These old plantations that still bear the intriguing names of former days, were the birth-places of Negro song on the islands. There are the biblically named estates of

"Canaan," "Jerusalem," "Bethlehem," and "Blessing," with "Envy," and "Upper" and "Lower Love," "Work," and "Rest," not forgetting the jeweled names of "Diamond" and "Ruby" which marked nearby plantations appropriately set in quavering chant and song.

Some of their songs embody the history of the struggle for freedom. The victorious Negroes of the revolution of 1848 sang this frenzied chant:

REVOLUTION SONGS
[From St. Croix, Virgin Islands, 1848]

OH, QUEEN MARY, WILL YOU HAB A GLASS OF WINE?

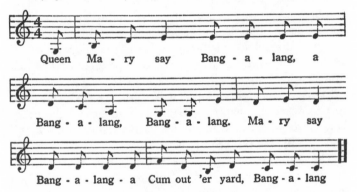

Queen Ma - ry say Bang - a - lang, a
Bang - a - lang, Bang - a - lang. Ma - ry say
Bang - a - lang - a Cum out 'er yard, Bang - a - lang

FAN ME, BUCKRA

Oh fan me...... Buck - ra Mis - sis, fan me,
Fan me, fan me, till de break of day.

QUEEN MARY

Queen Mary say Bang-a-Lang-a, Bang-a-lang, Bang-a-lang,
  Mary say Bang-a-lang-a, Cum out 'er yard, Bang-a-lang.
Oh, Queen Mary, will you hab a glass o' wine?

Queen Mary, wha' way we gwine burn?
  We gwine burn dare, gwine burn down Wes' End!
We gwine burn down; all de way gwine burn down.

FAN ME, BUCKRA

Oh Fan me—Buckra missis fan me
  Fan me, fan me, till de break o' day.

"Fan me, buckra" (white person) is the taunt that the
tables were to be turned and the slave the one now to demand service. "Queen Mary,"[1] an intrepid woman slave,
was the Joan of Arc of the rebellion. She led the march,
singing on the way as her infuriated followers planned to
"burn down West End" (Christiansted). A reminiscence
today of the old song is found in the name "burnt downs"
given to the whites of St. Croix. It is possible that Queen
Mary's song may have been an echo of the earlier rebellion
of 1759 when eighty-nine slaves were arrested; fourteen
put to death by torture, and others sold out of the country. Two who belonged to the "King estate," "Maria"
and "Will," were acquitted.

The Proclamation of Freedom of 1848 was "broadcast" everywhere by being "put on the drum-head"—a
custom of the islands in keeping with the old African
practice of the "bush telegraph." Messages are indicated by various rhythms beaten on drums made from
tree trunks. In St. Thomas one hears stories of enemies
having paid a price to the "queen" of the drum to have
a hated one "put on the drum-head" that he might become an object of satire, ridicule and mockery.

On folk song quest in the cane country, a short drive
from the center of the town of Frederiksted, brought the
author to the two roomed house of Mary Catherine, the

[1] She was taken to Denmark where she died.

"Princess' of "carossal" singing. Mary Catherine was finally persuaded to tell us of the melodies that she sang to us. Divided into groups, they were spoken of as "Torees" (stories, we surmised), "Calindas" and "Carossals." On the island were found a number of songs called "Carossals" or "Carossols," the meaning of which is obscure. It is the name of a native plant and also that of the dance that accompanies a class of tunes extemporized by the people. Two tunes, "Brownwell" and "Judge Horlick," were classed as Torees which our singer said must be sung "sharp." Gleefully she sang—

Marsa Judge Horlick, peep thro yo' window,
Go gell dem sweet rose cologne.
O do gell dem growin' in de garden— (smell them)
How all you lak our lates gullen? (queen)

Roll de drum, drummer, roll de drum!

The drum was used as an accompaniment. Both hands beat on the side of the keg. Judge Horlick (Horlyck) was a Danish judge, and the *torees* were sung as serenades to court his pleasure. This song was often sung at the holiday revels, by Mary Catherine and twelve others. All joined in the chorus while the drummer followed the instructions "Roll de drum, drummer," and ecstatically beat the keg and marked syncopated rhythms with the palm of his hands. Many of the tunes sung had the African manner of being divided rhythmically into groups of two eight notes in a measure of 3/4 and again a form of triplet played as 5/4 or syncopated identically like the music of the neighboring island of Puerto Rico.

"Coolie Brown" is an example of a "Calinda" which is a form of an African dance song known in all Creole countries and popular in Louisiana and in the French West Indies. As danced in Martinique and in Haiti, the men twirl canes or sticks and imitate a fight. The dance is known also as "Caliendo"—perhaps with Spanish influences. Mary Catherine punctuated "O Coolie Brown" with rhythmic hand claps—

> "O Coolie Brown, where you been so long?
> All a-roun' der town, Calinda,
> All a-roun' der town, Calinda,
> Cum out o' bonta we!—Ca-lin-da!
>
> "Mornin' star shell a' blow, Calinda,
> Mornin' star shell a' blow, Calinda,
> Cum out o' bonta we!—Ca-lin-da!

A jig described by the singer was nothing more than the familiar Negro dance "Juba" carried to all parts by the African. To the favorite social dance, the quadrille, an accompaniment is played by the flute "which you blow," the guitar "which you pick," and the drum "which you knock." There was, of course, the juiro "which you scratched."

Many of the songs are of a grossness and vulgarity not unexpected from primitive folk, yet more fundamentally clean than some of the variety and popular songs of the radio and stage of today. In a number of these songs there were seemingly meaningless rejoinders. Questioned, the singers of these productions patiently and musically intoned an explanation. The songs were "taunts."— "You quarrel wid me—I quarrel wid you. Put it in a song. Like dis—

> "Tiefman (thief), robber-man;
> Mama tief—mama robber;
>
> Young turkey run and bawl,
> 'E want de care o de mudder!
>
> Tiefman, robber man, ober berrie (overbearing);
> Mama tief, mama robber,
>
> De woman ober berrie;
> Tief de people, dem young turkey (a stolen turkey)
> "Carry on!—Go rail!"

Before leaving the island of St. Croix, Mary Catherine came to see the author at the one little hotel of the town that she might enjoy the novelty of hearing her old songs played on the piano. Greatly pleased at the dignity bestowed upon them, she became confidential. Her soft speaking voice droned a poem in free verse as she related something of her life—of how she had once led the singing on festival days.[2]

[2] The words of the songs of the Virgin Islands are often unintelligible because of the unusual, difficult dialect. No better place can be discovered for hearing the speech than down at the coal field on the East Side dock of St. Thomas where the men and women gather to carry coal on the ships. A group of laborers were seen standing in the shade of the warehouse waiting for the "Enare," a Norwegian vessel to be fastened to the dock for the purpose of bunking coal.

Watching the more energetic ones mending their baskets was heard a man accosting a co-worker: "Yep—devil of fightin' mon!" And indicating a large basket—"Heavy mon?" Fondling his basket, the man replies: "No, mon it, it good." The group ventures an opinion that a new one would be preferable. Interest becomes general. One asks the price to mend a basket—

"How much, mon?"—"One basket, one dollar. If me had mok one (make one), me char' five dollar!"—"O Mon!" is the expostulation.

"'Member, got to hand dry 'em, plait de straw—"

But the vessel is ready for bunking coal and a companion calls out—

"Leave 'lone—cum down to de ship, mon!"

They saunter goodnaturedly toward the coal piles, where women with baskets filled with coal were lolling on the ground, eating bananas and smoking T. D. pipes. A girl, passing one of the men, jokingly prod him in the ribs. "Go wan," he exclaimed, "I wan' no wife—got me foot in it now!"

The word "mon" (man) is used even in addressing a boy. Proverbs, unusual and quaint, are used in song and conversation. One reads—"Go on, mon, don't bother me; monkey nebber had no trouble till he swallow plum seed." And another—

"The moon can run as fast as it likes, but daylight will catch it."

The greeting of "Good night" upon first meeting is derived from a mistaken use of "Buenas noches" of Spanish Puerto Rico. The Creole language spoken here is a Creole with a Dutch basis. A Creole Bible shown the author, is one that was printed in "Dutch-Creole" for the benefit of the freed slaves, who knew how to read.

"No sing much now—work too hard;
  Sing lots when young; mak a work go fast—
Ironin' or cuttin' cane. No sing much now.

Wind and sun stagnate de cane; dry them;
  Me cut it, tie up, load it and carry it to factory.

No sing much now—work too hard,
  And head ache in de sun.
      Sing lots when young."

Many melodious street-cries are heard in the early morning in the Virgin Islands. The fish venders' tuneful cry
"Ice fish for breakfast; ice fish for stew," proclaims that
the fish has been protected from the heat of the tropical
sun, that it is good for the Virgin Island "breakfast"
hour, which is that of mid-day. In securing a number of
street-cries, the author noticed that the phrases were
much shorter and less musical than those of the near-by
island of Puerto Rico.

Of greater musical and ethnological interest were the
dance rhythms. A yard-boy, "Dargan," irresponsible yet
queerly faithful to the author's host, Bandmaster Adams,
by whom he was employed, liked nothing better than to
dance and to lie in the hot sun. He preferred to do his
spontaneous dancing unobserved and unnoticed. However, he was persuaded to dance the "Bamboula."

While on tour in the United States, the Navy Band of
the Virgin Islands played "Sam Polo," "The Bull Pas-
sin' "—a bamboula which is the well-known African Negro
dance of the West Indies and Louisiana. On those islands
are sung the following words to this melody.

Baby, Mama no tell no lie—Go Dear!
Baby, Mama no tell no lie—Oh!

Hush yo' mout' you foolish ting—your
  Mama gwine to work for money
Baby, Mama no tell no lie.

There are no folk songs in the Virgin Islands that hold
the poignant, religious note of the Negro Spirituals of
the United States although the slaves were not out of
touch with the religions of the various ruling white masters. Count Castenjöld, the Danish owner of the first estate on the island, gave permission to have his slaves
taught the Christian religion. His example was followed

SAM POLO
[A West Indian Bamboula]

Noted by Bandmaster Alton Adams, St. Thomas, Virgin Islands.

by others of the various races that peopled the country.

The following "West Indian Boat Song" from the
Virgin Islands, may be found in the *West Indian Sketch
Book*, London, 1834. It is repeated by White in *Ameri-
can Negro Folk Songs*.

> Hurrah, my jolly boys, Fine time o' day.
> We pull for San Thomas, boys, Fine time o' day.
> San Thomas hab de fine girl, etc.
> Nancy Gibbs and Betsy Braid, etc.

Massa cum fra London Town, etc.
Massa is a handsome man, etc.
Massa is a dandy man, etc.
Him hab de dollar, plenty, too, etc.
Him lub 'em much, him lub 'em true, etc.
Him hunt 'em round de guaba bush, etc.
Him catch 'em in de cane piece, etc. etc.

The "guaba bush" referred to is the guava plant from whence guava jelly, so well-liked in this section, is made. San Thomas (St. Thomas) is the principal port, but the "cane piece" is the cane country of the nearby island of St. Croix.

While it is to be expected that African influences should be strongly felt in Puerto Rico and other lands of the Spanish and French West Indies, very few pure Negroes are found in Puerto Rico. Today those mainly on the eastern end of the island are the black people who came from the Virgin Islands and the British West Indies. Contrary to the statement made by some travelers, the latter are a very clean people and deserve the local saying that "you can always ask for water and receive it in a clean glass." Their opposites in the same (peon) class, are the "jivaros" (jibaros), who are widely known in the mountains and valleys and who keep alive the song of the folk. Their tinkling guitars and ringing voices enliven the curving roads that lead the plodding laborers to the sugar controls, the factories, or to the coffee lands of the mountains.

Negro influences are found in the dance. Fernando Callejo speaks of the annual celebrations held during the slavery regime, by Negroes of different tribes, in the old market place of San Juan when the only instruments used to mark the rhythm of the dance-songs were the *bombas* and the *maracas*. The *bombas* (dances) take their name from the "bomba," the Negro drum which accompanies the dance. The refrain "Igi aya bomba" found in fragmentary form in an old areito (dance-song) is similar to one found in a Haitian bomba which reads, "Aya bomba, ya bombai—La masana Aanacona, Aya bomba bombai,"

The most popular dance form of Puerto Rico today is the danzon. In the primitive danzon there was a simple combination of notes in 2/4 time, called "tresillo de negras" after the Negro. The tango played in Puerto Rico is not to be confounded with the tango known in the United States. Here it is said to have been imported from Venezuela in the last century.

The true dance form of the *jivaros* is the simple "seis." This is interrupted by a recitation, a humorous "copla" called "bombai," which in this instance is a short melodic part of eight measures with interminable variations on one theme. In the modern Vals Jivaros, frequent syncopation is employed by leaving out the first beat of each measure and substituting a stroke on the box of the crude instrument which is used for the accompaniment. The melodic phrase is short, and the simple harmony is based on chords of the tonic, sub-dominant and dominant.

There are but few genuine Puerto Rican dances. The "meringüe" found in this section evidently came from Haiti by way of San Domingo. Here the flute sounds, the drum beats out a reply, and the picking of the guitar is heard while a couple dances. The fascinating danzon remains as the greatest inspiration to the native composer. While in San Juan, the author learned from Señor Jésus Figueroa, a cultivated Negro musician and orchestra leader, that the music was written to fit certain happenings, but that Campos and Mirando used famous poems. Juan Morrell Campos who was born May 16, 1857, in Ponce and passed away on May 12, 1896, combined instruments and evolved new and diverse rhythms for the danzon. With Manuel G. Tavarez (1843-1883), he brought a new elegance to the old form as composed by Don Eulogio Cortes and Don Ramon Santaella.

An aged musician, Julian Andino, gave the name of "terno-binario" to the rhythmic combination that was formerly suggested in the music of the Negro. But this is music of the trained composer; and, although showing strong native influences, it is somewhat apart from that of the primitive music-maker.

There is at present (1933) a number of young Cuban composers who are devoting themselves to the development of Cuban music which is rapidly taking its place as a distinct and interesting type of American art music. It is noticeable that these young musicians are not only employing their native African musical folk-contribution, but are also giving it public recognition. Alejandro Garcia Caturla, age 27 years, is one of the foremost men in this group whose compositions have been played by leading orchestras in the United States.

Writing of "Afro-Cuban" native music in the symposium, "American Composers on American Music," he says, " 'Afro-Cuban' music is our most original type of folk-song, and is a mixture of African primitive music with early Spanish influences. It employs many percussion instruments which have been developed in Cuba, and are to be found nowhere else, although they have their origin in African primitive instruments."[3]

Some of the world's most familiar and beautiful dance rhythmic forms lay claim to African-Negro influences. The Bamboula is the most widely known dance of African origin, and one which has kept its original name no matter in what clime it has found its home. It is said to have taken its name from the African drum, *bamboula,* which accompanies many of the dances. In New Orleans

[3] *American Composers on American Music,* edited by Henry Cowell, 1933. Chapter XXIII, "The Development of Cuban Music."

the song which accompanied the dance was also used as a
hunting song by the Creoles and Negroes of Louisiana.
The words were those of an old Creole proverb—"Quan
patate la cuite, nava mange" (When the potato is hot,
we will eat it) ; in other words, "Strike the iron while
it is hot."[4] The melody of this dance-song is common to
the West Indies and Louisiana. Friedenthal gives another
melody heard in the French Antilles. The theme, with
its striking rhythm, has been a favorite one for transcriptions. It was used by Louis Gottschalk for his piano
"Bamboula," transcribed for piano by S. Coleridge-
Taylor.

An elderly Creole neighbor told the author of this
dance in Place Congo, New Orleans, as he remembered it.
The performance opened with eighteen or twenty dancers
holding each other's hands and moving into places. The
first single movement was that of the women holding the
right hand of a companion and spinning around like tops
under clasped hands. All joined in the singing together
with prayers and danced uninterruptedly until nine
o'clock. The women were somewhat gayly dressed and
wore trinkets of Indian-like ornaments. This shows African origin.

The *vaudou* or *voodoo* corrupted into *hoodoo,* is a
dance of semi-worship, brought from Africa and practised
in all sections populated by the Negro. The python is
the god worshipped. In San Domingo, when the snake was
invoked in the *vaudou* dance, a refrain was sung:

> "Eh: Eh: Bomba: Heu, Heu:
> Canga, bafio, te:
> Canga, moune de le:
> Canga, do ki la:
> Canga li:"

[4] Lafcadio Hearn gives this old cryptic saying with many others
in his book of Creole proverbs.

These were the words linked to the extreme form of the *Vaudoux,* which was called "Danse a dou pedre."

Henry C. Castellanos, in *New Orleans As It Was,* states that, "according to the Africans of the Ardra nation who claim to have preserved unsullied the faith and ceremonies of their religion, they hold meetings in accordance with tradition borrowed from Africa, varied at times by Creole customs and other European customs as in matter of dress and ornament." St. John's Day, the twenty-fourth of June, was the day associated with this particular form of worship and the river plantations the favorite scene.

W. B. Seabrook has described the voodoo dance-songs of invocation to Damballa, Loco Agoue and all the old gods as being very beautiful. The voodoo rites of the Lehba sect, which he witnessed, were closed by a preliminary minor chant for full voice.

A favorite dance was that of the *Counjaille* or *Counjai* with love for its theme. According to Ware in *Slave Songs of the United States,* singers took the place of an orchestra. The leader was selected for his skill in improvising. He sustained the solo part, while the others shouted in chorus an obligato giving his compliments to some lovely dancer. Krehbiel in *Afro-American Folk-songs* states that an African word seems to lie at the bottom of the term Counjai. Lafcadio Hearn wrote from New Orleans to a friend, "My quadroon neighbor, Mamzelle Eglantine, tells me that the word *Koundjo* (in the West Indies *Candio* or *Candjo*) refers to an old African dance which used to be danced with drums." Today, the steps of the Counjai known as the coonjine are danced by the roustabouts who work on the Mississippi River. The relaxed and spread arms and knees are said to aid in carrying the heavy cargo.

An old African dance which falls under the Creole

dances of the New World is that of the Calinda which is spoken of in another chapter. In San Domingo, the Calinda was the principal amusement and the most popular dance of the early days. It was accompanied by a drum called tambour and a smaller one called *bamboula,* after the bamboo of which it was made. It was played with the wrist and fingers, slowly with one and quickly with the other. Dried calabashes, filled with seeds of corn or small stones were shaken by the Negroes. Sometimes the "orchestra" was enlarged by a banza, a sort of violin of four strings, but instead of being played with the bow, it is plucked. The dancers formed two lines or rows, the men and women opposite one another, three feet apart. They approach, join, separate, and then wait the drum signal which tells them to come together again.[5]

As a witness of this influence, Salvador Daniel states that the Fandango in Spain, to which the Calinda is likened, is a survival of a Moorish dance of Negro origin. It is accompanied by castanets and guitars. Of the fascination of the dance, it is written in the *Art of Music* —"You can feel the pulse of the semi-tropical, semi-African race; the flutter, passion and quivering seductiveness are a glimpse into the aesthetic depths of a national soul."

In recognition of these discoveries, the principal musical firms in France have recorded the *biguine,* a dance known on the African coast, under the name *malimba.* The dances are known in the French West Indies, but for lack of proper study the connection is not clear to the majority of those who consider themselves well informed on the history of music.

Gaston Vuillier, in his history of dancing, states that minstrels and troubadours composed *danzas,* and other Spanish dances. He quotes Father Martin who wrote in

[5] De Vaissiere, P., *Saint Domingue, 1629-1789,* p. 177.

1712 that the dance of Cadiz, famous for centuries, was not only in favor with Negroes, but also with ladies of high birth. Emil Pauer wrote in the *Monthly Musical Record* of September 1, 1872, that—"The better part of the national dance of Spain has relation with an African dance called '*la chika*' still in popular favor with all Negroes, particularly with the Congoes." The word Congo is used in connection with the dance Chica or Chika, in French Guiana and Louisiana, which is *la chica* in San Domingo and other sections of the West Indies. In Brazil, we find dance rhythms as well as instruments of Negro origin. The "Cucumbi" is still known in that country.[6]

When visiting Cuba in 1923, the author found many popular pieces written as *danzons*. The rhythms are not easy to play. The distinct 6/8 Criolla form, takes its name from the word Creole. In Haiti and neighboring sections, we find that the *méringüe*, a salon dance of that country, is identical to the Habanera of Cuba—at least, to the listening ear. The Haitian composer, Justin Elie, has preserved a number of folk melodies in a group of *méringües* written for piano soli.

"To me," writes Friedenthal in *Musik, Tanz und Dichthung bei den Kreolen Amerikas*, "Spain seems strongly to influence the dance and France the song and speech." It is true that in Creole folk music, the dance rhythms are mainly those of the Spanish-Creole while the folk songs, linked with the patois, remain French in structure and sentiment. Over all is the shadow of Negro Africa. The most fascinating and best known of the dance forms of supposed African origin is the "habanera."

According to Grove's dictionary, "A Habanera is a Spanish dance of an older origin than its name implies, having been introduced into Cuba from Africa by the Negroes, whence it was naturally imported into Spain.

[6] De Santa-Anna Nery, F. J., *Folk-Lore Brésilien*.

It is sometimes called Contradanza Criollo (Creole country-dance). It has a short introduction of two parts of eight or sixteen bars of which the first is in a minor key and the second in the major. This form is not always strictly followed.'' Although coming from Havana, the city of its birth and name, the "habanera" is known in the folk song of Brazil, Mexico, and, in fact, in much of the folk music of Central and South America.

In Mexico it is found as a salon dance. It is never sung, although the dancers sometime give an ejaculation akin to the African cry, "Aié," which is found at the close of many Creole songs. The dance as the author of this volume saw it in Mexico and Cuba, is in slow tempo. The form, says Friedenthal, "In the first part (minor), the melancholy part is played by the clarinet, while in the second part (major) the flute and violin enter together. In an orchestra, the bass is carried on by wind instruments, the horns taking part in the first eight bars only.''

In the volume *The Music of Spain*, Carl Van Vechten asks, "Was Nietzsche thinking of the Habanera inserted in the opera Carmen (which is based on the old Spanish tune), when he wrote 'The Case of Wagner'? This music is gay, but it has not the French or German gayety. Its gayety is African—destiny hangs over it; its happiness is short, sudden and without forgiveness.''

The ancestor of the "habanera" is the "tango" which was known in Argentina, as the Tango Argentino. The distinction is made that the tango comes from the Argentine while the habanero comes from Cuba. Raoul Laparra, composer of the opera "La Habanera," says of the "tango" form which he has transcribed, "It is a reflection of the Andalusian steps of the same name, which is of Arab character with sharp rhythmical contrasts, now morbid, now suddenly frantic, ending always in a few sonorous strokes of the heels coincident with the last sharp chords of the dance.'' Discussing these dances, Frieden-thal says, ''What impressions may not these fascinating, complicated and bizarre and yet transparent rhythms of the Negroes, have made upon the Spaniards who them-selves possess a refined sense of rhythm? The sound of the word tango was heard in La Plata from the sad days of the colony; it was the name the African Negroes gave to their percussion instruments. In the early days it was called the 'Tango of the Negroes.' During 1808 at a place not far from Montevideo the overseer, Elias, was called upon to close a building and prohibit the 'tango of the Negroes' because of the noise . . . A report from Rio de Janeiro, Brazil, stated that Mme. Renato Almeido, celebrated among Brazilians for talent and musical inter-ests, claimed the tango was originated by Negroes and that it was first played by colored carnival clubs in the River Platte cities.''[7]   W. C. Handy finds that there is a relationship between the tango rhythm and that of the Negro dance of the present, the ''Charleston.''

[7] The Negro Year Book—1931-1932, quoting Vicente Rossis's *Co-sas de Negros* (Cordoba, Argentina, 1926), Division XLI, p. 440.

CHAPTER VI

THE ORIGIN OF NEGRO SONG

BALLADRY—HISTORY OF FAMOUS TUNES—FOLK MUSIC FESTIVALS, WHITE—CLAIM OF "WHITE" SPIRITUALS—METHODIST CAMP-MEETINGS—CHRISTIAN SLAVE-HOLDING—CAMP-MEETING SONGS—ARGUMENT AS TO ORIGINS.

Balladry which encloses blood-thirsty, amusing or romantic narratives of the long ago, has attracted the attention of the historian chiefly because of the pictures of past customs and habits which are traced by the poetry of the people. Ballads have not always lent themselves to extemporized musical expression. Yet "Marlborough," the French ballad of many stanzas, has wandered the wide world over, in various racial settings. The author found a Spanish version of this old song in Latin-American dress, on the island of Puerto Rico. The tune remained the same.

There are about 305 English and Scottish ballads, and their variants, of primitive type, according to Professor Child of Harvard College. In the United States they are found in West Virginia, North Carolina, South Carolina, Tennessee, Missouri, Georgia and Texas. The model characteristics which have survived in the old English balladry in this country, are those of the Mixo-Lydian, Aeolian and Dorian—old ecclesiastical song modes—the oldest used in folk songs. These are not, of course, confined to songs of English origin. Writing of the actual existence of a "pure" Anglo-Saxon balladry, however, Dr. C. Alphonso Smith quotes the *Nation* (London) in declaring

113

that, "learned men have, of course, wasted much ink in arguing for and against the existence of ballads in Saxon England."[1]

The story of "Home, Sweet Home," is typical of how the ballad which originates with street singers, is assimilated by the people. This old familiar American song, first known in 1821, has been attributed to Henry Bishop, but John Howard Payne claimed that, having heard it sung by an Italian peasant girl, he sent it to Bishop who adapted the words of "Home, Sweet Home" to the melody and inserted it in his opera, *Clari, the Maid of Milan*.

According to the folk-lorist, Professor Lomax of the University of Texas, the ballad "The Maid Freed from the Gallows," is the only Negro song from American sources. Reed Smith in "The Traditional Ballad of the South," writes that the text of the song was obtained from W. E. Dehon of Summerville, South Carolina, who said he learned it from an old Negro nurse, Margaret, who belonged to the family in Charleston. "The Maid Freed from the Gallows," has a number of variants: "The Hangman's Tree," America; "Saylan," Jamaica; and "The White Captive," Texas. The music may be found in the *Journal of American Folk-Lore*.[2] In this particular, "The Prickly Bush" and "The Golden Ball" are of decided interest as shown in Child's English Country Songs.[3]

The best known Negro ballad in the United States, is the one called "John Henry." As "John Hardy," the story which may have originated in West Virginia, is familiar throughout the Southern States. A version of the real or mythical hero of tender heart and superior

[1] Smith, C. A., "Ballad Survival in the United States," *The Musical Quarterly*, Jan.-Feb., 1916.

[2] *Journal of American Folk-Lore*, XXV, p. 169.

[3] Child's *English Country Songs, Ballads*, vol. II, p. 364. No. 95.

brawn, is told in the *Folk Songs from West Virginia.*
The true ballad of John Henry has survived in many versions according to the sections in which the story is related. Professor Cox describes the hero as a famous steel
driver, a "handsome black roué, 6 feet 2, who weighed
225 pounds." One pay-day night he killed a man in a
crap game. Becoming converted while in prison, he was
baptized in Troy River, and confessed his willingness to
die. A picture of John Hardy on the gallows, was rescued
from a burning West Virginia City Hall by James Knox,
a Negro lawyer who was born in Tazewell County, Virginia. He presented it to the Folk-Lore Society.

"This old hammer killed John Henry, but this old
hammer won't kill me" is one of the many hammer songs
of the labor gangs.[4] Some authors think that it originated
in the Big Bend Tunnel in West Virginia, and perpetuates
the name of the powerful, lovable riveter whose story
Handy used for the like-named Blues. This picturesque
character described in the ballad "John Henry" has a
different life-story from that of "John Hardy" and was
known through ballads that originated in Mississippi, Virginia, and North Carolina.

It is well-nigh impossible to be precise or accurate as to
the origin of a ballad, a folk-song or even a famous song
such as the nationally known "Battle Hymn of the Republic." In 1924, when a controversy arose as to the
author of the tune "John Brown's Body lies a'moulderin'
in the grave," a "Former Brocktonian" (Brockton, Massachusetts) wrote to the Boston *Herald* on March 30, that
the song was heard by Samuel C. Perkins of the 12th regiment band from Brockton—at that time, North Bridge-
water—at the time the regiment under Colonel Fletcher

[4] Under "Rocks in de Mountains" this was sung by Negro crews
as a forecastle song. "Take dis hammah, gib it to de captain,
Tell him I'm gone, babe, tell him I'm gone."

Webster, son of Daniel Webster, was stationed at Fort Warren in 1861. The Negro slave who was singing the refrain, replied upon being questioned as to the song, that "there wasn't any more to it." Perkins thought it would make a fine marching song, and using a bass drum for a table, he wrote out an instrumentation for his band. This is said to be the first time the tune was musically set.

On the 24th of July, 1861, the band marched down Broadway on their way to the ferry in New York, singing and playing "John Brown's Body" to the great enthusiasm of the onlookers.[5] Another informant claims that a white captain, Henry J. Hallgreen, who died in Malden at the age of 95, wrote the words of the old song. He was captain of Company A of the Massachusetts Regulars and a Civil War veteran. Members of Perkins' band also added verses to the words of the old Negro slave.

C. A. Browne, writing a story of the famous tune for *The Musician,* tells of the first time Mrs. Julia Ward Howe, in company with her husband and Rev. James Freeman Clarke, together with Governor Andrew of Massachusetts, heard "John Brown's Body." In the midst of moving troops near Washington, every one sang popular army songs. The Rev. Mr. Clarke suggested that Mrs. Howe write words becoming to such a stirring melody as the excitable marching piece. She had thought of doing so, and Browne quotes the author as saying, "As I lay waiting for the dawn, the long lines of the desired poem began to twine themselves in my mind. For fear of forgetting them, I sprang out of bed, and, in the dimness, found an old stump of a pen . . . I scrawled the verses almost without looking at the paper." And so, from an old Negro refrain, was born the noble "Battle Hymn of the Republic."

[5] This band held their 80th anniversary in 1924.

Strong emphasis is now being placed on the advisability and the importance of preserving ancient melodies and ballads; among white musicians and educators the movement is having a lively growth. In the interest of the little known "mountain" folk song, as well as balladry and folk traditions, the first interstate Mountain Folk Music Festival, featuring banjo and fiddle tunes of the white race, was held on August 15, 1931, at Marion, Virginia. A second festival was held on August 13, 1932, with John Powell, Virginia pianist-composer, and Dr. George Pullen Jackson, of Vanderbilt University as leading participants. The interest of these particular educators is indicative of the trend these festivals are taking as relating to the history of "white" and "black" music of America. White Top, Virginia, was chosen as a meeting place as "the inhabitants are for the most part descendants of the original English and Scotch-Irish settlers who first penetrated the Southern Appalachian highlands. Ancient Anglo-Saxon folk music still exists here in purest form—" so wrote M. B. D., correspondent for *Musical America*. The folk hymns were introduced by Dr. Jackson, who gave a talk emphasizing the importance of "white" spirituals of the South, the Negro songs being sung by the Old Harp Singers, a white group from Nashville, Tennessee.

During the week of April 25-30, 1932, the Virginia State Choral Festival Association gave a second festival at which songs and dances as well as larger forms of modern compositions based on folk material were presented. A concert given by the National Symphony Orchestra with Hans Kindler, conductor, brought the festival to a close. It is worthy of mention that John Powell's "Natchez-on-the-Hill" was followed by "Shingandi," a primitive African ballet by David Guion, whose interest in Negro song is widely known.

In Charleston, South Carolina, one of the most individual cities of the world, a "Society for Preservation of Negro Spirituals" has been founded by white persons whose ancestors made South Carolina one of the most important states of the South. They have given public appearances as far north as Boston. The proceeds are devoted to charity. On July 15, 1915, the West Virginia Folk-Lore Society was organized, with John Harrington Cox and other officers who edited *Folk Songs* of the South in 1925.

Among these organizations, the Virginia Society is prominent in that its creator, John Powell with his associates have instigated a determined campaign to link not only the comparatively small number of songs of the illiterate mountain whites of the United States to the folk song of old England, but to claim as well the familiar folk songs of the Negro. In July, 1932, therefore, Eugene Kinckle Jones, a native of Virginia and the son of a trained musician, wrote in an editorial in *Opportunity,* a Negro magazine:

"It seems a little odd that until the Spirituals became accepted by music authorities abroad as the only original American music, Americans with few exceptions were not concerned with their origin, and still less their preservation. For two hundred years these songs had come up from the cotton fields and cabins . . . They were just "nigger songs" until the great world of music acclaimed them as the only music indigenous to America. Then it was that 'diligent scholars' started the painstaking and laborious task of finding their source, of collecting and amassing voluminous data by which ultimately they were enabled to announce that the Spirituals are not the creation of the enslaved black but rather the creation of the rural white."

John Powell's argument that the Negro heard the songs

credited to him as they were sung by Anglo-Saxons, and being inherently musical, he took them and made them his own, was further strengthened by the deductions made by Dr. George Pullen Jackson, a professor of German, who was born in Maine but has long taught language in the South. His claim of white origin for Negro song has made him a welcome visitor to the festivals featuring white "American" music. His latest work is a volume called *White Spirituals and their Singers*. In a preceding article on the *Genesis of the Negro Spiritual*, he stated that the religious folk-song of the Negro emanated from white racial sources. He gave no scientific method or procedure but simply made emphatic and arbitrary statements that lead the reader to conclude that he is in-intellectually dishonest.

The camp-meeting song of the colored people, so states Dr. Jackson, was the product of the Methodist revival movement. But, as Eugene Kinkle Jones in his editorial succinctly points out, "The revival tunes of Methodism may have power to move the devil harassed yeomen and mountaineers of the rural South, but there their influence ends. The Negro Spiritual had no such limitations. Teuton and Slav and Latin as well as American and English respond to its appeal . . . Like all cultural developments the American Negro Spirituals doubtless have many sources. But if one is anxious to evaluate the contribution of the Negro to American music, he should try to imagine what it might be if its sole inheritance had been the Methodist revival hymns of the South."

In appreciation of this contribution, Dr. W. E. B. DuBois said, "Little of beauty has America given the world save in the rude grandeur God himself stamped on her bosom! The human spirit in this new world has expressed itself in vigor and ingenuity rather than in beauty. And so by fateful chance the Negro folk-song,

the rhythmic cry of the slave—stands today not simply
as the sole American music, but as the most beautiful expression of human experience born this side the seas. It
has been neglected, it has been, and is, half despised, and
above all it has been persistently mistaken and misunderstood; but notwithstanding, it still remains as the singular spiritual heritage of the nation and the greatest gift
of the Negro people."⁶

These Negro defenders of their racial achievement have
other supporters. Paul Rosenfeld, in "An Hour with
American Music" writes, "As we know it, the Negro
Spiritual is an obviously sophisticated arrangement of
some more primitive song—we can merely guess at the
basic tunes." This remark would lead historians to consider the influences of the pagan blacks of Africa rather
than that of the illiterate whites of America. On November 15, 1856, a comment to this effect on the paucity of vocal music in the United States over seventy
years ago occurred in *Dwight's Journal* under "Songs
of the Blacks," over the signature "Evangelist." It read,
"The only musical population of this country are the Negroes of the South . . . Brother Jonathan is awkward at
the business and sings only on set occasions. He makes
little music at home or at most on the Sabbath Day. Our
people work in silence like convicts in a penitentiary.
Compared with our taciturn race, the African nature is
full of poetry and song."

Of all folk musical expression, English folk song is the
most barren. Their songs lack the freedom from monotony
which the people of Southern France acquire by their
short note groupings and frequent change of bar-time; the
brilliancy of the Spanish with their accented rhythms in
binary and ternary divisions; the unbridled emotion and

⁶ Du Bois, W. E. B., *The Soul of Black Folk*, p. 251.

sorrow of Russian song or the barbaric, rhapsodic moods of the embellishments of Gypsy song. This poverty of musical feeling in Anglo-Saxon temperaments was responsible for requests from the master class which made the musically gifted, though illiterate Negro serf, fore-shadow the graphone and radio by becoming performers of music for the indolent white listeners. Even some of the pious ones who had been converted at the revivals were known to have called upon their slaves to sing religious songs for them at their morning prayers or worship in the home. In this manner, the whites became doubly familiar with Negro hymns. The white man's Christ of lowly birth rather than the creeds as was practised, inspired the Negro slave to express his faith in musical forms of his own.

William B. Snow, in his unpublished poem "On Freedom," wrote of the dusky sons who "saw gods in woods, and spirits in the wind," and adds that "the imagination of the African, like his musical genius . . . seems to invest everything with a resident spirit of peculiar power. Accordingly, his mythologies are most numerous and poetical." From the *Edinburgh Encyclopaedia of Early Christian History* we gather that "a beautiful thread of implicit faith and fervent hope, of after life, assimilating to the hunting-ground of our own American Indians, and though sensuous still, a step far in advance of the black void of ancient philosophy, has always run through the higher mythologies of the Negro. So notorious, indeed, was the fact among early Christians, that that ubiquitous riddle, "Prester John," was, by believers, regarded as having a locale in Central Africa; while Henry of Portugal actually despatched two ambassadors, Corvilla and Payvan, to a rumored Christian court, south of the Sahara.[7] The oldest Latin translation of the Bible, mis-

[7] "On Freedom," *Autographs of Freedom*, p. 260. Richmond, Dec. 1, 1853.

called "Itata" was probably made in Africa and for the Africans.[8]

"The thread of implicit faith" made the mind of the Negro fertile soil for the teachings of the message of the Redeemer. In the West Indies from whence many slaves came to the United States, Christians of many denominations, including the Moravians, exerted themselves with great success to the conversion of the Negroes."[9] This was true even while writers deplored "the danger of false superstition, misnamed Christianity . . . becoming every hour more frightful." "But to true Evangelists," declares a reviewer in *Blackwood's*, "we must look for the averting of the most hideous calamities now imminent and to the book in their blessed hands, and expounded by their blessed lips, the Bible."[10]

In not every instance was the Christian Church in the United States reluctant to teach the Negro. In a letter of November 25, 1853, Mary Irving wrote from Thibodaux that she herself was permitted to teach the slaves, but that she deplored the short periods of study that were allowed; her pleading was that the enslaved might "have the key to the gate of Life Eternal."

There, too, were here and there, rare figures like Bishop Polk in Louisiana; C. C. Jones and Josiah Law in Georgia; W. D. Capers in South Carolina, and William Meade in Virginia, who made special efforts to evangelize Negroes. John G. Fee, a southern abolitionist in Kentucky, founded a church as well as a college at Berea, for both white and Negro students.

Nobility and courage gained by spiritual strength as

[8] Schaff, *History of the Christian Church*, volume II.

[9] Montgomery, James, *The West Indies and Other Poems*, London, 1814.

[10] Discussion of *Barbadoes*, a poem by M. J. Chapman, London, October, 1833.

opposed to the weakness and cruelty of blind bigotry, was the pattern followed by the slave bard who, never doubting, sang

> "I know de Lord's laid His hands on me,
> My Lord done just what He said;
> I know de Lord's laid His hands on me,
> He heal de sick an' raise de dead."

Compare this text with that of a Methodist revival hymn with its acknowledged doubt—

> "I bring to Thee, O Master,
> My burden and my grief;
> I do believe Thy promise,
> Help thou my un-belief!"

Dr. Jackson quotes from an 18th century hymn—ostensibly to show that the Negro was the borrower.

> "Awake, my soul, to joyful lays,
> Oh Glory Hallelujah!
> And sing the great Redeemer's praise,
> Don't you love God? Glory Hallelujah!"

Chorus—"There's union in heaven, and there's union in my soul.
Oh, Glory Hallelujah!"

The African song which reads—"Sweet Music in Zion's beginning to roll, Don't you love God? Glory Hallelujah!" embodies the questioning form found in many Negro Spirituals.

On this point the author of *The Negro and His Song* writes, "Many of the old Spirituals were composed in their first form by the Negro preachers for their congregations; others were composed by the slaves in the various walks of life, while still others were first sung by the mammies as they passed the time in imaginative melody-making and sought harmony of words and music."[11]

Surely the deeply imaginative Negro voiced his aroused religious feeling long before the time of the Methodist revival movement which Dr. Jackson contends was the origin of the product which he calls "white" Spirituals. Methodism flourished in America about 1790, particularly during 1800 to 1833. Since the revival movement did not

[11] We get a true picture of the old white camp-meeting as held in the South (before the time of the Negro Church and ordained ministers), by one who was not only a slave, but intelligent and capable of afterwards writing a vivid description of the proceedings. It was in the month of August, 1833, in the Bayside, eight miles from St. Michaels; Frederick Douglass writes (1)—"The camp-meeting continued for a week; people gathered from all parts of the country. . . . The ground was happily chosen; seats were arranged, a stand erected and a rude altar fronting the preacher's stand fenced in, with straw in it, making a soft kneeling place for the accommodation of mourners. In front and on the sides of the preacher's stand, and outside the long row of seats, rose the first class of stately tents. . . . *Behind* the preacher's stand, a narrow space was marked out for the use of the colored people. There were no seats provided for this class of persons, and if the preachers addressed them at all, it was in an aside.

"After the preaching was over, an invitation was given to mourners to come forward into the pen; and in some cases, ministers went out to persuade men and women to come in. By one of these ministers Master Thomas was persuaded to go inside the pen. . . . 'If he has got religion,' thought I, 'he will emancipate his slaves' but—in my expectations I was doubly disappointed."

"Captain Auld 'came through' with a profession of religion, but his relationship towards his slaves and the institution of slavery remained the same. The Captain's home became regular headquarters for the preachers, for after his "conversion" he became one of the most religious men in St. Michaels. Mr. Douglass tells of the many circuit preachers who were entertained there, who (with the exception of one—Rev. George Cookman, an eloquent English preacher) "seemed about as unconcerned about our getting to heaven as about our getting out of slavery." *Life and Times of Frederick Douglass*, p. 131.

begin to develop in the United States before the last quarter of the 18th century, it is difficult to believe that a race whose forbears were as musical as the Negro, should remain musically inarticulate for over 350 years—until they heard the wan, inane camp-meeting tunes which it is claimed, they sang as their own. If it is true, as Jackson says, that the revival leaders of a century ago had no recorded songs, but simply trusted to good memory, it is just as plausible that in their seeking for religious fervor, the camp-meeting attendants and mourners at the bench, unconsciously or deliberately borrowed the emotional hymns of the Negro. They are doing this very thing today.[12]

Eventually, the camp-meeting songs were recorded. In 1806 a book was published at Newbern, North Carolina. It bore the title-exhortation of "Speak to yourselves in psalms and hymns and spiritual songs."[13] The name "Spiritual" was that of the Negro's "prayer-song" which had taken the place of his old pagan "Spirit songs" of worship and divination. John Totten was the editor of another book, "Selection of Hymns and Spiritual Songs— as Usually Sung at Camp-Meetings." A 19th edition appeared in 1927. In 1928, Lamar & Whitmore, publishers, brought out a book for the Methodist which is called "The New Cokesbury Hymnal," the tunes of which are said to have been chosen by the people. Among the 225 hymns one finds the Negro songs, "Swing Low, Sweet Chariot,"

[12] See the treatment of this topic *in extenso* by Carter G. Woodson in an article in the *Journal of Negro History*, XIX, pp. 93-96. This is a review of George Pullen Jackson's *White Spirituals*.

[13] Before 1743, John Newbery, the father of Children's books, published his first children's book—*Spiritual Songs for Children* by J. Wright.

"Standin' in the Need of Prayer," "Down by the River-Side," and "I Know the Lord has Laid His Hands on Me."

But the publication of Negro Spirituals in hymnals does not make them "white." Dr. Jackson naively and generously (?) states that he will not deny that the Negro made three songs—"Steal Away," "Swing Low," and "Deep River." It must be conceded that if the Negro possessed sufficient musical gift to produce such a masterpiece of folk-song as "Deep River," alone, it is easily within his genius to contribute the group of lesser Spirituals attributed to him. Perhaps *three* folk songs are not too many for one race to have extemporized. James Weldon Johnson says to this effect, "Most difficult of all is it to believe that the Negro slaves were indebted to their white masters for the sources of these songs. The white people among whom the slaves lived did not originate anything comparable even to the mere titles of the Spirituals."[14]

Spokesmen for "white spirituals" claim that there are Hebrew influences in the songs of faith which are claimed by the Negro. Apart from the fact that the Biblical text of the Old Testament was assimilated by the slave in his acceptance of the Christian religion, there is a sympathetic affiliation which is not surprising. All students of Hebrew song know that as in the case of the German Jews of long ago (years before their present persecution), vent was given to their grief and bitterness in oppression. It is likewise true that the Hebrews incorporated into their song snatches of popular tunes of the particular countries in which they made their home. The use made of

---

[14] *The Book of American Negro Spirituals*, musical arr. by J. Rosamond Johnson, introduction by James Weldon Johnson, New York, 1925.

Negro music on the Spanish stage by Lope de Vega and Calderon shows how such an influence could have reached the Hebrews.[15] Their song in Spain, moreover, contained musical threads from early Africa acquired from contact of Africans with Jews in the Mediterranean. Was not the Temple music of the Hebrews taught them by Moses, who had been a disciple of the priests of Egypt and did not Egypt come under the influence of Ethiopia? The range of their old music is in many instances like that of Africa—very small, of only three notes. And, as with the Negro-American, it is associated with every act of their life.

It was evidently true that "the emotional need of the Negro caused larger themes, more varied than the African repetition" and as Dr. Heinitz says, "These slaves affected not only our dance music but the whole body of religious tunes. Sufferings of the Negroes, emotional conversion to Christianity, made more intense any native African tune."

Even as the author writes, however, the movement to propagate the "white spiritual" as the original native Christian song in the United States is carried forward. Samuel E. Asbury and Henry E. Meyer in an article, "Old-Time White Camp-Meeting Spirituals," for a volume of the Texas Folk-Lore Society, admit, however, that the words of the white spirituals are not as poetical as those of the Negro song.

The third annual White Top Folk Festival was recently held on August 11 and 12, 1933, when Mrs. Franklin D. Roosevelt was a guest and expressed herself as being desirous of being a "part of it." Dr. Jackson again featured the so-called "white spirituals" of the Southern Uplands and John Powell stressed the structure

[15] See C. G. Woodson's "Attitudes in the Iberian Peninsula," in the *Journal of Negro History*, XX, pp. 28-82.

of English-American folk tunes, thus laying the foundation for a universal acceptance of the claim that the traditional religious folk music of the United States is "white" in its origin. Educators, poets and writers were willing and interested listeners at this last festival.

Dr. Jackson, whom one would not like to charge with being a sciolist, states that the Fisk Jubilee Singers did not at first use Negro folk songs, but sang such songs as "John Brown's Body." They might have properly sung the old Battle Hymn, but it is beyond dispute that the famous school group made their reputation by delighting audiences with their "Slave Spirituals" as they were called. It was the idea of George L. White, who had heard the slave songs and had been impressed by them, to have the student group go North with their songs which had already charmed the people about Nashville.

Press clippings of that day are proofs of the type of program which the singers of Fisk gave. Writing of a concert held in Henry Ward Beecher's Church in New York in January, 1872, Rev. Theodore L. Cuyler of Brooklyn, in the New York *Tribune*, quoted the Rev. Chalmers, a delegate of the Scotch Presbyterian General Assembly as telling his home congregation that he had found the ideal church in America—it was made up of Methodist praying, Presbyterian preaching, and Southern Negro-singing. The Rev. Mr. Cuyler added that the "wild melodies of the emancipated slaves that touched the fount of tears" as sung by the colored students of Nashville, would have strengthened such an opinion. "Our people can now listen to the genuine soul-music of the slave-cabins before the Lord led his Children out of the land of Egypt."

That the Fisk Jubilee Singers featured the spirituals abroad as well as at home, is confirmed by tributes paid by such leading figures as C. H. Spurgeon, George Mac-

Donald and W. E. Gladstone, the prime-minister of England. Reference is made to the ''peculiar and plaintive melodies of the Southland in the days of slavery, which made up the major part of the program. A few selections of more artistic compositions were introduced—''[16]

In discussing the development of Negro song in general, Newman I. White correctly and fairly says, ''No matter how it developed, the Negro song is now definitely and peculiarly Negro, and that it is no more discrediting the Negro race to point out certain alien elements in its origin than it is a discredit to English poetry to have borrowed its rhyme from the French;''[17] and also, ''If Negro song owes a great deal of its origin to the white man's song, it has not been without its counter influence on the white man!''[18]

The folk-lorist, if he be musicologist as well, may search with pleasure and profit into the modes, phrases, scales and rhythm in order to find the underlying differences by which the religious consciousness of the two races are expressed. In the end he must admit this genuine feeling embodied in religious Negro song of which Alain Locke writes, ''A quaintly literal, lisping, fervent Christianity, we feel it to be the evangelical and Protestant counterpart of the naïve Catholicism of the tenth to the thirteenth centuries. And just as there we had quaint versions of Bernard of Clairvaux and St. Francis in the Virgin songs and Saints' Legends, so here we have Bunyan and John Wesley percolated through a peasant mind and imagination and concentrated into something intellectually less, but emotionally more vital and satisfying.''[19]

[16] *The Boston Journal,* a quotation from, among other testimonies as to the reception of these singers, printed on their programs and works in the author's collection.

[17] White, Newman I, *American Negro Folk Songs,* pp. 28-29.

[18] *Ibid.*

[19] *The New Negro.* Edited by Alain Locke.

With plangent voice the Negro Spiritual goes on. One can best reply to the diligent white scholar in the words of a quotation favored by the distinguished critic, Philip Hale, who writing of the pedants ''who dug and dove for the beginnings of folk song,''—''the deeper they dove the muddier they came up.''[20]

[20] Richard Grant White, writing with respect to Shakesperian commentators. Quoted by Mr. Hale in the *Boston Symphony Program Book.*

Chapter VII

NEGRO IDIOM AND RHYTHM

Development — Syncopation — Jazz — The "Blues" —
Will Marion Cook—J. Rosamond Johnson—James Reese
Europe—Exponents of Rag-Time—W. C. Handy—Form
—Discussions—Jazz Band Leaders.

Negro music is one of the foremost subjects of discussion in the modern world. "In good sooth," says *The Listener*, writing in the Boston *Evening Transcript*, "America should be sometime, the greatest of musical nations since she inherits the music of all the rest of the world, including that of Africa, Asia, and the Polynesian islands, to say nothing of the native Indian music, which is coming to the fore. But just now all these far-flung lines of musical inspiration are being jumbled into Jazz. In the music of the people, the influence of Africa preponderates at this moment. Indeed, it has seemed all along to the *Listener* that the Negro music or even the degeneration of it into Jazz, is a thing which is needed in the development of a really typical American music."

It has been claimed that Jazz will divide itself and follow two strains—"The Negro and the Intellectual." This aptly describes the situation. Many regard Negro music as synonymous with comedy and buffoonery, rhythmic oddities and random lines. But thoughtful musicians differentiate between music as expressed by trained and cultivated Negro Americans and Negro music of the above named style.

There are now two classes of native composers—the intellectual musician as exemplified in Harry T. Burleigh,

Clarence Cameron White, and a number of others who are now experimenting in Jazz as known through the dance and comedy. They are of the school of rising young composers of Negro descent who are creating music as an art. Their work follows the line of Negro Music as it has grown from the African or Negro folk song, expressive of the soul of a people in their varied moods, but the material is treated as by men of education, musical training and creative intelligence.

Their created works are those which are apprehended by the intellect and emotions rather than by the physical and sensational. Admittedly, they will experiment in rhythmical effect of whatever school. The Negro composer realizes that unless he uses folk themes subserviently, he must form his musical lines to correspond to the novel forms and odd scales of the songs employed. Not only will the structure of his composition be influenced by the modes in which the native song is found, but the rhythmic line must remain unchanged. It leaves only the content—the soul of the piece upon which he can lean for self-expression. Through the reflection of this image alone can he give forth an original contribution.

A. H. Fox Strangways in the *London Observer* significantly declares, "Music is a much bigger thing than any particular manifestation of it. It is true it is wrapped up in sound; and anyone who cannot naturally, or who does not, train himself to attend to sounds, can make little of it. But the root idea of it, underneath, is the desire of man to find a unity in the world without ignoring its diversity; to take the diversity as his subject matter and the unity as his plan. Musicians are often chess-players, sometimes mathematicians. That doesn't mean that they want to win off somebody else, nor that they aim at finality, but that they are lovers of vistas in whatever medium."

In the "new" national music now well-liked, the peculiar harmonies and tonalities employed run parallel with the accompanying Negro syncopated rhythms. Negro rhythm differs from the majority of racial musical rhythms in the great variety and complexity of its accents which ignore any division of time that follows the natural pulse of a regular metrical beat. Accents are anticipated or are held over beyond their expected time. The resultant syncopation early became known as Ragtime.

Modern Ragtime is supposed to have originated in the South and West. According to Ernest Newman, as syncopation it has been made use of from time immemorial and by the world's greatest musicians—Handel, Beethoven, Schumann, Liszt and Tschaikowsky. The modern musician has added innumerably to the list. The syncopation of the African song is the fore-runner of American Ragtime and the more reprehensible Jazz and Blues. At present, Jazz is spoken of simultaneously with syncopation or Ragtime, although fundamentally it is not the same thing. A few years ago, syncopation dealt with rhythm, while Jazz was the accompanying acrobatics and monkeyish antics on the part of the performers, and the grotesque use of the instruments.

The certain significance that the "Rag" presented in the bits of melody in the work or play song of the Negro, was overshadowed by the distortion of its content until the contribution, from a musical point of view, seemed destined to be a worthless one. So far did the Rag craze and Jazz spread, that in traveling and visiting many institutions of learning, the author found that the musical taste of the youth was being poisoned. To such an extent was this true, that a number of high-minded school presidents closed the mechanical instruments to the pupils who would listen to no other music except that of the "Rag."

Not only were the popular ballads in Ragtime destroying an appreciation of the classics; they also prevented an acquirement of taste for good poetry. The verses lacked literary value—the words were vulgar, the sentiment execrable. But so popular has Jazz become, it has spread all over the United States and Europe. Termed typical American, it nevertheless does not represent all America.

In the middle of the nineteenth century, the period of the "Funny Forties," the polka, quickstep, schottische and quadrille were enjoyed, as can be seen from the wealth of old sheet music published in these forms from 1839 to 1854. The favorite society dance of the past generation was the waltz, with the waltz kings, Johann and Eduard Strauss, in Vienna and throughout the world, as the leading composers. Inspired music of high standard, it lives on the concert stage today. Gradually the triple rhythm gave way to duple, the quiet waltz to the lively one-step, and thus the opening wedge was made for the more boisterous and exhilarating rhythms. As dance musicians, Negroes had always held a favorite place in the South, even before the Civil War when a lone fiddler as well as the small orchestra was used to amuse the family and entertain the guests.[1]

[1] A producer of this sort in the North, over fifty years ago, was a Negro of musical talent from Canada, who located in Detroit. There, with his wife and son, he formed what was called Finney's Quadrille Orchestra. Extra players were added to his little group, and as a demand was created for his services he divided his rapidly growing orchestra into a number of smaller groups augmented by white musicians. As the Negro population increased, Finney employed colored players altogether. Among these were his protegés, John W. Johnson and Will Stone. Fred Stone was the only euphonium Negro player at that time; he was also a pianist and more interested in the orchestra than the band. Charles Stone was a third brother. These young men organized the Detroit City Brass Band and an orchestra of forty or more men. Both Fred Stone and his brother performed on many instruments. John Johnson was

A distinct type of dance music, first introduced by untrained Negro players from the South, many of whom
could not read music, crept into vaudeville quarters after
having been brought northward from New Orleans, Memphis, St. Louis, thence to Chicago, and on to New York.
The old folk-dances, the Bamboula, the Counjai, the Juba
and the Calinda were of a time and scene apart, as they
have ever been from time immemorial. But the old
rhythms influenced the modern American dance music,
although this fact has at times been ignored.[2]

regarded as one of the finest cornetists in the West. His band compositions were widely played. The pieces written by Fred Stone
were catchy and tuneful. Among them were ''The Albacete
Waltzes,'' ''The Indian Two-Step,'' and ''Ragtime Baby,'' the
first Ragtime song written. The group later organized a dance orchestra in Philadelphia.

[2] Relative to the beginnings of the voluptuous dance forms of
today, Will Marion Cook, who featured the cake-walk in 1905, wrote
an illuminating letter to the editor of the New York *Times*, December 19, 1926. It was one in which he deplored the credit given
George White of the ''Scandals'' as the originator of the ''Charleston'' and the ''Black Bottom.''

''I have the greatest respect for Mr. White, his genius as an
organizer and producer of revues; but why do an injustice to the
black folk of America by taking from them the credit of creating
new and characteristic dances? From ''Old Jim Crow'' to ''Black
Bottom,'' the Negro dances came from the Cotton Belt, the levee,
the Mississippi River, and are African in inspiration. The American Negro, in search of outlet for emotional expression, recreates
and broadens these dances. Either in their crude state, or revised
form, in St. Louis, Chicago or New York the dance is discovered (?)
by white theatrical producers and sold to the public as an original
creation.

''The 'Charleston' has been done in the South, especially in the
little islands off Charleston, S. C., for more than forty years to my
knowledge. The dance reached New York five years ago. In
Harlem any evening a group of Negro children could be seen 'Doin'
the Charleston' and collecting pennies. This dance was first staged
in a real production by Frank Montgomery in 'How Come.' Leonard Harper, a colored man, used a few steps of the dance.

A Negro comedian, Shelton Brooks, is said to be responsible for "The Texas Tommy" and "Walkin' the Dog," two combinations of Jazz dances. The dancer, Josephine Baker, has followed in the wake of Ada Walker and Florence Mills as an exponent of Negroid dances and is now reaping financial reward and adulation in Europe as the most popular music-hall dancer of the day. She was engaged at the Folies Bergère in 1927-8. In 1931 she was chosen by the Fête Committee of Paris to be queen of the Colonies during the Colonial Exposition of that year at which African and West Indian French possessions were pictorially, commercially and architecturally represented.

The furore created by the Negro dance steps made an opportunity for the opening of a dancing academy by Billy Pearce who became the "Dancing Master of Broadway." Until 1932, Pearce's studio was the most important one in the theatrical world. His dancing teachers, all of whom were colored, came from Harlem and were expert in the new dances which included the tapdance. Broadway producers, stage and screen stars, pat-

"The first music with this fascinating rhythm was the 'Charleston Strut,' written by Tommy Morris and published by Jack Mills, Inc., about four years ago. (1922.)

"Jimmy Johnson, a Negro song writer, first conceived the idea of a Charleston song, and in his score of 'Runnin' Wild,' for Miller and Lyles, wrote the famous 'Charleston,' which was staged by Elida Webb, and the craze was on.

"It is doubtful if Mr. White even saw a 'Charleston' until he attended the final rehearsals of 'Runnin' Wild.' Similarly, for many years, the 'Black Bottom' has been evolving in the South. Irving Miller first produced the dance about three years ago in New York at Lafayette Theatre. Two years ago (1924) Louis Douglass, famous in Europe, thrilled all Paris as he and Josephine Baker 'Black Bottomed' at the Champs Elysée Theatre. Messrs. White et al. are great producers. Why with such immense flocks of dramatic and musical sheep, should they wish to reach out and grab our little ewe lamb of originality?"

ronized the Pearce studio: Ramon Navarro, Ed Wynn, Jack Hulbert, Jack Buchanan, Louise Brooks, Betty Compton, Libby Holman, Anita Loos, Bessie Love and Lily Damita, with many others were pupils at this school.[3]

The growth of Jazz orchestras ran parallel with that of

[3] Mr. Pearce, who came from Virginia, died in New York in April, 1933.

[4] Lieut. James Reese Europe, who was born in Mobile, Alabama, February 22, 1881, was one of the leading composers and directors of Ragtime music. He comes from a musical family of no mean gifts. This composer won international fame in this field by his compositions and demonstrations with bands and orchestras which he conducted about the time of the World War. His parents early migrated to Washington, D. C., and there he became a violin pupil of Enrico Hurlei, assistant director of the United States Marine Band. At the age of 14 the boy James entered a musical contest in which he was defeated by his sister, Miss Mary Europe, who won the first prize.

James Europe studied theory and instrumentation under Hans Hanke of the Leipzig Conservatory of Music, Melville Charlton and Harry T. Burleigh. Later he became the director of the "Williams and Walker," and "Cole and Johnson" companies. In composition, Mr. Europe's greatest successes were his marches. Of them the New York *Tribune* said that "all in all they are worthy of the pen of John Philip Sousa." After six years spent in conducting musical comedies, with the rapid rise of the dance he became associated with Mr. and Mrs. Vernon Castle for whom he wrote "Castle Walk" and "Castle House Waltz." He next became manager of many groups of jazz dance-orchestras in New York, at the same time organizing the Clef Club and Clef Club Orchestra which was mis-named a "Symphony" Orchestra. On March 11, 1914, Europe presented his orchestra of more than one hundred pieces playing works of Negro composers, at Carnegie Hall, New York. At that time, in an interview in the New York *Evening Post*, he said:

"You see, we colored people have our own music that is part of us. It's the product of our souls; it's been created by the sufferings and miseries of our race. Some of the old melodies we played Wednesday night were made up by slaves of the old days, and others were handed down from the days before we left Africa.

"Now I have between 150 and 187 musicians I can call on for work in the symphony orchestra, and I am continually adding to the dance. About 1900, Ford Dabney and James Reese Europe[4] came from Washington and organized jazz or-

their numbers and improving the constituent parts. For instance, I am just sending to South Africa for two French horn players, and to the Sudan for an oboe player. The British regiments in South Africa and the Sudan have remarkable bands, which receive musicians as young as twelve years and train them rigorously.

"Walter Damrosch or Mr. Stransky or any white leader of a symphony orchestra would doubtless laugh heartily at the way our Negro Symphony Orchestra is organized, at the distribution of the pieces and our methods of orchestration.

"For instance, although we have first violins, the place of the second violins with us is taken by mandolins and banjos. This gives that peculiar steady strumming accompaniment to our music which all people comment on, and which is something like that of the Russian Balalaika Orchestra, I believe. Then, for background, we employ ten pianos. That, in itself, is sufficient to amuse the average white musician who attends one of our concerts for the first time. The result, however, is a background of chords which are essentially typical of Negro harmony.

"Other peculiarities are our use of two clarinets instead of an oboe. As a substitute for the French horn we use two baritone horns, and in place of the bassoon we employ the trombone. We have no less than eight trombones and seven cornets. The result, of course, is that we have developed a kind of symphony music that, no matter what else you think, is different and distinctive, and that lends itself to the playing of the peculiar compositions of our race.''

The concerts of this orchestra as given in 1914, received both favorable and adverse criticism from white and colored sources respectively. *Musical America*, while commending a concert, said:

"If the Negro Symphony Orchestra will give its attention during the coming year to a movement or two of a Haydn symphony and play it at its next concert, and if the composers, who this year took obvious pleasure in conducting their marches, tangos and waltzes, will write short movements for orchestra, basing them on classic models, next year's concert will inaugurate a new era for the Negro musician in New York and will aid him in being appraised at his full value and in being taken seriously. It is impossible to applaud in Carnegie Hall his imitations of the vulgar dance music of Broadway originated by the tone poets of Tin Pan Alley.''

An open letter written by Mr. Adolphus Lewis, a colored music-lover of Philadelphia, voiced the opinion of many colored students of music. Mr. Lewis wrote:

"Of course, the music was typical of the light, happy-go-lucky chestras, and were heard at Florenz Ziegfeld's Roof Garden. At "The Marshall," a colored café and hotel in

Negro, but there are those among us who are trying to master the classics in music as well as along other lines, and to say that the program satisfied this class, would be gainsaying the truth. All the renditions of the Club were good, spicy and catchy . . . All races have their folk-song and dances, but all races try to develop their art from examples set by masters of other periods; and if we expect to do anything that is lasting from an artistic standpoint, we too, must study the classics as a foundation for our work.

"As a symphony orchestra the Clef Club was a miserable disappointment, but as a club of versatile entertainers and syncopated minstrels it is the 'last word' in that art."

At the very height of his popularity, and when this country entered the World War, Mr. Europe enlisted as a private in the Fifteenth New York Infantry, afterwards designated as the 369th Regiment. At the permission of Colonel Hayward, Mr. Europe organized a new band. Not content, the musician joined the ranks of the machine gun company and won sufficient recognition to cause him to be sent to an officers' training camp, where he was commissioned a lieutenant. For fifteen months the band was overseas and was heard everywhere with great delight.

Upon returning to the United States, the band started a tour of the leading cities. The concerts given at the Boston Opera House were so successful that a series were to be given at Mechanics Hall, but the tragic death of the director caused the concerts to be abandoned. On the night of May 9, 1919, Lieut. Europe was killed in the dressing room by an illiterate drummer whom he had reprimanded for unbecoming conduct.

The programs given by Lieut. Europe and the talented musicians who were associated with him, were the finest expositions of this particular style of music. Gilbert Seldes, who considered Lieutenant Europe a bit of a "Kappelmeister," stated in *The Dial*, that "Jim Europe seemed to have a constructive intelligence and had he lived I am sure he would have been an even greater conductor than Whiteman."

About this time, Will Tyers was writing dance music and marches which, like those of James Europe, were favorably compared with productions of Sousa. Negro musicians were at the height of their popularity for social dances. The syncopated rhythms which were used primarily in the dance, grew rapidly in favor.

Harlem managed by Jimmie Marshall, a musical group called "The Memphis Students" was organized with a membership of twenty. Jim Europe and other well-known musicians were the early members of this combination, which later became the Clef Club.

In 1905 the first Negro Jazz Band was heard at Proctor's Twenty-third Street Theatre. The orchestra consisted of banjos, guitars, mandolins, saxophones, drum, violin, two bass and a double-bass. The band was rehearsed by Will Marion Cook. Meeting with great success immediately, it appeared at Hammerstein's Victoria, and shortly afterwards the band opened the Olympia in Paris. Engagements followed at the Palace Theatre in London and at the Schumann Circus in Berlin. Compositions by the colored writer, Will Dixon, were played, while Buddy Gilmore, who originated the present style of trap (jazz) drumming, performed his acrobatic drum antics.

A third form of Negro syncopated music, the "Blues," arose and appealed strongly to followers of popular music. Its originator is William Christopher Handy, a Negro bandmaster, cornetist and composer. For some years the credit due him was given to white exponents, but he has now come into his own as "the father of the Blues." Handy was born in Florence, Alabama, November 16, 1873, the son and grandson of Methodist Episcopal ministers. While living in Memphis, Tennessee, he organized a band for which he arranged all the orchestrations. In 1909 he made use of the saxophone. The story of the first "Blue" song to be written is an interesting one.[5]   It

[5] Ethel Waters, in private life, Mrs. Clyde Mathews (born in Chester, Pennsylvania, on October 31, 1900), made her theatrical début singing "The St. Louis Blues," and became the foremost *blue* singer of the day. As a radio singer (1934-5), she is popular.

places the date of the new name in the domain of Ragtime as that of 1909-10. *Musical America* reported:

"In 1909 the fight for the Memphis mayoralty was three-cornered, the corners being Messrs. Williams, Talbert and E. H. Crump. There were also three leading Negro bands: Eckford's, Bynum's, and Handy's. As a matter of course the services of these three were engaged for the duration to demonstrate to the public the executive ability of their respective employers; through Jim Mulcahy, a ward leader, before whose saloon the Handy forces had often serenaded, his candidate turned out to be Mr. Crump. This was a matter of moment, involving the organization of sub-bands in order to cover all possible territory, and Handy was spurred to creative effort, which he happened to exercise through the aid, not of remembered tunes, but of that blues form which had, without analysis, somehow imbedded itself in his thoughts. His band opened fire at the corner of Main and Madison with a piece (named, of course, 'Mr. Crump'), of such vivacity that it caused dancing in the streets and an outbreak of public whistling. With such a song, and none like it forthcoming from Eckford's or Bynum's, the popular choice (Crump and Handy) was a foregone conclusion; the one became mayor, the other locally famous, the sought-after for all celebrations, the writer of manuscripts of his one lion-child for the belles between numbers at the dances, the magnificently tipped accordingly by their beaux; the proprietor of a whole chain of bands, sending out nearly ninety men to this quarter and that of a single night." Thus did a new form win immediate recognition for itself and its instigator and a political conflict at the same time.

In 1912, when W. C. Handy found it difficult to market his wares, he disposed of his copyright to the Bennett Company that had George Norton write words to fit the mel-

ody. The Pace and Handy compositions, lyrics by Harry
H. Pace and music by William C. Handy, became the
rage and the partners decided to migrate to New York.
Before 1916, the "Memphis Blues" had been followed by
many others in like vein, and they soon became favorites
on phonograph records. White musicians visited the Pace
and Handy publishing house in New York, listened to the
"St. Louis, Beale Street, the Harlem, Golden Brown, and
Loveless Love Blues," and departed to imitate the wailing, moaning, "careless rapture" or bad-man sentiment
of Handy's output. Primarily a lament over the loss of
a lover, the structural form of the exotic music was carried
from the cabarets to the vaudeville stage and to the not
over fastidious radio audience. When Handy was about
to be lost sight of as the originator of this distinctive
specialty in Negro song, he made the announcement that
he had released a new form, an evolution of the "Blues,"
and one which he believed would succeed the earlier style
for which he was responsible. This he called the *Gouge,*
and stated that he would protect its use by a trade-mark.
He declared that his invented music would meet the requirements of a symphony orchestra.

In a recent work, *The Folk-Blues as Music: 46 Blues,
an Anthology* by William C. Handy, with an introduction
by Abbe Niles, the composer describes the structure of his
music. He says:

"The structural peculiarities of the blues tunes may be
the result of those of the stanza, more likely the reverse is
the case but suffice it to say that the blues architecture is
admirably adapted to the impromptu song and versifica-
tion alike. Just as the stanza had three lines instead of
the two or four normal to simple verse, so the voice would
sing (always in two-four time) 12 instead of the normal
8 or 16 bars to the strain, each line being complete in 4

bars of the air. As each line usually expressed a thought which, with a period after it, would still make sense, so the air with the last syllable of each line would return to the keynote or the tonic third or fifth, so that the whole presented a period of 3 semi-independent phrases—(separated, as will be shown, by noticeable intervals) instead of one sustained flight—with successive bizarre effects of internal finality and of final incompleteness.

"Regularly in folk-blues the last syllable of each line

THE "ST. LOUIS BLUES"
BY W. C. HANDY

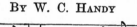

I hate to see   de evening sun go   down,

Hate to   see   de evening sun go   down,...

'Cause   my ba - by   he done lef dis   town.

Excerpt of rhythm from the "St. Louis Blues," by W. C. Handy.

thus coincides, not only with the key-note or another element of the tonic major triad, but with the first beat, third bar, of its corresponding four bars of music, leaving seven quick beats or three slow ones (according to time-signature) before the melody proper resumes its motion."

Handy's *Blues, an Anthology*, received wide notice by reviewers. Edward Burlingame Hill, writing in *The Christian Science Monitor*, spoke of the book as "material for close study of the Blue". . . "a practical and stimulating collection.'' Sigmund Spaeth in *The Bookman,* described the work as one that ''provides a variety of amusement and edification for the reader or performer, with no great demands, in general, upon his musical sense or ability.'' It covers the entire field of this type of folk secular music and includes excerpts from the piano concerto ''Rhapsody in Blue'' of George Gershwin.''[6]

Lieutenant John Niles in his book, *Singing Soldiers,* gives an example of what he calls ''The Deep-Sea Blues.'' It is a most amusing song extemporized by illiterate Negro soldiers who were sent from the Mississippi bottom to Hoboken, where they were put to work on the docks. One day, what they thought was the warehouse floated away. In Bordeaux they sang, ''Everybody in Hoboken town, Everybody an' me—Hopped upon a warehouse that was swinging around, An' went to sea. Oh, all day I'se a lookin' for trees, Lookin' for sand, Lookin' for land— 'Cause I've got dose awful weepin', sleepin',—Got dose awful sailin', wailin'—Got dose awful deep-sea blues.''

There is now in vogue a low type song of sentimentality called the ''torch song'' practised by the Nudists of the musical world, in which the whining voice complains of unrequited love. These songs probably are taken from the ''Blues,'' but they are in no sense a development or an improvement. Gilbert Seldes pithily says in *The New Republic,* ''None of these approaches in words or music the high level of the early blues—especially the work of Mr. Handy . . . Apart from being a good composer, Handy was in part recording and in part giving the essence of a simple emotion in terms which are well nigh universal.''

[6] In 1932, Handy was given a Class ''A'' rating in the American Society of Composers, Authors and Publishers. In 1933 the Vashon High School students sang his chorus, ''Opportunity,'' at the Vashon summer concert by the Saint Louis Symphony Orchestra. The song was highly praised as a fitting one for high school choruses.

Apart from the "Blues" and the singers of the "Blues," white conductors were working apace to make Jazz more acceptable. Paul Whiteman's search for a euphonius name for his Jazz band was anticipated five years earlier by Will Marion Cook when James R. Saville became manager of the Negro band and as a reorganized and incorporated body, arranged engagements on tour for "The American Syncopated Orchestra and Singers." Cook returned from Europe to direct the band that played to audiences of four to seven thousand persons.

Not until the past two or three years has Jazz arisen to the dignity of a subject for serious discussion by white and Negro students of music. The suggestiveness and vulgar humour of the lyrics, the crash and blatancy of the instruments, and the later distortions and physical gyrations by the performers which came simultaneously with the success of Jazz, prohibited discriminating people from considering either Ragtime or Jazz as a worth-while product. It was thought to be a passing fad of the hour, to pass with the free and unconstrained style of the dance. But a group of far-seeing musicians felt that there was an art kernel that could be winnowed from the chaff. Jazz had its defenders in those who saw in it a source of humour. As to its rhythm, E. Jaques-Dalcroze, the well-known exponent of eurhythmics, in writing his book, *Eurhythmics, Art and Education,* says, "It cannot be denied that Negro rhythms have had a salutary influence upon the development of our sense of rhythm. Twenty years ago our children were incapable of singing syncopation in the right time. Freedom of jazz bands, extraordinary vivacity and variety of their cadeneces, their picturesque turns and twists, their wealth of accentuation and fanciful counterpoint; all these have certainly infused new blood into musical rhythm."

The name "Jazz" is not new. Expressions of "Jazz

it up," were known in connection with music of a low type in southern cities. It is as difficult to determine the origin of Jazz as it is to locate the beginnings of a folk song. This new-old word was known in Cuba and Haiti from whence it is said New Orleans derived it. According to J. A. Rogers, a Negro writer, Jasbro Brown, who was a player of "Blues" or Ragtime in Chicago Negro cabarets, amused the patrons who shouted at him—"More, Jasbo, more jas, more."

"Jas" was likely a different "Brown" from the leader of the same name that Joseph K. Gorham, a theatrical man, persuaded to come North to Chicago. With his band of four pieces, clarinet, trombone and drum—and quite likely, a fiddle—the attraction was featured as "Brown's Band from Dixie."

About 1895, a Negro musician nicknamed "Stale Bread" had a small combination of five members which was known as Stale Bread's Spasm Band. They were of the levee groups of New Orleans. The song writer, Geoffrey O'Hara, claims to have heard Jazz played in this city about 1912, two years after Gorham discovered Brown's Band.

Discussing this question, James Reese Europe states that the first known Jazz Band was composed of a baritone horn, a trombone, a cornet and an instrument invented by the Negro. Akin to the clarinet, it was made out of the wood of a chinaberry tree, a well-known yard tree in the Southwest. But this musician makes no claim for having invented the name "Jazz Band." Henry O. Osgood and others name Bert Kelly as having done so in featuring his band in 1915.

About fifteen years ago, the buffoonery and distortion— a delirium tremens—of Jazz performers, was introduced with a growing prominence of the saxophone, drum and banjo, added to many implements of noise—rattles, whistles and pans. By 1924, a good Jazz band had no less

than five saxophones of different range—sopranos, altos
and a baritone. Gilbert Seldes surmised that "the equivo-
cal voice" of the combination, "seemed to have a special
affinity for the moans and wails of barbaric emotion, probably because it was in that connection that it was first
notably heard."

Jazz originated in Africa, and the slaves of centuries
ago brought it into Latin-America countries. In his book
So This is Jazz, Henry O. Osgood gives a definition which
he amusingly says anyone can use without credit or ac-
knowledgment—"Jazz: (orig. Africa) *v.* to enliven, to
pep up; *adj.* jazzy, applied to manners, morals and especially music—or pepped up most anything else."

Captain Jerome E. Hart who traveled in Africa over
nine years ago, claims that he heard Jazz at Axim, the
Gold Coast of Africa, played by a band of Kroo boys and
Ashanti and other natives. Their band consisted of a European cornet and trombone, banjo, big and little drums
and bells, but no saxophone. He describes their syncopation as "maddening."[7] It would seem quite likely that
this African band was playing American Jazz with added
African touches.

"Jazz" has been defined as a verb rather than a noun.
Writing in *The Forum* in the late summer of 1928, Sigmund Spaeth makes the deduction that—"Jazz is not a
form of music. It is a treatment applied to music, and,
incidentally, to all the other arts, and to modern life in
general. The Jazz treatment, in brief, is a distortion of
the conventional, a revolt against tradition, a deliberate
twisting of established formulas. As such, it is thoroughly
characteristic of the civilization of today. Every rebel in
art has "jazzed" the formulas of his predecessors. In
fact, "jazz" is a verb, rather than noun . . . . If jazz

[7] *Musical America,* August 1925.

effects are recognized as mere distortions of the conventional, it is easy to see that there is no such thing as jazz per se, but that all music may be subjected to a jazz treatment."

That Jazz can be made a musical performance has been proved by such orchestral and band conductors as Will Marion Cook and the late James Reese Europe together with a number of present day white orchestral leaders. The performances of the leading Negro band musicians have carried a definite and unmistakable message. But just as the white minstrels blackened their faces and made use of the Negro idiom, so have white orchestral players today usurped the Negro in his Jazz entertainment. However, there remains this difference—they are not caricaturing the medium, they are tremendously in earnest. Why did the Negro permit this to happen? The Negro is not altogether guiltless of failure to exploit his gifts, as accused by Gilbert Seldes, but it must be noted that he faced many difficulties and met with numerous obstacles. With the ready acceptance of white performers by influential managers, while heretofore leading theaters held closed doors to Negro attractions, it was far easier for the white Jazz exponents to place their new wares. Meanwhile, a number of white entertainers, wide-awake, frequented the Negro section (Harlem) of New York, and listened to the Negro musician improvising ragged and jazzed tunes in rhythm with the new dances; and, taking up this special type of music, they have popularized the form in leading hotel orchestras and on the stage.

Irving Berlin and other white theatrical stars presented dance steps of the Negro in keeping with the "hot" and "sour" tones of the orchestra and aided in the acceptance of the result as typical popular music of America. Ted Lewis, who heard Cricket Smith, a Negro barber who had an orchestra of banjo, guitar and fiddle, play improvised

WILL MARION COOK

Jazzy music, imitated the same rhythms for his present band of nine members. By this time, written instrumentation had been established, thus taking place of parts extemporized ad libitum by performers who knew little or nothing of musical notation.

On February 12, 1924, Paul Whiteman, a white jazz band conductor from California, in an attempt to place his music side-by-side with that of the higher standard, gave a concert in Aeolian Hall, New York. His New York band had already become well-known, and it now marked one more epoch in the growth of Jazz. The most important number on the program was "A Rhapsody in Blue," the piano part played by the composer, George Gershwin, whom Whiteman had commissioned to write a "Jazz symphony" for this concert. Other pieces, in the main, were "adaptations," "arrangements," and borrowed melodies, thus proving the paucity of Jazz as an original contribution. Even the heralded "Rhapsody in Blue" (which Gershwin wrote within one month's time), was orchestrated by a trained musician, Ferde Grofé. Elgar's well-known "Pomp and Circumstance," was added to the program, probably for a connecting link.

Whiteman's declaration concerning his undertaking, was amusing to serious thinkers. His object was "that with the hope that eventually *our* music will become a stepping stone which will be helpful in giving the coming generation a much deeper appreciation of better music." However, the band conductor did succeed in increasing the interest in Jazz, and his subsequent concerts on tour have been widely attended. Of the Lincoln's Day concert, W. J. Henderson of the New York *Herald* said, "He obtained admirable results in proving the euphony of the jazz orchestra." Whiteman, now the most talked of white Jazz conductor, designated his band a Modern American Orchestra; and while he advertised his concerts as a program of "True Form of Jazz," he attempted to subserve the original cognomen by calling his offerings the "Melodious Music of Today." Whiteman's première concert caused Olin Downes, music critic of the New York *Times*, in comparing the band's playing with that of the Negro (who was now becoming overshadowed), to say, "They play with an abandon equalled only by that race of born musicians—the American Negro, who has surely contributed fundamentally to this art which can neither be frowned nor sneered away."

Impetus was given the Whiteman experiment by a conference on Jazz arranged by the League of Composers and conducted by Vincent Lopez with his band from the Hotel Pennsylvania, New York, two days before the conspicuous Jazz concert was given. Lopez, of Portugese and Spanish blood, who assembled his band in 1917, is at present conducting one of the finest Jazz bands of the day. He, and others less prominent in 1924, were seeking new means of refining the new dance medium. Illiterate music-makers were attempting to compose Jazz concert pieces without any idea of the fundamental principles of composition and were making unnecessary efforts to make a bridge between the unique rhythmic dance music and true art music. The vulgarity of the medium persistently proclaimed itself in spite of the make-up and costuming it received at the hands of "arrangers."

During Music Week, on May 9, 1924, an echo was heard in Boston. A "Jazz Symposium" was held by Professor Hill, of Harvard College, Professor Marshall of Boston University, Mr. Gideon, Mr. Del Castillo and the Leo Reisman Orchestra. The month before, Mrs. Charles S. Guggenheim, chairman of the Philharmonic Orchestra of New York, announced that a chair of American Music to be devoted to the study and development of Jazz music was likely to be established at the American Academy in Rome. "Today all over Europe," she said, "the demand is great for American or jazz music. It is having a distinct bearing on the musical composers of the world. I firmly subscribe to the theory that this American School of Music should be developed and that in the not remote future a great American composer will be produced."

"Jazz" succeeded in securing a hearing in an artistic way. On the concert stage in 1924, Miss Eva Gauthier, a pioneer of the unusual, gave a group of popular songs which included "Alexander's Rag-Time Band," on her serious programs. This was not, however, to the pleasure of universal taste and liking and proved to be a lone venture. John Alden Carpenter's "Krazy Kat," a Jazz pantomime, based on newspaper cartoons of George Herriman, was produced in Chicago in 1923. This, however, was the work of a distinguished composer, and not to be compared to the undertakings of the talented Gershwin, whose Piano Concerto in F (with its "Charleston" rhythm) was first played on December 3, 1925, at a concert of the New York Symphony Orchestra conducted by Walter Damrosch. That same year, a concert was given by the International Composers, at which Eugene Goosens, conductor of the orchestra, essayed a Jazz number. At last Jazz had its première at the Metropolitan Opera House when Carpenter's "Skyscraper's Ballet" was given there on February 19, 1926. Truly Jazz was no longer in the under-world or in the music-hall stage.

European composers have shown this predicted inclination. Not only the famous Stravinsky, but a number of composers in France,—Arthur Honegger, Darius Milhaud and Jean Wiener, the first white composer to direct a Jazz concert in Europe, made use of the medium. Jean Cocteau, himself, played in a jazz band. Vuillermoz in *Musiques d'Aujourd'hui*[8] gives an interesting point when

[8] Freely translated by C.M.S.C., Oct. 13, 1923. Published in Paris.

he says, "It was not culpable sadism, congenital stupidity, or the desire to mystify, that inspired Stravinsky to write a 'Ragtime,' and certain other young composers to study the explosive reactions of Jazz. Nor do the commonplace railleries concerning the Negro art explain it entirely. The mysterious possibilities which this infernal machine displays instinctively attract the investigators.—Anything that tends to free musical discourse from its formulary slavery, its symmetry or its geometric plans, makes the modern composers thrill with expectancy—Musical physique is indeed starting a new chapter."

As to its barbaric seduction, Vuillermoz declared that— "Music has become bored by the delicate, cultural effects obtained from disunited orchestration, masterly harmony and scientific counterpoint. After centuries of refinement, therefore, it reverts to the primitive seduction of rhythmic clashing, cleverly managed. Jazz is not a game of chance. Its musical disorder is only apparent. Even its origin is security for this truth. The Negro race possesses a musical sense of rare subtlety and a rhythmic instinct of which we may rightfully be envious."

Serge Koussevitzky, the Russian musician, who, coming to accept the position of director of the Boston Symphony Orchestra, arrived in the United States during the year of the Jazz controversy, 1924, declared that it was very interesting from a technical point of view. He has proved the catholicity of his taste, and has been liberal in giving the modern composers a hearing on his symphony programs. The present situation forecasts the use of the new technical material, that which is regarded by the moderns as typical Negro music, by all Americans alike.

The trained Negro American composer, distinct from those who follow the line of Jazz, recognize that music must be more than a dexterous feat, and are now attempting to develop this characteristic American expression (which is Negro) in works of emotional sincerity which will have aesthetic value. With further liberation from objectionable features, Jazz bids fair in its present growth, to influence the music of the world. Its true worth will be determined by posterity; meanwhile the words of Paderewski, the great pianist and statesman-patriot of Poland, should be remembered:—"There is no corruption of manners in a Republic so great as that which follows a gradual decline from a prudent and modest music."

Of the present-day exponents of Jazz a few words should be added. There are a number of excellent Negro band leaders of syncopated music. In 1918, George Lattimore of New York took a troupe of 50 Negro musicians, known as "The New York and Southern Syncopated Orcrestras," to play in Europe. The director was Will Marion Cook. Their success included a command performance in Buckingham Palace. Lattimore became known as an impresario, and was successful in discovering and placing unusual, talented entertainers. Living in London, he has managed foreign acts and the stars thereof. When Earl Carroll assembled his talent for the musical extravaganza, "Vanities of 1932," he relied upon Lattimore to select his stage acts of foreign note.

Others of this type, according to a contract made in 1932, came as a group of well-known Negro bands under the organizers Irving Mills and Thomas Rockwell who assumed complete management. The organization, the largest of the kind in the country, included the band leaders Cab Calloway, Don Redmon, Baron Lee, and Duke Ellington (Edward Kennedy Ellington).

Duke Ellington is a composer of light music as well as the foremost conductor of Negro Jazz bands today. He has originated jazz rhythms, and in 1931, was awarded first place above white contestants in a contest for the most popular dance orchestral leader, arranged by the

Orchestra World and decided by popular ballot. His dance hits include "Mood Indigo," "Sophisticated Lady," and "Black and Tan Fantasy." His piece, "Creole Rhapsody," was awarded the annual prize offered by the New York schools of music for the best musical composition of the year 1933, which evidently meant works of a certain class. The prize piece, "A portrayal of Negro life," was featured by a concert of the schools on March 5, and played by Paul Whiteman's band. In the early summer of 1933, Ellington carried his band to Europe, and made a sensational London success. In August the manager of the Metropolitan Theatre, Boston, engaged the band by cable, for a gala Ellington week to begin August 18, as their first appearance upon their return to the United States.

The large number of Negro entertainers in light and popular music, now too many to include in a work interested primarily in music as an art, are men and women of diverse gifts and of decided talent. They are successful on both the vaudeville stage and the radio network. The Byron Brothers were for some years a popular group that received engagements from the leading vaudeville houses. Richard Byron invented in 1894 a double-necked guitar which was called the "Byrondolin."

Among the quartettes that are filling long engagements to broadcast, are the Southernaires who have been with the National Broadcasting Company for more than three years. The personnel of the Southernaires includes Homer Smith of Florence, Alabama, educated at Wilberforce University in Ohio, where he studied voice; Lowell Peters, second tenor, of Cleveland, Tennessee, educated at Knoxville College, whence he travelled with the college quartette throughout Europe; Jay Toney, baritone, of Kentucky, who was educated at Tennessee State Normal School, and sang in a quartette in Europe after fighting

MELVILLE CHARLTON

JAMES REESE EUROPE

W. L. DAWSON

BASILE BARRES

in the World War; and, lastly, William Edmondson of Spokane, Washington, who was educated at Spokane College, and for some time sang bass in a concert company. This group of young men have sung together since 1929. They make many of their own arrangements for their song offerings.

One of the most interesting programs broadcast during 1933, quite apart from the ordinary radio drivel, is the dramatic series based on Roark Bradford's Negro stories of John Henry, the hero of a Negro folk ballad. The charm of the dramatic work which was heard weekly over CBS (although spurious in part) is in the use of songs, particularly the work songs. These with the play songs and religious melodies were adapted by Juan Hernandez, a talented Negro actor-singer who takes the part of John Henry. The actor has a fine speaking voice of deep resonance. A leading role is taken by the exceptionally fine actress of color, Rose McClendon. For the première of this series of Negro folk-drama with music, the patron's committee included as members the two distinguished white musicians, Louis Gruenberg and Ernest Hutcheson.[9] Serious composers as well as those of immature talent are rapidly adding to a long list of those who are producing pieces in which they are experimenting in jazz rhythms and color. Thoughtful musicians are as one of the opinion

[9] The subject of John Henry was used some years ago by Handy who employed the old ballad for his blue song of like name. "John Henry," according to his version, was king of the riverters and drillers of the South. Proud of his exceptional strength, John Henry is heartbroken when he learns that a pneumatic riveter is to be installed. In a vain attempt to break the record time of the machine, his overstrained muscles gave way. His blows falling in rhythm to the melody which he sang, had been his swan song.

Handy, now in his maturer musicianship, has written a piece for orchestra called "The Evolution of the Blues," which has been orchestrated by Joseph Nussbaum.

that Gershwin is not the one who is to write the great American symphony, nor do they agree that a work in any one of the larger forms shall come out of the material which he exploits. There are at present cultivated Negro composers of whom much may be expected in the way of producing what will be the future American music. "Negro Symphony No. 1," by the Negro composer, William L. Dawson, was played during the second week in November, 1934, under the baton of Leopold Stokowski, at a concert by the Philadelphia Orchestra. It has caused wide, favorable comment. This is a step in that direction.

It is significant to note that in recent concerts of compositions by young American composers of 1935, that few if any are experimenting in Jazz as a means of expressing their feelings, moods or ideas. As Guido Pannain states in *Modern Composers*,—"Jazz is a means of expression but not a means of self-expression . . . it is a symptom of consciousness but not of reality." Ernest Newman, writing in the *Sunday Times*, London, says that the day of Jazz is over, "even with the crowd. Non-musical observers are now pointing out that America, with its Jazz, is now a back number as regards amusement-music. . . . Not Mr. Gershwin or any of that breed, but old Johann Strauss is what the world is running round after now in search of musical light-heartedness."

Let us hope that it is true that the makers of entertaining music have learned a lesson, and that they have come to realize that no seeker after Beauty can find inspiration in the common combination of unlovely tones and suggestive lyrics. Music should sound, not screech; Music should cry, not howl; Music should weep, not bawl; Music should implore, not whine.

CHAPTER VIII

MUSICAL COMEDY

MUSICAL COMEDIES AND REVUES—1820, 1898—NEGRO COM-
EDY STARS—WILL MARION COOK AND "THE ORIGIN OF THE
CAKE-WALK."—J. ROSAMOND JOHNSON—MUSICAL COMEDY
ON BROADWAY—RECENT NEGRO MUSIC-PLAYS—THEATRICAL
PLAYS WITH MUSIC.

From a judicious use of syncopation, Ragtime, quickly
followed by Jazz and the Blues, gave unrestrained zest
to the stage-dances. Negroes had been engaged in the
theatre, in the comedy type of entertainment, as early as
1820, when the "African Players" performed in New
York. In 1873, Lyles and Lyles, a musical comedy team
played "Free and Easy," a variety show. Twenty years
later there were many companies on the road. On August
4, 1890, Sam T. Jack's "Creoles" opened at Haverhill,
Massachusetts, with the novelty of Negro women on the
professional stage. John V. W. Isham followed in 1895 by
presenting the "Octoroons" abroad, in a comedy called
"Oriental America." About 1896, S. H. Dudley's "Smart
Set," including Walter Smart, who wrote his own songs as
well as the lyrics for his wife, Marion, one of the beauties
of the play, became known far and wide for the chorus
of extremely pretty colored girls.[1]

Ernest Hogan was one of the best known comedians who sang and acted. His real name was William
Fields. He assumed the stage name of Ernest Hogan in

[1] Before 1860 a concert troupe known as "The Extraordinary 7
Slaves," from Alabama, were billed in Massachusetts, "under guidance of Northern friends and guarantees, to purchase their freedom."

taking that of his patent medicine vending employer who
gave the young man his first histrionic opportunity in
having him do "stunts" of singing and dancing from his
wagon to attract buyers. He wrote many songs, one of
which, "All Coons look alike to Me," he is said to have
regretted writing. This song, he explained to a friend,
however, was suggested by his being in a place which was
raided because of the misdemeanor committed by one of
the party. In explaining to the police that he was not the
offender, the undiscriminating guardian of the peace replied, "All Coons Look Alike to Me." In all but similar
fashion was suggested to Kip Taylor "Please, Mr. Johnson, Turn Me Loose; I Got No Money But a Good Excuse." The composer, living in an Indiana town, frequently got into mischief with fellows playing on the
sand lots. Often when arrested they appealed to the
policeman in the language of this song.

In 1895, Hogan wrote the dance-song, "Pas Ma La,"
popularized in "By the Sad Sea Waves," a white comedy. Hogan became very prominent about 1899 and
traveled extensively. In 1902 he was with Gus Hill,
widely known as a producer until his death. From 1905
to 1907, Hogan starred in "Rufus Rastus," for which he
and Joe Jordan wrote the music to his own book. The
lyrics were by Lester A. Walton and Frank Williams.
Walton and Creamer wrote the lyrics for the "Oyster
Man," in which Hogan starred in 1907-08. The music
was by Will H. Vodery to the book by Miller and Lyles.

These productions tended to develop toward higher
ground. In 1898, the first Negro musical comedy worked
out by a Negro for Negro talent, was written and produced
by Robert Cole[2] and William Johnson. This was called

[2] Cole was born in Athens, Georgia, July 1, 1868, and died in
New York City on August 2, 1911. He was a graduate of Atlanta
University.

ROBERT COLE AND ROSAMOND JOHNSON

"A Trip to Coontown." Cole also wrote "A Shoo Fly Regiment." Among his popular songs we find "Louisiana Lize," "I must Have Been A Dreaming," "No One Can Fill Her Place," "Katydid," "The Maiden With Dreamy Eyes," and "The Cricket And The Frog." For a long time Cole amused a wide public with his "Tramp" act. All of these companies featured dance novelties.

In 1899 a new stage was reached when "Sons of Ham" was produced at the Grand Opera House, New York City, by Williams and Walker. The partnership between Bert (Egbert Austin) Williams and George Walker lasted until 1909, the time of the latter's death. The two comedians starred in "Abyssinia," from 1906 to 1907, and in "Bandanna Land" from 1907 to 1909—two widely heralded productions, the lyrics of which were written by Alex C. Rogers, the collaborator with Jesse A. Shipp in the writing of the book. The music was by Will Marion Cook, who also composed the music for "In Dahomey" in which Williams and Walker appeared from 1902 to 1905. The lyrics were by Paul Laurence Dunbar. On September 12, 1902, the piece was produced at the Globe Theatre, Boston, after which Cook took the aggregation of performers abroad. They gave one hundred and fifty performances at the Shaftesbury Theatre in 1903, with Williams as "Shylock Homestead," and Walker as "Rareback Pinkerton." The Boston *Herald* mentioned Bert Williams as having never appeared to better advantage . . . and that "His song 'I May Be Crazy But I Ain't No Fool' was the humorous pièce de resistance."

The best liked songs in this comedy were "On Emancipation Day" and "Happy Jim," sung by J. Leubrie Hill, together with "That's How The Cake-walk's Done." The play was seen again in Boston in March, 1905. The Boston *Evening Transcript* said, in comment thereupon, "Musical comedies with real music are rarities, but this is one;'' and in reference to Cook the reviewer added, ''The composer has succeeded in lifting Negro music above the plane of the so-called 'Coon Song' without destroying the characteristics of the melodies, and he has provided a score which is likewise unusually diversified. James Vaughn, who has written some of the added music, conducted the orchestra, and his piano accompaniments were one of the features of the performance.''

Before this time, Williams and Walker had been the stars in ''Two Real Coons,'' ''The Gold Bug'' and ''Senegambia Carnival.'' After Walker's death Williams, who had performed for some time alone, made a contract in 1911 to appear in the Ziegfeld Follies for ten years. Williams, who was born in Nassau, British West Indies, November 12, 1874, died in New York in 1922. He was a handsome man whose visage was masked by Negro make-up in order to fill character roles. He was last seen in ''Under the Bamboo Tree,'' a rewritten play of 1918-19. The New York *Evening Post* said of him, ''His admirable art was not for the orgiastic jazz, but for that plaintive humor of the 'blues' that is now coming to the front.'' Williams compellingly followed the path of Negro dance and comic song, but as an artist he was above his medium.

During these years, too, other artists were active. ''Put and Take,'' the lyrics and music by Spencer Williams, Perry Bradford and Tim Brymn, book by Irvin C. Miller, appeared on the boards in 1921-22, a year before ''This and That,'' with lyrics and book by Alex. C. Rogers, the music by C. Luckeyth Roberts. In 1912 Rogers collaborated with Henry S. Creamer in writing the lyrics and book of ''The Traitor,'' music by Will Marion Cook, in which he and Creamer appeared as stars.

The latter, with J. Turner Layton, wrote the lyrics and music of ''Strut Miss Lizzie,'' book by Creamer, in 1922. Mr. Layton was born in Washington, D. C., the son of

John T. Layton who was director of Music in the Washington Public Schools and the first conductor of the Samuel Coleridge-Taylor Society. The father was a bass singer, a pupil of Esputa. He died in 1915. The son received his academic education at Howard University and his musical training from his father who followed the classic school. The son has lately written songs of more than ephemeral quality. "The Little Gray Road of Love," "Thank God the Drums are Silent," and other ballads. Layton's co-worker, Henry S. Creamer, a product of New York schools, was born in Richmond, Virginia, June 21, 1879, the son of the Rev. H. Creamer. Young Creamer was one of the founders of the Clef Club, one of the first organizations to win notice in syncopated orchestral music. These two musicians now spend most of their time abroad where they have met with much success as exponents of Jazz. As song writers they have composed music for Nora Bayes, Al Jolson, Eddie Cantor, Eva Tanguay, Bert Williams and Mr. and Mrs. Coburn, who played at the Harris Theatre, in New York.

Miller and Lyles starred in "Darkeydom" in 1914-15; the lyrics were by Lester A. Walton and the book by Henry Troy, with music by Will Marion Cook. In 1927-28 they appeared in "Rang Tang," the music of which was written by Ford Dabney to lyrics by Joe Trent. The book was by Kaj Gynt. "Keep Shufflin'," a Miller and Lyles production of 1929, succeeded in reaching Broadway. In the meantime, 1924-25, they starred in their own vehicle, "Runnin' Wild," for which Jimmie Johnson wrote the music, and R. C. McPherson the lyrics.[2a]

James J. Vaughn, son of Wiley Vaughn, also deserves notice here. He was born in Boston and educated at the Rindge Technical School in Cambridge, where he became

[2a] The popular hit, "Good Morning Carrie," was one of the many by R. C. McPherson and Jim Brymn.

a noted football star. Bert Williams and George Walker, visiting Boston, heard the young man play the piano at a club which catered to a theatrical patronage, and noted his unusual gifts as a pianist. His first engagement was with Graham's Specialty Company, that featured the cake-walk in performances of Goodman's Alabama Troubadours. While in need of funds, he met Alex. Rogers in Philadelphia, and together the two men wrote the "Sultan of Zulu," which was bought by George Walker. Vaughan then became the musical director for Williams and Walker with whom he remained for eight years. He made a reputation as a Jazz pianist and wrote many songs for their productions. "Men and the Minstrel Bard," "It's Hard to Find a King like Me," "When the Moon Shines," and "When Susie Comes," became general favorites. In 1902, the musician went to Europe with the "In Dahomey" company.

For three seasons Vaughn was musical director of shows produced by J. Lubrie Hill, and opened Dudley's first picture house in Washington. He toured with "Black Patti" and her company, and collaborated with "Tutt" of the Tutt Whitney team. After a period of organizing orchestras in Albany, New York, in 1929 he joined the "Darktown Frolics" as director. Vaughn, now retired, makes his home in Boston. Tutt Whitney and J. A. Shipp were of "The Green Pastures" cast.[3] Lubrie Hill starred in "My Friend from Dixie," for which he wrote lyrics and book, and in "Here and There," by Alex. C. Rogers, from 1913 to 1916.

"The Policy Players," book by Jesse A. Shipp with music by Will Marion Cook, was a comedy in which Williams and Walker appeared in 1900. Williams starred in

[3] Jesse A. Shipp, b. 1859, died June, 1934. He took the part of Abraham in "The Green Pastures." Tutt Whitney died Feb. 10, 1934.

"Mr. Lode of Koal," lyrics by Alex C. Rogers, with music written by Rosamond Johnson in 1909-10. "Dr. Beans from Boston," lyrics by Henry. S. Creamer, book by S. H. Dudley and Henry Troy, with music by Will H. Vodery,[4] appeared in 1911-1912 with S. H. Dudley as the star. "Dixie to Broadway," the music by Mr. Vodery (practically the same play as "Dover to Dixie"), presented at the Broadhurst Theatre, New York City, on October 19, 1924, was the first real revue by Negroes. Florence Mills was the star during 1924-25. For 23 years Vodery arranged music for the Ziegfeld productions and also for those of the English producer, Charles Cochran.

Florence Mills, a singing comedienne and dancer, was an exponent of Negro dances and became the "rage" for her cake-walking and buck-dancing. She was born in Washington, D. C., January 25, 1895, and died November 1, 1927, in New York City. From vaudeville appearances with her two sisters, the slender, talented dancer soon earned a wide reputation in "Shuffle Along," a musical comedy with F. E. Miller and Aubrey Lyles as the stars, the lyrics and music by Noble Sissle and Eubie Blake. This musical melange had a long run, following the opening on May 23, 1921, in 63rd Street Music Hall, New York.[5] "Shuffle Along," a phenomenal success, was followed by "Liza," lyrics and music by Maceo Pinkard, the book by Irvin C. Miller, in 1922-23; but tunes from the former play such as "I'm Just Wild About Harry," "Love Will Find A Way," "Shuffle Along," and "In Honeysuckle Time," continued to be whistled and sung. For three seasons, 1921 to 1923, Sissle and Blake were the

[4] In 1929, Will Vodery, for a number of years arranger of music for Ziegfeld's Follies, was given a three year contract with the Fox Film Company, Hollywood.

[5] Lyles, who was born in Jackson, Mississippi, lived in Indianapolis, Indiana, and followed a musical profession in Chicago, died in New York City on August 4, 1932, at the age of 49.

foremost stars in Negro comedy. Blake pleased a wide public as a skillful Jazz pianist, and his keyboard manipulations were always a part of the show. Eubie Blake and Noble Sissle wrote their own book and music for their musical comedy, "Chocolate Dandies," in which they appeared in 1924-25.

It was in 1925 that musical plays with white casts featured Negro attractions. Miller and Lyles were in "George White's Scandals," and next appeared (in 1929) with Cora Green, a singer of "Blues," in Vincent Youman's "Great Day." In 1927, ten Negroes appeared in "Sidewalks of New York" while twenty were in the play "Americana." When Arthur Hammerstein opened his memorial theatre on Broadway, he presented fifty colored singing actors in the cast.

Sissle later traveled with his own orchestra, and Blake, also temporarily out of musical comedy, had an independent orchestra. His band in "Harlem is Heaven," produced by the Lincoln Pictures Corporation, New York, together with the dancing of "Bojangles" Robinson (1932) were the leading features of a hodge-podge attraction.

It was through the Sissle and Blake shows that the comedienne, Josephine Baker, best exhibited her talent as a dancer. She was seen in "Chocolate Dandies" before becoming a sensation in the music halls of Paris. Negro revues served to introduce singers of the "Blues." Ethel Waters became a Broadway star and since singing in "Africana," a revue conceived by Earl Dancer, lyrics and music by Donald Hayward, she is being heard as a popular radio singer of Negro song.

Negro actors of this period owe much to S. H. Dudley, a man of long stage experience, who rose from a small part as assistant to a patent medicine street hawker in Texas to the status of one of the greatest comedians of all time. He entertained in music halls, organized groups of musicians, wrote songs and "hits" for many vaudeville performers, and managed his own companies. As already stated above, he appeared in 1904, in the new "Smart Set," and became popular in vaudeville billed as "Dudley and His Mule." Some of his biggest hits were the familiar invitation, "Come After Breakfast, Bring Your Lunch, and Leave Before Dinner Time," "'Deed I Ain't See'd No Messenger Boy," and "Good Morning, Carrie." Dudley retired from the stage to enter business. He organized the Colored Actors' Union, and devoted his time to the management of a circuit of theatres with headquarters in Washington, D. C.

Foremost among the colored composers of musical comedy is Will Marion Cook, an erratic genius, a man of more than ordinary talent. He was born of educated parents in Detroit, Michigan. While a boy soprano, he began the study of the violin. For three years he attended Oberlin College, after which he went to Berlin where he became the pupil of Joachim, the violinist. Ill health forced him to return home, about the time "Ragtime" was spreading northward. According to Cook, this was about 1898. A number of Negro companies had been organized about this time, and at the suggestion of George Walker, Cook wrote some of the choruses. Lyrics by Paul Laurence Dunbar were set to melodies founded upon plantation hymns, and finally Cook's operetta, "Clorinda," or "The Origin of the Cake-walk" was produced at the Casino Roof Garden in New York, and created a sensation. The song "On Emancipation Day" became a pattern for later white composers, while the swaying rhythms of "That's How the Cake-walk's Done," greatly influenced the stage dances that followed. In 1919-1920 Cook toured America and Europe with his "American Syncopated Orchestra" which was the finest aggregation of musicians ever before heard in what is termed distinctly Negro music.

Cook later conducted the Clef Orchestra, a like organization of skilled Negro performers. He has held to his avowed intention to work only in the Negro idiom, but while doing so, he has produced music of undoubted worth. Cook, who was a pupil of Anton Dvorák, has received universal praise for his orchestrations. A London paper of May 16, 1903, stated, "The work of Mr. Cook, the composer, stands out prominently . . . in several of the numbers one could not listen to more excellent orchestration. He conducted with remarkable vigor and enthusiasm, and . . . his music displays true dramatic perception."

As an orchestral leader, Mr. Cook is musically well-equipped, and able to discern the excellent points in music of a syncopated type. He developed the primitive Jazz and selected trained musicians for interpreters. Of four characteristic songs written by the composer a few years ago, "Exhortation," a Negro Sermon, the "Rain Song," "Swing Along," and "Wid de Moon, Moon, Moon," Kurt Schindler said:

"Mr. Cook's work at its best means no less than finding the proper musical correlative to the Negro idiom, and thus adding a new territory to musical geography.

"Besides his larger works, Mr. Cook has been writing a great many songs in a more popular vein, but it is the development of his serious work along the lines of the 'Rain Song' and the 'Exhortation' which especially interests us, since here he will not only perform a lasting service to his race, but intrinsically enrich the entire musical world."

Mr. Cook has just completed a Negro music-drama "St. Louis 'ooman," which is based on life on the Mississippi River in the gay 90's. The lyrics have been written by his son who wrote "Stop the Sun, Stop the Moon."

By 1901, the group of Negro companies which were featuring the sentimental and comical ballad of the day, had reached their ascendancy. The press commented upon the passing of the "buck and wing" dancing that was to be outlived by the cake-walk, and a number of trained musicians came forward in the dual capacity of orchestral leader and musical-comedy promoter. They were largely responsible for the growth of Ragtime in the large cities, and their names became known wherever Ragtime succeeded in securing a foothold. Under Cook's baton, the cake walk reached its highest artistic expression.

J. Rosamond Johnson, who was born in Jacksonville, Florida, 1873, the son of a Baptist minister, worked simultaneously with Mr. Cook. Both he and his brother, James Weldon Johnson, received the advantage of an academic training. But while James Weldon pursued his studies through a collegiate course and developed as a man of public affairs and an author of recognized ability, Rosamond came to Boston where he entered the New England Conservatory of Music and received a thorough musical education.

Rosamond Johnson's career is an unusual one. From an exponent of distinct Negro music, as typified in Ragtime, both as a vaudeville performer and as a composer-producer, he rapidly rose from partnership with "Bob" Cole, comedian (a graduate of Atlanta University), to a successful directorship of musical comedies, thence to a professorship, but to return again to the vaudeville stage.

An early work, "The Red Moon," written and staged by Cole and Johnson, and performed by an aggregation of young Negro men and women, was one of the cleanest and brightest musical comedies of the day and from a musical standpoint, marked a decided advance in this sphere. "Wrap Me In Your Little Red Shawl," one of the "hits" of the operetta, was long remembered after the ill-starred "Red Moon" had passed from the stage. The presentation was a financial failure, but its influence lived.

At this time Johnson was collaborating with his brother, James Weldon, whose later poetry reached a high standard. At the same time, Cole and Johnson were writing "extravaganzas" for Klaw and Erlanger, white New York producers, and popular airs for Marie Cahill and other white musical comedy stars. "Under the Bamboo Tree," "The Congo Love Song," "Nobody's Looking but the Owl and the Moon," and "My Castle on the Nile" won national popularity.

After Cole's death, Johnson was engaged (in 1912) in vaudeville work with Charles Hart. "Lovely Daughter of Allah," a setting of one of his brother's lyrics was equally popular with "Excuse Me, Mister Moon," a song written for Alice Lloyd in the musical play "Little Miss Fix-It." In 1913, Johnson went abroad and while in London, directed musical comedy at Hammerstein's Opera House, where he gained new honors. He appeared in a new musical comedy act at the London Pavillion, then returned to this country in the Spring of 1914. His first appearance after his return was máde at the New Standard Theatre in Philadelphia.

Shortly after this Johnson accepted a position as director of music at the newly established Music School Settlement in New York. The musician remained at this institution for a few years, giving lessons and composing for voice, chorus and orchestra. It was at this period, that his best pieces were written. About 1917, when the author visited the New York Music School Settlement for colored pupils, Johnson whimsically said, "When I was single, I was in vaudeville, earning a lucrative salary; now that I am married, I am giving music lessons in a Music School Settlement!" It may be that the economic pressure and the untoward conditions resultant from the war persuaded him to return to the vaudeville stage. This he soon did and for two years he was engaged on the Orpheum and Keith Circuits with the "Rosamond Johnson Quintet."

Johnson rendered another service in 1925 when the Viking Press published his brother's excellent collection called *The Book of American Negro Spirituals*, for which he made the musical arrangements. Additional numbers were by Lawrence Brown. The introduction by James Weldon Johnson is a valuable contribution to the history of the Negro in music. After this, the musician proved most successful in a new field, and for two or three years thereafter the "Taylor and Johnson" programs of Negro Spirituals, presented by white concert management, met with much favor. The songs were sung in duet form in which Gordon Taylor joined his tenor voice with that of the basso cantante of Johnson's. The musician is now a choral conductor in New York City.

This prolific writer has composed pieces for solo voice, chorus, and orchestra. "Lift Every Voice and Sing," a national patriotic hymn sung by Negroes, is not only a melodically beautiful production but tremendous in its racial and national appeal. It is widely used by Negro organizations everywhere. Apart from this composer's lighter music in the Negro vein, are found serious songs, the words of which are by his brother.[6]

A list of his compositions include: "Walk Together, Children," which is a plantation melody transcribed as a majestic marching song for full chorus and orchestra. It was written for the Negro Pageant held in Washington, D. C., in 1915. Of this setting of a Negro camp-meeting

[6] The libretto of Enrique Granados' opera, *Goyescas*, which was written by Fernando Periquet, was translated from the Spanish by James Weldon Johnson in order that it might be presented in English at the Metropolitan Opera House in New York. The opera was given in 1916, under the direction of Gatti-Casazza. James Weldon Johnson, the translator is at present, Spence Professor of Creative Literature at Fisk University.

hymn, the Boston *Evening Transcript* of Feb. 17, 1917, said:

"The few touches which he has added in the development are those of the trained musician, with an accurate instinct for musical organization. Like all great music, whether of individual or folk-origin, it has the property of suppressing the conscious judgment and liberating the sensuous reactions into full play. Many observers have noted that the most promising signs in American drama are to be found in the popular 'topical' plays of George Cohan and a few of his fellows. The same hypothesis seems reasonable as applied to music. . . . Negro Ragtime appears to have the greatest vitality of any American musical strain and seems most likely to supply the materials for American orchestral works of incontestable originality."

For the past ten years, musical comedies with all Negro casts have reached Broadway, which is the height of ambition of all theatrical folk. After Lew Leslie's "Blackbirds" had the run of one year in New York—an unsurpassed record for this particular type of show—the manager organized a second company with Harriet Calloway as the star. Florence Mills appeared in the 1926-27 production for which the words and music were written by George W. Meyer. Aida Ward was the star of the "Blackbirds of 1928," in which the tap-dancing of Bill Robinson won applause.

Of Robinson's foot tapping Mary Austin wrote in *The Nation*, "The postures of his little dark body and the motions of his slender cane so puncture this rhythmic patter as to restore, for his audience, the primal freshness of their own lost rhythmic power." When a boy Robinson (known as "Bojangles" Robinson) danced in the streets of Washington for any amount the amused passerby cared to throw at his feet. He is now the highest paid tap-dancer in the world. When seen in "Blackbirds" in 1926, he divided the applause with the song hit of the show—"I Can't Give You Anything But Love."

Recent plays of a serious nature, dramas of Negro folk life, owe much of their success to the incidental music employed. Naturally they are in an entirely different genre from the revue, and appeal to thoughtful audiences. *Porgy* (dramatized by Dubose Heyward, a white writer), a Theatre Guild production of 1927, played to crowded houses. South Carolina musical street-cries and Negro Spirituals served to create atmosphere and to deepen the emotional appeal. Frank Wilson, actor and playwright, who had the leading role, is a singer of Negro songs of which he makes effective use in his own plays. He is an earnest and serious actor of artistic ideals. His play, *Meek Mose,* was given at the Princess Theatre, New York, with a Negro repertory company and marks the first time a Negro has appeared as producer of a dramatic work on Broadway. Lester A. Walton was the manager.

Heralded in 1930, by Richard Watts, Jr., dramatic critic of the New York *Herald Tribune* as "one of the loftiest achievements of the American Theatre," *The Green Pastures,* a Negro miracle play, proved to be a masterpiece. With a cast of ninety-five Negroes, it became a great attraction in the theatrical world. Richard B. Harrison, who played the role of "De Lawd" 1,658 times, passed away on March 14, 1935. This was a drama, a prize winning play from the book *Ol' Man Adam and His Chillun,* by Roark Bradford, the work of Marc Connelly. It is a religious play dramatizing Biblical scenes as the two white authors conceive the illiterate Negroes' visualization of the mysteries of the Book of Genesis— of a God of wrath who is a personal deity. *The Celestial Choir* of the play, that sings off stage or in the orchestral pit, are heard in Negro Spirituals "a cappella." The choir was first organized and conducted by Hall Johnson whose chorus had been reaping fame at the concerts at the International House and at the Lewisohn Stadium of New York City College. Ulysses Chambers,[7] tenor, followed Hall Johnson as director of the choir of *The Green Pastures* when the play went on tour. Chambers made the choral arrangements and trained the chorus for the second season of Lew Leslie's "Blackbirds."

Daniel Haynes was one of the leading singing-actors in *The Green Pastures* in which he played the dual role of Adam and Hezdrel. This versatile artist, successful on the stage and screen, was also an amateur painter and belonged to the Art Students League of New York. Haynes studied for the ministry in Atlanta, Georgia, his native city and came to New York with the idea of receiving advanced theological training. Instead he was drawn into accepting a place as understudy to the actor Charles Gilpin in *The Bottom of the Cup*. Owing to

[7] Chambers, who was born in Baltimore, is a teacher of piano and organ. He was educated at Morgan College in that city, and also studied privately with white professors of Peabody Institute. However, he received his first lessons in this field from his parents, both of whom were musicians. Advanced musical studies were followed at the musical Institute of Art, where he was graduated in 1916 and completed a post-graduate course in 1917. He studied further at the Teachers' College of Columbia University, where he finished a course in 1921 and was awarded the degree of Bachelor of Music and of Science. He has held many important positions as teacher and executant.

From the Supervisorship of music of the Baltimore colored Public Schools in 1921, he held, successively, similar positions at the Dunbar High School, Washington, D. C., and at the combined public schools of St. Louis. As organist, he has held positions at the "Lafayette," a white theatre of Newark, New Jersey, and at the Royal Theatre, Chicago. As tenor soloist and organist, Chambers has been connected with various white churches, including St. Luke's Cathedral, Trinity Parish and the Chapel of the Incarnation in New York City, and the First Presbyterian Church of South Hampton, Long Island. As solo organist he has been heard in the Wanamaker Auditorium in New York as well as in the largest cities in the United States.

Gilpin's illness, he opened the play at a moment's notice and was triumphant in the star role. Haynes next appeared in *Earth;* in *Rang Tang,* a review; and in *Show Boat* as the understudy to Jules Bledsoe. Haynes' work in the two motion pictures, *Hallelujah* and *The Last Mile,* added to his reputation as an actor and singer. The producer Reinhardt has declared that in *Hallelujah* Haynes gave the most artistic performance he has seen in an American photoplay.

Ziegfeld's *Show Boat,* drawn from Edna Ferber's story of romantic days on the Mississippi, gave an opportunity for Negro talent. The singing and dancing in this musical play which is far above the standard of the comedy and revue of the Jazz school, is excellently done, while Jules Bledsoe brought an individual interpretation to the outstanding song, "Ol' Man River," which has placed it side by side of the best liked art songs of the present day.

A number of recent concoctions in the form of Negro revues have been short-lived owing to the fact that they are unfinished, trivial even for that particular medium, and lacking in distinction. Among the plays that received mention we find *Blackberries of 1932,* a revue in two acts and twenty-six scenes by Eddie Green, lyrics and music by Donald Heywood and Tom Pelusco and dances arranged by Sidney Sprague and Lew Crawford. The play was staged by Ben Bernard and produced at the Liberty Theatre, New York.

Of the character of the Negro musical comedy today, S. H. Dudley, the veteran actor-producer, says, "It seems to me that there is room in New York for a Negro show different from the present one. I may be wrong. *Blackbirds* and other shows like it have been a success, but I would like to see something nearer the Negro's genius."

There are two factors which may account for the present dearth of first-class Negro musical comedies. First, the present economic conditions of stress in the United States and the world at large which prohibits at the moment any new venture that entails the risking of the necessary sum to further début artist recitals or the financing of the elaborate and costly revue entertainment demanded by modern theatre-goers. A large growing body of educated Negroes, moreover, are turning their attention to the dramatic stage, and are questioning the successful, serious Negro drama of the times, written by white playwrights. They realize that in order to produce a good musical comedy or an opera, one must have a knowledge of what constitutes "good theater." Nevertheless it has become more than a suspicion that distinctive plays can be written, in which the drama of the lowly can be treated as but one phase of the realities of Negro life. Young Negro writers, on the wave of the new art awakening in America, therefore, have accepted the advice of Alain Locke who, in writing of race-drama, has said, "The vehicle of all sound art must be native to the group." Americans of all racial affiliations are writing better stage music—it is not too much to expect that the Negro too will make progress in both the Negro folk-drama and his racial theatrical music. The distinct form of musical comedy and revues, frankly that of entertainment, and no more, will be benefited by an improved taste.

For some time—since 1921—groups of Negro men and women have been experimenting in a new artistic medium. They are found in colleges and in amateur dramatic organizations. The Howard University Dramatic Department organized from the school club by Montgomery Gregory, and guided by Alain Locke; the Morgan College Dramatic Club in Baltimore; and the Dramatic Club of Hampton Institute where students paint the sets, perform the roles and compose the chorus—these are at the head of a long list of Negro college dramatic groups which are seriously studying the drama and giving commendable performances.

In 1921, the Colored Players Guild of New York, under Dora Cole Norman, talented dancer, a sister of Bob Cole, the comedian, was formed to produce original plays. A few years later, the Krigwa Players, Little Negro Theater, a nation-wide movement sponsored primarily by W. E. B. Du Bois, and directed by Charles Burroughs in New York, won prizes and praise from Belasco and other authorities. These activities were actuated within the race, thus differing from the presentation of the "Negro Players" in three Negro dramas written by Ridgely Torrence in 1917.

Other such efforts should be noted. The Little Theater group in Washington, D. C., has been working under the direction of Willis Richardson, a Negro playwright, and Georgia Douglas Johnson, the Negro woman poet who is now writing Negro one-act plays. The Dixwell Community Players of New Haven, are acting alertly under the shadow of the Theatre of Yale University. The Aldridge Players of St. Louis, who have just celebrated their eighth anniversary (1927-1935), are producing Plays of Negro Life. The Gilpin Players of Cleveland, Ohio, for fourteen years have been widening their reputation in the longer, serious Negro plays written by white playwrights, but ever seeking new material. The San Antonio Little Theater Players are presenting Negro shows throughout the State of Texas. The Allied Arts Players of Boston have been presenting for five years romantic and historical plays in the "search for the jewel that hangs from Ethiopian ears."[8] These and other groups West and South

[8] Following the closing of the Allied Arts Centre, training school and sponsor of the Allied Art Players, individuals have been employed in government dramatic groups and in leading professional productions in New York and in Boston.

have started an influence that may prove tremendous in its appeal.

Not only are the Negro amateur theatres serving to create colored audiences capable of recognizing and appreciating productions of excellence, they are proving a means of giving the would-be-playwright a knowledge of the technique of the drama. The talented colored musician with something to say through the alliance of the arts and the theater, must perfect himself in dramatic technique if he is to write his own race-drama, the interpretation of which is now largely in the hands of white writers of the theatrical world.

Even as the author writes, a decided trend toward a certain form of music-drama is being evinced. For over three months, beginning in March, 1933, Hall Johnson's *Run, Little Children,* the title taken from that of a Negro Spiritual, was witnessed at the old Lyric Theater at New York. The scene is laid on the outskirts of a small southern town on an August evening. The second scene, that of the Hope Meeting House, gives opportunity for prayer-meeting scenes, shouting and preaching, praying and singing of Negro Spirituals. The folk material used in the first scene—in the orgiastic rites of the New-Day Pilgrims led by the prophet and the voluptuous Sulamai, was taken from the Bahamas. There Negro superstitions hold sway to a far greater extent than in the southern United States. The weakest part of this folk-play which was written and prepared by Mr. Johnson, leader of the Negro choir which was so favorably received in *The Green Pastures* (and independently as well), is said to be the portrayal of character, perhaps due to inexperience in play-writing.

This music-play has commanded the notice of the press. H. T. Parker, late music editor and critic of the Boston *Evening Transcript,* stated that, ''Outside the two spectacular scenes and his use in them of ritual and music and amassed song, he remains an inarticulate playwright in a flood of talk. . . . The root of the matter is in him, but for the present lack of adaptability and resource, he cannot bring it to stage-flower.'' Writing further, Parker concludes that ''the power that is implicit in 'Run, Little Children,' proceeds from the two scenes of spectacle and music. . . . Give Mr. Johnson primitive music and he is dramatist indeed. In these two contrasted scenes he has wrought something very like American music-drama.''

The film of Eugene O'Neill's play, *The Emperor Jones,* completed in July, 1933, was presented during the first week in October, 1933, at the Rivoli Theatre, New York City. The cinema was produced in Boston, beginning the week of September 23, with Fredi Washington and Paul Robeson in the leading roles. The title role is superbly acted by Robeson. The music was arranged by Rosamond Johnson. The movie version differs greatly from the original play, and it has no relation to Gruenberg's opera of like name. DuBose Heyward has written a long American sequence which includes scenes of the lowest class and types of Negro life. The scenes of folk life include an African ceremony with dancing and beat of the tom-tom, and the interior of a church in the United States, south, with ring shout and hysterical singing of the Spirituals, as inevitable as the pictures of Harlem night life, also portrayed. The statement by the press that the play-cinema ''represents three stages in the spiritual growth of the race'' is misleading, for the much-heralded use of folk music and musical sound proved to be abortive and devoid of any true ''spiritual'' portrayal. It is calculated to please the masses and to fill the coffers of those most interested. Offensive racial terms and scenes have been deleted.

Chapter IX

FOLK THEMES IN LARGER FORMS OF COMPOSITION

Folk Music and Art Music—Relationship—Importance of Works Based on Folk Themes—Interview with Henry F. Gilbert—Opinions—Composers' Use of Negro Themes—Serious Works in Various Forms—Symphony, Opera, Ballet—In Light Vein.

The creative artist of today is ever experimenting and seeking new ways—a new musical form or harmonic coloring by which old thoughts and the fundamental emotions may be expressed. Many, incapable of feeling great emotion, turn to the imitation of sounds rampant in a mechanical age. Following a concert given in Paris during the past season, *Les Beaux Arts* declared that the Spanish-American composers were more interesting because less shackled to the academic modernism than their Anglo-Saxon rivals, which was due to the fact that they willingly made use of their native rhythms and song which gave their compositions an exotic charm.

Of this tendency we have other witnesses. Apart from Chávez, director of the Conservatory of Music in Mexico, who alone writes universally, Alejandro Caturla, a Cuban musician, admitted his indebtedness to folk-lore, as did Amadeo Roldán, who makes use of the native folk-themes and local instruments. There are a few other young, earnest musicians, Alomiá Robles, Manuel Aguirre, and Roberto Carpio who are turning to their traditional music for inspiration. Amadeo Roldán, in "Rebambaramba," used local instruments to give picturesque vividness to his work. From far distant Peru, Carlos Sanchez Malaga, a musician strongly influenced by Inca music, ventures to say that "Music, from a creative standpoint, can no longer be universal—such music having exhausted its own possibilities of evolution, composers are forced to turn to folk music for the basis of their work."

To the colder, more phlegmatic and scholarly musician of the North, this remark might be thrust aside as the sentiment of an artist of the Latin race, who, in the terms of the southern Creole, may be described as "all heart." But history does not allow this to be easily done. It is well-known that there are folk-song themes of great nobility capable of being utilized with universal appeal. The Volga boat-song of the burdened Russian long-shoreman and "Deep River," the song of religious faith extemporized by the oppressed Negro bondman, are but two outstanding examples.

Tired of forced strivings and restless searchings, composers have again and again gone back seeking the "hills of peace" in the straightforward musical expression of the folk song, just as the composers of the German school did in the time of Beethoven and Brahms. The fundamental emotions of love and hate, sorrow and joy, have been found in haunting loveliness of melody. But an emotional theme must be presented with beauty in order to endure —to give pleasure to sophisticated listeners or to cultured audiences.

Music as an art may naturally be divided into two sections. Folk Music—that of the illiterate, the unsophisticated; of the unknown bard, welding a communal experience into a complete whole, whether it be that of sorrow or joy; and Art Music—the output of trained musicians whose creative works, composed according to an accepted standard of beauty, give aesthetic enjoyment to the cultured. While the two lines of tonal art lie ever apart, it cannot be said that "ne'er the twain shall meet."

Discussing the relationship between national music and folk music which are not to be confounded, Alexander Tansman, the Polish composer, defines "true music" as "that which is based on nationality; but in a very deep sense." He declares that "it is the essence of his country's folk music, ingrained in his being, which characterizes a truly inspired composer and gives his music a national flavor." Nevertheless, nationalism in music may be carried too far and result in propaganda or an exploitation that weakens the creative work of a composer. On the other hand, a universal theme may be interpreted through the race consciousness of an individual in such a manner that it possesses unlimited appeal regardless of nationality.

In Spain, a country strongly influenced by Italian music in the 18th and 19th centuries, after having been influenced by that of imported Africans five centuries earlier, Pedreel and Philip began the movement for nationalization of their music. This effort led to the study of Spanish popular song by such composers as Nin, Albeniz, Granados, Turina and Manuel de Falla. The last mentioned, though national in thought, is modern in the manner in which he presents his material. Vincent d'Indy and Julien Tiersot, with the folklorist, Weckerlin, and the song writer, Bordes, were deeply interested in their native French music.

Russian composers have clung closely to a nationalistic expression. The majority of their opera librettos are drawn from the prose-poems of their mulatto genius, Aelxander Pushkin, whose works were in the main, influenced by native thought and history. Moussorgsky's operas *Boris Godounov* and *Chovantshina* (completed by Rimsky-Korsakov), picture through the words of Pushkin and native Russian melodies, real and true Russian life. This great composer declared, "Reality is everything Simple truth, no matter how bald, courage and sincerity, these are what I strive after."

This composer's compatriot, Stravinsky, in his widely debated "Rite of Spring," complete with dissonances and rhythmic innovations, includes native folk material in the ballet. There are but few great composers of the classic or romantic era who did not show a healthy curiosity in folk-music. Haydn employed folk rhythms, Chopin employed Polish themes, Liszt and Brahms used those of the Hungarians. Today, Debussy and Ravel among the moderns, have delved not only into their own native song, but admit an influence of the music of the Javanese. Godowsky seeks to give program music of conflicting rhythms and chromatic color, suggested as he states by the sound of Javanese native music and orchestras.

Mahler and Bloch used Jewish folk themes, although Mahler was more interested in universal music. Bloch was more racial than national, for Hebrew music is more or less influenced by the nation to which it might belong since the dispersion of Jews from the Holy Land. Thus Ravel's Hebraic melodies are treated in Spanish style. Richard Strauss does not scorn to use native Italian melody to suit his purpose, while Sibelius is steeped in folk-song.

In England, Vaughn Williams, writer of music rich in melodic beauty, is strongly influenced by English folk-song which Cecil Sharp and other folk-lorists strived to preserve. Eight years ago (about 1828), was performed *Háry Janos,* a comic opera by the Hungarian, Zoltan Kodály, replete with Magyar folk music. Of the work, it was said that the composer "helped himself to the age-old treasure which is rich beyond dreams of melodic avarice." It might be noted in passing that the Allegro in Beethoven's Sonata in E for violin and piano is said to embody a Negro folk theme which was native to Louisiana, and belongs to the religious group of folk song of the race.

These melodies, a far cry from the "tin-pan alley" popular songs, have afforded inspiration to such composers as Henry F. Gilbert, John Alden Carpenter, Walter Kramer and George Chadwick as well as the newer men, Harold Morris and the Negro composers William Grant Still and Clarence Cameron White. Roy Harris, "out of the West," has had his music appraised as being related to the small stock of Scotch-Irish folk song which has survived in the United States through the cow-boy ballads. Thayer and Lieurance, Cadman and Farwell are best known for their cult of Indian tribal song, while Stillman-Kelley has not hesitated to go to the far East and has composed several works based on Chinese themes. Copland, Hindemith and Milhaud have delved in Jazz. In Europe, Mme. Johanna Müller has written an oratorio, "In Memoriam," based on Walt Whitman's poems on Abraham Lincoln, in which she uses Indian and other American folk themes. In Vienna, Alban Berg is probing the fount of Austrian song, while Ernst Toch, modernist, writes in national Austro-German spirit.

Folk song is as ageless as the traditions of a people.[1] Through unusual scale progressions, intricate rhythms

[1] The following are listed among many serious works written in various forms, the spirit of which is Negro.
Maurice Arnold—
  "Violin Sonata."
  "Plantation Dances" for orchestra.
Ernest Bloch—
  "America," a symphony in which Negro folk songs and blues are used as themes.
Robert Braine—
  "Concerto in Jazz"—Solo violin and orchestra.
Eddy Brown—
  "Over There" and "Nobody Knows."

and varied melodic strains it embodies both romance and history—the soul of a people. The modern composer no longer uses folk melodies as favorite quotations in his music, but seeks to establish a racial tonal atmosphere. Through art music, an individual charm and poetic content may be transmitted and move us to tears or to laugh-

Negro Spirituals, arranged for violin.

Cecil Burleigh—

"Plantation Sketches," op. 35, for violin and piano.

Concert numbers for advanced players.

Carl Busch—

"Negro Carnival"

The themes of this orchestral number include "My Old Kentucky Home," announced by solo oboe with harp accompanying.

Charles Wakefield Cadman—

"Trio in D major," for violin, 'cello and piano.

This is an example of idealized ragtime.

John Alden Carpenter—

"Little Nigger" and "Little Indian," for piano.

"Diversions," five pieces for piano.

"Four Negro Songs," for medium voice and piano.

"Krazy Kat," a jazz pantomine.

"Patterns," for orchestra and piano.

A hint of jazz in the second division.

"Skyscraper's Ballet."

André Simon Caplet—

"Epiphanie," a "fresco for 'cello and orchestra."

The third episode is called "Dance of the Little Negroes." The score description reads: "Melchior, the black and gold king, made his way in gorgeous procession to Bethlehem. There, greatly affected, he was enraptured, and to honor the King of the world, he bade his little Negroes dance."

Alejandro G. Caturla—

"Tres Danzas Cubanas" (1927) (1930).

"Bembé" (Afro-Cubana para 14 instrumentos) (1928).

Played by the Boston Chamber Orchestra, Nicolas Sloninsky, conductor.

George Chadwick—

"Symphonic Sketches."

ter. The poignancy of a child's funeral song heard in Puerto Rico, sung by mourning peons in the shadows of the ruins of Laparra, may be so transcribed by skillful hands that hearers in a far-flung concert hall may be moved to pity. Or the essence of Warren Storey Smith's cameo-cut song, "To Helen," may cause us to dream again

> Try as he may, Mr. Chadwick cannot write erotic music, but how exuberantly the "Jubilee" of the first sketch and the "The Vagrom Ballard" of the fourth flow along. If ever there was American Music also these two pieces are such. What is the Jubilee but symphonic music gone on a spree, but stopping occasionally to poetize along the way, and so to climb the heights of symphony concerts.—*The Boston Transcript,* following a production by the Boston Symphony Orchestra.

Aaron Copland—
"Piano Concerto in Jazz Idiom" (1926).
> Performed by the composer with the Boston Symphony Orchestra. Said to be a work of "fine sweep, rhythmic devices, and individual contrapuntal lines."

James P. Dunn—
"Overture on Negro Themes."

Samuel Gardner—
"In the cane-brake," for violin.
"Jazzetto" for violin and piano, simple rhythmic effect.

Henry F. Gilbert—
"Negro Rhapsody."
"Comedy Overture on Negro Themes."
"Humoresque on Negro Minstrel Tunes."
"The Dance in Place Congo."
"Two Episodes for Orchestra," 1 legend, 2 Negro episode.
"Negro Episode" (for piano).
"Negro Dances," for 4 hands.
"Negro Dances," for 2 hands.
"Suite."
> The suite in Negro idiom was the last composition written by this noted composer. It was composed in 1927 as a commission by the Elizabeth Sprague Coolidge Foundation for presentation at the Library of Congress Music Hall. The suite was first given at a concert of the Chamber Orchestra of Boston.

of beauty and of Greece—and of the beginnings of time. Legendry and balladry in the old civilizations remain undisputed. A few years ago, Arthur Farwell wrote in ignorance that the Negro race lacked myth and legend and therefore its music had only color to offer. While ad-

Leopold Godowsky—
    "An American Idyl"
    "An Ethiopian Serenade," for piano, from "Trian Kontameron."
Rubin Goldmark—
    "Negro Rhapsody."
    Given an initial performance by Cleveland Orchestra, Nikolai Sokoloff, conductor. Performed by the N. Y. Philharmonic Orchestra, Mengelberg, conducting.
Morton Gould—
    Suite of Short Poems. The third, "Jazz Caprice."
David Guion—
    "Shingandi," A Primitive African Ballet.
Henry Hadley—
    Symphony in D minor, "North, East, South and West"
    Performed for the Norfolk, Connecticut, Festival of 1911.
    The third movement is a scherzo and is of Negro character throughout. It does not touch the pathetic aspects of the racial character.
Victor Harris—
    "Medley from the Sunny South" for three-part chorus of women's voices with piano accompaniment.
    Employs two Spirituals and other Negro songs and closes with Dixie.
Arthur Hartman—
    "A Negro Croon," for violin.
    A use of pentatonics in D flat major.
Edward Burlingame Hill—
    "Jazz Study"—dedicated to Guy Maier and Lee Pattison.
Lucius Hosmer—
    "Ethiopian Rhapsody"—dedicated to the colored "Mammys of the old South." Negro rhythms and tunes are used in an ingenious manner.
John Tasker Howard—
    "Chant Nègre" ("The Old Ship of Zion").
    A piano setting of the old Spiritual which was sung to the composer by an ex-slave. Pianistic and effective.

mitting the peculiar properties of Negro music and its possibilities for beautiful development, he made the enquiry: "Is the Negro music waiting its time, and is it to have its period of development later?"

That period has evidently dawned. In an interview with the late Henry F. Gilbert of Cambridge, which was pub-

William Henry Humister—
    "A Southern Fantasy," for orchestra.
Abbie Norton Jamison—
    "Negro Death Song," for tenor.
A. Walter Kramer—
    "Two Sketches for Orchestra," Op. 37.
    "Chant Nègre," and "Valse Triste."
    "Symphonie Rhapsody on Negro Themes."
        "I'm Troubled in Mind" and "De Lord Delivered Daniel" are employed. 1923.
    "Chant Nègre," for violin.
    "Deep River"—A transcription for string quartette of H. T. Burleigh's arrangement of this Spiritual.
Ernest Krueger—
    "American Skteches."
Constant Lambert—
    "Rio Grande," for orchestra.
Ernessto Lecuona—
    "Danzas Afro-Cubanas," Album No. 3 (1930).
Clarence Lucas—
    "Holiday Sketches."
    "In Alabama."
        Scherzando movement introducing "Nobody Knows the trouble I've Seen."
Macmillan—
    "American Dances," one in A minor, one in E.
Daniel Gregory Mason—
    "On Negro Themes," for string quartette. In three movements. The second is a fantasy on "Deep River."
Milhaud—
    "La Création du Momde." A ballet.
Harold Morris—
    "Variations for a chamber orchestra."
        A piano concerto, Op. 36, first performed by the Boston Sym-

lished in the *Musical Observer* of June, 1919, the author asked the composer what he thought of the importance of works based on folk themes in the establishment of a school of American music. The reply was, "In late years a tendency has been apparent on the part of our younger composers to turn from an imitation of the musical art

> phony Orchestra, October 22, 1931, with the composer at the piano. The first movement introduces the rhythmic beat of the African drum, which is repeated in the last movement. The second movement is a set of variations on a Negro song. There is syncopation in the rondo. Mr. Morris, who is a Texan, uses the spiritual "I was way down a yonder, dum-a-lum." The symphonic work is in orthodox form, imaginative, individualistic and skilfully wrought.

Thorwald Otterstrom—

"Trabel On" (for piano).

"American Negro Suite" (for orchestra).

> *Musical America* said of the two movements from this suite, "The first is a rather sophisticated, but flowing and tuneful Negro song, 'Blow de' Trumpet Gabriel,' and a burlesque march 'Trabel On!' in Turkish patrol style. The orchestration is skilful—the composition was admirably presented." The suite heard in December, 1916, was performed by the Chicago Symphony Orchestra under the direction of Mr. Stock.

Clifford Page—

"Old Plantation Days."

> A cycle for mixed voices. The piece makes use of "Nellie Gray," "Old Black Joe," "Kentucky Home" and several Negro Spirituals.

> "Mary and Martha" and "Go Down Moses." The first named Spiritual almost unaccompanied, the second richly harmonized.

Kurt Pahlen—

"Six Negro Songs for Voice and Piano." Settings of poems by the Negro American poets, Langston Hughes and Countee Cullen. The poems were translated into German (1930).

Francis Poulenc—

"Rhapsodie Nègre," for small orchestra and a voice.

> The voice appears in the third movement of the work, "Honoloulou," under the title "vocal intermezzo," and again in the finale. It is original and effective. Dedicated to Erik Satie.

of Europe and to seek for artistic stimuli and spiritual incentive to creative activity within their own country. Hence we have had a number of compositions based on Indian, Negro and even Spanish themes. This is not necessarily American Music, but the existence of such works is significant as a beginning of a native musical culture

Maud Powell—
"Deep River."
> Transcribed for violin from Samuel Coleridge-Taylor's piano transcription.

John Powell—
"Rhapsodie Nègre" for Orchestra and pianoforte.
> Shortly after its completion it was first heard in New York City at one of the concerts of the Russian Symphony (1918). Following a hearing before an audience of the Philharmonic Orchestra of New York, the rhapsody was reviewed as follows:
> "The rhapsody is as truly psychologic, as complete a panorama of moods as the rhapsodies of Liszt and as inextinguishably alive. The form, the sequence of moods, seems unanswerable to an inner law of inevitability."

"The Banjo Picker," from "At the Fair," six sketches of American fun.
"Sonata Virginianesque," for violin and piano, written in three movements—"In the Quarters," "In the Woods," "At the Big House—(a Virginia Reel)."
"Sonata Noble," fourth movement.
> Mr. Powell's recent Negro discussions prove his music to be superior to his racial psychology.

Wallingford Riegger—
"Triple Jazz"—An American Polonaise in three-four time. (1923-1928.)

Amadeo Roldan—
"La Rebambaramba"—Afro-Cuban ballet. "Poema Negro."
"El Milagro de Anaquillé"—A Negro Cuban ballet. (Choreographic mystery in one act.)
> Conducted by the composer at Havana, Cuba, when the ballet was played by the Havana Philharmonic Orchestra, in the summer of 1932.
"Danza Negra"—Poem for voice and seven instruments.

which has actually been started. The rich fund of folk-lore and folk-song has certainly been the vivifying source whence have sprung the modern art cultures of the world.''

Mr. Gilbert's opinion was valuable since he has produced notable symphonic works based on Negro themes.

''A Chango''—Negro poem for quartet of instruments.
''Mulato''—for piano (1932).
Carlos Salzedo—
''Deep River,'' in Favorite Melodies, transcribed for harp.
Pedro San Juán—
''Liturgia Negra''—A suite for orchestra. ''Initiation'' evokes ancestral rites of Africans who were brought to Cuba (1934). The composer uses Afro-Cuban idioms.
Erik Satie—
''Parade,'' a ballet. This ballet is said to have ''started the movement to convert rag into musical values.''
Henry Schoenfeld—
''Violin Sonata''
Cyril Scott—
''Negro Air and Dance,'' for violin.
''Danse Nègre,'' for piano.
''Tallahassee,'' fantasie on Negro themes.
Leo Sowerby—
''E minor Trio,'' for flute and piano.
''Monotony'' and ''Synconata''
Mr. Sowerby, a Chicagoan, was first heard at Mrs. Coolidge's concert in the Berkshires, in September, 1919. His trio is written in a distinctive manner, dealing liberally in syncopations and harmonic colors.
Albert Spalding—
''Alabama,'' for violin with piano accompaniment.
The syncopation is produced in counterpoint effects, ably handled. Mr. Spalding has played ''Alabama'' on his concert programs. Speaking of Negro melodies, he says that they are of paramount value because they possess to a large extent the powerful quality of being sung or played with or without an accompaniment.
Albert Stoessel—
''Three Traditional Negro Spirituals,'' for male voices with

He was the first of American composers to gain recognition in Russia, and hailed in that country as a distinctive genius, whose orchestral works were to be included in the repertoires of the various symphony societies of that country; and fate so ordained that the second performance of the "Comedy Overture on Negro Themes" was given

strings and harp accompaniment, or piano ("Steal Away," "Swing Low, Sweet Chariot," and "Religion is a Fortune").

Stravinsky—
"Ragtime."
    Shows that the ultra-modern composer has not been unaffected by the interest in syncopated melody, and is a naturalistic picture by this remarkable composer.

Lamar Stringfield—
"The Legend of John Henry," a symphonic ballet.
    This piece was first performed at a concert of the North Carolina Symphony Orchestra, of which Mr. Stringfield is musical director.

Alexander Tansman—
"Spiritual and Blues" from "Sonatine Transatlantique."
    Played by José Iturbi on his recital tour of 1930-31.

Edgar Varèse—
"Integrales"—"A study for percussion instruments."

Villa-Lobos—
Danses Africaines for symphony orchestra.

William Walton—
"Façade."
    A unique number written in 1926 to accompany and intersperse recitation of poems by Edith Sitwell. The poems are to be given through a megaphone, in broken lines like the poetry of Vachel Lindsey. The piece was presented at the "Pops" in Boston on June 24, 1931. Rhythms of the tango, pasodobile and the polka are used as well as jazz.
"Portsmouth Point."

Mortimer Wilson—
"New Orleans Overture."
"Waltz of the Negro Dolls" (from the suite "From My Youth").
    Mr. Wilson's orchestral piece won the Reisenfeld prize for best American overture.

in Odessa by the Imperial Orchestra of Moscow on **the**
date of Germany's declaration of war against that country.
Mr. Gilbert's "Comedy Overture on Negro Themes" is
perhaps the most characteristic of modern works of the
larger forms of composition based on Negro folk motifs.
This composer used a two-four measure motive from a

Theophil Wendt—
  Six South African Songs, based on Native Melodies. Text writ-
  ten and adapted by the composer. For voice and piano.
Gaylord Yost—
  "Southern Melody."
  "From the South."
George Anthiel—
  Transatlantique, an opera.
  A delirious work which had its première at the Frankfort
  Opera on May 25, 1930.
Albert Chiafarelli—
  "Symphony in 3 movements," based on Handy's St. Louis,
  Beale Street and Limestone Blues.
Eric Delamarter—
  "Symphony after Walt Whitman."
    Mr. Delamarter uses two popular numbers, a mountain folksong,
    and two old Negro themes. His work is not an attempt to
    write Jazz.
Frederick Delius—
  Koanga—An opera based on George Cable's story of Creole life,
  The Grandissimes.
    This opera was first produced at Elberfeld State Theater in
    1904 with Clarence Whitehill in the leading role. The com-
    poser, Mr. Delius, in the winter of his life (seventy-one years
    of age), blind, and partially paralyzed, revised his opera
    with the expectation of seeing it produced in London under
    the direction of Sir Thomas Beecham. The composer had
    long been interested in Negro subjects. At one time, he
    heard Negro folk songs on his father's plantation in Florida
    in the United States, and he was particularly attracted by
    the harmonies produced in part singing.
  "Appalachia"—A tone poem for orchestra.
  Based on Negro themes and closing with a choral section.

Bahama song, an eight measure tune of the Mississippi steam-boat roustabouts—"For to see my Mammy, Oh—I'se gwine to Alabammy, Oh—." A fugue theme consisted of four measures of the Negro Spiritual, "Old Ship of Zion" given out by the brasses. Less well known is his "Negro Rhapsody" first performed under the direction

Louis T. Gruenberg—
"Six Jazz Epigrams," Op. 30. For piano.
"Jazzberries," 4 dances for piano.
"The Creation," for voice and 8 instruments. The poem, a Negro sermon by James Weldon Johnson.
"The Daniel Jazz," for voice and eight instruments. The poem by Vachel Lindsey.

Franke Harling—
Deep River—An opera with Jazz.
Described as a native opera, this work with the scene laid in New Orleans of French and Spanish atmosphere, was said to lack true operatic form. It was not drawn from the like-named Spiritual, but depended rather upon Negro folk idiom and jazz rhythms. Nevertheless, it remains an important venture. It was given in September and October, 1926, for two weeks at the Schubert Theatre, Philadelphia. It was produced by Arthur Hopkins with an all colored cast that included Jules Bledsoe.
In 1925, Negroes were given an opportunity to appear in Franke Harling's *A Light from St. Agnes* (the book by Minnie Maddern Fiske) when produced by the Chicago Civic Opera Company.

Charles E. Ives—
"Second Orchestral Set" (1902-1903).

Ernst Krenek—
Johnny Spielt Auf, a German opera.
This "Jazz opera" first produced in Germany, was heard in sadly garbled form at the Metropolitan Opera House in New York, when the role of "Jonny," a Negro jazz band conductor is changed to that of a black-faced music entertainer.

Maurice Ravel—
"Concerto" for left hand, piano and orchestra (1931).
First played in Paris by the war wounded pianist, Paul Wittgenstein, who has only his left hand; an exemplification of

of the composer at the Norfolk Festival (Connecticut) in June, 1913. "Americanesque" was based on three minstrel tunes, "Zip Coon," "Dearest Mae," and "Rosa Lee."

The composer's symphonic ballet, "The Dance in Place Congo," was produced at the Metropolitan Opera House in New York on March 23, 1918. Many interesting comments followed the production, some showing an appalling ignorance of the racial themes used. The piece which makes use of a number of Creole themes (not "Negro Creole" since there is no such race of people) was

the spirit rising above a material loss. The piece relies upon certain jazz idioms which the French-Spanish composer studied on his tour of the United States in 1928. "Chansons Madécasses." African rhythms are employed.

Deems Taylor—
"Circus Day," a suite orchestrated by Grofé.

Antonio Veretti—
Il Favorito del Ré (The Kings Favorite)—An opera.
This novelty was given at the Scala in 1932. The composer is one of Italy's modernists. He uses a jazz band in what was meant to be a satirical work. Although lavishly given, it caused an uproar and had only three performances.

Emerson Withorne—
"Pell Street," from "New York Days and Nights."
"Saturday's Child." A setting of poems by Countee Cullen.

Randall Thompson—
Symphony, No. 2, in E Minor. American in nature and style. Indication of themes of jazz.

A list of new pieces in the popular vein of light music include

John Green—
"Night Club"—A suite for three pianos and orchestra.

Ferdie Grofé—
"Mississippi Suite."
"Tabloid."

Herman Heller—
"Milestone Jazz"—A Spiritual, Soft-shoe dance, Cake-walk, The Texas Tommy, the Two-step, the Fox-trot and the Charleston, featured on one of his band programs.

given by the Boston Symphony Orchestra on April 26, 1918, and was reviewed at length with differences of opinion. One will suffice:

"Mr. Gilbert's music is no mean achievement * * * the rhythmic life of the music thrills the ear and goads the fancy. It is American, through and through, to write with such energy of rhythm, to dare so boldly what the silly pedants and purists will call 'vulgar' syncopations. The rhythmic verve of Mr. Gilbert's earlier 'Comedy Overture' is now rhythmic power. Again, the listener rejoices when the tang of 'Miche Banjo' the 'Bamboula Song' and other Creole tunes bites and snaps out of the music. Measures acrid, languorous, wanton, mere high spirits, lie equally within Mr. Gilbert's new range of imagination and achievement. Both rise highest in the beginning of the tone-poem, as the dance tunes turn into an infection on the spot, the air, the folk: and at the end when after the boom of the bell the music withers away into a dreary desolation. Yet between, the 'slow section,' dividing the dances lingers in a thick sensuous languor fertile of suggestion. Not hitherto has Mr. Gilbert sustained a whole piece at the pitch of 'The Dance in Place Congo.' " Boston *Evening Transcript*, April 27, 1918.

Well may we note also that in the past ten years many works both in large and small form, based on the Negro idiom, have been written by white composers. Apart from the arrangements of the Spirituals for song with piano accompaniment and for glee clubs, Negro themes and subjects have become exceedingly popular. In the realm of the unusual is the song cycle, "The Congo—A Study of the Negro Race" composed by Arthur Bergh, and first sung by David Bispham in New York. Bergh's cycle of three songs is written for a baritone voice and piano. The three sections are called "Their Basic Savagery," "Their Irrepressible High Spirits," and "The Hope of Their religion." The words—

"Then I saw the Congo creeping thro
the Black

Cutting thro' the jungle with a golden
track''

are spoken instead of being sung to a piano accompaniment, of a harmonization of the South East African melody "Thata Nabandu." This melody, noted by Junod,
occurs in the first and second sections, while in the third,
the spiritual "Didn't My Lord Deliver Daniel," appears.

The old dance theme of "Bamboula" is skilfully used
in a contrapuntal manner. Naturally the music is modern to suit the poem. The theme is that of superstition
being conquered by religion, and the cycle closes with the
melody of the old hymn "Hark Ten Thousand Harps and
Voices" overpowering the jungle cry of the god of the
Congo. It might here be added that the style of many of
Lindsay's poems is that of a primitive art—the chant—
half-spoken, half-sung words, the style not only of the early
Greeks, but of the African as well. Note C. Kambo Simango's reading of the African story "The Elephant
Hunt," beautiful in its rhythmic swing.

"The Congo" was read publicly by the poet whose
story of the inspiration that prompted him to write the
poem was thus told in the Boston *Transcript* of February
6, 1915. "Perhaps no one thing influenced me more than
the story I have before mentioned, Joseph Conrad's
'Heart of Darkness.' I wanted to reiterate the word
Congo and the several refrains in a way that would
echo stories like that. I wanted to suggest the terror, the
reeking swamp-fever, the forest splendor, the black-lac-
quered loveliness and above all the eternal fatality of
Africa, that Conrad has written down with so sure a
hand."

In the operatic field, the latest success in America, is
the opera "Emperor Jones" in English, written by Louis
Gruenberg after the play by Eugene O'Neill. This was
first given in January, 1933, at the Metropolitan Opera

House, New York, with Lawrence Tibbett in a magnificent portrayal of the Negro adventurer. The opera lacks vocal line. The most telling melody is the Negro Spiritual "Standin' In Der Need of Prayer" which is used in the last act. Under direction of others the opera was given on May 2 and 5, 1933, with Mr. Tibbett and with Negro choruses in Chicago. The composer, Mr. Gruenberg, has long been interested in the Negro idiom as the catalogue of his pieces disclose.

An unusual offering called "Processional," "A Jazz Symphony of American Life and a Rhapsody in Red" depicting life in a little American mining community, with a background of a jazz band, was sponsored by the Theatre Guild. Meanwhile, we find other indications of interest in Negro musical contributions. Pietro Mascagni, visiting America thirty years ago, said in 1903 of Negro songs, "They are real music and we Europeans have almost lost the sense of true music."

Chapter X

MUSICAL PIONEERS

Turning back the pages of history, we find it remarkable that in a period as early as from 1847 to 1876, had arisen a number of Negro musicians and singers whose work was of sufficient merit to demand recognition from the white press and from cultured people of the country. In various large centers such as New Orleans, Memphis, Philadelphia, Boston, New York City, and Detroit, groups of musicians who made a wide reputation as performers of dance music, rapidly arose. New Orleans, Philadelphia and Boston were the exceptional cities. Particularly in New Orleans, the home of the "French Opera," the group turned to the classics as their standard.

Eugene V. Macarty, a Negro musician of a century ago, has been remembered by historians of New Orleans. He was born in that city in 1821, and studied piano under J. Norres. In 1840, having won the interest of the French ambassador to the United States and Creole friends, he was accepted as a pupil in voice, harmony and composition at the Conservatoire Imperial in Paris. In his native home, he became known as a man of versatility. He was a singer who possessed a rich baritone voice, a composer of light music, an actor of ability, and a man of public affairs. He was also considered an excellent pianist.

Basile Barés, pianist and composer, was born in New Orleans, January 2, 1846. He was a student of piano under Eugene Prevost, at one time director of the French Opera House orchestra, and of harmony and composition under Professor Pedigram. During 1867, he spent some time in France and played in Paris, after which he returned home. His dance compositions, a number of which the author has in her collection, were very popular. They were published from 1869 to 1870. His salon pieces, in the style of that period, show an effective use of the ''glissando,'' an embellishment that was in vogue and often found in the Mexican and Spanish-Creole music of that section. His best-liked pieces were ''Les Cents Gardes,'' ''Minuit Polka de Salon,'' ''Basile's Galop,'' ''La Créole,'' ''Merry Fifty Lancers,'' ''Elodia,'' (polka mazurka), ''Violettes Waltz,'' ''Delphine Valse Brillante,'' ''La Capricieuse Valse,'' and ''Les Variétés du Carnival.''

Samuel Snaér, a versatile musician, was born in New Orleans about 1834. He played the violin, 'cello, organ and piano, and was organist at the Church Sainte-Marie, on Chartres Street. He possessed a good tenor voice, but did not sing professionally. Joseph A. Moret, a later violinist, was among his first pupils. While active as a teacher of piano and violin, he also devoted time to composition. His first work, ''Sous sa Fenêtre,'' was published by Louis Gruenwald. Desdunes spoke of Snaér as being excessively bashful. He did nothing to further his own career and preferred to live a retired life in New Orleans where he died.[1] A catalogue of his compositions include ''Rapelle-toi,'' ''Le Chant du Depart,'' ''Grand Scène Lyrique,'' ''Le Vampire,'' ''Graziella,'' (overture for orchestra), ''Le Bohemien,'' and ''Le Chant des Canotiers.'' Besides his orchestral pieces he wrote many in the dance forms of the day—polkas, waltzes, mazurkas and quadrilles. Barés was a man of fine literary tastes as well as a musician.

[1] Desdunes, R. L., *Nos Hommes et Notre Histoire*, Montreal, 1911.

The vocalists, Mrs. Lucy Adger and John Mills, with the violinists, F. J. R. Jones and Edward Johnson, and the pianist, M. Inez Cassey, were sponsors of oratorio societies. Sarah Sedgewick Bowers (later Mrs. Bell), was a fine singer; and according to the *Daily Pennsylvanian* of May 3, 1856, she was "endowed by nature with the wonderful gift of song." She gave recitals of operatic arias and classical songs in Philadelphia and New York and was active musically with her gifted brothers. The singer was a member of the well-known Negro families— the Turpins and the Howards, who maintained beautiful homes and fostered salon music in their social life. The most noted member of the musical Bowers family, was Sarah's younger brother, Thomas.

William Brady, who died in March, 1854, was actively engaged in composing songs and pieces in dance rhythms, —polkas, quadrilles, and waltzes—and also anthems and other pieces for church services. His "Anthem for Christmas," published in 1851, is among his best known compositions. James Hemmenway, composing light music about 1829, and A. J. Connor, composing and publishing music from 1846 to 1857, have been mentioned elsewhere.

Another composer of this period who also published music in Philadelphia, was the violinist, Edwin Hill, who was the first Negro to be admitted to the Philadelphia Academy of Fine Arts (1871). Among Mr. Hill's compositions, about thirty in number, one finds songs and anthems. His son, Edwin Hill, Jr., is now known among the local musicians as a teacher of violin and a choral conductor. He has written a number of sacred songs and piano pieces, and has arranged groups of spirituals. His "Keep Me from Sinking Down" is a prize piece written for violin.

Thomas J. Bowers, tenor, known as the "American Mario," was born in Philadelphia in 1836. His father was for many years, the warden of St. Thomas' Episcopal Church, which first opened its doors on July 17, 1794, under the guidance of Absalom Jones. This historic church was the outgrowth of a fellowship with the earlier "Free African Society" organized in 1787. It is of special interest to musicians in that much sacred music written about 1800 was composed for services of this church. An elder son, John C. Bowers, having received lessons in piano and organ, became organist of St. Thomas' Church. At the age of eighteen, Thomas, who had been taught by his brother, followed John as church organist. He then began the study of voice under Elizabeth Greenfield-Taylor and in 1854 appeared in a local concert as her pupil. Shortly afterwards, he was engaged for a concert tour and traveled in the eastern and middle western states. Colonel Wood, a former manager of the Cincinnati Museum, arranged concert appearances for him in New York and Canada. In Hamilton, a difficulty arose concerning the admission of a Negro party of six to first-class seats. The contention that Negroes were not allowed to occupy first-class seats in Canada, was protested by the purchaser, Dr. Brown. He was upheld by the singer, who refused to give the concert should there be any discrimination shown. His argument that he did not leave home to encourage racial prejudice won the point and established a principle for Bowers and his colleagues.

The Sedgwick Company with Bowers as the tenor soloist, was highly praised by the press. His repertoire included arias from the standard operas and songs from the oratorios of the old masters. It was said that he sang only those ballads that were of musical worth. The critics early called him the "American Mario" in comparison with the noted Signor Mario of that day.[2]   The Boston

[2] The Italian tenor, Conte di Candia Mario, was the most celebrated singer of that day.

THOMAS J. BOWERS

Journal spoke of him as "possessing a voice of wonderful power and beauty," while the reviewer of another paper wrote, "As most of our citizens have heard the 'colored Mario,' it is unnecessary for us to speak of his singing, as it is generally admitted that his tenor is second to none of our celebrated opera-singers."

The *Daily Pennsylvanian* of February 9, 1854, commented on a concert given by Bowers in Samson Street Hall in Philadelphia, and concluded that, "He has naturally a superior voice, far better than many of the principal tenors who have been engaged for star opera troupes. He has, besides, much musical taste." The author's informant, Dora Cole Lewis of Philadelphia and Boston, says that even in later life Bowers was a man of handsome appearance, well-dressed, and of fine stage deportment. Critics of that day spoke of certain mannerisms in the use of gestures; a habit which until recently has been deplored as being more fitting to the opera stage.

So much attention has been given to the folk songs of the illiterate and to Negro buffoonery, that few have realized how arduously the lone artists strove to achieve musical recognition. In a letter to a friend, Bowers in his maturity wrote, "What induced me more than anything else to appear in public was to give the lie to 'Negro serenaders' (minstrels), and to show to the world that colored men and women could sing classical music as well as the members of the other race by whom they had been so terribly villified."

Peter P. O'Fake, was a versatile musician who was active in New Jersey at this time. He was a skilful artist and became proficient on the flute and violin mainly through his own efforts. He was born of intelligent parents in Newark in 1820. At the age of twenty-seven he played a violin solo, De Beriot's "Sixth and Seventh Airs with Variations," at a concert given by the Jullien Society of New York. In spite of racial prejudice, O'Fake was often called upon to take part in the activities of various white musical organizations, and at one time he conducted the orchestra of the Newark Theatre (1848). The musician organized a small orchestra which was engaged for entertaining purposes by the wealthy citizens of Newark. His dance compositions, mainly those written for the popular quadrilles of the day, had a certain vogue, but were not of lasting value. In 1856, the musician became director of the choir of an Episcopal Church in Newark, a position which he held for some time.

Among the singers of the early period was Elizabeth Taylor-Greenfield who was born in Natchez, Mississippi, in 1809, brought to Philadelphia when one year old and reared by a Quaker lady, Mrs. Greenfield. Her musical gifts were early shown and encouraged. Following her patron's death in 1844, she went to Buffalo, New York. In October, 1851, she sang before the Buffalo Musical Association and was received with such acclaim that her voice was likened to those of Jenny Lind and Parodi; and the sobriquet "The Black Swan" was bestowed upon her.

The Buffalo *Express* said of her performance on this occasion, "On Monday, Parodi in all her splendor, sustained by Patti and Strakosch, sang at Corinthian Hall to half a house. Last night Miss Greenfield sang at the same place to a crowded house of respectable, cultured and fashionable people of the city. Jenny Lind has never drawn a better house, as to character, than that which listened with evident satisfaction to this unheralded and almost unknown African nightingale. Curiosity did something for her, but not all. She has merit, very good merit; and with cultivation she will rank among the very first vocalists of the age. She has a voice of great sweetness and power, with a wider range from the lowest to the highest notes than we have ever listened to; flexibility is not wanting, and her control of it is beyond example for an untaught vocalist. Her performance was received with marked approbation and applause from those who knew what to applaud.''

At Albany, New York, in January, 1852, she was heard in the lecture room of the Young Men's Christian Association before a representative audience which included Governor Hunt and his family, members of both houses of the Legislature and other State officials. On February 3, 1852, she sang in Boston at the Melodeon. The Boston *Evening Transcript* said, "She sings with great ease, and apparently without any effort. Her pronunciation is very correct, and her intonation excellent. Her voice has a wonderful compass, and in many notes is remarkably sweet in tone.''

After Miss Greenfield's tour of the Northern States, aided by New York music-lovers, she went to Europe with the hope of studying and of singing in public. She arrived in London on April 16, 1853. An interesting entry is found in the *Memoirs* or *Diary* of Harriet Beecher Stowe who was in London at the time Miss Greenfield arrived without funds. The singer was disappointed in a proposed concert management. Mrs. Stowe, learning of her, gave her her protection and introduced her to the Duchess of Sutherland who arranged a musical at the Stafford House. Of this reception James M. Trotter gives a most interesting account in his book *"Music and Some Highly Musical People."*

Miss Greenfield's success was immediate. The London *Times*, the *Morning Post* and the *Observer* commented on the range of her voice, its power and sweetness. Many concerts were given in London under the patronage of titled ladies, and on May 10, 1854, she was commanded to sing at Buckingham Palace for her Majesty, Queen

Victoria. Her accompaniments were played by Sir George
Smart, organist and composer to her Majesty's Chapel
Royal. The singer returned to America in July, 1854.
The New York *Herald,* referring to her stay abroad, said,
"The Swan now sings in true artistic style and the wonderful powers of her voice have been developed by good
training." Miss Greenfield then located in Philadelphia
where she opened a studio for vocal students. She died
in April, 1876.[3]

Some other interesting musicians of that time, the
Luca Family, consisting of the father and three sons,
made their home in Connecticut. Alexander C. Luca, the
father, was born in Milford in 1805. He became a shoe-
maker by trade and studied music in the village singing
school. He removed to New Haven, where he married a
Miss Lewis, who also possessed musical taste. For some
time he held the position of chorister in a Congregational
Church and at the same time organized a small concert
company with his wife, his sons, John and Alexander,
Dinah Lewis, his wife's sister, and himself.

The family had their first wide hearing at the May
anniversary of the Antislavery Society held in the Tabernacle in New York City in 1853. Young Cleveland was
then a member of the company and was called a "wonderful boy pianist." Their respective talents were John
W. Luca, the eldest son, bass-baritone and violinist; Alexander C., tenor and violinist; Simeon G., tenor and violinist; and Cleveland, pianist. The group traveled throughout New England and the Middle West until 1859. After
the death of Simeon in 1854, Jennie Allen of New York
joined the quartette.

The son Cleveland migrated to Liberia about 1860 and
composed the National Anthem of that country. He died

---

[3] *The Theatre Arts Monthly* published a rare old print of Elizabeth Greenfield in the issue of June, 1931. "The Grand Old Days."

there March 27, 1872. For some time the Luca Family became the associates of a white company known as the Hutchison Family. Later, John joined the celebrated Hyer Sisters, while Alexander directed another company. In September, 1857, the Niagara *Courier*, commenting on one of the Luca Family programs, said, "The introductory piece, Fantasia, from 'Lucia,' evinced the highest order of musical culture, the most excellent taste, with that superior power of execution which long practice only gives."

An instrumentalist of this period; Henry F. Williams, was born in Boston, August 13, 1813. He possessed natural talents, played many instruments, and was engaged by P. S. Gilmore of the celebrated Gilmore's Band. He wrote many pieces which were published by Oliver Ditson from 1842 to 1866. Among his compositions, most of which were of a sentimental order, was an anthem, the authenticity of which was doubted by the noted pedagogue, Lowell Mason. Finally admitting Mr. Williams as the composer, and impressed by his ability, Mason advised him to go to Liberia, Africa, in order to win recognition, as he felt that race prejudice would deter him in America. This advice he refused to heed.

A well remembered name is that of Justin Holland who was born in 1819, the son of a farmer, Exum Holland, who made his home in Norfolk County, Virginia. At the age of fourteen he came to Boston and located in Chelsea. He is said to have shown marked musical gifts at the age of eight; but, having no opportunity of furthering his love of music, he was overjoyed at the chance which came his way of taking guitar lessons under Simon Knaebel, a member of Kendall's Brass Band. He later took lessons with William Schubert, guitarist, and Pollock, flutist; and in 1841, recognizing the limitation of his general education, he went to Oberlin College. In 1845, he located in Cleveland, Ohio. There he gave guitar lessons and studied French, Italian and Spanish that he might have access to technical works on guitar playing, many of which were written in foreign languages. When living in Boston, he became entranced at the playing of Mariano Perez, a Spanish guitarist, who was heard with a visiting company at the Lion Theatre, and he determined to learn for himself how to explain how certain effects were produced. Holland had not at that time access to many scientific works which treat the subject of acoustics, and so he writes, "I . . . thus discovered the true theory of the harmonic tones to be the vibrations of a single string in a number of equal sections, more or less, and all at the same time; and that their production was at the pleasure of the operator as he desired higher or lower tones. Having fully verified my discoveries, I then corrected the erroneous theory on this subject of the great guitarist, F. Sor."

Before the publication of his instruction book, Holland made many arrangements of standard pieces for solo guitar, and wrote more than thirty-five original works. His publishers included John Church, Cincinnati; G. W. Brainard and D. P. Fauld, Louisville; and S. Brainard's Sons, Cleveland. His most important contribution is *Holland's Comprehensive Method for the Guitar*, which was published in 1874 by J. L. Peters of New York. An advance notice of the book contained a criticism from one Dressler of *The United States Musical Review* in which he said, "I must confess that it is already, in its present state, the best in this country; the most thorough, explicit, progressive, agreeable, and satisfactory work ever written in this country or in Europe. The method is very elaborate, and contains many points not heretofore touched on in works of the kind. Mr. Holland's abilities as a composer of music, and his skill as a performer upon the

JUSTIN HOLLAND

guitar, render him pre-eminently qualified to write such a work; and supplying, as it will, a want long felt, it will achieve popularity at once, we firmly believe.''

In 1876, a revised edition, *Holland's Modern Method for the Guitar*, was published by Oliver Ditson, Boston. According to that house, the book remains until today, the favorite method of guitar playing. For the composer's musical standing in 1877, as a result of these efforts, we turn to Carl Merz who wrote in the *Musical World* of that year, ''Mr. Holland is a great lover of art, a gentleman of culture who reads fluently several languages and whose labors are highly esteemed by publishers as well as by lovers of the guitar. He lives in Cleveland where he enjoys the patronage of the lovers of music, irrespective of color.''[4]

The guitarist lived a useful and full life. Apart from his teaching which included piano-forte instruction as well as that of the guitar and flute, we find him writing on matters of social reform as early as 1844. He numbered prominent young men and women among his pupils. The daughter-in-law of Governor Briggs of Massachusetts, formerly a Cleveland girl, and his son were of this group.

At this period, Cincinnati, Ohio, became a music-loving centre, mainly brought about by combined efforts of Negro musicians who worked together for enjoyment of the art. The Mozart Circle, of twenty-five members, directed by William H. Parham, was organized about 1875. Their first cantata, ''Daniel,'' was given in July, 1875, shortly

[4] *Der Freimaurer (The Freemason)*, a monthly published in Vienna, Austria, gave a biographical account of the musician, in 1877. Added to his interest in Masonry, Mr. Holland made good use of his knowledge of certain languages, by establishing a friendship between the colored Masons of Ohio and those of the Grand Lodges of Peru, Portugal, Spain, France and Germany. In 1878, the guitarist's young daughter, Clara Monteith Holland, began to be known as a pianist and a skilful player of the guitar.

followed by "Esther." The soloist was William H. Morgan. The Circle seems to have grown out of the choir of Allen Temple, which had been organized by the pastor, the Rev. Thomas H. Jackson, who was a singer. In 1857, a choir was organized by Rev. J. R. Bowles for his church in Chillicothe, and under the leadership of James D. Hackley, it became known as one of the best in Ohio.

From the first, the cause of good music and encouragement to Negro trained musicians, came from the Negro Church. This fact is probably unknown by writers who think of the church as fostering only religious "revival" tunes, shouts, and spirituals. In the East, the choirs afforded an outlet both for trained singers and Negro organists, even though in most instances it was a labor of love. The pioneer work of the majority of instrumentalists and vocalists, those who aspired to a concert career, was accomplished through church societies which were always willing to arrange a concert, for a division of the profits. For many years the Negro Church remained the artist's most willing "manager."

Interest in vocal and instrumental ensemble grew apace. About 1872, the Colored Opera Company was formed in Washington with John Esputa as musical director. On February 3 and 4, 1873, they gave "The Doctor of Alcantra," by Eichberg, in Lincoln Hall. Criticisms from *The Daily National Republican* and the Washington *Daily Chronicle* were favorable. The last named paper reported, "The full opera-dresses scattered liberally through the audience reminded one not a little of the scene at a concert by Carlotti Patti or the Theodore Thomas Orchestra. Quite a third of the audience was composed of white ladies and gentlemen, largely attracted, perhaps, by the novelty of the affair; and among them were many representatives of the musical circles of the city. . . . The choruses were effective. In dramatic ability there was

little lacking, and the singers were quite as natural as
many who appear in German and French opera.''

The principals in the Washington cast were Mrs. Agnes
Gray Smallwood, soprano; Lena Miller and Mary A. C.
Coakley, contraltos; Henry F. Grant and Richard Tomp-
kins, tenors; William T. Benjamin and George Jackson,
baritones, with Thomas H. Williams, bass. Mrs. Smallwood received special praise for her "beautiful ringing
voice, dramatic method, and carriage of unusual grace.''
The company appeared in Philadelphia on February 21,
1873, at Horticultural Hall and was highly praised by
the Philadelphia *Inquirer,* which said of their chorus,
"Their singing is really unsurpassed by the finest chorus
in the best companies.'' Other papers were equally impressed by the efforts of this little group of ambitious
singers, who gave later performances in Ford's Theatre
in Washington.

In Boston, Nellie Brown Mitchell organized a Juvenile
Operetta Company which gave their first performances
on May 16 and 17, 1876, at a "Centennial Musical Festival'' which she herself originated. The group, augmented by local talent, gave a performance in Haverhill
on the thirteenth of December of that year. For some
years, Mrs. Mitchell presented juvenile groups which she
and her sister trained.

The Philharmonic Society of New York City which
was organized in 1876, had a junior division in which
youth with musical taste were required to study and pass
a test before being admitted to the senior section that appeared in public performances. P. H. Loveridge conducted the society of twenty members, that included Walter F. Craig, first violinist; William Lewis, 'cellist; P.
Williams, flutist; and Elmore Bartelle, cornetist.

An earlier ensemble was the Progressive Musical Union
of Boston, organized about 1875. For their first public

concert given March 9, of that year, the president, Elijah
W. Smith, wrote the following poem:

"Progressive: ay, we hope to climb
    With patient steps fair Music's height,
And at her altar's sacred flame
    Our care-extinguished torches light;
And, while their soft and cheering rays
    Life's rugged path with joys illume,
May Harmony's enchanted wand
    Bring sunshine where before was gloom!

And though we may not walk apace
    With Mendelssohn or Haydn grand,
Nor view with undimmed eyes the mount
    Where Mozart's shining angels stand;
Yet in the outer courts we wait
    Till knowledge shall the curtain draw,
And to our wondering eyes disclose
    The mysteries the master saw."

Musical New Orleans remembers with pride the "Philharmonic Society" which was in existence about that
time. It was composed of a group of trained musicians
under the direction of experienced conductors such as
Constantin Deberque and Richard Lambert. The latter
musician, a teacher of music, was the father of the talented Lambert brothers. The Philharmonic, an all Negro
group of instrumentalists, was organized for the study
and presentation of the classics.

While meritorious concert performances were being
given by trained Negro virtuosos before 1846, brass bands
were also organized simultaneously with the growing musical associations. Many bands were the outgrowth of small
orchestras. The most noted of these was known as "Frank
Johnson's Band" which was organized by a man of that
name in Philadelphia. As an orchestral and band conductor he toured the United States with his own group from
1839 to 1841, played before Queen Victoria in 1841, and

returned to continued popularity in this country. Johnson was a skilful performer on the bugle besides playing
many other instruments. He died in Philadelphia in
1846, and at his funeral, the silver bugle presented to
him by the English queen, was placed under the casket.
The organization was continued under the leadership of
Joseph G. Anderson, and the band was heard on tour
until his death in 1874. After that turn in affairs it became
known as the Excelsior Band. "Frank Johnson's Band"
created considerable comment at the time of its conception, in that all the members were good sight-readers.

As early as 1855, an Ohio Band known as the "Scioto-
Valley Brass Band" was organized under the leadership
of Richard Chancellor and John Jones of Chillicothe. The
"Roberts Band" was organized in 1857 under the directorship of William Davis and Thomas Harris. In 1859,
with Thomas Harris and A. J. Vaughn, leaders, a combination of the earlier, original groups, the "Union Valley
Brass Band," became noted throughout Ohio. William
H. Starr, a performer on brass instruments and a teacher,
was the director.

William H. Dupree, born in Petersburg, Virginia, first
a cab driver at the Court House, later a distinguished
citizen of Boston, was a member and manager of this
band until 1863, when he went East and enlisted in the
Negro Fifty-fourth Regiment. There he became manager
of the regimental band.[5] During the Civil War, John
Moore was leader of the Fifty-fifth Regiment Band. He
died in Philadelphia in 1871.

In Baltimore, before 1878, C. A. Johnson, an organist
and concert promoter, added to his musical reputation as
conductor of "The Monumental Cornet Band." There

[5] Lieut. Dupree, for long one of the most influential patrons of
music in Boston, passed away June 22, 1934, at the age of 95, in
Neponset, Boston.

were a number of competent band directors in Boston, among whom were James L. Edwards, Francis P. Cleary, and George W. Sharper. The latter directed the "Excelsior Brass Band" which later became known as "The Boston Brass Band." Sharper, a barber by trade, was an excellent cornetist. In the far South, "Kelly's Band" and the "St. Bernard Brass Band," of New Orleans, were trained and conducted by E. Lambert who performed on several instruments.

Certain cities tended to become popular as centers with Negroes conspicuous in music. Old programs of the year 1874 bear the names of the best remembered pioneer musicians of Boston. At this time the pianist, Samuel W. Jamison, was at the height of his popularity. Jamison was born in Washington, D. C., in 1855, and died in Boston in February, 1930. He began his studies in Boston at the age of eleven as the pupil of James M. Tracy and F. K. Boscovitz, a Hungarian pianist. He later studied under B. J. Lang, and had the distinction of playing with the Boston Symphony Orchestra. In 1876 he was graduated from the Boston Conservatory, but was heard in concerts a year earlier when he received praise for his Chopin and Liszt interpretations. Jamison, who later devoted his time to teaching pianoforte, remained a brilliant pianist until his death.

Benjamin J. Janey, tenor, a private pupil of New England Conservatory professors, a flutist as well as a favorite singer, was often heard in duets from the Italian operas with Nellie Brown (later Mrs. Brown Mitchell) and Fannie A. Washington, a local contralto singer, who had a measure of Conservatory training. Duet and quartette singing flourished in that day. A popular combination included Miss Brown, Miss Washington, Mr. Janey and Mr. Fisher. Harry Fisher, baritone, and Wallace King, tenor, appeared in concerts on tour, as did the Stewart

Concert Company composed of Hamilton Hodges, George H. Barnett, and the William E. Lew Quartette. Of this younger group, Hodges became internationally known as a fine and artistic singer. A sketch of his career may be found among the early interpretative musicians.

One of the best known pianoforte teachers about 1877, Rachel M. Washington, organist and pianist, was the first Negro graduate of the old Boston Conservatory. Apart from her teaching, she held the post of organist at the old historic (Negro) Twelfth Baptist Church of Boston.

James Caseras, pianist and organist, was one of the best organists in the East. His musical training was received abroad before coming to this country from England, sometime before 1877. He held the post of organist at a Catholic Church in Springfield, Massachusetts, for some years, and also appeared as a pianist in Boston.

David T. Oswald, of Worcester, a finished violinist, was known from Boston to New Brunswick, as a promoter of first class musical entertainments, as well as for the excellence of his public playing.

Frederick Elliot Lewis, born in 1846, was a well-known musician of Boston. His father, of New England birth, was a performer on the flute, piano-forte, 'cello and violin, while his mother was a choir singer. He took his first lessons in piano from his mother. About the age of twelve he began the study of the organ and harmony and continued his piano lessons under Rachel Washington. A most gifted and eager student, he afterwards studied other instruments under local teachers. In 1861, he made his debut as a violinist in a concert given in New Bedford. While a student of the organ, Lewis tested organs for Hook and Hastings, organ manufacturers.

His purpose in studying so many instruments was carried out that he might be the better fitted to write orchestral and band music. Lewis was a member of the large orchestra that played at the World's Peace Jubilee held in Boston in 1872. From 1861 until 1878 he was engaged in arranging and composing music for piano, orchestra and band. His Fantasia for piano, Opus 3, is in the style of Gottschalk's pianoforte pieces. For some years he maintained a well equipped studio and enjoyed the association of the prominent musicians of the city. He was a member of white music societies, one of which was the Haydn and Mozart Club of Chelsea, an instrumental group which he sometimes conducted as first violinist. He also enjoyed the esteem of the musicians Julius Eichberg, director of the Boston Conservatory (at that time), and P. S. Gilmore, the band director.

John T. Douglas, violinist, was born in New York City, 1847. He studied in New York and in Europe, and is remembered as a devoted lover of music. He gave David Mannes (now a celebrated violinist of New York) his first violin lessons when he was a young lad without means. Mr. Mannes has not ignored the favor of his Negro teacher. Douglas was acquainted with several instruments, but was known as a fine guitarist as well as a proficient violinist. He composed many pieces for orchestra and for piano. Those that the author of this volume has examined are in the salon style of the "eighties." For some years the musician traveled, and taught music in New York where he died a few years ago. Like many ambitious musicians, he met with frustrations which saddened his later years.

In the East, the De Wolf Sisters, Sadie and Rosa, soprano and contralto, became known as singers of exceptional merit. They were born in Charlotte, North Caroline, but early came to Boston where they were heard in Sunday night concerts and as members of "Walker's Quintet." For two years they were engaged on a vaudeville circuit, after which they joined Sam Jack's Creole Company, August 4, 1890. The sisters retired after twelve years' stage experience in a refined type of vaudeville that would illy fit the coarse acts which gradually found a wide public. Rosa De Wolf died in Boston on May 23, 1917.

A remarkable musical prodigy of the "eighties" was the phenomenon, Thomas Greene Bethune, known as "Blind Tom." He was born without sight, in Columbus, Georgia, on May 25, 1849, and was of unmixed blood. He possessed absolute pitch, an unerring ear and a marvelous memory. He was said to have a repertoire of seven thousand pieces which he had learned by having them played to him. He traveled extensively and created a stir in America and in Europe. A review in *Music and Drama,* New York, appearing on June 3, 1882, said, "To write Tom's performance down as worthless and inartistic, was to fly in the face of facts. . . . Many a country piano teacher could have learned from him something about the production of good tone and the proper use of the pedals."

Of those especially gifted persons whose contribution was of real musical value to the race, we find two sisters, Anna Madah, and Emma Louise Hyers, who at the age of seven and nine years showed a predilection for music to such a degree that they were placed under a German instructor in Sacramento, California, the city of their birth. They were students of voice and piano, and languages. Later they received instruction from Josephine d'Ormy. Their parents refused to allow them to appear in public until their debut on April 22, 1867, when they were presented before an audience of eight hundred at the Metropolitan Theatre in Sacramento.

In speaking of their remarkable voices, the press mentioned sweetness and purity of Madah's voice as shown in her singing of "Costa Diva," and Verdi's "Fors e' lui che l'anima,'' and of the fine contralto possessed by Louise. Their father, who seems to have shown considerable wisdom in furthering his talented daughters' careers, insisted upon further study before allowing them to undertake an extended tour. On August 12, 1871, they made an impression at a concert given in the Salt Lake City Theatre. They were assisted by a baritone by the name of Le Count. The first part of the program was devoted to selections from the first and second acts of Donizetti's opera "Linda di Chamounix." The western press, particularly the daily papers of Missouri, Illinois and Ohio, praised the singers widely in reviews, which if space permitted, would be interesting to reprint as examples of musical criticism of that period. Anna's singing of E flat above the staff with the greatest ease, and her bird-like trills, caused her to be likened to Jenny Lind, while Emma's voice was said to be one of remarkable quality and richness "rarely heard."

The father, who traveled with the sisters, engaged Wallace King of Camden, New Jersey, who was the rising tenor of the day, and John Luca, the baritone of New Haven, as assistant artists. Concerts were given at the Young Men's Christian Association Hall in Brooklyn, New York, and at Steinway Hall in New York City. The audiences were cultured, the halls crowded and the criticisms flattering. The New York *Tribune* said, "These are two young colored girls who have received a musical training in California, and who are by no means mere 'Jubilee' singers, as the programme of last evening clearly shows." The press commented on the "high order of music, operatic and otherwise" which was performed, and of their voices a reviewer in the New York *Evening Post* wrote, "Miss Anna Hyers possesses a flexible voice of great compass, clear and steady in the higher notes. Miss Emma, the contralto, has a voice of great power and depth; qualities which, in impassioned strains, give it a richness not often heard in chamber concerts.'' Wallace King's singing was spoken of as ''exquisite.''

After the Boston concert, where they sang before Eben Tourgée (who became director of the New England Conservatory of Music), P. S. Gilmore and other musical people, the Boston *Journal* said of the tenor, ''Mr. Wallace King has a pure, sweet tenor voice of remarkable compass, and sings with excellent taste.'' After appearances at the hall called the Meionaon, in Tremont Temple, the sisters remained in Boston for some time, in order to continue their musical training, after which they traveled throughout New England where they commanded crowded houses. King continued to receive special notice, and attention, too, was given to ''the combination of the voices in some wonderfully fine four-part singing. Luca, the baritone, also sang duets with King. Again following a concert at Mechanic's Hall at Worcester, the ensemble was complimented. The *Daily Press* said that ''the quartette singing was unaccompanied, and was the finest that has been heard in this city for years. The voices blended beautifully, and were full of expression.''

The sisters were engaged to sing at the Peace Jubilee concerts in Boston. They remained in this section and in 1875 filled engagements at the Boston Theatre where they appeared in the Sunday night ''sacred'' concerts, with an orchestra of forty pieces, conducted by the white orchestral leader, Napier Lothian. The custom of noting the number of recalls has not changed with the years, for we read of the delight of an audience that insisted upon thirteen encores.

Two years later, about 1877 and 1878, the Misses Hyers widened their activities by taking part in a drama, ''Out of Bondage,'' a play in four acts written expressly for them by a white writer, Joseph B. Bradford of Boston.

Samuel Lucas (Milady) was a member of this company when they toured throughout the West in 1878. Miss Celestine O. Browne of Jamestown, New York, was the pianist.

Emma Louise Hyers died some years ago. Anna Madah Hyers became the wife of Dr. Fletcher of Sacramento. Visiting California in December, 1920, the author had an opportunity to call on Mrs. Fletcher. In the autumn of her life, she lived quietly, but was actively interested in art music, especially as it pertained to the Church. She was most gracious in showing souvenirs of her happy career.

Nellie E. Brown (Mitchell), soprano, who was born in Dover, New Hampshire, early came under the tutelage of Miss Caroline Bracket, a vocal teacher of Dover, who advised her to prepare for a public career. In 1865 she began her life time service as a church singer as a member of the Free-will Baptist Church (white) of Dover. In November, 1872, the young soprano was engaged as soloist of the Grace Church, Haverhill, Massachusetts. After four years as salaried singer she resigned to accept an engagement as director of the choir of the new Methodist Episcopal Church in her native city. Since 1874 she had "commuted" between the two cities, in order to sing leading soprano parts in the latter choir. Before this, she came regularly to Boston in order to study at the New England Conservatory and counted Mme. J. Rametti and Professor O'Neill among her teachers. In November, 1874, she sang in Steinway Hall, New York City, with much success and appeared in concerts from Canada to Washington, D. C.

The New York papers spoke of her beauty of voice and "rare charm of manners." During the year of 1876 she was actively engaged in organizing groups of young people for musical presentations. In July of the same year she was engaged to sing at the Sunday School Parliament held on the island of Wellesley, in the St. Lawrence River. The soprano not only conducted some of the programs, but she was also one of the leading soloists together with P. P. Bliss, the well-known writer of sacred songs, and his wife who was also a singer.

During her career Nellie Brown had the distinction of being the leading soprano of four leading white churches in Boston, among which were the Winthrop Street Church of Roxbury and the Bromfield Street Church. She married Lieut. Charles L. Mitchell of the famous Negro regiment, the Fifty-fifth Massachusetts, whom she survived. After retiring from the concert stage, she devoted her time to teaching and singing in local affairs. While her first recognition was gained as a singer of French songs and Italian operatic arias, she did the old Scotch and Irish songs particularly well. Her later reputation was sustained by her charming singing of high-class ballads. Until her death which occurred in Boston in January, 1924, Nellie Brown Mitchell maintained the gracious sweetness of her manner, and an amiability and willingness to encourage younger musicians.

Flora Batson was a younger singer who was born in Providence, Rhode Island, in 1870. She possessed a remarkable soprano voice of great range as well as sweetness. As a ballad singer, she traveled throughout the United States, in Europe, Australia, and New Zealand and touched African soil. In 1887 she organized a concert company, and on the twenty-first of March of that year, she was heard and acclaimed at Music Hall, Boston, after which she became popular on southern tours for her high class entertainments. She was engaged as a soloist for a large temperance revival in New York where she sang for three months. At the height of her career she married Mr. Bergen, a white business man, who for sometime was her manager. She died suddenly in Philadelphia, on December 2, 1906.

As early as 1876 Negroes of culture were working in the furtherance of good music in Cincinnati. To this point many white fathers in the South sent their manumitted mulatto offspring, before the days of emancipation. Here, one of these, Fannie Adams, a vocalist and teacher of piano, was received as a member of the Cincinnati Choral Society and another, John F. Ransom, baritone, active in white and colored musical circles, labored as organist and choral conductor. In 1870 he played the organ at Olivet Baptist Church in Chicago. He has for long been identified with local musicians in Boston as an earnest teacher.

There were many other musicians of unquestioned ability who were active. McDonald Repanti, of New Orleans, who studied piano under his brother, Fierville Repanti, a teacher and composer who went to Paris where he died before 1878, became a well-known pianist before making his home in Mexico. Maurice J. B. Doublet, who studied violin under L. Gabici, was born in New Orleans in 1831. His son, J. M. Doublet, who was born in 1860, was one of his talented pupils. Thomas Martin was one of the noted guitarists of this section, and taught both white and black pupils. Charles Martinez was another guitarist and violinist who was an experienced player of other instruments. He died about 1878. Dennis Auguste, who was born in 1850, was educated by Col. Félix Labatut, who had the talented boy study with Eugene Prévost after having lessons under Richard Lambert and Professor Rolling. Joseph Mansion, of a well-known Creole family, was an excellent amateur violinist. He, of a family of educators, was a member of the House of Representatives.

An interesting figure in the musical life of Boston for

a long time was Mrs. Arianna Cooley Sparrow, who was the daughter of the pretty quadroon whom Harriet Beecher Stowe depicted as one of her characters in her *Uncle Tom's Cabin*. Mrs. Sparrow sang in the Tremont Temple Choir, and later was the soprano of the Berkeley Street Church quartette. For a long time she was a member of the Handel and Haydn Society. Due to excellent training under the well-known teacher, H. L. Whitney, Mrs. Sparrow retained the natural sweetness of her voice and purity of tone that enabled her to sing acceptably in St. Augustine Episcopal Church, Boston, when over eighty years of age.

In Philadelphia, art music was cultivated by earnest musicians such as Margaret Jones (grandmother of the sculptress, Meta Warrick Fuller), Hans Shadd, Daniel Purvis and the Mastens—Margaret, Sarah, and the brother, Daniel. This group of amateur musicians, educated and refined, fostered the love of oratorio singing, and made possible a wider appreciation of the professional musician. Sarah Masten (Lewis) who died July 28, 1931, won an award in the National Musical Contest held at New York City in 1878. As early as 1839, however, talented persons were studying and performing in the Quaker City. William Appo, long active as a teacher and at one time one of the principal members of the excellent "Frank Johnson's Band," also taught music in New York City, and by the year of 1878, had retired to a quiet life on his farm.

In Boston, the New England Conservatory attracted many of these earnest Negro students of music, a number of whom became church singers. Georgina Smith, who later became the wife of Dr. G. F. Grant, and whose daughter Mabel became in turn a church organist, filled the post as organist of the North Russell Street Church, the mother of the present African Methodist Episcopal Zion

Church. She studied voice at the New England Conservatory and appeared in the public concerts of the school. The Boston *Globe* and the *Journal* spoke of her fine stage presence, her pure, sweet soprano, and the manner of her singing "which could but receive the warmest plaudits."

The younger daughter of Mr. and Mrs. John J. Smith of Boston,[6] Adelaide Smith Terry, equalled her sister Georgina as a favorite singer forty to fifty years ago. W. H. Copeland, tenor, and B. J. Janey, flutist, both having studied voice under teachers of the New England Conservatory, met with some measure of success. Mrs. Phoebe A. Glover and her sister, Mrs. Hester C. Jeffreys, made an enviable local reputation as the "Whitehurst Sisters." They were the daughters of a musically gifted mother, and their inherited vocal gifts were enhanced by cultivation and training. Mrs. Glover in turn gave her daughter, Georgine, a thorough musical education at the Boston Conservatory, where she was a pupil of Petersilea. She is today a teacher of piano in Boston.

The greatest of the Negro prima-donnas of yesterday was Mme. Marie Selika (Mrs. Sampson Williams). About 1879, while visiting in San Francisco, California, Mrs. Frances Bailey Gaskin heard the young soprano sing; and, recognizing the exceptional quality of her voice, the former persuaded her to come to Boston. This she did, and while making her home with Mrs. John B. Bailey, the mother of Mrs. Gaskin, she continued her studies and became proficient in German, French and Italian.

In 1880 Mrs. Williams gave concerts in various centers and under the efficient management of Lieut. Dupree, who aided and encouraged many young struggling Negro artists, she created a furore by her marvelous coloratura singing. For a stage name she took that of "Selika," the

[6] John J. Smith was one of the first Negro members in the Massachusetts Legislature.

MADAME SELIKA

heroine of Meyerbeer's opera, *L'Africaine*. A fine testimonial concert was arranged for her by John Boyle O'Reilly, who was a personal friend of John Bailey.

Soon afterwards Madame Selika visited Europe with her husband, who was an aspiring baritone singer, known as "Viloski." She achieved immediate success. The Paris *Figaro* said, "Madame Selika sang in great style. She has a very strong voice of depth and compass, rising with perfect ease from C to C, and she trills like a feathered songster. Her range is marvelous and her execution and style of rendition show perfect cultivation. Her 'Echo Song' cannot be surpassed. It was beyond any criticism. It was an artistic triumph."

Of her appearance in Berlin, the *Tagblatt* reviewer wrote, "The concert by Mme. Selika was given yesterday before a well filled house, and this distinguished artist gave us a genuine pleasure. Mme. Selika, with her singing roused the audience to the highest pitch of enthusiasm, and after her first aria, she was twice recalled, and could quiet the vociferous applause only by rendering a selection with orchestral accompaniment. Of this wonderful singer we can only say that she is endowed with a voice of surpassing sweetness and extraordinary compass. With her pure tones, her wonderful trills and roulades, her correct rendering of the most difficult intervals, she not only gains the admiration of amateurs but also that of professional musicians and critics."

After some years of successful concertizing, Mme. Selika and her husband located at Philadelphia. Mr. Williams, the soprano's husband, has been described by those who knew him as having a fine stage presence and a charming manner. His voice, however, was far inferior to that of Mme. Selika, whose desire that he be engaged on joint programs with her, often caused her to lose excellent opportunities. After Mr. Williams' death which occurred in Philadelphia about fifteen years ago, his devoted wife went to New York City where she has for the past few years been a teacher of voice at the Martin-Smith School of Music in Harlem.

Frederick P. White, a cultivated musician of Boston, was born in Providence, Rhode Island. Among his instructors was the noted teacher, B. J. Lang. White began his career as accompanist for Mme. Selika and finally became one of the best accompanists of more recent years. Upon one occasion, when Mme. Selika's trunk and box of music had been delayed, on concert tour, White played the entire program of operatic arias and songs, without notes. His talent embraced more than a gift of good memory, as can be seen from later criticisms. For over twenty-five years, he was organist at the (white) Methodist Episcopal Church in Charlestown, Massachusetts. He is now organist and teacher of piano in Boston.

William E. Lew, an associate of Frederick P. White, was one of the most progressive musicians of a group that fostered both solo and ensemble work. Of an old New England family, he is a direct descendant of Barzilia Lew, a Negro musician in the army of King George, who took part in the French and Indian War and the Revolutionary War as a member of the Continental Army. The author has had the privilege of examining the original papers granted by the English king.

William E. Lew and his sister, Edith, soprano (afterwards to become Mrs. Frederick White), played music for four hands and sang duets as children entertainers at church and society affairs. Apart from the study of piano, voice and harmony, he began the practise of choral directing as early as 1884. At that time Wallace King was director of the African Methodist Episcopal Zion Church choir, with Alice Thibeau, organist. There Mr. Lew directed cantatas, and also sang at the Twelfth Baptist

Church where Rachel Washington was organist with John R. McClenny, chorister.

Shortly after this, William E. Lew, now an excellent tenor, gave up local work as a chorister and organist in Cambridge, to join the Sam Lucas Concert Company of Boston.[7] In such work he continued with this and other agencies until 1887. From 1888 to 1900, he directed glee clubs, choirs, and special quartettes. In 1903, Mr. Lew joined the original Smart Set Company as chorus conductor. He was the first Negro musician to direct a white orchestra on a southern tour. Since 1906, he has devoted his time to teaching—first at southern colored institutions, and more recently in New York, where he is a pianoforte instructor in public schools, favoring the new class method of teaching. Mr. Lew is treasurer of the Oxford Piano Teachers Association of New York, of which Allen C. Albee is president. He is the only Negro member of the After School Piano Forum.

By 1913, twenty years ago, an over-lapping new group of earnest musicians labored conscientiously to increase an appreciation for good music by Negro audiences, and to

[7] Other members apart from Mr. Lucas, included Miss Carrie Melvin of Providence (later Mrs. Lucas), violinist and cornetist; Wallace King, tenor; James Waddy, basso; the De Wolf Sisters and the lately formed Lew ensemble. This was the well known Lew Male Quartette which consisted of J. Bunch Stanton, first tenor; W. E. Lew, second tenor; M. Hamilton Hodges, first bass; and George H. Barnett, second bass. For several seasons the successful company traveled throughout New England under the management of the Redpath Lyceum Bureau. In 1887 the Bureau sent the quartette to the Stewart Grand Concert Company of Madison, Wisconsin, for two seasons, and in 1888 presented them at Chautauqua assemblies. Between 1884 and 1886, the Lew Quintette, with Miles G. Minor and Paul Desmond, became an attraction of the Redpath Bureau, and sang for the Young Men's Christian Association and other such audiences. When Mr. Hodges went to Australia in 1896, Edward Rollins became the first bass.

win recognition for colored interpreters of classic music. Of these Mme. Estelle Pinckney Clough, of Worcester, a dramatic soprano, who was heard on concert tours and in amateur operatic productions, and Mme. E. Azalia Hackley of Detroit, were prominent. In recent years, Mrs. Clough maintained a successful studio of voice in Worcester and enjoyed a large white clientele. For a number of years she was heard in leading roles in the operas fostered by Theodore Drury. In 1900, this manager, a tenor, organized a semi-professional company under the name of the Drury Opera Company, and for thirty-three years, he has intermittently given standard operas in Boston, Providence, Philadelphia and New York. "Carmen" was sung at the Lexington Avenue Opera House in 1900. In May, 1901, the New York papers gave space to the production of *Il Guarany*, the best known opera written by the Negro composer, Gomez. Mr. Drury appeared as the Indian chief, Péry. The orchestra was composed of Negro musicians. On May 11, 1903, *Aida* was produced in New York with Estelle Pinckney Clough in the title role, George L. Ruffin as Amonasro, and Drury as Radames.

In the Spring of 1934, Trinity Church, Boston, Massachusetts, honored Ruffin[8] upon the completion of fifty years' continuous membership in the choir. When about 8 years of age, then singing in the boy's choir under direction of J. C. D. Parker, Phillips Brooks noted the remarkable sweetness of his voice. He sang at the Church of the Advent until his voice changed, when at the age of sixteen, he returned to Trinity Episcopal Church, and sang consecutively under direction of Horatio Parker, Wallace Goodrich, Ernest Mitchell and Mr. Snow. Ruffin is an organist as well as a singer, and apart from his singing at Trinity Church, he plays the organ in St. Augustine's

[8] George L. Ruffin was born in Boston, the son of Judge George L. Ruffin and Mrs. Josephine St. Pierre Ruffin.

Church. He was the first Negro member of the Handel and Haydn Society, and is among the senior tenors of the noted Boston "Cecilia Society." He formerly took leading roles in amateur operatic productions.

Dekoven Thompson, a well-known musician of Chicago, was born in St. Louis, Missouri, in 1879, the son of Rev. James E. Thompson, who removed to Chicago when the boy was two years of age. He passed away in New York City on May 26, 1934. He was the writer of many successful ballads, the best remembered of which include "Love Comes But Once" and "A Heart Disclosed" which were sung by Mme. Schumann-Heink. "If I Forget" is also sung by the famous contralto.

William H. Bush, organist, was born in New London, Connecticut, February 15, 1861. He is the son of a mechanic, Aaron Bush, and a musical mother who was encouraged to give her son lessons under Charles B. Jennings of New London. When a young man, he was given cast off parts of old organs by a Negro organ builder, Preston Hamilton, and made a pipe organ for himself. When eighteen years of age he was permitted to use the organ of the (white) First Congregational Church and until his twenty-third year, he studied organ, English and German under private instructors. An opportunity to prove his ability as an organist came when Jennings, because of a disabled hand was unable to play, and in an emergency he was called in to take the place of his teacher as church organist. After six months he was engaged by the Methodist (white) Church at a salary of one hundred and fifty dollars a year. Continuing to perfect himself in the study of composition and musical theory as well as organ, he finally became organist at the Second Congregational Church, the richest in the city.

Bush went weekly to New York for study with Dr. Samuel Warren and in 1887 gave his first recital at Grace

Church, New York. With the assistance of Dr. Warren, he gave annual concerts for thirty-five years. Bush was made chorister as well as organist at the Congregational Church. In 1904 he was chosen as one of the musicians to represent his state at the St. Louis Exposition where he played before an audience of five thousand persons. The organist is a lover of Bach. As a teacher he has been most successful. He is a member of the American Guild of Organists.

M. Hamilton Hodges, baritone, of Boston, possessed fine natural talent. He began his musical activities as first bass in the Lew Male Quintette. Hodges then joined the Stewart Concert Company and traveled extensively through the Middle West. He later joined the McAdoo Jubilee Singers, the leader of whom was a fine bass singer. After traveling abroad with this company, he settled in Auckland, New Zealand, in 1896, and there he became prominent as a concert singer and teacher of voice.

In 1898 Hodges returned to this country on a visit, and gave many recitals in and about Boston. Here he won favorable criticisms from the distinguished American critic, Philip Hale of the Boston *Herald* and other reviewers of note. He was assisted by Frederick P. White, accompanist. The excellence of the two artists may be comprehended by this criticism by H. T. Parker, musical editor, which appeared in the Boston *Evening Transcript*, of January 26, 1910.

"In a group of songs by Schubert, two by Strauss and Von Fielitz, a group of French songs by Masse, Bemberg and Goddard, and English songs by Mallinson and Wallace, Mr. Hodges used a baritone voice of great richness, full of subtle inflections, full of adjustments of tone to the mood of the songs, and with reserves of great power and sonority. When he used the soft tones of his middle register, as he was invited to do by several of the lighter songs, it was without a hint of monotony. He gave his

sotto voice as varied a color as his full voice. This effect
brought to Mallinson's song 'Four by the Clock,' the
vague and eerie quiet of the moments that precede the
dawn, and left in due prominence the rhythm of the pianoforte accompaniment which marches to the regularity of
the pendulum's swing or the sifting of sands in the hour
glass.

"Two others of the group of songs by Mallinson compelled admiration for their music, for the singing and for
the work of the accompanist. Mr. Frederick P. White
made the accompaniment what it rarely is in a recital of
any kind—an integral part of the performance."

The year 1912 found Mr. Hodges in New Zealand. In
December of that year he sang the part of "Mephisto-
phles" in a performance of Gounod's *Faust* given in
oratorio form by the Wellington Musical Union of Australia. His services were in demand as an oratorio singer
in many parts of the country. In 1913, he was engaged to
sing in the *Messiah* which was produced by the Finding Choral Society, and in Coleridge-Taylor's *A Tale of
Old Japan*, which was given by the Wellington Royal
Choral Society.

In February, 1913, he gave exacting programs with such
excellence that the New Zealand *Free Lance* said of
his recitals, "Mr. Hodges is helping to raise the standard
of musical taste in this community, for he includes nothing
tawdry in his program. He has a cultured, artistic judgment, and as he is always on the alert for new music of a
high standard, we are indebted to him for a knowledge of
many fine songs." In 1925, Mr. Hodges returned to Boston, where he died in 1928, at the age of 59.

Joseph Douglass, violinist and orchestral conductor, is
the grandson of Frederick Douglass. He was born in
Washington, D. C., on July 3, 1871. After studying with
local teachers, he entered the New England Conservatory
of Music in Boston as a student of the violin. Further
study was followed abroad. Returning to the United

States from London, he arranged many concerts under his own management and was heard for a long period in violin recitals throughout this country. His concert work was interrupted to accept the charge of the violin department of the Music School Settlement for Colored People in New York. He later resumed concert playing and then became a teacher of violin in the Howard University Music Department. He later conducted a theatre orchestra in Washington and taught privately. He died in 1935.

Leonard Jeter, now a matured 'cellist, was born in Newport, Rhode Island. He was one of a musical family. He was a pupil of Schroder, and later of Leo Schulz. For a long time Jeter was active as a concert artist. He makes his home in New York City, where he is engaged in orchestral practise. His playing is that of a thorough musician.

Mme. Siseretta Jones, another artist, was born in Portsmouth, Virginia, but came to Providence, Rhode Island, over 66 years ago. She died June 24, 1933. When a young woman she developed a remarkable dramatic soprano voice. She was soon engaged for a tour to South America and the West Indies. Returning to this country after two years spent in travel, Mme. Jones was engaged as principal artist at the Madison Square Garden Jubilee from April 26 to 28, 1892. Following this successful appearance the soprano was booked to appear with Levy's Band at a number of white expositions. At this time a theatrical paper, *The New York Clipper* spoke of her singing as that of "The Black Patti." Her maiden name, however, was Matilda S. Joyner.

Other engagements followed. Mme. Jones appeared at the Pittsburgh exposition as soloist with Gilmore's Band in 1893, under the management of Major Pond, when she was said to have received two thousand dollars for one week's engagement. She later appeared at the White

House by the invitation of President Harrison. Other invitations for private musicals followed; and she sang at the homes of Chief Justice Fuller, Senator Andrews and other distinguished persons. Traveling throughout Europe, Mme. Jones was received by royalty and met with much success. She was later director of the Black Patti Troubadours, heard mainly in Western and Southern cities for nineteen years. The two principal performers in this company were Bob Cole, as "Willie Wayside," the tramp, and Billy Johnson, in descriptive songs. "The Spanish Review" was a favorite number.

Sidney Woodward was one of the finest tenors that the race has produced. He was born on a Georgia plantation October 16, 1860. Early orphaned, he encountered many hardships while working his way through school. In 1889, by the assistance of Miss Clark, a student of Frank E. Morse of Boston, who heard the young man sing in Peoria, Illinois, he made his way to Boston and became a pupil of Mr. Morse and later of Mme. Edna Hill. About 1890, Woodward undertook an extensive Southern concert tour in order to add to his means that he might prolong his vocal studies. In Galveston, Texas, his talent and ambition won the interest of the author's father, Norris Wright Cuney, Collector of Customs, who, giving him substantial aid and encouragement, enabled the singer to continue his travels in the State after his Galveston concert.

In Boston, Woodward's first public appearances were so successful that he was engaged as first soloist at the People's Baptist Church. Later he accepted a position at another white church, that of the Second Congregational Church, where he remained for five years at a salary of five hundred dollars a year. He continued his vocal studies and gave a recital in Chickering Hall on February 15, 1893. Philip Hale, writing of him in the Boston *Journal*, said, "He sings as a rule with ease, his tones are pure and well sustained, his attack is decisive, and he does not abuse the portamento; he knows the meaning of the word legato, he phrases intelligently, and holds himself in control, and his enunciation is admirable.''

In 1892, Woodward's beautiful voice won for him the friendship of Mme. Nordica, who became his sympathetic friend and helped him to rise to higher levels. Between 1897 and 1900, after Woodward had joined a Musical Comedy company, John W. Isham's ''Oriental America,'' in order to reach England, he was engaged in singing throughout Ireland, Scotland, Wales, Germany, Austria, Holland, Belgium and Russia. In England, he sang a number of times at the garden parties given at Buckingham Palace. After the singer's return to the United States he served as a teacher of voice at the Florida Baptist Academy in Jacksonville, Clark University in Nashville, and at the Music School Settlement in New York City. During this last period, he gave a concert in Carnegie Hall, New York, in celebration of his thirty-first anniversary as a singer. He died February 13, 1924.

Harry A. Williams, tenor, of Cleveland, Ohio, who is identified with this period, received his first lessons in voice in that city, after which he went to Paris where he studied under Delle Sedie and Sbriglia. From Paris, he went to London, where he became a pupil of Tosti and Luigi Denza. For the greater part of the time, he lived in the home of the latter where he met many famous musicians. Finally, he was appointed a teacher of voice at the London Academy of Music, of which Denza and Pollitzer were directors. He returned to the United States and made his home in Cleveland, where for a number of years he was a successful teacher of voice. Invited to take charge of the vocal department of the Washington Conservatory of Music which had been established by Mrs. Harriet Gibbs Marshall in 1903 in Washington, D. C., he

FLORA BATSEN BERGEN

SIDNEY WOODWARD

ABBIE MITCHELL

GERALD TYLER

removed to that city. While there, he organized and directed the Washington Concert Orchestra, with Bernadine Smith as concert master. Although Mr. Williams possessed a beautiful voice of lyric quality and sang with finish and distinction, he preferred to teach and until today is recognized as a proficient vocal instructor. He makes his home in New York City.

Some years ago, attention was called to an exceptional and beautiful lyric soprano which was heard at Hammerstein's Roof Garden in New York City. It was the voice of Rachel Walker, who went to Europe where she met with signal success. She won the notice of Mme. Marchesi, the famous teacher of voice, and while in London, became a pupil of Sir Henry J. Wood. After a concert in Paris, the correspondent of that city for the New York *Journal* wrote, "Her voice is one to catch the ear and hold it. Pure, clear, sympathetic, it unites the lyric qualities of the soprano, with the passion and power of the dramatic soprano, a commingling which may appear analogous to those who hold that such characteristics may not be in one voice. Her tones are rich and melodious, and the difficult aria brought out the beautiful cultivation of the voice. In the scene and prayer from 'Iphigenia,' she stood before her audience transfixed into the part she acted. Of soulful face and fine physique, she might well be taken for the passion-stirred heroine of Gluck's masterpiece."

While abroad Miss Walker sang before Her Majesty, the Queen of Spain, the Duchess of Albany; Her Royal Highness, the Princess of Saxe-Coburg and Gotha and the Gaekwar of Baroda. She received compliments from the great modern French composers, Massenet and St. Saens. She returned to America in 1914 at the threatened outbreak of the war. During the season of 1914-16, she sang in many Northern cities in concerts and in Negro musical festivals. Since 1924 she has lived quietly in her native city of Cleveland, Ohio.

Mme. Anita Patti-Brown of Chicago, one of the most successful singers of the race, is widely known as the possessor of a naturally fine voice the skilful use of which was enhanced by training under noted teachers in Chicago. She was for a number of years, one of the leading sopranos of the race. Mme. Patti-Brown has traveled extensively, under her husband's management, and has filled concert engagements not only in the United States, but in the West Indies, South America and England.

Mme. Mayme Calloway-Byron, soprano, of Chicago, Illinois, is the possessor of a very fine dramatic voice of wide range and power. Her principal work was done abroad, so that she is not known as widely in this country as her artistry deserves. Her training was that of the operatic school. In Europe, Mme. Byron had the distinction of appearing with the Philharmonic Orchestras of Munich and Dresden. From Europe, after passing through many unpleasant experiences incident to the World War, which included the loss of valuable jewels and souvenirs of her artistic triumphs, Mme. Byron returned to America, and made her home in Chicago. While filling concert engagements on the Pacific Coast, she was assisted by her young daughter, who has decided pianistic talent. Hearing her sing in 1917, the author was impressed with her artistic interpretation of the German lieder as well as the high order of her vocalism as displayed in her operatic selections.

The foregoing survey is by no means a complete record of the many Negro men and women who were active in the field of music in the pioneer period. We can but recognize that from 1840 to 1880, within forty years, there arose in this country a considerable number of Negroes who were not only ambitious and earnest, but who possessed talent befitting their desires and were able to attract the attention of the thoughtful and intelligent people of America.

The Negro musicians of New Orleans deserve here a little more than general treatment. They lived and labored in a different environment from that of any other musical group in this country. Many of them were of French extraction. A goodly number, having parents of wealth, were sent to Paris to complete their education.[9] For these very reasons they have been misunderstood. One marvels at the tendency, now evident, to describe these people as "Negro Creole." To call their music "Negro Creole" is absolutely incorrect and shows a woeful ignorance of the history of that particular section—a distortion of facts which even rising prejudice does not ex-

[9] An interesting description appeared in an early newspaper—"The Free Colored People of Louisiana"—*The New Orleans Picayune*. (Reprinted in the *Anglo-African Magazine*, Aug., 1859.)

"Our free colored population form a distinct class from those elsewhere in the United States. Far from being antipathetic to the whites, they have followed in their footsteps, and progressed with them with a commendable spirit of emulation, in the various branches of industry most adapted to their spheres. Some of the best mechanics and artisans are to be found among our free colored men. They form the great majority of our regular settled masons, brick-layers, builders, carpenters, tailors, shoe-makers, etc., whose sudden emigration from this community would certainly be attended with some degree of annoyance; while we count among them in no small numbers *excellent musicians*, jewelers, goldsmiths, tradesmen, and merchants. As a general rule, the free colored people of Louisiana, and especially of New Orleans—the 'creole colored people,' as they style themselves—are a sober, industrious, and moral class, far advanced in education and civilization. From that class came the battalion of colored men who fought for the country under General Jackson, in 1814-15, and whose remnants, veterans whom age has withered, are taken by the hand on the anniversary of the glorious Eighth of January, by their brethren-in-arms, and proudly march with them under the same flag."

cuse. Another work is devoted to the folk music of the Creoles, who were brought under French influences, and whose manners and tastes even until today, are of that school.

An important name of the early school of musicians of New Orleans, from 1840 to 1879, is that of Lambert. Richard Lambert, a member of a talented family of seven, was a teacher of music in Louisiana. His son, Lucien, who was born about 1828, received his first instruction in New Orleans, where he became known as a pianist, teacher and composer. Unhappy under southern racial prejudice, he went to Paris, where he continued his studies. He was called to Brazil to be the chief musician at the Court of Dom Pedro. When about fifty years of age, he entered the piano manufacturing business in that country. A list of his compositions include—"La Bresiliana," "L'Americaine," "Paris Vienne," "Le Niagara," "La Juive," "Le Depart du Conscrit," "Les Ombres Aimées," "Cloches et Clochettes," "Pluie de Corails," "La Rose et le Bengali," and the piano transcriptions, "Au Clair de la Lune," and "Ah! vous disais-je Maman."

Sidney, another son of Richard Lambert, was also a brilliant pianist, who wrote for the piano and other instruments. For his method of piano-forte study, he was decorated by the King of Portugal and called to that country to be a musician at court. He later became a teacher in Paris, France, where he added to his list of compositions which include "Murmures du Soir," "Anna Bolena," "L'Elisire," "L'Africaine," "La Sonambula," "Transports Joyeux," "Les Cloches," and "Si j'étais." John Lambert, who was born about 1862, early showed unusual talent. He was educated at St. Joseph School in New Orleans, and studied many instruments. He was a cornetist of note.

One of the most widely known musicians of that section,

was Edmund Dédé, who was born of free parents in New
Orleans in 1829. They had migrated from the French
West Indies. He, however, seems not to have been of
mixèd blood. He learned to play the cornet, then studied
the violin under C. Deburque, a Negro violinist, and continued his studies with L. Gabici, director of the orchestra of the old St. Charles Theater. In 1848, his father
sent him to Mexico in order to complete his musical education. In 1857, he went first to England and then to
Paris, France, where he entered the Conservatory. There
he became a pupil of Halévy and Alard and won a number of medals.

For many years Dédé was the director of the orchestra
of "L'Alcazar" in Bordeaux, France. In 1894, he returned to this country to visit relatives. The steamer on
which he was sailing was wrecked at sea and with other
passengers he was taken aboard a Texas coal steamer and
landed at Galveston, Texas. He remained there for two
months and was acclaimed by the best musicians of that
section, both white and black. The author's parents, ever
appreciative of musical talent, entertained him. After
giving many concerts, Dédé went to New Orleans, where
he received a royal welcome.

The program given below is a copy of one which the violinist gave in this country in 1894.[10] After playing in
many cities as far North as Chicago, he went back to

[10] The following is a Dédé program given in New Orleans.

Program
"Salle des Amis de L'Esperance
Rue Tréme, entre Dumaine et St. Phillipe
Grande Soirée Artistique
pour les adieux, et en Benefice du
Prof. Edmund Dédé,
Donnée sous le patronage du
Club Amis de L'Esperance,
avec le concours des Amateurs et des Artistes

France, never to return.   Shortly before her death in
1920, Mme. Erado, an aunt of Dédé, sent the author the
words of a song which he had written as his farewell.
The burden of the poem was his return to France: "My
adopted mother, France, who so often has consoled me—
Eternal is my destiny to live far from my native country, the land of my birth; but the prejudice that pursues,
it is implacable—my country which refuses my love, it is
the land of my birth."

Dédé died in Paris in 1903.   He had been married for
some years to a French lady, and a son, George, is said
to have survived him.   The violinist-composer's works include ballet music, "Ables," "Les Faux Mandarins" and
"La Sensitive," played by many orchestras, "Le Palmier
Overture," and a number of songs.[10]   His last composition
was an opera in four acts called *Sultan d'Ispahan*.   A
dramatic aria from this work, "Le Serment de l'Arabe,"
was revived by the concert singer, William Richardson, as
an example of art music written by early Negro composers.
It is written in the style of Verdi and the Italian school.

du Club Ida, et de distingues Professeurs de la ville.
Dimanche, 21 Janvier, 1894
I Concerto de Violin Op. 64..Mendelssohn
accompagné par Mme. Serge
'Rigoletto' de Verdi...D. Alard
par Mlle. Lucie Barés et le Prof. E. Dédé
Il Trovatore—Verdi—Fantasie pour violin, exécuté par Ed. Dédé,
accompagnement de quatuor par Mm. Nickerson, Mauret, E.
Colin et P. Dominnguez.
Si J'etais Lui (nocturne)
Poésie de M. V. E. Rillieux, musique de Ed. Dédé
chante par M. H. Beaurepaire.
L'orchestre sous la direction du Prof. Nickerson
Le piano sera tenu par Mme. Serge et M. Basile Barés, Professeurs."

Dédé was the owner of a valuable Cremona violin which was
lost when he was shipwrecked.

CHAPTER XI

MUSICAL PROGRESS

PRESERVATION OF NEGRO SPIRITUALS—LATER-DAY FOLK
SONG SINGERS—MRS. E. AZALIA HACKLEY AND MUSIC FES-
TIVALS—NATIONAL ASSOCIATION OF NEGRO MUSICIANS—
CHORAL SOCIETIES—PEDRO T. TINSLEY—SAMUEL COLE-
RIDGE-TAYLOR'S FIRST VISIT TO AMERICA—SCHOOLS OF
MUSIC—PRIZE WINNERS AND MUSICAL CONTESTS

To the world at large, the Fisk Singers had revealed the
beauty of the Spirituals, but as they were without adequate settings they were unknown as solos on the concert
stage, until the composer, Harry T. Burleigh, arranged a
number of them for this purpose with piano accompaniment. From time to time Burleigh issued additional
groups until he awakened a new interest in the melodies.
He has been followed by many white musicians, but none
have surpassed his artistic and sympathetic accompaniments. Not only did he know the idiom of the song and
the feeling manifested therein, but his excellence as a
singer and composer enabled him to produce work of art
while not destroying the traditional mood of the folk song.
Burleigh's songs, meriting the attention of serious artists,
found a place on concert programs of the celebrated singers of the day. Although recognizing his calling as a
composer of art songs, we must consider his success with
the folk-song settings as tremendous.

Almost simultaneously with Burleigh's contribution
was the movement among Negro musicians to give the
Spirituals a wider hearing from the concert platform.

Until today the extensive use of the old plantation melodies has been repugnant to many people of African descent. Not having felt nor undergone the hardships of vassalage, they were too far removed in freedom of spirit and not far enough separated by duration of time to welcome the allusion to slavery and felt that the plantation hymns were but a reminder of the misfortunes of a race. They resented, too, the attitude of many Caucasians in their wish to restrict Negro singers to folk songs and in their expressed desire to hear students in Negro schools sing plantation hymns to the exclusion of other music. About 1909, students of Howard University refused to sing the songs and went on a strike. The same revolt was all but repeated at that institution in 1919. Wilberforce during these years avoided trouble by taking the attitude that Negro folk songs were beneath the notice of a university and tabooed them from the very beginning.

Development in music, then, has not always meant an increasing interest in the Negro's special contribution. A teacher of piano and choral singing is found in nearly all of the schools and colleges for Negroes. A number of these institutions are employing better equipped teachers than formerly, and many are enlarging their single piano course to a department of music which embraces piano, violin, voice, choral work and theoretical studies. Instructed by teachers who have received their training in the conservatories of music in the North, the students, in spite of the prevalence of ''Jazz,'' which has retarded their musical growth, have begun to understand and appreciate classical music. They have refused, then, to be restricted to the singing of the Spirituals.

We must admit, too, that the race termed ''Negro'' is no longer African. After centuries of American habitation, a new people with characteristics naturally devolved from the admixture with the white and Indian blood has been created in America.[1] Just as we find musicians of other races without any particular concern regarding the folk material of their nation or race, so are there many Negro lovers of music who have no special interest in the folk songs. This sentiment prevails among laymen as well as among musicians. On the other hand, there has arisen a group of serious men and women, who have not only shown a willingness to accept plantation songs as a heritage, but in doing so, lose no time in brooding over the cruel past or the unjust present.

In the march of civilization, every race has had its day of trial, and since from every experience the soul of an individual is developed, the Negro musician accepting this patrimony, realizes that it represents but one phase, and one only, of the musical life of the race. They know that the songs of the untutored can never be the full expression of the cultured, but like the nature lover who appreciates the beauty of the wild flower of the field and mountain side, as well as the cultivated blossom of the garden, they recognize the charm of the simplicity, naïveness and straightforwardness of the folk song.

It is with this spirit that such an organization as "The Nalle Jubilee Singers" was established a few years ago by Miss Mary Nalle of Washington, D. C., with Harry A. Williams as director. "The American Folk Singers" under the direction of Henry Lee Grant of Washington, and the "Folk Song Singers" organized in 1914 by Mrs. Harriet Gibbs Marshall, president of the Washington Conservatory of Music, and directed by Will Marion Cook, were similar commendable undertakings.

At that time, E. Azalia Hackley, a Negro soprano of

[1] Under instructions from Congress, the census law provided that the population schedule shall include an inquiry into the number of "Negroes, Mulattoes, Quadroons and Octaroons." The returns of 1870 were tabulated, while those of 1880 were not.

Philadelphia, a former student under Jean de Reszke in Paris, retired from the concert platform and devoted her talent to training groups of singers. In various places she planned and directed "Folk Song Festivals," and succeeded in reaching large groups of people in every important city in the Union. This work was carried on with noteworthy success until 1921, when a physical collapse while conducting festivals in California, caused her to retire. She departed this life in Detroit, Michigan, in 1923.

"The Folk Song Festival" of Mrs. Hackley not only drew attention to the melodic beauty of the music, but also gave the youth of the race a new respect for racial folk material, and an incentive to interpret it. A typical review of her work said, "An admirable musician herself, the chorus under Mrs. Hackley's leadership sang with a purity of tone, a precision and control that did not lessen the fervor and abandon which gave color to these Spirituals."

In 1919, a National Association of Negro Musicians was formed for the purpose of "stimulating progress, to discover and foster talent, to mold taste, to promote fellowship, and to advocate racial expression." The discussions at the first conference included "methods for systematic education of the public as to broader significance and truer appreciation for Negro Music." The Association has steadily grown and has eminently filled its purpose. The membership includes music-teachers of Negro schools, leading professional musicians and various music clubs throughout the country. It is now the foremost Negro musical organization, with branches in twenty-eight States.[2]

[2] The fifteenth annual convention was held in Indianapolis, Indiana, August 12 to 17, 1933. The honorary (past) presidents of the Association are Henry L. Grant, Dr. Clarence Cameron White, Dr. R. Nathaniel Dett, and J. Wesley Jones. The officers until

In New York, the headquarters of musical comedy and Jazz, the progress of serious music was hastened by Daisy Tapley, mezzo-soprano, assisted by Minnie Brown, soprano, who instituted and conducted for a number of seasons (without personal financial gain) a number of concerts called "Educational Series." In this artist series, leading musicians of the race were presented in winter recitals in Brooklyn and New York until 1920.

In the same effort two choral societies of a quarter of a century ago, took the lead in the excellence of their work and in the standard which they maintained. The first in regard to age, was "The Choral Study Club" of Chicago, which was organized in 1900, under the leadership of Pedro T. Tinsley. By his perseverance, uncompromising artistic ideals, and exceptional ability for instructing and directing he brought the club to a high level. Tinsley, by the time he died, in December, 1921, had become a baritone soloist and chorister of the highest gifts. It would be difficult to recall an individual who did more to upbuild musical taste in the Middle West. His one ambition was to increase the musical appreciation of the Negro youth of Chicago. To this end he gave unstintedly of his strength and talent.[3]

1933 included Mrs. Lillian M. Le Mon, president; Camille L. Nickerson, vice-president; J. Wesley Jones, executive secretary. At the sixteenth annual convention held at Pittsburgh, the officers elected were Maude Roberts George, president; Kemper Harreld, Atlanta, vice-president; Clara Hill, Indianapolis, recording secretary; J. Wesley Jones, Chicago, executive secretary; George Hutchinson, Chicago, treasurer; Effie Diton (Mrs. Carl Diton), New York City; Lillian Brown, Indianapolis; Lillian Lemon, Indianapolis; and Camille Nickerson, Washington, D. C., directors.

[3] Associated with Tinsley in the organization, were three musicians who continued uninterruptedly at their post—M. Gertrude Jackson and Mrs. Pelagie Blair, accompanists, and J. Gray Lucas, president of the Club. Compositions presented included Max Bruch's "Flight of the Holy Family," Prothero's "Castilla," Cowen's

The Samuel Coleridge-Taylor Society of Washington, D. C., which was organized in 1902 under the conductorship of Prof. John T. Layton, has been one of the most potent aids in the advancement of musical culture in the capital of the nation. The first concert was given on April 23, 1903, at the Metropolitan African Methodist Episcopal Church, when the complete cantata, "Scenes from the Song of Hiawatha," by S. Coleridge-Taylor was given, with Kathryne Skeene Mitchell as soprano, Sidney Woodward as tenor, and Harry T. Burleigh as baritone in the leading roles.

The Society came into being at the instigation of Mrs. Andrew F. Hilyer who had met Coleridge-Taylor when she was visiting London in 1901. Upon her return to Washington she expressed her desire to Miss Lola Johnson (later instructor in music of the Negro Public Schools of Washington) to form a choral group that could perform the works of the distinguished Negro composer. The correspondence between them and Coleridge-Taylor was engaging. In April, 1903, the composer wrote from London, "No performance has ever interested me half as much as this 'colored' one (of *Hiawatha*) and I would give a great deal to be with you all." On June 1, 1903, the Board of Managers of the Coleridge-Taylor Society invited the composer to visit Washington and personally conduct his *Hiawatha* trilogy. In November, 1903, he arrived in the United States and on the sixteenth of that month directed in Washington the presentation of this tremendous chorus. This was the first presentation of the

"St. John's Eve," Mendelssohn's "Lauda Sion," and S. Coleridge-Taylor's "Blind Girl of Castle Guille," "Bon-Bon Suite," and "Hiawatha," given with orchestral accompaniment on the tenth anniversary of the Club. Mme. Skeene Mitchell, soprano; George Holt, George Johnson, tenors; T. Theodore Taylor, Harry T. Burleigh and William H. Richardson, baritones, have appeared as soloists with the Choral Study Club.

COLERIDGE-TAYLOR SOCIETY, WASHINGTON, D. C., 1900, WITH THE GREAT
COMPOSER AS DIRECTOR

entire work in America. The soloists were Mme. Estelle Pinckney Clough as soprano, T. Arthur Freeman as tenor, and Harry T. Burleigh as baritone. The orchestral accompaniment by members of the United States Marine Band was inadequate, but the chorus of two hundred voices achieved success. The audience was one of the most remarkable ever assembled in Washington. Unfortunately, however, the concert had to be given in Convention Hall, where the acoustic properties were of the poorest, but prominent members of Washington's official and social life and nearly all the leading white musicians were present. The program of the second night was devoted to part songs and short pieces written by Coleridge-Taylor. His "Three Choral Ballads" were sung for the first time in public. Two songs for tenor, "A Corn Song" and "Beat, Beat Drums" were sung by T. Arthur Freeman, and "African Dances," a suite for violin and piano, was played by Clarence Cameron White, with the composer at the piano. The Washington *Post* of November 17, 1903, said, "The work of the chorus was magnificent from start to finish. Their tone, shading, phrasing, precision and response to every move of the composer's baton was a lesson in choral singing. Their climaxes were magnificent and thrilling, and they did full justice to the splendid composition."

A loving cup from the Coleridge-Taylor Society, which bore the inscription, "It is well for us, O brother, that you came so far to see us," a baton made of cedar which came from the home of Frederick Douglass, a gift from the pupils of the M Street High School (now the Dunbar High School), and an autographed photograph from Theodore Roosevelt were among the gifts received by Coleridge-Taylor before his departure for a short visit to other cities in the United States. On July 31, 1906, *Hiawatha* was repeated with Burleigh, Holt, and Mme. Mitchell as soloists.

Anticipating a second visit to conduct three of his works, *The Atonement, The Quadroon Girl,* and *Hiawatha,* the composer wrote Mrs. Hilyer in September, requesting that instead of the unsatisfactory orchestra from the United States Marine Band, a certain number of string players be engaged and the wind parts be filled in on the piano-forte and organ "by that extraordinarily clever Miss Mary Europe and someone else." He also requested that Lent and White be asked to select the strings and Burleigh the soloists. On November 21, 1906, this Music Festival was held under the direction of Coleridge-Taylor, and the accompaniment for *The Atonement* was played by the string section of the Philadelphia Symphony Orchestra. Lola Johnson, mezzo-soprano, and Charlotte Wallace, contralto, sang solo parts in *The Atonement.* On April 23, 1908, the Society gave the *Hiawatha* trilogy again in Washington, and the following month presented *The. Atonement* in Baltimore, with the soloists Mme. K. Skeene Mitchell as soprano, T. Wilcot Swan as tenor, and William H. Richardson as baritone.

The comments on these performances were flattering. The Washington *Post* said of Miss Europe, "Her work at the piano was delightful. Her good tone and clear technique were observed all through the accompaniment." James Gibbons Hunneker, who attended· the performance, said, "The work of Samuel Coleridge-Taylor marks an epoch in modern composition, his wealth and weirdness, and his richness of orchestration being almost a musical revelation to modern writers."

Following the death of John T. Layton and that of Mrs. Hilyer, which occurred about two years later (December 14, 1916), the Coleridge-Taylor Society disbanded, but in 1921 it was revived under the directorship of Roy W. Tibbs. On May 19, 1932, *The Atonement* was again given in Washington under the sponsorship of the

"Committee on Coordinating Activities among Colored People for the George Washington Centennial Celebration," sub-committee on music. The soloists were Mrs. Lillian Evans Tibbs (Mme. Evanti), soprano; Mrs. L. H. Burrell, contralto; G. Stanley Brooks, tenor; and Charles H. Wesley, baritone. The accompanists, Miss Mary L. Europe and Mr. Van Whitted of ·Howard University Conservatory of Music, with Dr. Melville Charlton as organist. As conducted by Roy W. Tibbs, the work was highly praised.

Other such organizations deserve mention. Among these are the Amphion Glee Club of Washington, D. C.; the People's Choral Society of Philadelphia; the Musergia of Louisville, Kentucky; the Coleridge-Taylor Music Club of Fort Worth, Texas; the Progressive Choral Society of Chicago; the Chorus ·Study Club of combined choirs of Chicago (James A. Mundy, conductor); the Coleridge-Taylor Club of Norfolk, Virginia; the Festival Chorus drawn from various colleges of Atlanta, Georgia, under the directorship of Kemper Harreld; and the Bel-Canto Singers of Philadelphia, organized by William Cowdery in 1914 to maintain a vocal scholarship for talented young Negro singers. They paved the way for more recent endeavors. Such groups have also been instrumental in giving opportunities to Negro soloists for oratorio and cantata singing.

The Mundy Choristers of eighty voices took part in the open air Stadium concerts given in Chicago in 1931 under the auspices of Loyola University. This group, one of the leading choruses of the United States, is under the direction of James A. Mundy, who is a teacher of voice and chorister in· Chicago. He has been instrumental in presenting a number of Negro solo artists in that city. In 1933, a Twentieth Anniversary Festival was held in his honor at Orchestra Hall, Chicago.

In the far Southwest, the Beaumont Community Chorus

in Texas combined with the Beaumont Music Study Club, members of the National Association of Negro Musicians, have celebrated National Music Week in a large way and have sponsored artist recitals, thus bringing Negro artists to that section of the country. The Fort Worth Music Association, formerly directed by Mrs. Manet Harrison Fowler, president of the Houston (Texas) Summer School of Music, assisted by other branch organizations successfully sponsored one of the most impressive annual meetings of the National Association (1929). Music-lovers of both races, white and colored, attended the sessions and artist recitals, while the city of Fort Worth halted traffic in order that the parade of floats, "Miles of Music," might pass through the business section of the city. The outstanding feature was the excellently drilled chorus of 1,000 voices under the direction of Mrs. Martha B. Wynn.

In the Northwest, the Coleridge-Taylor Society of the state of Washington, enjoys more than local reputation due to the activities of the president, Mrs. Nettie Asbury, a writer on musical interests of the race, for western journals.

In Terre Haute, Indiana, the Harry T. Burleigh Musical Association presents talent and gives musical and dramatic performances. In Louisiana, the United Choirs of New Orleans of 150 voices under the direction of Mrs. Marion Dozier Walker, hold annual songfests before large mixed audiences drawn from neighboring states.[4]

Negro colleges have long fostered choral singing. The Hampton Choral Union, composed of the Negro church

---

[4] The colored Chicago University of Music, housed in the edifice which was formerly the home of Mme. Schumann-Heink, was incorporated in 1921 with Pauline James Lee as president. Summer as well as winter courses were offered. This institution, at one time conspicuous enough to be the scene of Gertrude Sanborn's *Veiled Aristocrats*, has not recently functioned efficiently.

THE HAMPTON CHOIR

choirs in Hampton, Virginia, organized by R. Nathaniel Dett when director of music at Hampton Institute, takes the same rank. The Hampton Institute Choir reached a high standard under the guidance of Dett and was considered one of the finest choral bodies on the semi-professional stage. This choir of forty trained voices first gained special recognition by appearing at the Music Festival in the Library of Congress, Washington. Engagements followed at Carnegie Hall in New York, in the Atlantic Seaboard States and at Symphony Hall in Boston. On April 23, 1930, after having gained an enviable reputation, the chorus sailed for Europe for a tour made possible by the generosity of George Foster Peabody. Appearances were made in Westminster Abbey and the Salzburg Cathedral and under royal patronage in England. The city of Paris officially welcomed the choir. There they made records for the Pathé Talking Picture Company. Concerts were given at Rotterdam, Amsterdam and the Hague, as well as in Germany.

As the first Negro director, Dr. Dett is to be congratulated in that he had the courage to prepare programs featuring art music as well as Negro folk music which made it possible to judge the work of his group by world standards. *La Feuille d'Avois* of Vienna states, "There was absolute mastery of the most difficult passages, incomparable blending, beauty of subtle shading, marvelous discipline, all united into the finest cohesion." Benjamin Stolberg's criticism in the "Atlantic" that the director may "already be guilty of racial sensitiveness—and ashamed of Negro Spirituals" is in keeping with the thought that every Negro singer should "specialize" in Negro songs. Critical praise of the choir's singing of old Russian hymns as well as classic selections, justified the director's judgment. The choir was compared to the best Russian choruses. In 1933, Dett having resigned from Hampton

Institute, the choir came later under the direction of
Clarence Cameron White, and it has recently appeared
at the White House by invitation of President Franklin
D. Roosevelt. An important comment on this appearance
was, "The Hampton Institute Choir, under the direction
of Dr. Clarence Cameron White, appeared in concert last
evening at the First Congregational Church, sponsored by
the Mus-Art Club of Lincoln Congregational Church and
the music department of public school division 10-13.

"For pure tonal beauty the choir surpasses any heard
here in some time, and much of that is due to the expert
use of a restrained volume that seemed to attain a pene-
trating sweetness and roundness. The interpretations of
the varied program were marked by great elasticity in a
purely technical sense and a genuineness of feeling that
was the combined individual response to the music. While
most of the phrasing was based on the musical idea
rather than on that of the text the effect was impressive
in its beauty.

"Whether in the classic group which opened the program, the four Russian numbers which followed or works
by Anglo-Saxon composers, the choir caught the initial
atmosphere and reproduced it with smoothness of changing dynamics and polished vocal color. Dr. White directed with a whole-hearted concentration which demanded the utmost in good musicianship from his singers.
A group of numbers sung by male voices formed an en-
joyable moment in a program that held the interest
from beginning to end. The final group was made up of
choice Negro spirituals. A large and attentive audience
received the visiting singers with enthusiastic acclaim."—
Washington Star, May 11, 1935.

Without seeming to give undue prominence to Fisk
University as the instigator of choral music one must in
all fairness refer to the new Fisk Choir which is the pro-

longation of the early Mozart Society of this institution. Composed of sixty vested singers conducted by Ray Francis Brown, a white musician, they have made a fine reputation on the professional stage. On January, 1933, they opened their national tour in Cincinnati and were later heard in Carnegie Hall, New York; in the Severance Hall in Cleveland, Ohio; in the Bushnell Auditorium in Hartford, Connecticut; and in Symphony Hall in Boston, as well as in other prominent cities. The tour was under the patronage of Paul D. Cravath, Walter Damrosch and Bishop Manning. The New York concerts were conducted by Dr. T. Tertius Noble, organist and choirmaster at St. Thomas Episcopal Church of New York, an English musician who came to Fisk the year previous as guest conductor and was so greatly pleased with the possibilities of the chorus that he was happy to conduct the group in his own compositions.

Additional numbers were directed by Ray Francis Brown, organist, and for six years director of the Music School of Fisk, and Negro Spirituals by Mrs. James A. Myers, for eighteen years director of the disbanded Jubilee Singers. The soprano soloists were Martha Sutton from Nashville and Catherine Van Buren from Pittsfield, graduate students from the Music School. Apart from compositions by Dr. Noble, and folk songs, the program consisted of numbers by Bach, Palestrina, Gretchaninoff and other composers. Managers of the tour had the cooperation of the distinguished violinist-teacher, David Mannes of New York.[5]

The Tuskegee Institute Choir, a very fine body under the direction of William L. Dawson, director of the Music School of that institution, sang at the White House by

[5] The Fisk University Choir has been heard later in national broadcasts with Edward Matthews, baritone soloist, who was engaged as director of Negro Folk Music at Fisk University.

252 NEGRO MUSICIANS AND THEIR MUSIC

invitation of President Hoover. In 1932 a contract was made with this chorus for one month's engagement at the opening of Radio City, the big amusement venture, in New York. Arrangements were also made for international broadcasts.

Another Negro singing group which has appeared at the White House for both Herbert Hoover and Franklin D. Roosevelt, is the Morehouse College Quartette from Atlanta, Georgia.[6] Great credit for this and other such efforts should be given Kemper Harreld, violinist and teacher, director of music at Morehouse College, who has done much to further the appreciation of music. He has successfully arranged and conducted annual Music Festivals in Atlanta for the combined colored colleges. His education was received at the Chicago Musical College and under private teachers in Berlin, Germany.

Other such efforts also deserve mention. An excellent group from the oldest college for colored youth on free soil, is the Wilberforce College Octette of four young men and four young women. Their tours and broadcasting in 1933 serve to call attention to the seventy-fifth anniversary of this Ohio institution. The Virginia State College Choral Society, from Petersburg, and the Mansfield Singers from Claflin University are receiving merited attention and praise. In Washington, the Howard University Glee Club under Roy W. Tibbs and Choir of 90 voices under Lulu V. Childers, director of the Music School, have made a record. Shaw University Singers have been invited to sing with the North Carolina Symphony.

There are a number of choral organizations of more recent history now doing commendable work. The Ham-

[6] The members of this college group, in 1933, are Simon C. Clements, Edward R. Rodriguez, Kenneth R. Williams and Wilson P. Hubert.

VESTED CHOIR, PALMER MEMORIAL INSTITUTE, SEDALIA, N. C.

ilton-Johnson Negro Chorus of Brooklyn, New York, directed by Wilbur P. Johnson, has filled important engagements about New York. They took part in the first Long Island Music Festival which was held at Port Washington, Long Island, under the sponsorship of the New York Federation of Music Clubs.

A young chorus of two or three years' standing, is that of the Greater Boston Negro Chorus, which has been trained and directed by Mrs. Dorothy Richardson, a contralto singer and a chorister. Mrs. Richardson possesses a beautiful, well-trained voice and is in demand for many forum and lyceum audiences, both as a soloist and with her chorus. Her local activities include a position as soloist at the Community Church of Boston, services of which are held at Symphony Hall.

The Greater Boston Negro Chorus in the International Music Festival held on February 22, 1933, won the second prize in Class B—the mixed chorus contest, while the male chorus of this group, composed of thirty voices, won the first prize above the German Male Chorus and the well known Viking Male Chorus. This choral group was also a prize winner in the contest of 1932 when Granville Stewart, a tenor singer, assisted Mrs. Richardson in the training of the singers. This group was the first prize winner in 1934, and in February, 1935, in the mixed chorus class.

Another Boston choral group doing meritorious work is the Ancrum-Forster Choral Society, composed of music students of the Ancrum School of Music, a Negro institution organized and directed by Mrs. Estelle Ancrum Forster, pianist and organist, a graduate of the New England Conservatory of Music. Mrs. Forster's chorus has filled radio and concert engagements.

Of the choral groups before the public today, the Hall Johnson Negro Choir of twenty mixed voices, has had the most spectacular success. This organization is under the direction of Hall Johnson of New York, a trained musician. It has filled concert engagements at Town Hall in New York; it has functioned in theatrical appearances in Negro music drama; and it has been widely heard in radio programs. For five consecutive summers the Hall Johnson Singers have been one of the attractions at the annual Lewisohn Stadium Concerts given in New York City. At the fourth annual concert, they were accompanied by the Philharmonic Symphony Orchestra, under direction of Wilhelm von Hoogstraten. On June 24, 1932, they sang concerted numbers at Madison Square Garden at the inauguration concert of the Cosmopolitan Opera Association of New York, Max Rabinoff, director.

At the final concert of the Columbia Series in Carnegie Hall on April 4, 1932, the Choir appeared with Marian Anderson, contralto, as soloist. Hall Johnson has won fame by specializing in Negro folk song singing. As he says, "Beyond adequate clarity of diction and a fair precision of attack no attempt is made to secure a perfect choral ensemble as generally accepted." But the results obtained by this choir prove that the director has done far more for his group, as is conclusively shown in the singing of his enlarged chorus in his play "Run, Little Chillun!" In *Musical America,* "Mephisto" says of his work, "Johnson has a real creative talent, and his treatment of the choral voices is decidedly his own; he orchestrates for chorus." Walter Damrosch says, "They sing with fine precision, beautiful tone quality, and with a deep inner emotion which fairly sweeps the listeners along."

According to the last United States Census report, of 1930, there were 10,583 colored musicians and teachers in the United States. This number has doubtless increased because of recent tendencies to stimulate the study of music. Within recent years the leading Negro colleges have de-

HARRIET GIBBS MARSHALL

K. SKEENE MITCHELL

E. AZALIA HACKLEY

PEDRO T. TINSLEY

veloped schools of music out of their former departments
of music. To this end, they are securing leading professional and experienced Negro artists and instructors.
Working toward the same end are a number of privately
managed institutions of which the Washington Conservatory of Music is perhaps the oldest. The school, in progress for thirty years, was founded by Mrs. Harriet Gibbs
Marshall, the first Negro graduate of the Oberlin Conservatory of Music, and formerly director of music in the
Negro Public Schools of Washington, D. C.[7] The institution offered a complete course of music under able teachers. In 1920, Mrs. Marshall retired from active duties at
the head of the Conservatory in order to devote her time to
her husband, Captain Napoleon B. Marshall, who had been
severely wounded in the World War. While ·Captain Marshall was located as a United States Government attaché in
Haiti, Mrs. Marshall engaged in gathering the folk music
of that country and produced a book of such productions.
Since her husband's death (1933), she has been working
toward the establishment of a Negro National Conservatory for the study and development of Negro Music, and
is again the director of the Washington Conservatory of
Music and School of Expression.

In the summer of 1911, the broad-minded and noted
white musician, David Mannes, launched a project to establish a Music School Settlement in Harlem, New York
City. For a number of years this school did efficient
work and planted seed for future development. Annual

---

[7] Mrs. Marshall, at that time a well-known pianist, is the daughter of the late Judge Mifflin W. Gibbs of Little Rock, Arkansas, a
graduate of Oberlin College, elected city judge in 1873 (the first
Negro to hold like office in the United States) and in 1877 appointed United States Consul to Tamarive, Madagascar. The talented daughter, Harriet, possessed executive ability as well as
pianistic talent and developed a complete course of music at her
school under able teachers.

concerts of Negro Music were given at Carnegie Hall. Mrs. Natalie Curtis (Burlin) and Rudolph Schirmer were among the directors. Distinguished Negro musicians of talent have served in this institution. The Martin-Smith Music School of New York has a large student body and maintains an orchestra. The school was founded by David I. Martin, assisted by Helen Elise Smith (now Mrs. Nathaniel Dett) and was incorporated in 1919.[8] Mr. Martin was for a short time instructor of violin at the colored Music School Settlement of New York. He left that institution to establish a school that would "give all deserving children an opportunity regardless of their ability to pay for instruction, to train professional musicians as missionaries to work in conjunction with other educational institutions, and to make special provision for pupils of unusual aptitude and talent to continue their work in more advanced schools, after they have completed the Normal Course." Mr. Martin's death occurred in 1924, but the school has continued.[9]

In 1905, the Philadelphia Concert Orchestra was founded, and incorporated in 1908 with E. Gilbert Anderson

[8] Miss Smith, pianist, was the first Negro pupil graduated from the pianoforte department of the Damrosch School of Musical Art in New York City. She has served as a teacher at Hampton Institute.

[9] In December, 1925, the musician's portrait painted by E. A. Harleston, a colored artist, was unveiled in the great hall of City College. The precocious talent of Mr. and Mrs. Martin's own gifted children—Eugene Mars, violinist, and David, 'cellist, was commented upon by the New York press and music journals of a few years ago.

When the sixth anniversary concert of the school was held at Carnegie Hall, the New York *Sun* (December, 1922) said, "The first movement of Schubert's Unfinished Symphony compared not unfavorably with the recent work of the Harvard students and the rhythmical prowess of the orchestra was ably developed under the baton of David Martin, the director."

conductor. The Orchestra Association was founded in 1907, with Andrew F. Stevens, president, an executive committee of eight and a board of directors eighteen in number which sponsored the concerts of the Orchestra. A Woman's Committee of Philadelphia with branches in Wilmington, Delaware, West and North Philadelphia, Camden, New Jersey, and Chester, Pennsylvania, lent support to the Orchestra. A request performance given on April 25, 1910, during the fifth season of the orchestra, is a specimen of the artistic programs presented. The Symphony program book with historical notes by Algernon B. Jackson, disclosed works by Verdi, Mendelssohn, Offenbach, and the Beethoven Symphony No. 1 in C Major. Clarence Cameron White was the soloist in Mendelssohn's Concerto for violin and orchestra, in E minor, Op. 64. In the present day when there is much discussion concerning concerts for children, it is worth noting that the Philadelphia Concert Orchestra, a Negro organization, had given over twenty-four years ago, their third Children's Orchestral Concert.

A recent symphonic group that is winning applause in the musical world is the Baltimore City Colored Orchestra, which was organized November 3, 1929. After being first financed by unknown citizens, an appropriation from the city was given the enterprise in 1930. The first public performance was held at Douglass High School, directed by Charles L. Harris. At the 1931 concert, Ruth McAbee, soprano, was the soloist. The combined concert of the city-financed orchestra of 85 musicians and 300 singers, given in the Spring of 1932, attracted an audience of 2,500 music lovers. The program included an orchestral work by James O. Jones, a Baltimore Negro musician; Haydn Symphony, Opus 26; and selections from Wagner and Will Marion Cook. The Baltimore *Sun*, editorially, said, "The colored citizens of this once highly musical community now seem to have Baltimore's only great organized chorus; and that at a time when the nation's de luxe musical organizations are groaning over record deficits . . . Baltimore's more modest musical adventures are bringing lively pleasure to the community and at the same time keeping within their tiny budgets.'' Of the successful appearance with the Baltimore City Chorus in 1933 with W. Llewellyn Wilson as director, *Musical America* said, ''The potent ability of these ensembles was evident.''

An unusual ensemble which is active in New York City at present is that of the well-known choir, organized by Eva Jessye who is the only Negro woman conductor on the radio. The groups furthered by Miss Jessye give programs of Negro music which are well planned as to both historical and musical merit. The Folk Song Dancers are interpreters of racial musical thought, and the group comprises educated and trained mimes of artistic ability. The unique programs of the combined ensembles, quite distinct from the folk dancing or racial presentations of the music comedy stage, have the endorsement of representative musicians and educators. The list includes the names of Dr. Percy Goetschius, Dr. Sigmund Spaeth, Dr. Hugo Reisenfeld, Rabbi Stephen S. Wise, S. L. Rothafel (Roxy), and Lawrence Stallings.

A concert given by the Victorian Concert Orchestra in Boston in 1933, served to call attention to this band of colored musicians which has existed for nearly 30 years. In early 1906 the organization was founded by Charles H. Sullivan who until his death, 1933, was its faithful manager. It rapidly grew under the directorship of Clarence Cameron White, who conducted the band for six years (beginning in 1914). The orchestra continues to afford a medium for ensemble practice in the classics.

The Desdunes Band of 35 members under the leadership of Dan Desdunes, the son of Rodolphe Desdunes, a

ZULU SINGERS IN LONDON

AN AFRICAN SCENE

gifted Creole of color of New Orleans, was organized in 1911, and for nearly twenty years participated in all of the larger civic events of Nebraska. Mr. Desdunes had his first engagements with S. H. Dudley, as leader of a small Texas circuit orchestra. He passed away April 24, 1929. His father was the author of *Nos Hommes et Notre Histoire*, which includes biographies of Creole musicians of New Orleans.

In this connection efforts in Africa deserve mention. The African is beginning to turn attention to his native song. In 1931, we find the Kumasi Trio from West Africa coming from the Gold Coast to London to record seventy-two native tunes in the Fanti language. That same year the Zulu Singers, a group of ten, visited London for the purpose of making phonograph records for H. M. V., the Gramphone Company. A mixed double quartette of the singers gave concerts before large audiences. The gifted native director, R. T. Caluza, had arranged African songs with piano accompaniments. In his collection of 100 melodies are found war, funeral and dance songs. The program songs were sung in four part harmony to an accompaniment of drum and tambourine. Charles H. Wesley, professor of History at Howard University, on leave as Guggenheim Fellow for research on slavery in the West Indies, on hearing the Zulu Singers in London, said, "The programs of these singers are varied ones. The usual type is a developmental program which demonstrates the rise of Zulu music from the early period to the present." .... In listening to the singing Wesley found it apparent that the "folk songs of the Negro in America have many similar idioms in Africa, even Zulu Africa. In the singing, the movements and the rhythm of the Zulu Singers there is an elementary background of emotional life which one may parallel in parts of America and in the West Indies."

In recognition of the services rendered by these artists aids and awards have been received by Negro musicians and students. A John Simon Guggenheim Memorial Foundation Fellowship was awarded in 1925 to Nicholas G. J. Ballanta of New York City and Free Town, Sierra Leone, Africa, to continue scientific studies of the musical conceptions of the African peoples and compare these ideas with the musical conceptions of the older systems of European music. A second grant was awarded Ballanta Taylor in 1927, to continue his researches into musical conceptions of the African people. In 1930, Marian Anderson, contralto, was awarded a grant for study in Germany. From the Julius Rosenwald Fund Clarence Cameron White, violinist-composer, received a grant of $3,000 for creative work and for the purpose of foreign study in 1930. He received a second grant in 1931 for the leisure in which he might complete an opera—*Ouanga*. In November, 1932, having completed his opera in Paris, he gave a concert performance of the same in Chicago, Illinois, and was awarded the David Bispham Medal by the American Opera Society.

In 1931 Camille L. Nickerson, pianist, received a Rosenwald fellowship of $1,000 to enable her to make a study of Creole folk songs and to continue her studies at the Oberlin Conservatory of Music. Miss Nickerson was born in New Orleans, Louisiana, the daughter of W. J. Nickerson, teacher of music, and is a graduate from the Oberlin Conservatory. She is at present a member of the faculty of Howard University Conservatory of Music. She has arranged both Creole and Negro folk songs, a number of which are presented by Edna Thomas from manuscript copies. Her "Death Song" was sung by R. Todd Duncan, baritone, at the 1932 concert given by the faculty of Howard Conservatory. So far, none of her works have been published.

In 1925, the "Holstein Prizes" donated by Casper Holstein, a Negro of New York, awarded through the magazine, *Opportunity*, included prizes in musical composition. Edmund T. Jenkins took the first prize of $75 for "African War Dance," for full orchestra; and the second prize of $50 for his "Sonata in A Minor," for cello. A second prize went to Florence B. Price, Little Rock, Arkansas, for "In the Land O' Cotton." To Hall Johnson, the third prize was given for "Way up in Heaven." The awards were made in 1926. In 1927, Mr. Holstein again donated $1,000 for contest awards; those in musical composition were won by Hall Johnson, New York, first prize of $50 (for a composition of from two to six instruments), for a "Sonata." To Florence B. Price, Little Rock, Arkansas, went the second prize of $25 for "Memories of Dixieland"; two prizes to Hall Johnson; an award of $50 .or "Fiyer," vocal composition for solo voice, and an award of $50 for "Banjo Dance," a choral work. To Andrades Lindsay, Brooklyn, New York, for "Concert Fugue" (piano), and to Tourgee DuBose, Talladega, Alabama, for an "Intermezzo" (piano), a division of the prize offered for a piano composition in smaller form. To J. Bruce, a first award of $40 for the arrangement of the Negro Spiritual, "All I Want." To Ernest F. Peace, Washington, the second award for an arrangement of "Nobody Knows de Trouble I've Seen."

The Negro in music has been noted also by the Spingarn Achievement Award, established in 1914 by J. E. Spingarn, chairman of the executive committee of the National Association for the Advancement of Colored People. This provides for a gold medal to be given to the man or woman of African descent who during the year shall have made the highest achievement in any field of human endeavor. In 1917, Harry T. Burleigh was awarded the medal for excellence in the field of creative music. In 1925, Roland Hayes received the medal for the "reputation which he has gained as a singer . . . and because in all his singing Mr. Hayes has so finely interpreted the beauty and charm of the Negro folk song."

Taking the record of Negro musicians into consideration, the Harmon Foundation also has given such awards. In 1927 R. Nathaniel Dett, at that time musical director, Hampton Institute, Virginia, received the first award, a gold medal and $400 for his vocal and instrumental compositions. In 1927, Clarence Cameron White, at that time director of music, West Virginia State College, Institute, West Virginia, received the first award, a gold medal and $400 for his work as violinist and composer. E. H. Margetson, organist of the Chapel of Crucifixion, received a second award, bronze medal and $100 for his symphonic orchestrations and for both instrumental and vocal compositions. In 1928 J. Harold Brown, Indianapolis, Indiana, received a second award, a bronze medal and $100 for the earnestness of his musical endeavors and for his orchestrations. Harry T. Burleigh, New York City, received in 1929 a first award, gold medal and $400 for his arrangement of Negro Spirituals and for instrumental suites; Harry L. Freeman, New York City, received a first award, a gold medal and $400 as the composer of the first Negro grand opera; and Carl R. Diton, New York City, received a second award, a bronze medal and $100 for his compositions which include the first movement of a symphony in which African rhythms are employed.

In 1927 the Juillard Musical Foundation awarded fellowships of $1,000 each to provide means for study under masters in the United States and Europe to Ernestine J. Covington, Houston, Texas; to Cornella Lampton, Chicago; to Alexander E. Gatewood, Kansas City, Missouri. In 1926 Miss Covington was awarded the scholarship for the third consecutive year. In 1931 the Margaret McGill scholarship in singing was awarded Annie Wiggins Brown of Baltimore, Maryland.

In 1930, the Wanamaker Music Contest for prizes totaling $1,000, under the auspices of the Robert Curtis Ogden Association and the annual conventions of the National Association of Negro Musicians, were awarded. Class 1— William L. Dawson, Chicago, first prize, $150, for "Jump Back, Honey," and Penman Lovingood, New York City, second prize, $100. Class 2—William L. Dawson, first prize, $150, for "Scherzo," and N. Clark Smith, Chicago, second prize, $100, for "Negro Folk Song Prelude." Class 3—Druscilla Tendy Altwell, El Paso, Texas, first prize, $150, for "Wade in the Water." Class 4—J. Harold Brown, Indianapolis, prize $250 for "African Chief," choral work.

In 1931, the winners of the Wanamaker prizes were: Class 1—William L. Dawson, first prize for "Lovers Plighted"; James E. Dorsey, second prize, for "Sandals." Class 2—J. Harold Brown, first prize, for "Allegro"; Eugene Alexander Burkes, Newark, New Jersey, second prize, for "Sonata." Class 3—J. Harold Brown, first prize, for a "String Quartette"; N. Clark Smith, second prize, for "Swing Low, Sweet Chariot." In 1932, the prize in the fourth class, for a symphonic work, was doubled to $500. At the earlier convention of 1927, the winners were—Wellington Adams, Washington, D. C., in class 1 and 3; Frank Tizol and Harry E. Rush in class 2; Fred M. Bryan and Wesley Howard in class 3; Marietta Bonner, J. Harold Brown, Richard Oliver, Fred D. Griffin and Mrs. C. B. Cooley, class 4; Oscar Howard, John A. Gray and George Ducket, class 5.

In 1932, Margaret Bonds won a Wanamaker Prize for a song which she composed as a scholarship pupil of the National Association of Negro Musicians, and Mrs. Florence B. Price won a prize for a symphonic work which she was invited to play at a concert sponsored by the Friends of Music at the Century of Progress Exposition held in Chicago. She is a graduate of the New England Conservatory of Music, and has studied composition in Chicago. Miss Bonds, who was also asked to appear in the artist series at the Fair, is a graduate of Northwestern University Music Department in the class of 1933.

Others of much note deserve here at least a brief remark. In the final 1925 Music Week Contest held at Carnegie Hall, New York, the singing of Doris Trotman gave her the rating of 92½ per cent which won the gold medal. In the California *Eisteddfod* of 1927, a state-wide musical contest, Antell Marshall, not quite twelve years of age, won the first prize of $2,700. The scholarship was awarded for excellence in memory work, and technical proficiency—phrasing, tone quality, rhythm, tempo and pedaling. In a memory contest held for young musicians in Akron, Ohio, the city and state medal and music scholarship to Ohio Wesleyan University, Delaware, Ohio, was won by Edith Player. Ruby Mae Green, in an open contest held by the New York Music Week Association at Carnegie Hall, received the highest rating over all the interborough contestants. Again in the far West, three colored boys, Leon and Otis Rene of New Orleans, and Benny Ellison of Pittsburgh, received the prize of $500 awarded by the managers of the California Maid Exposition for the best written song. In July, 1932, David Johnson, student at the Institute of Musical Art, New York, was awarded the gold medal for the highest rating in the New York Music Week Association contest.

CHAPTER XII

MUSIC IN WAR SERVICE

PATRIOTS OF 1815-1860—SPIRITUALS IN THE WORLD'S WAR
—SOLDIER SONGS OF 1862—VOLUNTEER MUSICIANS—ARMY
BANDS—MUSICAL STUDENTS AT THE FRONT—SONGS
INSPIRED BY THE WAR.

The Negro's contribution to military music should not
be despised. In the famous Battle of New Orleans, under
Jackson in 1815, the men of color came marching down
the old Bayou road, singing "Le Marseillaise" and their
own Creole war song, "En Avan' Grenadié"—"Go forward, grenadiers, he who is dead requires no ration."
This old song of fearless courage, originated at an earlier
period. It sprang into life as a battle cry of the native
San Dominicans when they were fighting the mother country (France) for their independence.

In all the wars of the United States the Negro has
been vitally concerned, and he has often expressed in song
what he has not dared to utter as a discourse setting
forth his opinions. Thus have sung father and son, the
one for independence of America, the other for freedom
of race, and the youth for freedom of the world.[1] The

[1] A poem by Walt Whitman, "Ethiopia Saluting the Colors," a
reference to this era, has been set to dramatic music by Harry T.
Burleigh. By strange concurrence, a fitting reply to the query,
"Who are you, dusky woman—Why rising by the roadside do you

Negro knew that his freedom was at stake in the war between the sections, and as soon as he had a chance he came into the army in the spirit of this song:

> I've listed and I mean to fight
> Yes, my Lord.
> Till every foe is put to flight
> Yes, my Lord.

the colors greet?'' is embodied in a rare letter of Abraham Lincoln's which is found among the manuscripts in the Pierpont Morgan collection. It reads:

EXECUTIVE MANSION

Washington, March 26, 1863.

Private

Hon. Andrew Johnson.

MY DEAR SIR:

I am told you have at least thought of raising a Negro military force. In my opinion the country now needs no specific thing so much as some man of your ability and position to go to this work. When I speak of your position, I mean that of an eminent citizen of a slave state and himself a slave-holder. The colored population is the great available and yet unavailed of force for restoring the Union. The bare sight of fifty thousand armed and drilled black soldiers on the banks of the Mississippi would end the rebellion at once. And who doubts that we can present that sight, if we but take hold in earnest?

If you have been thinking of a plan, do not dismiss the thought.

Yours truly,

A. LINCOLN.

The records assure us that President Lincoln's wishes were realized. On the banks of the Mississippi, two regiments and officers for a third were formed under command of General Butler. Their courage in defending the Union excited the admiration of all Americans.

There was an old king in ancient days, Down by the river,
Was wicked in all his works and ways, Down by the river,
Old Pharaoh was that wicked king, Down by the river,
He would not let God's people sing, Down by the river side.

When I was down in Egypt's land, Down by the river,
I heard a mighty talk about the promised land, Down by
     the river,
The promised land I now behold, Down by the river,
The promised land all strung with gold, Down by the
     river side.

END THIS WAR

From the state of Louisiana came "The Runaway's
Song," one of defiance:

> "O, General Florido,
> Indeed fo' true dey can't catch me,
> Dey got one schooner out to sea;
> Indeed fo' true dey can't catch me."

This old melody was afterwards popular as a boat song.
Another improvised chant which after the war was adopted
for a chantey, was known as "Stood Wall Jackson." This
was sung to the author in 1917, when seeking Creole folk-
songs at New Iberia, Louisiana. The hero of the song was
Stonewall Jackson, but the distortion of the name into

that of "Stood Wall Jackson" is but one of many amusing examples of the interpretation given unfamiliar words or names by the aged and unlettered singer.

Colonel Higginson, who in 1862 cast his lot as commander of black soldiers for the Union, wrote of the marching song, "Gwine in de Wilderness" as one at which "every step instinctively quickened so light and jubilant the rhythm." The song ended in a cry of "Hoigh," after each verse, which reminded Colonel Higginson of an Irish yell. We find a similar cry at the close of many of the Creole folk-songs, and it is characteristic of a great number of African songs.

Fortunately, this commander kept a diary, and in it he daily jotted down his impressions. Of his soldiers' improvised verses, he says, "They were descriptive of the happenings of the moment and then in a jubilant chorus, the little drum-corps in advance, a jolly crew, their drums slung on their backs and the drumsticks perhaps balanced on their heads, they sang

"We're gwine to de Ferry,
De bell done ringing;
Gwine to de landing,
De bell done ringing;
Trust, believer,
O, de bell done ringing;
Satan's behind me,
De bell done ringing."

"Hangman Johnny," which was sung at this time, was always hushed upon Colonel Higginson's approach. The second verse began:

"De Buckra 'list for money"
O dey call me Hangman Johnny! O ho, O ho!"
But we'll all hang togedder,
O hang boys, hang."

Since "buckra" was the cognomen for a white person, Colonel Higginson surmised that the song referred to the

fact that the white soldier was receiving pay, while the
Negroes were then fighting without financial reward.[2]
An interesting song which may have been of African
origin was sung when marching or embarking. The closing refrain was unexplainable.

"My Army cross over,
My Army cross over,
We'll cross de mighty Myo
   My Army cross over (thrice)
O Pharaoh's army drownded,
My Army cross over."

"The mighty Myo," thought Colonel Higginson, came
from the "Mawa," signifying to die—a term in the African dialect of the Cameroons.

The Negro claims also the origination of the song
"John Brown's Body." In August, 1862, on St. Simon's
Island on the coast of Georgia, a district populated only
by Negroes, twenty-five black soldiers attacked a Con-
federate band. The Negro leader, John Brown, was
killed. Colonel Higginson speaks of this martyr as being the first armed Negro to fall in the war. His father,
a soldier in his regiment, believed until his dying day,
that the song "John Brown's Body" was sung in honor
of his young soldier son.

Negro bands have figured in featuring music among
Negro soldiers. The Ninth Cavalry Band, under Wade
H. Hammond, was very widely known for its fine work.
Bands organized by Walter Loving in the regular service
and the Philippine Constabulary Band also showed the
Negroes' ability in this sphere. The Negro military mu-
sicians not only entertained their own units, but those

[2] Higginson, Thomas Wentworth, *Army Life in a Black Regiment*,
Chap. V. About 180,000 colored soldiers fought in the Civil War.
John Moore was the colored leader of the Fifty-fifth Regiment
Band. He died in Philadelphia, 1871.

of the whites less gifted in this art. This special aspect is a long unwritten chapter in the history of the Negro.

Among the English bands, that of the colored West Indian Regiment was classed with the British Guards' Bands. Their visit to Canada in August, 1922, was a most successful one. Of their playing on Warrior's Day at the Toronto Exhibition, the Toronto *Evening Telegram* said, "The sight of dark-skinned bandsmen of the West Indies Regiment moving amongst them, come to entertain them with their beautiful music gave point both to the fact and to the music. For, notwithstanding the word of clever people to the contrary, we want nationality in music. . . . The band never fails to do beautiful work, sometimes astonishingly beautiful work. . . . We say the same of its conductor, Bandmaster Nash."

Would that all nations of today might determine to fight their battles by the leavening power of music and declare with the folksinger—

"Going to lay down my sword and shield
     Down by the river-side,
Going to lay down my sword and shield
     Down by the river-side,
To study war no more."

When the United States entered the World War, the whole nation turned to song as did the black soldier in the days gone before. From every side came pleas for a "singing army." A few years before, in order to preserve more of the Negro folksongs, Mrs. Burlin, at the suggestion of George Foster Peabody, the senior trustee of Hampton Institute, and several others connected with that school, had visited the sea island of St. Helena and had become beloved by a population of six thousand Negroes of un-mixed blood. When the war came, and the men were called to the colors, she decided to use the folk-songs as a means of bringing comfort and courage to the soldier and to the families who were left behind.

Through the interest of Mr. Peabody, J. E. Blanton, half-brother of Dr. Robert R. Moton, principal of Tuskegee Institute, joined with the War Camp Community Service in popularizing the old Spirituals and visited many camps where he taught the boys to sing the folksongs and Mrs. Burlin's "Hymn to Freedom." This was the old melody, "Ride on, Jesus," for which she had written new words. The song was published by Schirmer and carried its message to the hearts of the singers. Of this work, Mrs. Burlin said:

"Through toil and suffering song has kept the heart of the Negro still unembittered; through prejudice and mis-understanding it has upheld him; through the stress and sacrifice of this white man's war it has cheered him on. And those who recognize its power are surely not wrong in feeling that in the inspired music of the black man lie a prophecy of the possibilities of the race and an earnest plea for that democracy at home which cannot be won by bomb or bullet, but by sympathy and understanding and a realization of the contribution which each race can make to the civilization of the world."

Negro songs were sung by both the colored and white soldiers in America and abroad. A Ragtime song often sung by the southern Negro boys in France, ran—

"Mah Mammy's lyin' in her grave,
Mah daddy done run away,
Mah sister's married a gamblin' man
An' I've done gone astray.
    Yes, I've done gone astray, po' boy,
    An' I've done gone astray."

When Lieut. Europe and his band returned to Camp Upton from Europe, he remarked, "We jazzed all over France but we also surprised them when we represented

America at the big fete held in the Tuilleries Gardens in Paris, playing classical music with equal ease.'' In March, 1918, the band opened the first recreation center for American soldiers at Aix-les-Bains, a French resort. After this they were returned to Paris to play in the hospitals and parks. This 369th Infantry band represented American troops on the August fete day in 1918. There in Paris the band was given a vote of honor which ranked it with those of the British Grenadiers, the Royal Italian, and the Garde Republicaine, or, in other words, naming it as one of the four best bands in the World War.

During the war a number of bands became known for the marked ability of their leaders and for their success in bringing comfort and cheer to the soldiers at the front and solace and joy to the wounded at the hospitals. One of these was that of ''The Buffaloes,'' the colored regiment of New York. The regiment was called the ''Singing 367th Infantry.'' Lieut. Thompson was the conductor. Then there appeared the 349th Artillery Band, conducted by Lieut. Norman Scott; the 351st Field Artillery Band, conducted by Dorsey Rhodes; the 807th Pioneer Band, conducted by Will Vodery; the 372nd Infantry Band, directed by Lieut. George E. Duff; the 350th Field Artillery (Illinois Eighth), conducted by Lieut. Tim Brymn; the 368th, directed by Lieut. A. Jack Thomas. The well directed band under Alton A. Adams of the Virgin Islands is the only Negro organization of the sort in the United States Navy.[3]

[3] The following is a program given by this band at Carnegie Hall, New York:

PROGRAM

Onaway, Awake, Beloved..................................*S. Coleridge-Taylor*
For You Alone...*Ghiel*

MR. CHARLES WATERS

Concertino for flute and piano...*Chaminade*

WALTER LOVING, DIRECTOR, PHILIPPINE
CONSTABULARY BAND

Apart from the instrumental music as featured by the military bands, we know that Negro song played an important part in giving morale to the troops. There were, however, a number of composed songs that were inspired

Negro Spirituals—
    "Mammy o' Mine...*Pinkard*
    "See it Through," regimental song.......*Sergeant George Battle*

"BUFFALO" QUARTETTE

Overture to "Mireille"...*Gounod*
Entr' Acte..*Delibes*
Album Leaf..*Wagner*
March from "Aida"...*Verdi*
March ....*Chambers*
Anvil Chorus
Hallelujah Chorus from "Messiah"...*Handel*
Onedolin

CORPORAL LESTER MILLER
(MRS. McFARLAND, accompanist)

Dance Music of Negro origin (5 numbers)
"Madelon"

    The most noted band stationed outside of the United States is that of the Philippine Constabulary Band, which played with great success in this country at the Million Dollar Pier, Atlantic City; the Belasco Theatre, Washington; the Hippodrome, New York; and Symphony Hall, Boston. The band was featured at the World's Fair in St. Louis and at the inauguration of President Taft in 1909. The group was recalled to Washington to play at President Taft's first public reception at the White House, and to give the initial concert at the opening of the Grand Esplanade in Washington. The Constabulary Band was organized October 15, 1924, by Walter Howard Loving, who had entered the regular army as a musician and had served with the 24th U. S. Infantry until the outbreak of the Spanish-American War. He organized the Band of the 8th U. S. Volunteers and the 48th U. S. Volunteers and served with the latter as 2nd Lieutenant until the regiment was mustered out of service in 1901.
    In September, 1901, he received a commission from President Taft, who at that time was Governor-General of the Philippines, to organize a band for the Philippine Government. From an organization of thirty men, the leader developed an excellent band of ninety

by the war. Among these, is found "There's a Service Flag in the Window," both words and music written by Colonel Charles Young, who was a fine amateur musician and a collector of African folk-songs. The war song was

members which came into great prominence when playing at the San Francisco Exposition.

On February 21, 1916, the conductor was retired with the rank of Major. Judge Gilbert, in behalf of the Manila community, presented Major Loving with an engraved gold watch, platinum chain and a purse of gold, with these remarks:

"We the citizens need you. Regardless of race or color; regardless of religious or political views; regardless of station, high or low, we will need you."

The band was next conducted by Lieut. Navarro. By 1919, the band had greatly deteriorated, and Major Loving was again assigned to duty. He re-organized the band and after four years' leadership, was retired with the honor of having brought the organization back to its former efficiency. Major Loving was born on December 17, 1872, in Lovingston, Virginia. Graduating from the Washington, D. C., High School in 1892, he went to Boston to attend the New England Conservatory and there received a thorough musical education. He has recently lived in Alameda, California.

A program given for the benefit of the Philippine Islands Anti-Tuberculosis Society, November 6, 1923, reads:

Andante con Moto from Fifth Symphony......................*Beethoven*
Allegretto Scherzando from Eighth Symphony...........*Beethoven*
Caprice Italien..*Tschaikowsky*
Second Concerto for Piano and Orchestra...............*Rachmaninow*

There were interpolated numbers by Mrs. Wilma Hillberg, pianist, and Mr. Vladimir A. Elin, baritone.

The 349th Artillery Band, an excellent small band, was directed by Lieut. Norman Scott, of Wilmington, Delaware, who died of pneumonia in France. He was succeeded by McReynolds of the 9th Cavalry.

The director of the 351st Field Artillery Band was Dorsey Rhodes, a clarinetist, and a graduate of the Institute of Musical Art, New York. He later had charge of the Howard University Band, Washington, D. C.

One of the talented young musicians of this band was Ernest Hays, of Baltimore, Maryland. He played the saxophone in the dedicated to his friend, Charles Burroughs of New York, in admiration of his dramatic ability.

"The Colored Soldier Boys of Uncle Sam," a marching song, was written by W. J. Nickerson, one of the pioneer musicians of New Orleans, Louisiana, while "Go on, Mule," an army camp folk-song, was the output of J. Fletcher Bryant and R. Nathaniel Dett. Nannie G. Board of Louisville, Kentucky, a teacher in the State Agricultural and Industrial Institute at Nashville, Tennessee, won first place for producing the best original war song in a competition arranged by the United War Work Campaign Committee of the State of Kentucky.

Foremost among the art songs inspired by the war, is "The Young Warrior," by H. T. Burleigh. The English poem is by James Weldon Johnson, whose reputation as a man of letters equals, if not exceeds that of his brother, J. Rosamond Johnson as a musician. The song was trans-

band, but as he was a graduate in the Organ Class of 1916 at the New England Conservatory, advanced studies being interrupted by his call to the colors, he was able to give much pleasure by his organ playing in a chapel at Le Mans, France, where for some time the band was stationed. Hays is now a member of the music faculty at Hampton Institute.

The 807th Pioneer Band, Lieut. Will Vodery, leader, spent some time in France. Among the well-trained and talented musicians in this band were Oral Cooper, tenor, and Louia V. Jones, violinist. The latter was called in the service on the eve of his graduation from the violin department of the New England Conservatory. During the closing sessions of the school he played the Mendelssohn Concerto, Op. 64, with the Conservatory orchestra. As he evinced talent of a high order, a brilliant future was predicted for him. In the band, he played the saxophone, but had an opportunity while in France of giving pleasure by his violin-playing.

Wesley I. Howard, violinist, was assistant band-master of the 809th Infantry Band. A post-graduate of the New England Conservatory, he spent a year in further study at l'Ecole Normale and the Conservatoire National of Paris. He, too, did solo work in France, when for one year he acted as assistant band-master.

lated into Italian by Edvardo Petri, and having a martial motif, it became a marching song of the Italian Army. It was first made known by Pasquale Amato singing it at an Italian benefit concert at Hotel Biltmore. It met with extraordinary success.

Other war songs written by Harry Burleigh were "One Year—1914-1915," words by Margaret M. Harlan, and "The Soldier," the poem by Rupert Brooks. *Musical America* said, "The intensity of this 'One Year' is colossal. Singers will grip their audiences mightily with it . . . It is one of those cases of true simplicity of style wherein greatness is to be found; vital in every sense in this war essay!" "The Victor," another song composed by Burleigh, is dedicated "to all those who gave their lives for the Right."

As a singer, Harry Burleigh rendered valuable volunteer war service in New York. During the period of the war, his art songs were featured by William H. Richardson, colored baritone, who without remuneration gave his services for one year, both as concert soloist and director of Community "Sings." Helen Hagan, graduate of the Yale Conservatory of Music, one of the most prominent Negro concert pianists, succeeded at the close of the war in going to Europe, where she gave cheer to weary and sick soldiers.

Many excellent, though lesser known, Negro musicians joined forces in fostering community singing throughout the United States at that time. Others found that necessary funds could be supplied through the channel of music, and playing hands and singing throats provided the price of material for knitting fingers.

As one, their hearts echoed the old Negro folk-song—

"We will end this war, brethren,
    Down by the river,
End this war, down by the river.

There was an old king in ancient days,
    Down by the river,
Was wicked in all his works and ways,
    Down by the river—Down by the river side."

On September 6, 1919, a significant statement was made
relative to Negro song which Jerome Swinford, leader of
the United States Glee Club of the Hampton Roads Naval
Base, had employed for his singers who were given official
recognition and approval from the Navy Department.
Musical America said, "Mr. Swinford believes that he has
found in the Negro Spirituals the connecting link that
will carry community music from the popular airs of the
day into the realms of music of the better sort."

O, Hallelujah, O, Hallelujah, O, Hallelujah, Lord,
    Who'll jine de Union?
Say, ef you belong to de Union ban',
    Who'll jine de Union?
Den here's my heart, an' here's my han',
    Who'll jine de Union?
I love yer all, both bond an' free,
    Who'll jine de Union?
I love you ef-a you don't love me,
    Who'll jine de Union?

CHAPTER XIII

WORLD MUSICIANS OF COLOR

NAUBAT KHAN KALAWANT—MABED IBN-OUHAB, SEVENTH
CENTURY — BILAL — IBRAHIM — CHEVALIER DE SAINT
GEORGES—GEORGE BRIDGETOWER—HISTORY OF THE KREUTZ-
ER SONATA—JOSE WHITE—ANTONIO CARLOS GOMEZ—
SAMUEL COLERIDGE-TAYLOR—THE ALDRIDGES—"MONTAGUE
RING" (AMANDA IRA ALDRIDGE)—BRINDIS DE SALAS—
OTHER MUSICIANS ABROAD—IGNATIUS SANCHO.

It is interesting to discover that musicians of Negro
blood have been of sufficient importance to have had their
names carried down through the centuries. For the record of the first men and women of humble beginnings
whose talents impressed the nations with whom they were
identified, we turn to ancient sources; from a seeming
obscurity we add them to our list of gifted musicians. In
spite of the fact that the Arabians were a people without
folk-arts, such as pottery and art crafts, during the sixth
to the ninth centuries, they enjoyed a period of progress
which had its full flower in poetry and song. Negroes
among these people at that time made important contribu-
tors to their culture.

Of the Negro, Naubat Khan Kalāwant, Viña player of
the early seventeenth century, employed at the Court of
Jahangir in India, we have the following:

"Ali Khan Karori, who was one of my revered father's
old servants and was the dārogha of the drum-house (Na-
gārak-hāna), I appointed with the title of Naubat Khan,
and promoted him to the rank of 500 personal and 200
horse."[*]

*Memoirs of Jahangir, 1605-1627.

NAUBAT KHAN KALAWANT

Thirteen centuries ago, Arabia gave to the world a poet of humble birth, Antar, whose romance is the inspiration today for dramatist and musician. A century later, a singer in like station, added glory to Arabia. The lives of both poet and musician had many common experiences. The name of the poet, Antar Bin Shaddad, lives through the art of music; the name of the musician awaits a poet to revive the knowledge of his former existence.

Mabed Ibn Ouhab, the date of whose birth is wanting, was born a slave, the son of a Negro father and he, himself, a mulatto. As a youthful slave, Mabed faithfully

"LAHN"

MABED—7TH CENTURY

tended the flocks for his master, but an opportunity was provided for him to take music lessons from Saib Khather-Kachith. Both Antar and Mabed won their freedom because of their marked superiority and extraordinary gifts.

One day, Ibn-Sourëidj and El-Gharid, two of Arabia's celebrated singers, were traveling to Medina to accept the honors that were to be conferred upon men of renown. Arriving at a spot near a bathing pool which was near the city, they met a young boy who was carrying a net to ensnare birds. The lad was singing a "lahn," a well known strain. So beautiful was the voice that the two singers accosting the boy, asked him to repeat the song. This he did and in such a remarkable voice and manner that Ibn Sourëidj turned to El-Gharid and said, "Hast thou ever heard anything to equal this? If it is thus that a bird-boy sings at Medina, what chance have the professional singers in the city? For me, my mother may lose me, if I do not return immediately!" El-Gharid was of the same opinion and both renounced their journey and returned to their homes.

Ibn-Soureïdj's opinion of the voice of the youth Mabed was of great importance, for he himself a freed man, was not only a celebrated singer who was said to "touch the heart-strings by his magnetic emotion" but an instrumentalist of note who was an attaché of the Court of the Calif Othman, about 650 A. D.

The Calif Jezid, a musician himself, learning of the discovery of the talented youth, desired to hear him and sent a courier of Medina with an order to bring Mabed to him. The Calif, wishing to hear the "lahn" which Mabed had set to music, ordered a large basin of water perfumed with musk, saffron and rose-water, and, seating himself on the edge of the basin, a curtain hiding him from Mabed's gaze, he plunged into the perfumed water as he cried out to Mabed, "Sing to me the lahn." Thrice he ordered him to sing—"Once more the incomparable lahn" and Mabed responded with:

"Alas! there are no longer these men—noble hearts! Submitting to fortune, all went the way of their desires.

In rapid course of events, time carried them away. One after the other, they have disappeared. Thus time sweeps away all and annihilates.

The separation causes my eyes to weep, and takes away from them, sleep.

Ah! separation is full of tears, when one loves!"

As Mabed ended the song, the servants replaced the Calif's vestments and brought little boxes of perfume. The singer was presented with 15,000 pieces of gold and told by the Calif to go back to Medina, but "keep this secret about that which you have seen. He who wishes to keep the favor of Princes must be discreet.''

Mabed next studied music under Saib-Khather-Kachith, a man who had been manumitted by Abdallah Ibn-Djafar and Djemila. Mabed's intelligence, beauty of voice, and the merit of his compositions soon acquired celebrity, and we next hear of him as a musician at the palace. Thus he fulfilled the prophecy of Ibn-Soureïdj, ''If this young man lives he will be the great singer of the country.'' A poet speaking of Mabed, declared that ''Towais has shone in the art of singing and so has Ibn-Soureïdj, but Mabed alone has reached the heights in his career.''

While in the service of the Calif Yezid, who reigned but three years and a half, Mabed died at Damascus in the palace of the Prince in 628. His son, Kerden, speaking of the last rites said, ''When the hearse came out of the palace, Salama, a slave of Yezid's, a woman musician who had been a pupil of my father's, took hold of one of the supports of the carriage and with eyes filled with tears, recited the verses of El-Alhouet, which her father had set to music and which alluded to the actual separation of death.'' It was the *lahn* that had first brought Mabed into favor at the Court. The Prince Oualid Ibn Yezid and his brother marched in front of the hearse.

Mabed's personal valuation of his compositions is found in the declaration, ''I have composed airs that a tired man cannot sing or the man who is weighted down with his water-bag. I have composed melodies that a man leaning on his elbows cannot sing without raising himself up straight. I have written those that a man who is seated down cannot sing without rising!''

Mabed has been described as of tall stature, of prepossessing looks but squint-eyed. Alexandre Christianowitsch, to whom we are indebted for facts concerning Arabian music and musicians, says of the *lahn* written by Mabed:

"It possesses all the beauty of the Oriental catilena; the grief, that vague thing that you cannot analyze. It can only be compared with a zephyr which just touches the ear—by a beautiful balmy night. It is a complete dream."

Isaac, son of Ibrahim El Mosouly, a noted musician of the time, one who was at home in poetry, law and music, places Mabed as "A singer who was well-informed. A consummate artist and one of the most agreeable of singers. His compositions denoted a superior talent to all his rivals. He was the prince of singers, he was the first artist of Medina!"

Ibn-Souréidj was a contemporary of Mabed and was

CAMEL CHANT

Folk song noted in 1851 by H. Churi.

himself a freed man. He is described as having been of dark complexion—"wine-colored," with eyes in which there was a flare. Although suffering from physical defects—he was lame—he became noted because of his musical gifts. An older man than the celebrated singer, Mabed, he served as an attaché to the Court of Calif Othman (644-656 A. D.).

We surmise that this was the time of the camel-chants, noted in early Arabian folk-song—those modulated plaints that the camel-drivers chanted with the belief that they would charm their beasts and stir them to a more rapid pace.

When the grand square of the Kaaba was to be enlarged, the Persian workmen brought with them the Persian lute. Ibn-Sourëidj was charmed with the instrument and afterwards used it in accompaniment to his singing. Of four great singers of Arabia, El-Gharid, Mabed, Ibn-Mohriz and Ibn-Sourëidj, Youmes is said to have named the latter as the greatest.[1]

Lafcadio Hearn, who for years made a study of Oriental literature, mentions Bilal, a black Abyssinian, who possessed the sweetest and finest voice in all Islam. The singer, when noticed by the annalist, was thin and tall, of dark complexion, with thick graying hair. For long he sang only for the Kalif Omar. He was taught the Call to Prayer by "Our Lord Mahammed." When traveling to Damascus, Omar was beseiged by the people to let the noted Black Muezzin sing the prayer for them. Although nearly a century in age, Bilal had retained his wonderful voice. Hearn says of him, "They aided him to ascend the minaret. In the midst of great silence the great African voice burst out into the ADHAN as it has still been sung for more than 1,200 years from all the minarets of Islam."[2]

The name of Bilal, of Arabia, is of great significance in the history of music, for he was the singer who introduced the *Call to Prayer*, known throughout all Islam. He was born "Rabáh" and was an Abyssinian slave who belonged to a man of the tribe Djumah. Bilal was persecuted by unbelievers for his ardent faith in Mohammed which resulted in his winning the protection of Abu Bekr, who bought him his freedom. Fleeing with Mohammed to Medina, he made his home with Abu Bekr and continued a faithful follower of the Prophet, who declared a bond

[1] The story of the mulatto Arab musicians are in part, translations from Christianowitsch—"Esquisse Historique de la Musique Arabe aux temps anciens,"—Publ. Cologne, 1863.
[2] See also the "Gulistan."

of brotherhood between Bilal and the Khath Ame Abu Ruwaiha. The former slave had the honor of being named one of the Five non-Arabians to whom Omar assigned grants. When Mohammed was finally prevailed upon to have a musical number to be used to call worshipers to prayer, Bilal received the appointment as the Muaddin of the Prophet, and was the first person to sing the noted adhān.

The singing of the adhān is a highly developed art in Islam, and is carefully studied and practised. The melody varies somewhat, in that it is treated with many embellishments, dependent to some extent on the skill of the singer, but the tune must be correctly fitted to the words. There are seven declarations of faith, one a repetition of the first—"Allah is most great." A familiar arrangement begins, "There's no deity but God."

Bilal was Mohammed's companion on all his campaigns, and carried the prayer-spear, anaza, before the Prophet's public prayers at the great festivals. After the capture and occupation of Mecca, Bilal had the honor of being the singer of the adhān from the roof of the Caaba. After Mohammed's death, the Muaddin, eager to take part in the Holy War, accompanied Abu Ubaida into Syria. While in the conquered land, he was requested to sing the adhān. So touchingly was this done, that Omar and the people wept. The stories of the age of Bilal are conflicting. Lafcadio Hearn speaks of Bilal being 100 years of age at this time, while another account states that Bilal died in Damascus in A. H. 20 (641 A. D.) about the age of sixty. He was buried in adjacent Dariyā.

Ibrahim-al-Mahdi, a renowned singer and musician of Arabia, reigned for a short period as Caliph of Islam. He was the son of the Caliph Muhammed al-Mahdi and a black African slave girl named Shikla or Shaka, and was directly descended from Hashin, the grandfather to the

Prophet Mahomet, and a brother to Haroun al Raschid. Al-'Babbas was his uncle. Ibrahim was born at the close of 162, that is, in July, 779. According to one writer, he was of dark complexion which "he inherited from his mother Shikla who was a 'Negress'." In his manhood he was given the nickname of "al-Tinnan, the dragon"—because of his large physique. In 817 Ibrahim when thirty-eight years old, was chosen to succeed his father as Caliph instead of Al Mamoun whom the people renounced because of his favors to the descendants of Ali rather than to the reigning family, the Abassides.

At the beginning of his reign, Ibrahim received the name of Al Mubarak, "the blessed," but his period as ruler was destined to be short. For failure to receive pay the troops rebelled, and he was defeated and forced to retire to Bagdad. In June, 819 (Hedja 203), his nephew, Al-Mamoun, was proclaimed. Ibrahim made his escape disguised as a woman but was finally arrested. A few years later, in 825-6, Al Mamoun pardoned him. When arrested by one of the Negro police and brought before his nephew he was said to have proudly exclaimed, "If you punish me you will be just; if you pardon me, you will be great." Al Mamoun was moved, and prostrating himself in prayer exclaimed, "Then I pardon you."

In his own words, Ibrahim-Al-Mahdi tells of an incident which took place while he was in hiding after being forced to abdicate. He had asked shelter from a man standing in a doorway who proved to be a barber and the householder. Once inside the comfortable hall, Ibrahim became suspicious that the man might betray him. He was served with refreshments, after which his host brought forth a lute and asked the fugitive to sing, saying, "It will be a great honour for your slave."

"How do you know that I am a good singer?" asked Ibrahim. The barber-host exclaimed, "By Allah! your

reputation is too great for me not to know it; you are
Ibrahim, the son of Mahdi.'' He was then asked to sing
three songs in which Ibrahim was said to have excelled.
The musician admitted his identity and asked, "Where
did you learn of these three airs?'' His host replied, "I
have been in the service of Ishak, son of Mausili (the famous musician), and I often heard him speak of the great
singers and the airs in which they excelled.'' So pleased
was the man with Ibrahim's singing and playing, he refused the gold pieces that were offered for his hospitality.

It was Ibrahim's singing and playing which served to
introduce him to the young woman who became his wife.
One day, passing a linen-merchant's house, Ibrahim noticed a beautiful hand and wrist at the latticed window,
and eager to meet the owner of the pretty hand, he used
clever subterfuge to enter the house. He slipped in with
a number of invited guests who were expected, and the
host was led to believe that his friends had brought him
as a special guest. After refreshments were served, a
young slave girl entertained with singing to the strain of
the lute. Ibrahim criticised her performance at which she
threw down the lute and taxed the host on the rudeness
of his supposed guest. To cover his confusion, Ibrahim
asked for a lute and sang so exquisitely, that the slave
singer threw herself at his feet, while all present marveled
at his musical skill. Three times he sang which aroused
great enthusiasm. After all the guests had left, his host
pressed him to tell him who he was. When Ibrahim gave
his name, the merchant exclaimed, "I should have been
surprised, sir, had anyone of a rank inferior to your own
possessed such skill. To think one of the royal house was
with me all the time and I knew it not!''

The host was curious as to why Ibrahim had entered
his home, and upon being told of how he was attracted
by the beautiful hand at the lattice, the merchant called

all his slaves in succession to examine their hands. At
last the host called his sister, and as soon as Ibrahim saw
her he cried out, "It is she!" It was love at first sight,
and the merchant called ten men friends as witnesses, and
then and there gave his sister in marriage to Ibrahim,
with a dowry of twenty thousand dirhems. The happy
lover gave one bag of money to the bride and distributed
the other bags among those present. Mamoun, who was
then Caliph, ordered Ibrahim to present his generous
father-in-law at Court, where he became one of the faithful courtiers.

At one time Ibrahim was taunted because of his Negro
blood with the question: "Is it thou who art the Negro
Khalif?" To which the ruler replied, "I am he whom
thou hast deigned to pardon; and it has been said by the
slave of the Banu 'l—Hashás—'When men extol their
wealth, the slave of the family of Hashás can supply by
his verse, the defect of birth and fortune.' Though I be a
slave, my soul, through its noble nature, is free; though
my body be dark, my mind is fair."

Ibrahim passed away on Friday, 7th Ramadan, which
is July, 939 A. D., at Surr-man-rá râ. He was of the Ab-
bassides dynasty of Caliphs of Bagdad, which was the
most celebrated of all the Islam dynasties. During his
reign, he built the mosque at Ar-Ru-Safā. The many
stories told of Ibrahim reveal him as a man of great generosity and tenderness which quite unfitted him to be a
strict ruler of the people. A scholar of fine attainments,
he cared more for literary pursuits and for his music. He
is best remembered as one of the great singers of Arabia.
He played several instruments but was a skilfull performer on the lute. Ibrahim lived at the time when the
use of Arabian music was at its height; and he was the
leading figure of one of two rival schools of musical
thought. He was termed a "progressive" as opposed to

the "conservative" musician, Ishaq-al-Mausili.

The history of European music also reveals a number of musicians of Negro blood who gained distinction as executants of note. Noticeably among these men of world fame was the Chevalier de Saint Georges. This violinist, born at Basse-Terre, Guadaloupe, on Christmas day, 1745, was one of the most brilliant virtuosos of France. He was a Creole of handsome appearance, the son of a Negro mother and a French father, M. de Boulogne, a comptroller-general. In his novel, "Le Chevalier de Saint Georges," Roger de Beauvoir states that the boy was named after the finest vessel in the harbor of Guadaloupe—thus the Christian name of Saint Georges was given the child whom the father brought to France and placed under competent instructors. He was taught fencing under a famous master, La Boëssière, with whom he made his home.

Early evincing musical talent, he became a pupil of Jean Marie Clair. He studied composition with Gossec, who in 1776 dedicated to him his "Six Trios for two violins and Bass." The young musician developed as a fencer, dancer, and artist. Having become very proficient with the foils, he fenced with noted men, among whom was the celebrated Italian, Faldoni, and was heralded as the most skilled fencer of France.[3]

His father left him a comfortable inheritance, which enabled him to become a member of the aristocratic society of Paris and a popular idol of the day. Nevertheless, he did not neglect his musical studies. He was always a serious student; and during the winter of 1772-1773, he was heard at the Concert des Amateurs as violin soloist in two original concertos written for violin with or-

[3] On the 9th of April, 1787, a fencing match was arranged between Saint Georges and Mlle. la Chevalière d'Éon de Beaumont. This took place at Carlton House in London. Among the distinguished spectators was the Prince of Wales, afterwards, George IV.

chestral accompaniment. The compositions were praised highly by the press. These first pieces were followed by six string quartets. Published in June, 1773, this establishes the important fact that Saint Georges was one of the first French composers of string quartets. His work is contemporaneous with that of J. Ch. Bach (1772) and Haydn (1768).

Shortly after gaining fame as a violin soloist, the Chevalier de Saint Georges is said to have played concertos with Jarnovitz. Saint Georges followed Gossec as director of the Concert des Amateurs. He continued to compose and finally in 1777 turned his attention to the theatre. In June, he produced *Ernestine,* a comedy in three acts, at the Comèdie Italienne. The music was charming and graceful, but the libretto by Laclos was not liked, so the work did not survive. Only fragmentary melodies exist. Following a second series of quartets in 1778, *La Chasse,* a new comedy with ariettes, was performed at the Comédie Italienne. It brought him the favor of Mme. de Montesson, the talented wife of the Duke of Orleans, who made him director of the concerts at her theatre. There in a beautiful concert hall, dedicated to the Muses, Saint Georges appeared with prominent people of the day. His concertos were more successful than his dramas. He became an intimate friend of the Duke of Orleans; and, having an office assigned him in the Duke's hunting establishment, he was given the title of Lieutenant of the Hunt of Pinci.

Most versatile of men, he essayed interpretative roles and acted in comedy in the home theatre of Marquise de la Montalembert. His next piece written for the theatre was *The Anonymous Lover,* the manuscript score of which is in the Paris Conservatory.

The composer knew little of the art of economy, and as

he was both liberal and generous he was forced to turn to his skill as a fencer in order to add to his purse when, upon the death of his friend, the Duke of Orleans, whom in 1787 Saint Georges accompanied into exile, he lost his position in the hunting establishment. He met the most noted fencing-masters on the continent, but returned to Paris to resume his musical activities. His *The Girl Boy*, a two-act piece, was presented on August 9th, 1787, at the Comédie Italienne and was highly praised.

Political adventures intrigued him. As early as 1761, he had been one of the gendarmes of the royal guard; and for two years, about 1791, he was a captain in the National Guard. It was during this period that Saint Georges gave concerts with Louise Fusil and Lamotte, a horn-player, at Lille, and in Belgium took part in martial operations.

As leader, "Chief of Brigade," he fell under the suspicion of graft, the cry of the hour, and of making private use of regimental funds. He was dismissed from the service although he gave proofs of his innocence and loyalty to his country. After having suffered imprisonment for over a year, many came forward to attest to his honesty and bravery, among whom were his successor, Target, the Mayor and other officials of Lille. The evidence was so conclusive that he was reinstated in command of his regiment; but, finding a chaotic condition due to political intrigue, he finally ended his military career. He made a visit to San Domingo, returned to Paris and died, a poor man, on June 12, 1799.

Greatly gifted, Saint Georges was also noted for being charitable, brilliant and vivacious, and of a most engaging personality. As a violinist, it was stated that he was one of the most brilliant of French virtuosi—vigorous and exact in his bowing, daring and skilful in bravura passages,

LE CHEVALIER DE SAINT GEORGES

and poetic and expressive—his notes appearing "like many dazzling sky-rockets."[4]

In 1776, the following stanza was written by Moline under the portrait of Chevalier Saint Georges.

THE BEGINNING OF THE *RONDO* OF THE SECOND QUARTET

BY SAINT GEORGES

Rondeau di Menuetto.

etc.

> "Offspring of taste and genius, he
> Was one the sacred valley bore,
> Of Terpischore nursling and competitor;
> And rival of the god of harmony.
> Had he to music added poesy,
> Apollo's self he'd been mistaken for."

[4] *Le Chevalier de Saint Georges* by Roger de Beauvoir. Calmann Lèvy, editor, page 23. In his list of compositions, we find: Three Sonatas for violin and pianoforte (or clavecin), 1781; Three Sonatas for two violins, 1801 (in the British Museum) and Symphonies Concertants for two principal violins, one of which has orchestral accompaniment; Six Quartettes for 2 violins, alto and bass, Op. I—Sieber, publ. 1773; Ten Concertos, Op. 2 to 8—Bailleux, publ. 1775; Five Comedies—*Ernestine;* a few selections to be seen in the Paris Conservatory; *La Chasse; l'Amant Anonyme; La Fille garçon* and *Le Marchand de marrons.* The complete score of *l'Amant Anonyme* (The Anonymous Lover) is housed in the Paris Conservatory.

Of this versatile artist, the Abbé Grégoire says: "When Saint Georges, who was considered the best swordsman of his time, was to fence or exhibit his musical talents, the newspapers announced it to the idle capital. His bow and foil set all Paris in motion."[5] According to Lionel de la Laurence (translation by Frederick H. Martens for *The Musical Quarterly*) "Saint Georges' quartets are written in a clear, flowing, ethereal style. More supple, more singing than that of Gossec, his melodies, notably in the rondos, well characterize the sentimental and melancholy mulatto . . . . In all St. Georges' works the thematic material shows grace with a touch of Creole languor."[6]

Ignatius Sancho, a writer who made his home in England, was the composer of various pieces of music, one whose talent and musical taste are best remembered in his mentioned "Theory of Music." Sancho, called by Fuller "God's Image Cut In Ebony," was born in 1729 of slave parents on board a slave ship off the coast of Guinea en route to the Spanish West Indies. His father committed suicide rather than submit to being enslaved, and his mother early passed away. At the age of two, the child was taken to England and given to three maiden sisters. Finding these owners severe to the boy and unappreciative of his unusual promise, the Duke of Montague who lived at Blackheath befriended him and gave him an opportunity to study. He was given the name of Ignatius when baptized at Carthagena and the surname "Sancho," after Don Quixote's Sancho, was added. At the death of his patron, the Duchess of Montague took the youth into her home and gave him the place of butler.

[5] On November 12, 1912, a street in Basse Terre was given the name of the noted musician.

[6] Ferris, William H., *The African Abroad*, vol. 2, p. 828; Grégoire, *An Enquiry concerning the Intellectual and moral Faculties of the Negro*.

At her death, she left him an annuity, while he also enjoyed the friendship of George, the 4th Duke, son-in-law of his benefactor. Sancho married a young woman from the West Indies, and by his letters one learns of his steady devotion to Anne and their six children. His extraordinary learning, acquired through his own efforts, brought him to the attention of the educated people of the day. Among these was Lawrence Sterne.[7]

In addition to his friendship with Sterne, Sancho enjoyed intercourse with members of the circle of the theater, painting and music. His love for the theater led him to aspire to become an actor in such roles as Othello and Oroonoko, but he was unfitted for the stage. He did write two plays, however, and admiringly followed his friend, Garrick. In 1768, Gainsborough who performed on various instruments and enjoyed the society of musicians and writers as well as painters, made a portrait of Sancho at Bath. The painting was later engraved by Bartolozzi. Hogarth is said to have painted Sancho in 1742 as the Negro boy in the picture *Taste in High Life*.

[7] In 1766, a letter written to Laurence Sterne in appreciation of his attitude towards slavery was the introduction to a loyal friendship. The contents expressing thanks for the minister's liberality touched thus upon the writer's own race and struggles: "I am one of those people whom the vulgar and illiberal call 'Negroes' " .... and later, "Dear Sir, think in me you behold the uplifted hands of thousands of my brother Moors."

In Sterne's reply, he wrote, speaking of a friendless young Negro girl—"But why *her* brethren? or yours, Sancho, any more than mine? At which tint are the ties of blood to cease?" In subsequent letters, Sterne wrote—"You know, Sancho, that I am your friend and well-wisher" and again from Coxwold he cautions him—"I hope that you will not forget your custom of giving me a call at my lodgings next winter—in the meantime, I am very cordially, my honest friend Sancho,

"Yours, L. Sterne."

The writer's need of funds was the cause of his opening a grocery store in 1779, but his business interests did not prevent him from following the muses. He wrote pamphlets, discussions on the events of the day, composed pieces and published *A Theory of Music* which was dedicated to the Princess Royal. He submitted a piece to one Mr. H—— through his wife Mrs. —— to whom he wrote on June 17, 1779, "Pray make my kindest respects to your good partner and tell him, I think I have the right to trouble him with my musical nonsense.—I wish it were better for my own sake—bad as it is, I know he will not despise it, because he has more good-nature." At an earlier period (November 5, 1777) he sent one of his compositions to Mrs. C——. Addressing her from Charles Street, he says, "The little dance (which I like because I made it)—I humbly beg you will make Jacky play."

While Sancho wrote in his early manhood that "my chief pleasure has been books," he writes later of evenings at a friend's "fine place, good songs—much company—and good music." His musical taste was highly regarded and his opinion sought. In a letter to one Mr. R——, he says, "Well, I have critically examined thy song—some parts I like well. . . . I will certainly attempt giving it a tune—such as I can—the first leisure—but it must undergo some little pruning when we meet." He shared his musical pleasures with friends. He sent a letter from "Charles Street," April 9, 1778, to his correspondent, Mrs. H—, saying, "I present—to Mr. H—, that he may judge of fiddler's taste and fiddler's consequence in our great metropolis—the ticket was a present from the great Giardini to the lowly Sancho—and I offer it as a tribute of musical affection to thy worthy partner."

Sancho passed away on December 14, 1780, and was

Ignatius Sancho.

buried in Westminster, Broadway.[8] In 1803 his son William published an edition of his father's letters.[9] This publication accounts for Sancho's being known more as a man of letters than as a musician.

[8] In 1777, Sancho had some thought of coming to America and in December wrote to a friend, Mr. S—, a letter which prophesied the future greatness of the United States. He declared, "When it shall please the Almighty that things shall take a better turn in America —when he conviction of their madness shall make them court peace —and the same conviction of our (English) cruelty and injustice induce us to settle all points in equity—when that time arrives, my friend, America will be the grand patron of genius—trade and arts will flourish—and if it shall please God to spare us till that period —we will either go and try our fortunes there—or stay in Old England and talk about it."

[9] At that time he maintained a bookstore in his father's old shop in Charles Street. The Gainsborough painting was presented by a daughter of Ignatius Sancho, to her father's friend, William Stevenson of Norwich. It was sold in 1889 with the Stevenson estate. A fine example of the charm and excellence of Sancho's writing is seen in a letter written to "Mr. J— W— E—" in January, 1780— the last year of his life. It is worthy of being published as an essay. In a copy of Sancho's memoirs that was owned by Wendell Phillips the abolitionist penned the lines—"On the value of books," to the heading of this beautiful letter.

Sancho's happy family life and devotion to his wife should not pass un-noticed. The writer-musician wrote to a friend in 1777, "You cannot imagine what hold little Billy gets of me—he grows —prattles—and every day learns something new—and by his good-will would be ever in the shop with me. The monkey! he clings round my legs—and if I chide him or look sour—he holds up his little mouth to kiss me;—I know I am the fool—for parent's weakness is child's strength:—true orthodox—which will hold good between lover and lovee . . . . Dame Sancho would be better if she cared less.—I am her barometer—if a sigh escapes me, it is answered by a tear in her eye; I oft assume a gayety to illume her dear sensibility with a smile—which twenty years ago almost bewitched me;—and *mark!*—after twenty years' enjoyment—constitutes my highest, pleasure!" Laurence Sterne—"'Letters, sermons, etc." Saintsbury edit. Letters of the late Ignatius Sancho, an African, etc. Printed by J. Nichols—London. MDCCLXXXIV. Third edition.

Before 1790, an interesting character by the name of George Polgreen Bridgetower had been introduced in the best circles in London. He was familiarly called the "Abyssinian Prince." The details of his family history are not known. It is said that his father came from Africa and migrated to Poland where he married a German or Polish woman, who afterwards lived in Dresden and died at Budissen on September 11, 1807. John Frederick Bridgetower and his wife, Marie Ann, were the parents of two sons, both talented musicians, one a 'cellist and the other, George, the violinist, who was born in Biala, or Viala, Poland, in 1779.

In 1790, Bridgetower, the father, was seen in London with young George who was then known as a violin prodigy of exceptional gift and talent. The mother at this time was living in Dresden with the other son. We hear nothing further of this youth, whose initial was "T," except that he evidently became a 'cellist of some note as he took part on an important program with his brother in 1803. The son, George Augustus Polgreen, was destined to have his name linked with Beethoven, the great German master, and to become the first interpreter of the famous work known as the "Kreutzer Sonata."

A pass dated July 27, 1803, which was probably a permit to travel to Dresden and London to play, gives a personal description of young Bridgetower. Filed in Vienna police records, the permit reads, "George Bridgetower; character, tonemaster; born in Viala, Poland; twenty-four years of age, middle height, smooth brown face, dark brown hair, brown eyes and somewhat thick nose." From a picture of this period, we find that Bridgetower was handsome in appearance.

The boy was a pupil of Giorn (or Jarowic) and also of Haydn. At the early age of ten he showed great talent.

GEORGE POLGREEN BRIDGETOWER.

1782?—1860.

In his youth he became a musician in the service of the Prince of Wales, who later became George IV. His first concert appearance was in Paris at a "Concert Spirituel," given April 13, 1789. His playing was of such excellence, that another concert was given eight months later at Bath and attended by 550 persons. The *Morning Post* of December 8, 1789, stated in a review, "Ranzzini was enraptured and declared that he had never heard such execution before even from his friend La Motte, who was, he thought, much inferior to this wonderful boy. The father was in the gallery and so affected by the applause bestowed on his son, that tears of pleasure and gratitude flowed in profusion. The profits were estimated at 200 guineas." The *Bath Journal* published a letter from the lad's father who wrote appreciatively of the warm reception given his talented boy. On February 19, 1790, George made his first public appearance in London at the Drury Lane Theatre, where he played a violin solo between parts of the *Messiah*. On the second of June, he and Clement (then a lad of about the same age), gave a concert under the patronage of the Prince of Wales.

Bridgetower continued his studies under Barthelmon, Giornovichi and Altwood, while at the same time he became first violinist at the establishment of the Prince of Wales at Brighton. In 1802, while yet a lad, we hear of his visiting his mother in Dresden. He took advantage of the baths at Teplitz and Carlsbad and had his permit extended so that he might spend a few months in Vienna. Appleby speaks of him at this time as being a very industrious man although inclined to be melancholy.

We find Bridgetower at the Handel commemoration of 1791, when, with young Hummel, he was seated at the side of Joah Bates, organist, and pulled out his stops for him. He was engaged as a performer at the Haydn-Salo-

mon concerts[10] of 1791, and at the concerts of Barthle-
mon's in 1792 and 1794 when he played a concerto of
Viotti's. Further notice of Bridgetower appears in Bos-
sler's *Musical Correspondence* of July 7, 1790, in a letter
of June 6 from Abt Vogler, which reads:

"On Wednesday, June 2, I attended a concert in Hano-
ver Square, where two young heroes of the violin vied
with each other, and all lovers of art and music for three
hours enjoyed the most pleasing entertainment. The
interspersed concerts were every time most warmly applauded.

"The quartet, however, was by young violin virtuosi,
whose combined ages would not be forty years, and the
playing of which surpassed every expectation. The first
violin was played by Clement from Vienna, the second by
Bridgetower of Africa who is ten years."

Bridgetower spent much time in playing in Vienna,
while successful appearances in Dresden, both in public
and exclusive affairs, gave him entry into the highest
musical circles. Many appreciative letters were received,
and at one of the private musicals he made the acquaintance of Held.[11]

Anticipating the arrangement of English concerts, a letter of January 14, 1803, reads,—"Billy Cole sent me
your sealed letter to Brighton which I, myself, placed in
the hands of the Prince and it was read in my presence.
His Royal Highness considered the letter very appropriate and was pleased to grant him permission. So much

[10] The first Haydn concert took place May 16. Bridgetower played
concertos with Salomon at the remaining five of the series in Han-
over Square Rooms.

[11] At his first Dresden concert, July 24, 1802, given under the
direction of Schulz, the program read: No. I—Symphony, Mozart;
No. II—Violin Concerto; No. III—A Symphony, Viotti; No. IV—
Serenate, Viotti; No. V—Symphonique Piece; No. VI—Violin
Variations.

Facsimile of a letter written by Beethoven to Baron Alexandre de Wezlar. Reproduced from the original in the possession of Mr. Arthur F. Hill, F.S.A., and by his kind permission.

for the present.'' The note was signed by Frederick Lindemann, a member of the Prince of Wales' orchestra. On the 18th of March, a concert was given at which Mme. Eliot, who subscribed for eighteen tickets, opened the patron list. Mlle. Grunwald was to sing, but her father wrote that his daughter had contracted a cold and would be unable to appear. The program, given without the songs, was as follows:

Part I No. I Symphony...Beethoven

   No. II ....

   No. III Violin Concerto..........................Bridgetower

Part II No. I Violoncello Concerto....Mr. T. Bridgetower[12]

   No. II ....

   No. III Rondo for Violin

After several weeks, another concert was given on April 26. Mme. Eliot was again a patron and subscribed for twenty-five tickets. Other concerts were planned for the year 1803, and at this time Bridgetower asked the assistance of Beethoven. This was willingly given, and the first of a series of concerts took place in May.

A police license was necessary in order to give concerts, and at Vienna, May 9, 1803, Bridgetower made an application in which the following reasons were given for making the request:

1—At present the musician has the honor of being in active service of the Crown Prince of England.

2—He has already played violin concertos in many parts of Europe.

3—He has received the support of famous musicians and now wishes, he himself, to add publicly to his reputation. The concert is thought to have taken place on the 24th of May. The following statement appears on the reverse side of the permit given by the Vienna police:

[12] Brother of George.

"At this (date indefinite) between the 16th and 24th of May, the celebrated A Major Sonata Op. 47, dedicated to Rudolph Kreutzer of Paris, said by Schrieber to have been originally written for Bridgetower, was performed." The patron list included many titled and noted persons among whom were—Le Prince Esterhazy, Le Prince Lobkowitz, Le Prince Schwarzenberg and l'Envoyé d'Angleterre. As the concert date was near at hand, Bridgetower urged Beethoven to complete the Sonata for pianoforte and violin, that he might have his part. Only the first part had been written, the piano part simply sketched in here and there. About four-thirty one morning, he called Beethoven and again asked for his copy. As there was not time to write the work out, Bridgetower played the theme and variations in F (Andante con Variazioni) from Beethoven's manuscript. This took place in the Hall Augarten at eight in the morning. During these times, this was not an unaccustomed hour for rehearsal.

The Allegro in 6/8 time was said to have been beautifully written, originally the part of Op. 30 in A Major for Violin and Piano dedicated to the Emperor Alexander. Later Beethoven took this out as being too brilliant, although "the fascinating Tarantelle was in his judgment, especially adapted to the temperamental Bridgetower." The variations remained in the Sonata.[13]

---

[13] The following is an interesting communication from Czerny, which Thayer quoted: "In the V Sonata for Bridgetower, the first part was written in four days, the other parts in two days. The finale taken from an earlier finished Sonata." He gives the theme which appears in the first movement as one taken from Kreuzer and adds, "I was assured of this by a French artist (1805). Perhaps this is the reason for the dedication."

Thayer states that in later years Bridgetower spoke to him about Beethoven, and told him that when the Sonata Op. 47 was composed, all the parts had been collected, and on the first leaf was a

Bridgetower enjoyed the friendship and association of the exclusive circles. We learn of the famous physician and Prague professor, Dr. Joh. Th. Helm, with Count Prichnowsky, making a visit to Vienna in the Spring, and, meeting Beethoven on the street, were invited by him to hear a rehearsal of his string quartettes at the home of Schuppanzigh. Helm wrote, "We met a number of the best musicians gathered together, such as the violinist Krumbholz, Moser of Berlin, the mulatto Bridgethauer; also a Herr Schrieber and the 12 (or 14) year old Kraft."

About 1795, a little group of noted musicians met informally at a Mr. Tomkinson's to try over and to review new music of Germany. Those who regularly assembled there included, J. B. Cramer (of the "Cramer Studios"), pianist; his half brother, F. Cramer; J. R. Salomon; Bridgetower, "a mulatto and celebrated violinist"; Watts, tenor; Morant, also a tenor—who became the husband of Dussek's widow; Dahmen; Lindley and Crossdale. At one of these impromptu musicales, the new Trios Op. 1 of Beethoven were played.

Bridgtower's introduction to another circle by his friend Beethoven is recorded in the latter's (not dated) letter, saying, "Come, my dear boy, at 12 o'clock to Count Dehm's where we were day before yesterday. They will perhaps wish to hear you play something—that you will

dedication to him. Before leaving Vienna, however, he quarreled with Beethoven over a young woman, and Beethoven then dedicated the work to Kreutzer.

He continues, "As I accompanied him (Beethoven) in this sonata, I suggested in the first part of the Presto, 18 measures for the pianoforte instead of nine. Beethoven jumped up and threw his arms around me and said, 'Again, my dear boy,' and held the pedal down during the course of this, unto nine measures—Beethoven's expression in the Andante was so chaste, which was always characteristic of his slow movements, that the sympathetic unison demanded a repetition."

see. I cannot come before half past one—until then I will take pleasure in thinking about seeing you today.'' Probably in 1803 Beethoven in another letter thus introduced Bridgetower to Baron Wetzler:

"At Home, on May 18. Although we have not spoken, I do not hesitate for all that, to speak of the bearer, Mr. Bridgetower, as a master of his instrument, a very skilful virtuoso worthy of recommendation. Besides concertos, he plays in quartetts in a most praiseworthy manner and I wish very much that you would make him better known. He has already made the acquaintance of Lobkowitz, Fries and many other distinguished admirers. I believe that it would not be unwise to bring him some evening to Theresa Schonfeld's who I know has many friends —or else at your home.''

Bridgetower's works were worthy of notice. Manuscripts found in the British Museum, bear his signature. Chief among his compositions there is the *Henry* ballad dedicated to her Royal Highness, the Princess of Wales, which was formerly sung by Miss Feron. The pianoforte studies are forty-one in number. Other works thought to be his are two books of *Minuets for Violin, Mandolin, German Flute and Harpsichord, Composed by an African, Inscribed to His Grace, Duke of Buccleugh and to the Right Honorable John, Lord Montague of Broughton.* The studies *Diatonica Armonica* mentioned above, were published in 1812.

Bridgetower visited Rome in 1825 and again in 1827 after which he returned to London. The date of his marriage is unknown, but he is said to have outlived his wife, and to have bequeathed the sum of $5,000 to his wife's sister, a Miss Drake. A daughter who lived in Italy is said to have been his only offspring. During the latter part of his life, he became practically unknown. His death occurred at 8 Bedford street, in the southern part of London, February 29, 1860.

José White, a Negro Cuban violinist, born in Matanzas on January 17, 1833, the son of an amateur musician, began violin lessons when quite young. When visiting Cuba in 1855, Gottschalk, American Creole pianist, heard the talented boy play and advised that he be sent to France to study. White entered the Paris Conservatory of Music; and the next year, in July, 1856, he won the first prize for his violin playing.

Le Pays of August 5th stated, "As for Mr. White, he showed himself so much superior, that there ought to have been created in his favor an exceptional prize. He has played with an extraordinary animation, not like a pupil, but like a master,—like a great artist who commands his auditory. The jury itself was electrified. In order to compete with that young man, there ought to have been masters there."

White, at that time over eighteen years of age, was said to be of prepossessing looks.—"He carries his head high, and his look is proud and intrepid," said the *Gazette Musicale*. Alard took great interest in the young artist and spared no pains in making his ability known.

In 1858, when White was called home by the illness of his father, Rossini, the composer wrote him,

"Allow me to express to you all the pleasure that I felt Sunday last at my friend Mr. David's. The warmth of your execution, the feeling, the elegance, the brilliancy of the school to which you belong, show qualities in you as an artist of which the French school may be proud. May it be, Sir, that through my sympathetic wishes I may bring you good fortune by finding again in good health the one for whom you fear today.

"Accept my blessings, Sir, I wish you a happy journey and a speedy return.

"G. Rossini."

Shortly after White's arrival in Cuba, his father passed away. Before his return to France, he gave many concerts in his native land. His first concert after his return to Paris won for him the reception due a master. *"L'Illustration"* said of him, "He possesses an extreme dexterity in the use of ·the bow, and makes the staccato with as much audacity as perfection. He has the agreeable tone, the elegant style, the proper expression and is not affected. Here, then, he is placed in the first rank in that glorious phalanx of violinists which Europe envies us."

He next visited Spain, and played there before the Queen who presented him with a set of diamond studs and bestowed upon him the decoration of Chevalier of the order of Isabella, the Catholic. The musician was further honored by the Queen by her acceptance of the dedication of a piece which he had written.

Upon his return to France in 1864 White played at the Tuilleries before His Majesty Napoleon the Third and the Empress Eugenie. During the absence of Alard, the professor at the Conservatory, White was called upon to take charge of his classes. Teaching at the Conservatory in 1865, he was next admitted as a member of the Société de Concerts. A gold-ornamented violin bow, was a prized gift of appreciation from Alard, his former teacher.

In Herz Hall, in 1867, he played his own concerto, written for violin and orchestra. It was thought by some to be of unnecessary length. However, the *French Musicale* added,—under date of March 3:

"Mr. White's concerto is very temperate—the fabric of it is very well cared for; the main themes are well separated from the very commencement; the harmonies are unmistakably elegant and fine; the orchestration is written with a firm and sure hand, without fumblings or failings. He had the good fortune to receive from the delighted

A. CARLOS GOMEZ

audience that surrounded him, a double wreath presented together to the violinist and to the composer.''

The next five years White spent in teaching, playing and composing. His studies for violin were approved by Auber, director of the Conservatory and chairman of the Committee on Musical Studies, and were used in the course. White had won the friendship of Ambrose Thomas, Gounod and other leading masters.

In 1876, White visited the United States, and on March 12, 1876, he appeared in New York at a Philharmonic Concert given by the Theodore Thomas Orchestra when he played the Mendelssohn Concerto and the Bach Chaconne. On March 26, he appeared in a concert given at the Boston Theatre, assisted by Levy, the cornetist. The press praised his style and masterly interpretation. After making a favorable impression in this country, the violinist went back to France and visited Brazil. He returned to Paris and died in that city in 1920.

His compositions include a quatuor for stringed Instruments, several fantasies, six studies for violin, pieces for one and two instruments, and "La Bella Cubana," "Stryienne" and "Romance sans Paroles" which were lately to be had at the music house of G. Schirmer in New York.[14]

An outstanding racial figure in the realm of opera is Antonio Carlos Gomez, born in Brazil, July 11, 1839. *Musical America* in February, 1924, says, "It was in Campinas, a city in Brazil of considerable importance as a coffee center, that the mulatto Gomez, composer of the opera, "Il Guarany," and generally noted Brazil's chief

[14] *Biography* by Paul Dupont—Paris, 1874. José White was the owner of the fine violin called "Swan's Song," said to be the last made Stradivarius violin. *The Strad*—July, 1909. Detailed press comments, James M. Trotter, *Music and Some Highly Musical Peoples.*

musician, was born. There is a statue of him, baton in hand, bronze music desk behind him, in a prominent little square in the center of the town—a fragile fellow of typical Brazilian lack of physique, overweighted by a mass of unbearded locks. Campinas appears to have a special trend toward music, for this was also the birth place of Guiomar Novaes.''

Before Gomez had reached his majority, he was sent to Europe by the Emperor of Portugal. He received his musical education at the Conservatorio of Milan, and in 1861, his first work ''A Noite de Castello'' was produced at Rio de Janeiro. His first appearance as a composer was made at Milan, January, 1867, when he produced a piece called ''Se na minga.''

Thus meeting success, he gave, in 1868, a revue *Nella Luna*. The work by which he is best remembered is the opera *Il Guarany* which was first produced at La Scala on March 19, 1870. After being heard in Italian cities, it was performed at Covent Garden in England, July 13, 1872. It was revived on May 16, 1874, and when heard a few years later, February 17, 1879, at Moscow, it was warmly received. The opera was not heard in the United States until November, 1884, when it was given by the Italian Opera Company at the Star Theatre. *The New York Tribune* of November 8, was not enthusiastic, but the *New York World* said, ''The libretto adapted from a South American novel with an aboriginal texture, has the merit of situation and color. The merits of the opera are dramatic action and local color. It is picturesque, romantic and vivid. The performance was a most vigorous and excellent one.''

The opera of *Fosca,* given at La Scala on February 16, 1873, was unsuccessful. Then followed *Salvator Rosa,* a lyric drama in four acts, the libretto by M. Ghislanzoni, which was first produced at the teatro Carlo

SAMUEL COLERIDGE-TAYLOR

Felice in Genoa, on March 21, 1874. The music was said to be superior to that of *Il Guarany*. When the season re-opened at La Scala, *Salvator Rosa* brought the composer fifteen recalls. The press spoke of "the warm and brilliant coloring, ample measures of scenic effect and admirable precision in its technicalities."

Of a fourth opera which was not well-received, Cherubini, Junior, writing for *The Music Trade Review* from Milan, March 29, 1879, stated, "It appears to me that Signor Gomez left the field of pure Italian melody for which his warm nature and his musical education are fitted, in order to throw himself into the mare magnum of Wagnerism. . . . Perhaps the principal reason of the failure comes from the circumstance that the subject is always portrayed with dark colors of hatred and crime; among those a ray of brightness never appears to afford relief to your oppressed senses."[15]

The opera of *Lo Schiavo* (The Slave) was produced for the first time on September 29, 1889, at Rio Janeiro when the composer's countrymen paid him great honor. The performance was conducted by the composer. It was considered the most important event in the musical history of Brazil, and the Emperor, Empress and the entire Court attended the performance.

Two years later, 1891, *Condor* was produced at Milan. An ode entitled *Il Saluto del Brasile* was performed at the Philadelphia Exhibition on July 19, 1876. Another work of similar character, *Colombo*, a cantata, was written for the Columbus Festival in 1892. Gomez was appointed director of the Conservatory, Pesaro, in 1892; but, owing to ill health, he returned to Brazil. Shortly after an appointment as director of the Conservatorium at Para, Gomez died on September 16, 1896.

[15] Signors Tamagno, Kashman and De Rezke with Mlle. Emma Turolla, and Mme. D'Angeri were in the cast.

Samuel Coleridge-Taylor, born in Holborn, near London, England, on August 15, 1875, is recorded in history as the greatest Negro composer and one of the greatest English musicians of his time. He was the first musician of African blood to receive world recognition. The musician was affiliated closely with the lovers of Negro music and was greatly interested and moved by the folk-music of his race. His biographer, in giving his reasons for dwelling on Mr. Coleridge-Taylor's racial qualities, says that "the musician never forgot them, never feared to defend them, and his music is so fraught with their characteristics that to ignore them, had it been possible, would have been a deliberate misinterpreting of my subject."

The composer was the son of a Negro of Sierra Leone, educated in England, a member of the Royal College of Surgeons and a licentiate of the Royal College of Physicians. The composer's mother was Alice Hare, a young white woman of London. As the father was of unstable character, the marriage was an unhappy one; and the parents soon separated. The young mother removed to Croydon with her infant son, and in this section the musician lived and died.

Coleridge-Taylor first became acquainted with the violin at the age of five when a small instrument was given him by Holman, an elder member of the family who had befriended Mrs. Coleridge-Taylor and her boy. During his boyhood, he possessed a sweet, pure voice and sang at St. George's Presbyterian Church and later at the Church of St. Mary Magdalene at Addiscombe. His first teacher was Joseph Beckwith, an orchestra conductor who was attracted by the lad's evident love for music. In 1890, the youth entered the Royal College of Music where, studying violin, piano, harmony and composition, he remained until 1897. His teacher in composition was Sir Charles Villiers Stanford, who became his good friend.

In 1895 the young student won the Lesley Alexander prize in composition. His first effort in composition was a setting or arrangement of the National Hymn which he attempted at the early age of nine years when a pupil at the primary school.

The composer's career, however, had already begun. In 1891, Novello and Company published his Anthem "In Thee O Lord." Two years later, in the fall of 1893, he gave his first public concert, one of chamber music. The program which was given at Small Public Hall in Croydon, embraced three songs, a clarinet sonata and a pianoforte quintet in G minor, all works of the young musician. In 1895, while pursuing his studies, he became a teacher of violin at the Croydon Conservatory of Music, and one year later he was given the directorship of the Conservatory String Orchestra. Teaching was never to his liking. Owing to his limited means during these years, he continued to follow his calling. Among his pupils was the mother of Liza Lehmann.

A concert given on September 12th, 1898, at Shire Hall, Gloucester, launched him decisively on a notable career. The "Ballade in A minor" had been written for the Committee of Three Choir Festivals. The commission came through the kind suggestion of Sir Edward Elgar, and the work was a triumphant success. It brought the young man unmistakable recognition as a serious composer, and from this time on he wrote continually. "Hiawatha's Wedding Feast," first performed by the choir and orchestra of the Royal College of Music, under Sir Charles Stanford, made him famous. But none of these efforts brought financial gain. Young, unknown and untried as a composer, a public yet to be won, he willingly sold the copyright of *Hiawatha* for a very small sum. For the second and third parts he received all told only two hundred and fifty pounds.

On December 29, 1899, at Holy Trinity Church, South Norwood, Coleridge-Taylor married Jessie S. Fleetwood Walmsley, a young English girl whom he met seven years before when both were students at the Royal College of Music. The marriage was an ideally happy one. Two children came to them, Hiawatha, a son, and Gwendolyn, a daughter.

The composer's activities were many. In 1902, he became conductor of the Royal Rochester Choral Society, a position he held until 1907; in 1904, he received the conductorship of the Handel Society and in 1906 he founded the String Players Club, an organization which he greatly improved. The theatre intrigued him, and in this field he was particularly successful. He wrote incidental music for many Shakespearean productions of Sir Herbert Tree; at the same time he continued his teaching, and conducting of the Croydon Orchestral Society and the Westmorland Festival. In 1903, he became professor of composition at the Trinity College of Music.

Apparently a touch of America proved to be a turning point in Coleridge-Taylor's career. About 1899, the Fisk Jubilee Singers were again touring England under the direction of Frederick Loudin; and, hearing the Negro melodies, the composer was greatly touched by them and from this time, many of his works were based on Negro themes. On March 12 and 14, 1900, the Cecilia Society of Boston, Massachusetts, gave a performance of "The Wedding Feast," but his first personal interest in America began in 1901, with the invitation to visit this country to conduct a performance of his Hiawatha Trilogy. In a letter, undated as was his habit, Coleridge-Taylor wrote to Miss Lola Johnson in September, 1901, that it would be impossible for him to visit the United States in the autumn as he would be rehearsing the music for Mr. Beerbohn Tree's new play *Ulysses*. He added that the purpose of his visit "was not for the production of *Hiawatha* so much as to give an impetus for choral singing among colored people." . . . "If the colored people mean to perform *Hiawatha*, they must do it as well or better than their white neighbors." This visit which took place two years later, has been described in another chapter noting the formation of the Coleridge-Taylor Society of Washington, D. C. The composer was heard in concerts in Philadelphia and in Chicago. In December of that year he returned to England. Recitals of his smaller compositions were given at Mendelssohn Hall, New York, and at Washington, St. Louis, Chicago, Milwaukee, Detroit, Toronto, Pittsburg and Boston.

In 1909, Mr. and Mrs. Stoeckel, while on a visit to London, invited Coleridge-Taylor to come to Norfolk, Connecticut, to conduct his own compositions. At the fifteenth and sixteenth concerts of the Litchfield Choral Union, the composer conducted the first two parts of *Hiawatha,* and *Bamboula,* a rhapsody dance written for the occasion On this second visit to America, he was the guest of Carl Stoeckel, the well known patron of music. The assisting artists were Reed Miller, tenor, Harry T. Burleigh, baritone, and Felix Weir, violinist. There was a distinguished audience, and the artists, Fritz Kreisler, Yolando Mero, Alma Gluck, Gertrude May Stein, George Hamlin, Herbert Witherspoon, Henry P. Schmidt and Arthur Mees, joined the hospitable host, Mr. Stoeckel, in according the composer every courtesy. His experiences in this country were most happy, and his American affiliation with both races gave him great pleasure.

Upon Mr. Coleridge-Taylor's return from an American visit he expressed his surprise at finding so great an appreciation for pure music and commented upon the musical taste of this country and its recognition of musicians. Meanwhile, in 1905, Oliver Ditson Company of Boston published his *Twenty-four Negro Melodies, Transcribed for the Piano"*; the themes were drawn from the African, West Indian and other Negro-American sources. Coleridge-Taylor wrote a friend in September, 1904, "I really must say that your American publishers, Ditsons, are the only publishers who have ever written to express their thanks and appreciation of my work, and yet I thought Americans were much more matter-of-fact than the English." Since that time a number of smaller works have been published by this house. The beautiful cantata, *A Tale of Old Japan,* was begun at Norfolk, Connecticut, at the time when the composer was the guest of that broadminded and appreciative lover of music, Carl Stoeckel.

Among the pieces which were based on American themes are "Overture to Songs of Hiawatha," which he wrote after the "African Suite"; "Symphonic Variations on an African Air" ("I'm Troubled in mind"), and a "Violin Concerto," the second movement of which was based on the plantation melody "Many Thousand Gone." The re-written "Concerto" was dedicated to Maud Powell. The composer's admiration for the patriot Toussaint Loverture resulted in the concert overture for orchestra of like name. *African Romances* was a setting of six poems by Paul Laurence Dunbar. An opera, *Thelma,* on which he devoted two years labor, was found to be unacceptable for production and was a great disappointment to the overworked composer.

In the midst of many engagements, the musician was suddenly taken ill, and after a few days of suffering, on September 1, 1912, at the early age of thirty-seven he passed away. The busy world stopped long enough to do him honor. The most significant memorial testimonial concert given in this country was that of January 13th, 1913, which was held at Jordan Hall, Boston, Massachusetts. The artists who contributed their services were Harry T. Burleigh, William H. Richardson, baritones; Maud Cuney-Hare, pianist; Jaques Hoffman, violinist, and Ludwig Nast, violoncellist (members of the Boston Symphony Orchestra); Frederick P. White, organist and Melville Charlton, accompanist. An address was given by W. E. B. DuBois of New York, whose work the musician had so greatly praised.

Concerning Coleridge-Taylor's favorite authors, his biographer, Berwick Sayers, speaking of the musician's sympathetic appreciation of Browning, the English poet, says, "Without being aware of his history, he felt curious racial affinities with the former and held a theory that the expressed sympathy of the poet with the darker races was the outcome of actual blood relationship with them." Not only did the racial heritage of Browning intrigue the musician, but the theory that Beethoven had colored blood in his veins interested him, and he felt that the features and other physical characteristics of the great master confirmed the rumor.[16]

Coleridge-Taylor's children have evidently endeavored to live up to his ideals. "Whene'er the Sun Goes West," a song for soprano voice, was written by Gwendolyn Coleridge-Taylor in memory of her father. The words are by the son, Hiawatha. The daughter, Gwendolyn, married H. C. Dashwood in London, on April 19, 1924. Extracts

[16] An interesting description of Beethoven's grandfather is found in a rare manuscript in the Royal Library of Berlin:

"Short and massive, broad shoulders, short neck, large head, round nose and dark brown complexion." There is an uncommon portrait of the composer—"L. Van Beethoven (from an engraving by A. Brückner)." The medallion by Jacques Eduard Gatteaux, is Negroid in features. But—of whatever blood, this great immortal conquered all material, physical conditions and bequeathed to all children of men the universal radiance of his profound spiritual character. It was the power of a great soul that appealed to the kind heart of Coleridge-Taylor.

from "Hiawatha's Wedding Feast" were played at the wedding. She is gifted both as an interpretative dancer and as a singer, and has appeared in recitations set to her father's music. She has also written several songs and pianoforte pieces and a trio for 'cello, violin and piano. Her brother is also musically gifted. He is conductor of the String Players Club which was founded by his father. At the time that *Hiawatha,* an operatic work based on the story of the Indian hero, the music of which was written just before the composer's death, was staged at Albert Hall, London, May 19, 1924, the interpolated dances were adapted by young Coleridge-Taylor who directed these and other ballet music. Eugene Goossens conducted.

Hiawatha is now given annually in Albert Hall, London, and is now being spoken of as a "famous production." For two weeks in June, 1932, this work was presented daily by T. C. Fairbain, with members of the Royal Choral Society, directed by Dr. Malcolm Sargent. The lighting, dancers, chorus, orchestra, scenery and costuming share in the praise accorded the production. The London correspondent of *Musical America* wrote in the August, 1932, issue, "The performance increases one's admiration each year. The way in which Mr. Fairbain has solved his problems, so that the whole vast production can be reassembled each year deserves unreserved admiration and praise. And it is a pleasure to record that *Hiawatha* paid its way and made a profit."

Amanda Ira Aldridge ("Montague Ring") is an English woman musician whose career is of particular interest as she is the daughter of the great Negro tragedian, Ira Aldridge, who was born at Belair, Baltimore, Maryland, in 1810 and died at Lotz, Poland, in 1867, an American

LURANAH IRA ALDRIDGE

FREDERICK OLAFF IRA ALDRIDGE

JOSEPH WHITE

BRINDIS DE SALA

actor whose fame was achieved abroad.[17] He married a
Swedish singer gifted with a beautiful voice. She not
only appreciated the histrionic gift and racial heritage of
her distinguished husband, but also the promise of their
three talented children, two daughters and a son, bearing
his father's name. The boy became a pupil in piano of
Oscar Beringer and showed remarkable promise, but he
died at the early age of twenty-three.

A daughter, Luranah, born in London March 29, 1860,
was a dramatic contralto, of renown. She studied in London, Paris, and Berlin, and was engaged for several seasons at the Royal Opera House, Covent Garden, London,
and also at most of the principal continental opera houses.
In 1896 she participated in the Bayreuth Festival. When
she sang in Paris, Charles Gounod wrote to Sir Augustus
Harris of Covent Garden, that Luranah Aldridge had
the most beautiful voice he had ever heard. In the midst
of her career, ill health caused her to leave the stage.
After twenty years of invalidism from rheumatism she
died November 20, 1932, and was buried in the Kensington
Cemetery at Gunnersbury, near Kew Gardens.

The second daughter, Amanda Ira, is a composer and
teacher of note in London. She was born March 10, 1866,
in Upper Norwood, a suburb of London, where she spent
her childhood. Her mother saw to it that her gifted children be kept in a musical environment and had them
attend all of the musical performances held at the Crystal
Palace. When a young girl, her fine voice and exceptional
mind indicated a professional career. At that time fifty
free scholarships by competition were offered at the Royal

[17] Aldridge who first appeared at Covent Garden Theatre, London,
on April 10, 1863, later appeared with such success as ''Othello''
and ''Shylock'' that he traveled over the continent in these and
other roles, both with English and German companies, and was
compared with the leading tragedians of the day.

College of Music, open to British subjects. Amanda won one of these and became a student under Jenny Lind. At the request of the late King Edward, then Prince of Wales, the "Swedish Nightingale" had consented to train nine gifted students. Interest was taken in the progress of the young colored singer, herself of Swedish blood, and the scholarship was extended to a fourth year. When Jenny Lind retired Amanda was placed under the tutelage of Sir George Henschel. She later studied elocution with Dame Madge Kendal, the famous actress; and harmony and counterpoint with the late Sir Frederick Bridge and Dr. F. E. Gladstone.

Miss Aldridge says, "I have played the piano from the time when my fingers could reach the keyboard, but I only began to compose when I was in my 'thirties'; up to then and up to now, I have been a teacher of singing." After Miss Aldridge's successful establishment as a teacher of voice, she adopted the name of "Montague Ring" in order to keep her work as a composer apart from that of a singer and instructor. Her first compositions were in a light vein and in dance rhythms. Two of her songs are settings of poems by Paul Laurence Dunbar. Two others, "Two Little Southern Songs: Kentucky Love Song—June in Kentucky," were settings of lyrics by a well-beloved English poet, Fred G. Bowles. Her pieces in the African idiom are original, imaginary compositions and are not based on folk themes. They are sympathetically, and musically written with true African flavor. The teacher-composer accounts for this in stating that her mother, although Swedish, influenced the development of the pride in the African blood of her children as tribute and appreciation of the Negro race to which her husband belonged.

Miss Aldridge writes in a romantic, melodious vein, and has not turned to the ultra-modern school. As she

MONTAGUE RING

expresses it, she always "thought" musically and her mother never wearied of trying to induce her to write down the melodious phrases that she was continuously humming or playing. *Musical America* and other journals have given her songs favorable notice. In London her compositions are played by leading orchestras and military bands and are danced at principal opera houses. Her Moorish and African dances have been used as incidental music and interpolated dances for theatrical performances.

Jenny Lind early predicted that as her pupil was not only gifted as a vocalist and as a pianist, but also possessed correct judgment, with experience she would become a master of singing. Her predictions proved true. The London *Times,* the *Daily Telegraph,* the *Queen,* and the *Musical Times* have commented upon Miss Aldridge's "rich, deep voice, used with skill and judgment," and upon the finish of her pupils. A recent issue of the London *Times* says, "The pupils of Miss Ira Aldridge all, or nearly all, have in common one invaluable attribute of a singer—that is style."

The *Norwood Press and Dulwich Advertiser* thus pays Miss Aldridge a high tribute in commenting on the remarkable success at the Bournemouth Musical Festival by George Wetherill, an Alleynian tenor, who won both the Gold Medal and the Bronze Medal: "We understand that this young artist has been exclusively trained by Miss Ira Aldridge, through whose studio many famous artists have passed. Mr. Wetherill possesses unusual natural gifts, and these have been brought out by highly skilful tuition."

Miss Aldridge has had the distinction of having for her pupils such personages as the Viscountess Fincastle, Lady Bisset, Lady Westland, Mrs. Henry Cust, Lady Bowen, and His Honour Judge Howland Roberts. Americans who have studied with her include Marian Anderson, Negro contralto, Roland Hayes, the Negro tenor whom she also coached in languages as well as voice culture, and Paul Robeson, Negro baritone-actor.[18]

Brindis de Sala of Cuba, a Negro violinist of European fame, did concert work in Germany and received many decorations which included tokens from the German Emperor and the King of Italy. He was tall, straight, and graceful with skin darker than mahogany, a man of general culture, speaking fluently six languages. Sketches of his career appeared in journals of his day. The *Liberator* reprinted biographical data contributed to a Paris paper by Sabino Lasado in 1859. Claude Brindis de Sala was born in Havana, Cuba, in 1800 and was of African blood. His mother was a nurse in the family of Count Don José Maria Chacon, and the kindly feeling and close friendship engendered by her position as wet-nurse, was bestowed upon the gifted son. The boy exhibited remarkable musical talent at an early age, and he was placed in the Academy conducted by Professor Ignatius Calvo. The island was then under the government of the Marquis of Somervelos who was impressed with the talent of the student. The Marquis considered his artistic ''treble voice unequaled'' and offered him his patronage.

When scarcely out of his boyhood, Brindis was appointed musical director at the entertainments of His Excellency and held this post until the end of the Count's administration. In 1837, having an opportunity to display further his abilities as a conductor at an entertainment given in honor of his Excellency, Governor Michael Tacon, he was appointed to direct the band for several official affairs which included the inauguration of the Palace of Arms. His compositions and musicianship

[18] As composer, Miss Aldridge has a long list of pieces to her credit.

aroused popular acclaim and praise from the Marquis of St. Philip and St. James, and foreign visiting noblemen. General Ulloa of the Marines appointed Brindis director of the orchestra for the royal feasts celebrated in honor of the young queen, Isabella II. The musician dedicated to her a richly-bound collection of his compositions, and served the Queen as sub-lieutenant in the Negro regiment of Havana.

Successfully passing an examination conducted by the Corporation of Havana, Brindis de Sala was awarded the degree of "Maestro Composer and Musician." He continued his orchestral work as leader of various philharmonic and dramatic societies.

Brindis de Sala spent a number of years abroad in study and in concert work. From the Paris Conservatory in France, he was engaged at the Covent Garden Concerts in London. Wishing to perfect his artistry, he went to Leipzig, where he became a student of the violinist, Ferdinand David. As a concert artist, he created a sensation in European cities and passed through many experiences because of his dark skin. By the Berlin critic, Otto Lessman, he was styled "The King of Octaves." He was finally called to Berlin, where he was appointed soloist to the Emperor. Among his other honors it is noted that he was a chevalier of several foreign orders; that the King of Portugal appointed him a Commander of the "Order of Christ;" and that he was given the title of Baron by the German Emperor. He married a German lady, and their sons became cadets in the German Army.

In later years, the violinist traveled in the British West Indies, Cuba and South America.[19] He died in 1912 in

[19] While in Cuba in 1898, Mr. Portuondo had the opportunity of taking lessons from him. The distinguished musician had been disappointed by the fact that his valuable violins had gone astray—mis-sent to the port of New York, they were returned to him in

Buenos Aires.[20] A brother of the violinist was also musical and played the violin.

such a condition that it was impossible to play upon them. Mr. Portuondo, Sr., a maker of instruments and a musician as well, offered to repair the violins. Brindis de Sala was skeptical, but after a few days, when the instruments were in perfect condition, he clasped them to his breast with the exclamation "Only in Germany could they have done this!"

[20] Speaking of other musicians of color in Cuba, Raimunde Cabreba in *Cuba and Cubans* writes—"In music, White, Cervantes, Diaz, Albertini and Jimenez, distinguished alumni and winners of first prizes at the Conservatory of Paris, artists whose genius has been admired in Vienna, London, Paris and other great centres of Europe and in America . . . some of the former like the mulatto White are exiled from their native soil."

In an earlier period, Francis Williams, a Jamaican of Negro parentage, who died about 1774, published a song in England called "Welcome, Welcome Brother Debtor." According to Prof. Chamberlain, it made such a sensation, that several white men claimed it as their own. Francis Williams wrote excellent Latin verse and in 1764, took the degree of Bachelor of Arts at Cambridge.

CHAPTER XIV

TORCH BEARERS

CREATIVE MUSIC—PRESENT-DAY COMPOSERS—
INTERPRETATIVE ARTISTS—SINGERS—PIANISTS
—VIOLINISTS AND MUSICIANS IN GENERAL.

The individual Negro composer, caught in the controversial trends of the time, is in a state of development, and his output naturally differs from the product known as "Negro Music" which is collective and more or less defined. There are those among the younger talented ones, affected by the general low taste of the age, who cry out loudly for a hearing of what they mis-name "Negro Beauty," to be found "in the bellowing voice of a jazz shouter, singing Blues," and insist that ears are closed unless they willingly give audience to the blatant, incoherent cacophancy of their nurturing. In their haste to arrive, they would ignore the training which gives the ability to attend to beauty in sound, in words as well as in musical tones. Paradoxical as it may be, the "Blues" in music has been converted into a literary expression used by the majority of the rising school of American poets, and "Jazz" has sought the sister art of poetry for a new medium of utterance. In turn, the giddy young jade has amusingly reverted to music, for both white and black poets are giving musical settings to jazz poems by such writers as Johnson, Hughes, and Cullen.

To the few who have refused to be influenced by the market demands, there has come a spiritual unrest, and with renewed vision they are creating music as an expres-

sion of their own life and ideals. In reality, the Negro
musician is more truly American than members of the
later arrived hyphenated races—French, Swiss, German
or Hebrew; and he is more apt to produce the distinctive
American music of the future. In doing this, he will have
to stand shoulder to shoulder with the talented Latin-
Americans who also of America—although not of the
United States—are rapidly being recognized here and in
Europe.

Fortunately, like all students the world over, the Negro
who is truly an artist seeks to appreciate the refined, romantic taste of the Italian school, the primitive, emotional
fervor of the Russian song, the intellectual insight of the
German lieder, the refined delicacy of the French, and the
sensuous allure of the Latins of the tropics. Only by gaining a basic unity can he acquire the keen and delicate perception to place his alien medium in the rank of great
music. While attempting to employ his folk music in art
compositions, the Negro composer believes that he may
also interpret a universal theme through his own individual consciousness in such a manner that it will possess
unlimited national appeal. Adept in the use of contemporary musical form and harmony, he is more inclined toward *diatonism* than *atonality* and is in heart a fervid
romanticist.

The interpretative musicians—singers in particular—
are placed in a difficult situation. In the South from
which so many of our talented young men and women
have come, it is difficult to hear good music sung or
played by famous artists. In Atlanta, Georgia, for years
the Negro was not allowed to attend the performances of
the visiting grand opera company. It was only in 1930
that the Philharmonic Society of New Orleans opened a
section of seats and allowed Negroes to become a part of
its audience of 3,000 subscribers. In Washington, the

capital city, Negro musicians are either refused admission or segregated at symphony and artist's concerts. In spite of racial handicaps, added to the usual difficulties which all sincere artists meet, regardless of race, the Negro musician who is thoroughly prepared finds it not impossible to gain recognition in the United States.

On the other hand, upon completing his musical studies in this country or in Europe, from the time of his début, the Negro singer finds himself, unlike any other racial artist, subject to inhibitions. Today, to be a Negro vocalist is to be an exponent of Negro Spirituals, and there are many music-listeners and concert goers who would confine them to their folk song alone. Unlike the selections of the soloists of the past generation, programs of singers of fine voice and training are marked by the inevitable "closing group of Negro Spirituals." There are but few who have had the courage to present art programs to their own taste irrespective of the hall-mark of Negro religious song. In doing so, they brave criticism from both races, and find a limited hospitality in the concert hall. The details of the struggles and triumphs of some of these individuals are interesting.

The rise of Harry T. Burleigh, singer and composer, the most distinguished of the Negro musicians and one of the most noted of his time, well illustrates this point. He was born in Erie, Pennsylvania, on December 2, 1866. For many years he has made his home in New York City. His maternal grandfather, held in bondage in Somerset County, Maryland, was given his freedom after he had made several attempts to escape. His maternal grandmother was the daughter of a Scotch woman born in Edinburgh, Scotland, who emigrated to Michigan, where she married an Indian. Burleigh's paternal grandfather and grandmother were mulattoes of Newburgh, New York.

This composer's parents were employed in Erie by a

family named Russell, who at that time had the renowned artists of the day play in their drawing-room. The lad, Harry, then a pupil in the Erie High School, learned that Rafael Joseffy was to give a musical at the Russell home, and in his eagerness to hear the pianist, he stood in the snow for hours that he might be on hand and listen through the drawing-room window. He was taken ill from exposure, and his mother, learning of his action, asked Mrs. Russell if her boy could not be given some household duty by which he might be able to listen to her guest-musicians. Appreciating the boy's love for music, Mrs. Russell had him open the door at her next musical. At this time the visiting artist happened to be Teresa Carreño, and with her was Mrs. MacDowell, the mother of Edward MacDowell, America's noted musician. It was his good fortune to meet her later in New York City.

In his early manhood Burleigh sang in the churches and in the Jewish synagogues in Erie, and at the same time worked as a stenographer while clinging to the thought of seriously studying music. In 1892, at the age of twenty-six, with the assistance of friends, he came to New York and won a scholarship at the National Conservatory, where for four years he studied voice culture, solfeggio, history of music, Italian, stage deportment and fencing. Christian Fritsch, Rubin Goldmark, and John White were his teachers. During the last year of his studies, owing to his outstanding talent, he was given the instruction of pupils in voice and allowed to act as clerical assistant to Mrs. MacDowell, by which means he repaid Mrs. Thurber, the founder of the institution, for her interest in his musical education. In the Conservatory orchestra he played double bass and later tympani and looked after the music of that organization. It was during the second year at the Conservatory that he had the privilege of meeting Anton Dvorák with whom he was frequently found.

HARRY T. BURLEIGH

In the Dvorák home, Burleigh found time to copy the musician's manuscripts and to sing Negro Spirituals at his request.

These were rare opportunities for the gifted young student, but he had no regular income and therefore found it difficult to support himself. His tuition was met, but there were living expenses to be considered. For a while he was able to meet his needs by singing and training Negro church choirs, but the pay was inadequate to carry him through the following school year. To overcome these difficulties, he worked during the summer season in a hotel at Saratoga, New York.

Burleigh was now ambitious to become a church singer, but the question of race prejudice proved to be an immense handicap for a Negro with such an objective. About this time, too, a well known lady who had for years sung in the aristocratic St. Thomas' Church was dismissed when the parishioners learned that she had Negro blood. Undaunted, however, Burleigh, hopeful of being included among the applicants for the vacancy of baritone soloist of St. George's Episcopal Church, secured an introduction to the rector, Dr. Rainsford, through the kindness of Mrs. Thurber. On Dr. Rainsford's recommendation in 1894 he entered the lists and out of sixty applicants, was chosen for the position.

Six years later, in 1900, the singer reached a similar post at Temple E-man-u-él, the richest Jewish synagogue in the country. For the first two years after his graduation from the National Conservatory of Music, he taught singing at that institution, but soon his interpretation of Negro Spirituals as well as his artistic vocal gifts, brought him in demand for private musicales and public performances, and he devoted all of his time to singing. During his career as a singer, Burleigh was often heard in Lon-

don, England, and sang before his Majesty, King Edward
VII, and many people of distinction.

His first efforts in composition were three little songs
"If you but knew," "A Birthday Song," and "Life."
About 1904 the William Maxwell Music Company published his "Love's Garden," soon followed by "Jean." The
latter song was widely liked and sung. These early beginnings in the writing of music were more than the trial
of unused wings—the songs were more than pleasant and
singable ones, for in them was displayed a fine command
of the principles of harmony and the gift of poetic imagination. From that day Burleigh's reputation as a composer steadily advanced.

The next stage in the development of this musician
was his sponsorship of the Negro Spirituals. These tremendously popular folk songs of the acclaim of the present time, had been mainly interpreted by quartettes and
choral groups. Burleigh visioned a higher level for these
productions. He not only instituted the singing of the
deeply emotional, religious song of the Negro by solo
voice, but turned his attention towards setting them in a
musicianly manner that they might be used by trained
concert singers and also be enjoyed by discriminating
audiences. Their folk song appeal was already undisputed. His simply arranged collection called *Plantation
Melodies, Old and New*, published by G. Schirmer,
showed a modest beginning. Today his sympathetic settings of the religious folk song and his superb art songs
have earned for him the title as given by Walter Kramer
in *Musical America*, "Composer by Divine Right."

One outstanding feature of Burleigh's song-writing is
that of choice of text. He says, "For me a poem must
have more than just an ordinary sentimental reference
before I can set it, or rather before it makes any impression on me. I read hundreds of perfectly good poems

that I would never think of setting to music. There has been a neglect on the part of our composers, I think, of the kind of poems which in my estimation call out musical thought of real fiber.''

While in the maturity of his powers as a vocalist, Burleigh retired from the concert stage but continued to sing at St. George's Church and at Temple E-man-u-él in New York City. In 1919, the members of St. George's presented the singer with a gift of a valuable watch, which marked his twenty-fifth anniversary as soloist in the choir. On March 30, 1924, a Vesper Service of Negro Spirituals as arranged by Mr. Burleigh was staged as a tribute to the composer. The program read, ''Mr. Burleigh carries his thirty years' membership in this choir remarkably well indeed. With the years he has changed, but he has not grown old. There has been an ever deepening regard for him with the passage of time. He is a great composer, singer and musician and a faithful servant in the Chancel of this Church. May this day bring to him a moiety of that great satisfaction he has given to thousands and cheer his generous and devoted heart.''

In 1925, commemorating the completion of twenty-five years of continuous membership in the Choir, Temple E-man-u-él presented Mr. Burleigh a testimonial inscribed on parchment and bound in gold-tooled Morocco leather, the contents of which read, ''You have contributed much to the maintenance of the high standard of excellence for which we have striven in the musical portion of our services. Your melodious voice and your artistic compositions have added greatly to the devotional attitude of the worshippers within our sanctuary.''

Burleigh has risen somewhat too with the assistance of another friend, George Maxwell, who was managing director of G. Ricordi and Company from 1911 to April, 1931. This friend's death led A. Walter Kramer to say in *Musical America* (July, 1931) that ''George Maxwell's wholehearted championing of H. T. Burleigh was a fine thing. It was he who was responsible for making the Burleigh Negro Spiritual settings internationally known as well as for publishing his too little known art-songs.'' Burleigh has for long been a reviewer for Ricordi and Company who have published the greater number of his compositions.

A few of Burleigh's finest art-songs are these: ''In the Wood of Finvara,'' ''The Prayer,'' ''Memory,'' ''The Grey Wolf,'' ''By the Pool of the Third Rosses,'' ''The Sailor's Wife,'' ''Ethiopia Saluting the Colors,'' a song cycle, ''Saracen Songs,'' ''Passionale,'' ''A Corn Song,'' ''Down by the Sea,'' ''Have You Been to Lons,'' ''Five Songs by Laurence Hope,'' and a large number of settings of Negro Spirituals the last of which are—''Who's Dat Yonder'' and ''Dry Bones'' (1931). Of the five songs, the poems written by Laurence Hope, an English woman who lived for years in East India, at that time Krehbiel, musical editor of the New York *Tribune*, wrote, ''In all of them the pianoforte and voice are beautifully and truthfully consorted in the utterance of the poetic sentiment.'' W. J. Henderson, critic and musical historian of that day, said of ''The Saracen Songs,'' ''Mr. Burleigh's poetic conceptions are paired with his masterly musicianship and at the same time he has shown a wise consideration of the lover of music.''

While still a contemporary of younger musicians, Burleigh who has met the world standard in his chosen artistic field, still stands as the most famous of Negro musicians. His career as a singer, untainted by sensationalism differed somewhat from that of an earlier group of talented vocalists of the race in that he had the advantage of an educated mind as well as a trained voice. His generosity to struggling musicians and to all worthy causes is a well-known trait of his character. The mental attainment which this composer has reached is unquestionably one of the principal causes of his being one of the foremost writers of music to the English text.

Burleigh's only sister, Eva, whom he survives, was a trained musician who was known in educational circles and institutional life in New York City. A son, Allston, has both dramatic and musical ability and has taken roles in the serious plays of Negro life.

Such a career, of course, has merited various honors. Howard University conferred the degree of Doctor of Music upon Burleigh, and in 1917, he was given the Spingarn achievement award. A signal honor is now being planned by the State Museum and visual Education in Harrisburg, Pennsylvania, where exhibits from the state's four outstanding composers, Stephen Foster, Ethelbert Nevin, Charles Wakefield Cadman and Harry T. Burleigh are to be installed in the Museum. The Burleigh collection is to include photographs of the composer, the house in which he was born and ''at work in his studio,'' with original manuscripts of his favorite compositions, and a collection of his published music.

Clarence Cameron White, violinist-composer, born August 10, 1880, at Clarksville, Tenn., the son of Dr. and Mrs. James Wm. White, also faced a struggle. His early boyhood was spent in the college town of Oberlin, Ohio. As his parents later made their home in Washington, D. C., he was educated in the public schools of that city and at Howard University. Showing decided musical talent, he was sent to Oberlin College, where he entered the Conservatory and remained for five years. There he studied the violin and had orchestral practise as first violinist in the school orchestra of all white pupils with the exception of himself. Upon completion of his studies at the Conservatory, he returned to Washington and was given the position of director of the string department of the newly formed Washington Conservatory of Music, which was founded by Harriet Gibbs Marshall.

The violinist spent the summer of 1906 in study in London, England, and upon 'his return to Washington he was appointed teacher of public school music. Meanwhile, in the summer of 1905, the musician had married Miss Beatrice Warrick, a talented young pianist, a member of the well-known family, the Warricks, of Philadelphia, Pennsylvania, and Washington, D. C. Desirous of further development, White and his wife went to London in 1908, when he became a student under M. Zacharewitsch, the noted Russian violinist and teacher. At the same time he studied composition under Samuel Coleridge-Taylor.

During White's two years' stay abroad, he was first violinist in the String Player's Club of Croydon, said to be the finest string orchestra in England at the time, and conducted by Coleridge-Taylor. Returning to America in 1910 he located in Boston, Massachusetts, where he opened a private studio. He further engaged in composing and concertizing with his wife as his accompanist. From 1924 to 1930, he was director of music of the West Virginia State College at Institute, West Virginia, and was also engaged for violin recitals on tour. He devoted his summers to study in order to increase his knowledge of band and orchestral instruments. The ripening musician had early displayed a talent for composing salon and teaching pieces, for he had a singular gift of melody.

As this power grew, White sought possibilities in the Negro folk music as a source of art forms and particularly in pieces for the violin and piano and for voice. Carl Fischer Company, the well-known New York publishers, accepted his compositions written during his stay in Boston, and they were soon played by Fritz Kreisler, Irma Seydel, and other noted violinists. The following

CLARENCE CAMERON WHITE

are his best known violin compositions: "Bandanna Sketches"; "Chant" (Nobody Knows de Trouble I've Seen) "Negro Dance" (Sometimes I Feel Like a Motherless Child), "Lament" (I'm Troubled in Mind), "Slave Song" (Many Thousand Gone), and the suite *From the Cotton Fields*: "Cabin Song," "On the Bayou," and "Spiritual." "Memories from a Negro Cabin," "Bear the Burden," "I'm Goin' Home," and "Down by de Ribber Side" (for voice), are spirituals that had never before been published in any setting. The "Bandanna Sketches" were later arranged for orchestra and military band.

In concerts of original compositions given in 1922, White gave the following additional numbers by Samuel Coleridge-Taylor, "Ballade in C minor," "Four African Dances" and "Sonata, Op. 28," their first presentation in America. At the completion of a continental tour, the *Musical Courier* voiced the general opinion, "His playing is most finished and artistic." It was in recognition of such worth that in 1927, the Harmon Foundation awarded the violinist-composer the first prize for musical achievement, of $400 and a gold medal.

In 1928, Clarence Cameron White and John F. Matheus, Professor of Romance Languages of the West Virginia State College, and a writer of short stories and plays, made a summer visit to Haiti for the purpose of studying Haitian folk lore and to collect native musical and literary material. An early result of the visit was *Tambour*, a two-act play written by Mr. Matheus with incidental music by Clarence Cameron White. The native dance number, a "Meringüe," has recently been published by Carl Fischer Company. The play had its first presentation in Boston, Massachusetts, in 1929, when it was given by the Allied Arts Players, a Little Theater group whose performances were highly praised by the reviewers of the daily press.

In 1930, White was awarded a Rosenwald Fellowship of $3,000 for creative work, and a leave of absence from his duties was secured for the purpose of foreign study and leisure in which to write an opera. The award was extended a year in 1931. In Paris, France, he was a student of composition and orchestration under Raoul Laparra, the distinguished French composer. His opera, *Ouanga*, libretto by John F. Matheus, based upon the life of the Haitian liberator, Dessalines, first ruler of Haiti, was an important result of this study. Plans are soon to be made for a performance of this opera. The stage training and professional experiences of such singers as Abbie Mitchell, Jules Bledsoe, Lillian Evanti and Florence Cole Talbert make possible the selection of a strong colored cast of principals.

While in France, the composer wrote short numbers for violin; and on May 29, 1931, "Quatuor en do mineur," "Prelude, Dawn, Jubilee Hallelujah," a string quartette based upon Negro melodies, was played in Paris at the Ecole Normale de Musique, by faculty members of the school. The program included a quartette by Beethoven, a quintette by Ernest Bloch, and, "Deux Impressions Populaires" by Isadore Freed. It is interesting to note that this is the first performance of a string quartette by a Negro composer in Paris since the days of the Chevalier de Saint Georges.

Although handicapped by the artist's usual lack of means, White has courageously worked toward his goal and has never for a moment swerved from the high ideals of a true musician. He is an outstanding example of the consistent growth of a composer who mastered his technic so as not to be restricted to a verbatim interpretation of Negro melodies. His use of the themes has proved the stylistic adaptability of the same and his compositions show a universal unity based upon a diverse racial expression.

Upon White's return to the United States, the American Opera Society presented *Ouanga* in concert form, at the Three Arts Club, North Shore Art Center in Chicago. A brief story of the opera was told by Professor Matheus, and explanatory remarks were made by the composer. John Greene, baritone, and Cleo Wade sang star roles with Fred Farrel, pianist-accompanist, who also played the orchestral parts. At the close of the performance, White was presented the David Bispham medal which is awarded to American composers who write operas of outstanding merit and reach a standard whereby a definite contribution is made to American opera. He is the thirty-fifth recipient in a list which includes Henry Hadley, Frederick S. Converse, Deems Taylor, Walter Damrosch and other distinguished composers. In 1928, Atlanta University conferred upon him the degree of Master of Arts. In 1933 Wilberforce University honored him with the degree of Doctor of Music. In 1932, White was made the director of the Hampton School of Music. He resigned in 1935 and returned to Boston. Reviewing some of White's compositions, *Musical America* said, "They are numbers which no violinist who can appreciate charm of melody and keen sense of violinistic effect can fail to like—all three ('From the Cotton Fields'), have been conceived for the instrument with real imagination and refined musicianship."

William Grant Still, after similar struggles, stands in the front ranks of young composers in the modern idiom. He was born of educated parents, in Woodville, Mississippi, on May 11, 1895. His father possessed musical taste. His mother, Mrs. Shepperson, of Little Rock, Arkansas, was a teacher of literature in the high school. After completing his secondary training in Little Rock, the young man attended Wilberforce University and later studied at Oberlin College. He took special lessons in composition from George Chadwick of Boston at the New England Conservatory, and later from Edgar Varèse in New York. After locating in that city, Still became engaged in arranging and orchestrating musical comedy melodies, but soon deliberately turned his back on light music and began to experiment in a serious way in Negro musical characteristics. He now devotes all of his time to composition and has to his credit a growing list of worthy productions, many of which are in the larger forms.

Among his works for large orchestra is the *Afro-American Symphony*, rendered by the Rochester Symphony in 1931, in the American Composer's Series in Kilbourne Hall, the orchestra of sixty-five players being conducted by Dr. Howard Hanson. Other representative works chosen were by the white composers, Sowerby, Griffes, Farwell and Gleason. *Africa*, land of romance (symphonic poem), another of this order was performed by Barrere's Little Symphony, Rochester Symphony, and at the Festival of American Music held in Bad, Hamburg, Germany. Selections from *Africa* were presented by Paul Whiteman at his Modern Concert held at Symphony Hall, Boston, February 12, 1933. *From the Journal of a Wanderer* (symphonic poem) was presented by the Chicago Symphony and Rochester Symphony orchestras. *Darker America* (symphonic poem) was rendered by the Rochester Symphony and American Composer's Guild. And of the same order is *From the Heart of a Believer*.

His works for chamber orchestra include *From the Land of Dreams* (suite), presented by American Composer's Guild; *Levee Land* (suite), by the same group of musicians at Frankfort-on-the-Main, Germany; *From the*

WILLIAM GRANT STILL

Black Belt (suite), rendered by Barrere's Little Symphony, Civic Repertory Theatre (1932), and by the Eastman School Little Symphony (May 3, 1933), at the Third Annual Festival of American Music directed by Dr. Howard Hanson in Rochester, New York. A comment from *Musical America* on these productions read, "The outstanding works, from the point of originality, beauty of orchestration and vitality, were: first, Mr. Still's suite, which with its humor and charm, received a real ovation, directed to the composer who was in the audience." The suite includes the following sections: "Li'l Scamp," "Honeysuckle," "Dance," "Mah Bones is Creakin'," "Blue," "Brown Girl," and "Clap Yo' Hand." To this group belongs also *Log Cabin Ballads* (suite), produced by Barrere's Little Symphony.

His stage works include *Sahdji*, a choral ballet with music by Still, the scenario by Richard Bruce and Alain Locke; and *La Guiablesse* (a ballet of Martinique), composed for Ruth Page, who wrote the scenario, and produced at the May Festival, 1933. When the former ballet was performed on May 22, 1931, at the Eastman School of Music with Thelma Biracree, principal dancer, and originator of the choreography, and other white participants, the reviewer for *Musical America* stated, "The music is vital and primitive, expressive of the tribal rhythms of the jungle. The score contains beauty. Mr. Still achieves a vivid atmosphere with very simple means one of the most striking bits being the closing comments of the chanter, sung without accompaniment, as the curtain falls."

Mr. Still's principal works are in manuscript. *Africa* is published by C. C. Birchard. In *American Composers of American Music*, a symposium edited by Henry Cowell (1933), the twenty-seventh chapter, "A Negro Composer's Point of View," is written by Mr. Still. In 1934 Still was one of the recipients of the Guggenheim Fellowships.

The career of R. Nathaniel Dett reflects the same triumph over obstacles. The youngest of three brothers, he was born of educated parents in Drummondsville, Ontario, Canada. His mother is well known in the North for her work in the interest of Negro women's clubs. Of his early fondness for music, Dett says, "I played the piano ever since I can remember; no one taught me, I just picked it up: I used to follow my two older brothers to the house while their lessons were in progress." The teacher finally offered to give the young music-lover free lessons, but he taxed her patience by always changing a composition "to make it sound better."

His talent came to the notice of Prof. John R. Frampton of the Music Department of the Iowa State Teachers' College, and arrangements were made for him to enter the Oberlin Conservatory of Music in Ohio. He was graduated there in 1908 and was the first Negro to receive the degree of Bachelor of Music for original composition.

After his graduation he accepted the directorship of music of Lane College, Jackson, Tenn., where he developed the Lane Choral Society. Three years later he went to Lincoln Institute, Jefferson City, Missouri, then to Hampton, Virginia, to take charge of the choral work of that institution. Under his leadership, the Hampton Chorus of four hundred voices has given many well-known works with leading white and Negro soloists.

On December 27, 1916, Dett married Miss Helen Elise Smith, a musician of New York City, who had charge of the pianoforte department of Hampton Institute. In 1920, he secured a leave of absence for one year that he might further pursue his musical studies in Boston. There he had the advantage of instruction under the pianist-composer, Arthur Foote, while he took lessons in composition

R. NATHANIEL DETT

at Harvard University in Cambridge. At this College he won two prizes, the Boote prize in composition and the Bowdoin prize for an essay, "The Emancipation of Negro Music."

While in Boston, Dett was heard in piano recitals and also had the pleasure of having his choral works presented by organizations noticeably among which was the "Cecilia Society" one of the best white singing societies of New England.

His duties as director at Hampton Institute, however, he resumed. Nevertheless, he gave much time to composition. Among his later works is a modern suite, "Enchantment," four numbers for piano; six "Negro Folk Song" derivatives; two songs, "Magic Moon of Molten Gold" and "A Thousand Years Ago or More"; and various settings of "Folk Songs of the South" for three-part chorus with solo voices.

His "Danse Juba," as played by the distinguished Australian pianist, Percy Grainger, and other pianists of note, has tended to popularize his compositions. His best works are found in the choral form: "Listen to the Lambs," for mixed chorus; "O Holy Lord," an anthem for eight-part mixed chorus; "Music in the Mine," an unaccompanied folk-song scene, written for solo tenor voice and chorus (a miner and people of the mine). "The Chariot Jubilee," for tenor solo and chorus of mixed voices with accompaniment of organ, piano or orchestra, was written at request of the Syracuse University chorus and its conductor, Prof. Howard Lyman. By *Musical America*, it has been termed, "A master piece of its kind —a truly inspired piece of choral writing." "Listen to the Lambs," has been sung by the choir of the Church of the Ascension, Columbia University Chorus, and Syracuse University Chorus. "O Holy Lord" was first presented by the Elgar Choir in 1917 at the Field of Honor Memorial Services for Canadian soldiers fallen in battle. Dett's choral works have been extensively used by singing organizations of both races.

Dett has also arranged many Spirituals. His best known piano compositions are two suites: "Magnolio" and "In the Bottoms," and written along more modern lines, the "Enchantment Suite" which is an interesting and atmospheric oriental number for piano. The suite includes "Incantation," "Song of the Shrine," "Dance of Desire" and "Beyond the Dream."

During the summer of 1929, Dett studied under Madame Nadia Boulanger of the Fontainbleau School, Paris. He then devoted the greater part of his time apart from his directorship at Hampton Institute to the Hampton Institute Choir of forty finely trained voices. The Choir made a successful European tour in 1930, after which they again toured the United States. Their appearance in April, 1931, at the Odeon in St. Louis, Missouri, was a memorable one. Further details of Mr. Dett's work as a chorister are noted under the Chorus section.

Evidently R. Nathaniel Dett is one of the group of active musicians whose work in the interest of Negro music is of permanent value. Referring to him as a pianist-composer, a reviewer in the Chicago *Tribune* wrote, "It remained for the pianist of the evening, R. Nathaniel Dett, to show how the characteristic accents of Negro music may be developed into genuine art forms without resorting to imitations of the white man's music. Mr. Dett performed two suites of his own compositions entitled, 'Magnolia' and 'In the Bottoms.' From the former one may select the movements entitled 'The Deserted Cabin' and 'Mammy' as significant examples of this elevation of the folk song to the forms of greater compass, wider contrast and deeper meaning." One may add that these works are based on original themes as devised by the composer. In

DETT CHORAL SOCIETY, WASHINGTON, D. C.

1926 Oberlin College conferred the degree of Doctor of Music upon him, which is the first instance of a leading institution of music thus honoring a Negro musician.

Among the composers who are advancing the cause of good music in the race and in the United States, is Carl R. Diton, of Philadelphia, Pennsylvania. He received his education and musical training at the University of Pennsylvania in Philadelphia. As a protégé of Mme. Azalia Hackley, the young musician had the advantage of study for one year in Munich, Germany. Upon returning to the United States, he spent a short time in fulfilling concert engagements in piano recitals in the North and West. In 1915, he accepted a position as teacher of piano at Paine College, Augusta, Georgia. Shortly afterwards he was called to accept the post of director of music at Wiley University, Marshall, Texas, where he did much for the development of good musical taste. His next position was that of director of music at Talladega College. Diton's work there was outstanding; but, being desirous of residing in a music center, he resigned his position and returned to Philadelphia, his native home.

From the beginning of his career, the musician was active as a composer. In February, 1914, he won first prize in the national competition in New York, opened to Negro composers. At that time, Diton said to the author, "For some inexplicable reason I get more inspiration in writing for contests than I do in any other way. Consequently all my best work has been done in that way, although I failed in many cases to get prizes. My piano rhapsody was entered in the colored contest and—my four 'Spirituals' won the first prize." In a Nebraska contest, Diton wrote "The Hymn of Nebraska," one of the best of his competition pieces, although it failed to win the prize. A simple hymn was what the rules of the contest called for, while "The Hymn of Nebraska" was in the form of an oratorio. "Swing Low, Sweet Chariot," transcribed for the organ, is a free transcription "a la fantasia." The composer was moved to write this number when improvising a few years ago on the great organ in the Morgan Tabernacle in Salt Lake City. The noted organist, Clarence Eddy, has played the piece with much success.

Of Diton's prize numbers, "Pilgrim's Song" (I'm a Poor Wayfarin' Stranger), the "Deep River" setting, "Little David Play on Your Harp," and "Ev'ry Time I Feel the Spirit," *Musical America* says, "Mr. Diton's work commands respect and admiration. He not only knows the spirit of this music, but has a sense of how to set it to advantage for chorus. Choral societies throughout the country should use these five numbers. They are individual and will make a stirring effect."

While studying the art of composition, the musician maintained a studio for piano pupils and at the same time took lessons in voice. Ambitious to become a singer, Diton came to New York for vocal training and was fortunate in being given an opportunity to become a student in the Juilliard School of Music. By this institution he was graduated from the Department of Singing in 1930.

In recognition of his various services, the Harmon Award of $100 and a Bronze Medal was bestowed upon the musician in 1929, after he had completed a unique concert tour of the South, undertaken with the purpose of carrying the message of good music to distant parts. Diton is at present continuing his vocal studies, singing, and concertizing, but the greater part of his time is spent in teaching in New York City.[1]

Melville Charlton, who was born in the city of New York in 1883, is perhaps the leading organist of the Ne-

---

[1] His songs, arranged for five part chorus, are published by the house of G. Schirmer.

gro race. He is, however, a church and concert organist whose ability is not measured by racial lines. His general education was received in the public schools and in the College of the City of New York. He won a scholarship at the National Conservatory of Music, where he studied harmony, counterpoint, fugue and composition. Charlton first played the organ at St. Philip's Episcopal Church before a congregation that composed many of the older Negro families of New York. After a few years' service he resigned and accepted the position of organist at the Religious School of Temple E-man-u-él, the wealthy Jewish Synagogue in which Harry T. Burleigh sang.

In November, 1915, Charlton received his certificate as an associate member of the American Guild of Organists, for which one of the examiners was Horatio Parker, director of Music of Yale University. His organ playing has been commended by Emil Pauer, a former conductor of the Boston Symphony Orchestra; by Max Spicker, and leading theologians who have heard him as organist of the Union Theological Seminary, one of the positions which he later occupied in New York City. As a piano accompanist, Charlton was engaged in concerts with Harry T. Burleigh throughout the East. He still functions in both capacities and also gives attention to the art of composition. "Poem Erotique," published by G. Schirmer, is his best known piano production. Other short pieces have been written for organ and for the voice. In recognition of his efforts, Howard University conferred upon him in 1930 the degree of Doctor of Music.

The awards and prizes through competitions and contests which have been furthered by individuals and foundations within recent years, have no doubt encouraged young composers as well as writers and poets. While the ideal is not the one for which a true artist strives, it has been the means of giving the struggling musician a prospect of being heard and in many instances badly needed financial assistance.

Before the contests brought forward much excellent talent, Harry Lawrence Freeman of New York had succeeded in making his name known as a composer. He chose the difficult field of opera, and has presented original works under his own management. In September, 1928, his opera *Voodoo*, was produced at the Fifty-second Street Music Hall in New York. In 1929, he was awarded a Harmon gold medal and a prize of $400 for achievement. In 1930, scenes from his various works were staged at Steinway Hall, New York. A list of his operas include *The Martyr, The Prophecy, The Octoroon, Plantation Vendetta, Voodoo, The Tryst, Zuluki,* and *Valdo.* The Paramount film company has purchased *Voodoo,* to be presented on the screen in a condensed version.

J. Howard Brown, pianist and organist, who received for the third time the Rodman Wanamaker prize in composition and also a Harmon award, holds the degree of Bachelor of Music from Fisk University, where he received his musical education. He also received the degree of Bachelor of Music from the Horner Institute, Kansas City Conservatory. For four years he was director of music in the Northeast Junior High School of Kansas City, Kansas, and also taught piano at the Metropolitan School of Music of that city. He has been director of music in the Crispus Attucks High School at Indianapolis, at the Florida State College at Tallahassee, and has charge of the theoretical department of the Cosmopolitan School of Music and Fine Arts, a Negro conservatory of music.

Lawrence Brown, pianist, composer and arranger of Negro music, was born in Florida, studied in New York, and appeared in concerts in leading cities of the United States after which he continued his studies in London, England. For a short while he was associated with Roland

Hayes as his accompanist. He pursued musical studies for four years in London, where he appeared before the King and Queen, Princess Victoria, Lady Astor and other persons of social prominence. He has written interesting settings of Negro themes for violin and piano, and for 'cello and piano.

Delving seriously into the history of Negro music, Brown spent the Fall of 1925 in folk song research in the South of the United States, and during the season of 1925-26 he presented rare and unusual songs to his own accompaniments in joint concerts with Paul Robeson as singer. Brown is widely known as one who seeks to preserve every peculiarity of Negro music both in content and rhythm. As a composer he has restricted his efforts to this field, and he has been most successful as a master of Negro song.

Following New York appearances with Paul Robeson, the actor and Negro folk song singer, in the spring season of 1930-1, *Musical America* said of him, "Mr. Brown not only played fine accompaniments but lent variety and a further racial color to the program by joining in the melody with the singer." The musician has made Victor records with Paul Robeson. At present he is engaged in concert work in Europe and in America.

William L. Dawson, trombonist and composer, is at present director of the Music School of Tuskegee Institute.[2] After finishing, in 1921, with the class at Tuskegee, where he got his start in Music, Dawson attended Washburn College, Topeka, Kansas, studying composition and

---

[2] Known primarily the world over as an industrial school, Tuskegee has lately enlarged the music department and has secured the services of noted colored musicians toward developing a school of music of high standard. Mr. Dawson was a member of the graduating class of Tuskegee Institute in 1921. For five years he was one of the Tuskegee Singers.

orchestration. In 1925, he received the degree of bachelor of music from the Institute of Fine Arts, Kansas City, Missouri. He also studied composition under Felix Borowski at the Chicago Musical College and under Adolph Weidig at the American Conservatory for four years. In 1927, Dawson received the degree of master of music from this Conservatory.

As trombone soloist, he has appeared under the management of the Redpath Chatauqua, and for four seasons, was first trombonist of the Chicago Civic Orchestra, conducted by Frederick Stock and Eric DeLamarter. The position was won by competitive examination. In August, 1929, Dawson assembled an orchestra and gave a program on the Plaza, during the Century of Progress Band Conductors' Contest, sponsored by the Chicago *Daily News*. The musician was chosen to be one of the directors during the 1933 World's Fair of Chicago.

In the educational field, Dawson has held positions as director of music at the Kansas Vocational College, and at Lincoln High School in Kansas. Since his first lessons in piano and harmony under Alice Carter Simmons at Tuskegee, he has been interested in composition, and has thrice been a Wanamaker prize winner. During the second week in November, 1934, the composer's "Negro Symphony" had its world première when played by the Philadelphia Symphony, Leopold Stokowski, conducting.

James E. Dorsey, baritone, was born at San Antonio, Texas, November 22, 1905, the son of Blanche Wade Dorsey, a well-known singer in Texas. From the Chicago public schools, he entered Tuskegee Institute, where he took the course in electrical engineering. During his last year he traveled with the Tuskegee Quartette. In 1924, he went to Lincoln University, where he turned decisively to the study of music, although he had been studying the violin from the time that he was seven. While a student at Lincoln, he studied theory of music under William Happich, director of the Symphony Club of Philadelphia, and voice under Mme. E. Roth of Philadelphia. He organized there the Music Club of thirty-five voices, which he later conducted on a short tour to principal cities. He now holds the post as director of music at Lincoln University.

Possessing creative talent, apart from his school duties he devotes his time to composition. Aside from his Wanamaker prize work, "Sandals," his compositions include choruses for mixed voices; arrangements of "Negro Spirituals" for male voices; eight songs for voice and piano; four fugues; "Rondo and Allegro"; "Fantasy on Thanksgiving," theme for four hands; "Aria" for baritone and orchestra; "Theme for Variations for String Quartette," and a number of songs with pianoforte accompaniment.

Shirley Graham, a student at Oberlin Conservatory, occupied in research in African music, utilized Negro material and characters in an opera, *Tom-Tom*, which had its première at the summer opera season at the Cleveland Stadium held from June 29 to July 6, 1932. Clifford Barnes conducted Miss Graham's opera the cast of which included Jules Bledsoe, Charlotte Wallace Murray, Lillian Cowan, Hazel M. Walker, Luther King and Augustus Grist. The dancing was under the direction of Festus Fitzhugh, a young Negro from the Cleveland Playhouse Settlement. The scene of the opera is laid in the African jungle, but changes in the second and third acts to the United States, south and north. Both text and music were described as "expressive and often deeply moving."

Edward Jenkins, born in Charleston, South Carolina, the son of a Negro educator, was one of the promising young American composers who won his laurels abroad. In 1914, he became a student at the Royal Academy of Music in London, where in 1915 he won the Orchestral Scholarship for two years, the Ross Scholarship for three

years and the Oliveria Prescott Prize. In open competition he won the Charles Lucas Silver Medal for the composition of "Three Ballet Airs" for full orchestra; and
at the annual examinations, he received the Bronze and the
Silver Medal for sight-singing and clarinet playing. He
won the Battison-Haynes Prize by his work in composition.

In London, Jenkins was active as a church organist and
also as clarinetist at the Savoy Theatre and at the Grand
Theatre in Llandudno, Wales. During the season of 1931,
his "Negro Rhapsodie-Charlestonia," was performed in
the Kursaal at Ostend with unprecedented success. The
conductor of the orchestra was François Rasse. This promising career was cut short by early death.

William Andrew Rhodes of Boston, church organist and
composer, was born in Greensboro, North Carolina. He
is a graduate of the New England Conservatory and has
filled successful local concert engagements as pianist and
composer-accompanist. In 1932, he was awarded the E.
P. Brown Prize in Class IV for a group of three songs
with piano accompaniment and a choral piece. In 1933,
he was again the winner of the same prize for his "Prayer
of the Crusaders" for mixed chorus—A Capella. Rhodes'
arrangements of Negro Spirituals have been widely sung
by leading soloists and choral societies.

N. Clark Smith, a matured musician, long maintained
a reputation as a bandmaster and choral conductor. He
also won prizes for his compositions in the Negro idiom.
For many years he conducted the band at Tuskegee Institute and made annual tours. He arranged many Negro folk songs and edited a small book of Negro Spirituals
with piano accompaniments. His best known pieces are
songs, "Prayer for Emancipation"; "Rocks and Mountains" (male voices); "Plantation Song Cycle" for baritone, and "Couldn't Hear Nobody Pray," chorus with orchestral accompaniment, which won a prize at the Dunbar

Song Leaders' Prize Contest, held on May 29, 1922, in Washington, D. C. Also a Wanamaker prize winner, he was chosen to organize the Pullman Company Porter's Chorus, which he conducted in various centers. Thereafter, until his death, on October 8, 1935, he was supervisor of music in the Sumner High School of St. Louis, Missouri.

Edward Margetson, who makes his home in New York City, was born in St. Kitts, British West Indies, and some of the most beautiful compositions he has written are songs of the Caribbean Sea. His "Echoes from the Caribbees," is a group of songs for solo voice with piano accompaniment. A madrigal and motet—"When You No More" and "Far From My Heavenly Home," have appeared. Margetson received his musical education at Columbia University. He is active as a teacher and church organist in New York City. As a composer, he has received critical praise for unusual skill in writ-choral music of extraordinary power.

Edward H. Boatner, baritone, was born in New Orleans in 1918. The son of an itinerant minister, he early became interested in Negro religious song. His first musical instruction was received at Western University at Quindaro, Kansas. He later studied at the New England Conservatory, and under private teachers in Boston. For one year he had a scholarship at the Boston Conservatory of Music. In 1922, Boatner was one of the winners in the state vocal contest of the National Federation of Music Clubs. As a composer, he has been mainly interested in Negro Spirituals, a number of which he has arranged. His song, "Trampin'," produced in 1931, was the first publication of William Maxwell, who was for years a member of the staff of Ricordi & Company.

Nicholas George Julius Ballanta, a native African musician, was born in Freetown, British West Africa, in 1894. His grandfather's melodious African name was changed to that of Taylor by the church missionaries. Young Ballanta studied music without the aid of a teacher. He was sent to London for Sir John Stainer's work on harmony, the principles of which he mastered. By mail, prior to 1921, he was able to pass the intermediary examinations of Durham University, England, for the degree of Bachelor of Music. Coming to New York in 1922, he made an impression on Dr. Frank Damrosch, and he was awarded a scholarship at the Institute of Musical Art.

Ballanta-Taylor traveled in Alabama, Georgia and South Carolina; and at the Penn Normal, Industrial and Agricultural School he studied music and engaged in folk song research. He received a diploma from the New York school in 1924. In 1925, his book of 103 recorded Negro Spirituals gathered on St. Helena Island was published. The musician's transcriptions and his foreword are of unusual interest. A Guggenheim fellowship enabled him to travel and do research work in Africa, where he has collected native songs.

Frederick J. Work, director of music at Bordentown, New Jersey, who has been favorably known as a chorus director and for his interest in Negro folk songs, has turned his attention to the art of composition. Among his manuscript works, the "F Major String Quartet" given at the Philadelphia Art Alliance's Annual Concert of Manuscript Music, May 1, 1934, evoked commendation from the critics as a "skillfully worked out composition—the real thing."

John Wesley Work, rescuer of Negro folk song, and the first to record the melodies for the phonograph, was born in Tennessee, August 6, 1873, the son of John Work who had had the benefit of musical training in New Orleans. His grandfather, Stephen Boyd, was a well-to-do free man. Like his father, young Work began early to sing. After entering Fisk University in 1891, he organized the Glee Club at the time that Adam Spence was directing there the Mozart Society. Graduating in 1895, he attended Harvard University to study Latin after having taught in a small school for a short period. He was called to Fisk to teach this language but threw most of his energy, enthusiasm and heart into an attempt to restore Negro Spirituals to a proper place as folk songs worthy of respect. In this he had the encouragement of President Cravath.

Work collected material, reorganized the Fisk Glee Club, trained choruses and traveled with the Fisk Quartette. Krehbiel said of him, "A concert goer might live a lifetime and never hear such beautiful homogenity of tone, as that which they produce." Together with Agnes Haynes, a teacher at Fisk whom Work had married, and his brother Fred, he made systematic research and collected songs which were published as *Folk Songs of the American Negro*. He was also the composer of the beautiful Fisk college song.

Between 1915-1923, with a change of administration, came difficulties usually encountered by those who work unselfishly for a cause. There were misunderstandings and discontent, and a decided change of policy in the Fisk Music Department followed. The Glee Club was taken from Work's leadership, and he was replaced as head of the Latin and History Department. Lucrative positions were offered him at Tuskegee, Hampton and the Colored State Normal at Nashville. The presidency of Roger Williams College was open to him; but, devoted to Fisk, he remained until insufferable conditions forced him to resign. Disillusioned, he went to Roger Williams, but died two years later, in the spring of 1926, when on his way North to seek rest. Until the end he remembered the advice given by President Cravath to the eager, young, enthusiastic worker, "Let nothing come between you and your God-given task." John Wesley Work's fame rests secure as the founder of the movement for the restoration of Negro folk song.

Gerald Tyler, a pioneer musician of St. Louis, Missouri, was graduated from Oberlin Conservatory. He later studied voice under Herbert Witherspoon. Besides acting as assistant director of Public School Music in St. Louis, and teaching voice and piano, he wrote many songs and incidental music. His vocal pieces include the "Syrian Lullaby," "Dirge for a Soldier," "Heart o' Fancy," and "Ships that Pass in the Night." Of the last mentioned, the Boston *Evening Transcript* said, "It is music that was deeply felt and eloquent and withal simple in structure." Tyler was one of the three musicians chosen to write the centennial drama music in commemoration of the one hundredth anniversary of Missouri's admission to the Union. The music was rendered by the Morning Choral Club and the St. Louis Symphony.

Virgil Thompson, another musician, first became known by an unusual opera, *4 Saints in 3 Acts*, a novel title. He returned from Paris to supervise the production given with forty colored singers, the choreography by Frederick Ashton of London. The opera was first performed on February 8, 1934, at Hartford, Connecticut, and was given for three weeks at the 44th Street Theater, New York City, with a return engagement following. The seemingly incomprehensible libretto written by the free verse poet, Gertrude Stein, created widespread comment as did the innovation of having an all colored cast appear in an opera in English in which there was no attempt to feature folk-songs or Negro spirituals.

In spite of the critics and the public declaring that they could not decipher the meaning of the story with its senseless word-patterns, the work was in many respects a success due to the excellent singing and acting of the chorus and the principals. Edward Matthews was acclaimed for his beautiful singing in the role of St. Ignatius, as was Altonell Hines and Beatrice Robinson Wayne in leading roles. The entire cast was praised for their diction, which a reviewer declared "established an all-time precedent for opera in English." The Hartford performance was given by the *Friends and Enemies of Modern Music* at the Avery Museum of Modern Art.

The orchestra was directed by Alexander Smallens. The chorus was trained by Miss Eva Jessye of New York. The music was scored for an orchestra consisting of strings, a harmonium, two saxophones, and a large accordion; an unusual combination to fit unusual paragraphs. However, a critic declared that the libretto is not altogether unintelligible if you know the history of St. Theresa of old Spain, St. Ignatius, and the companion saints. Simple cellophane made striking settings for the artistic lighting. The opera opens a new chapter for the colored race in this field.

CHAPTER XV

INTERPRETATIVE MUSICIANS

Of those Negro musicians devoted exclusively to interpretation Roland Hayes, tenor, deserves the most conspicuous place. He was born in poverty, June 3, 1887, in Curryville, Georgia. His career has been most remarkable. From a plantation he went to Chattanooga, Tennessee, when fourteen years of age, and five years later he found work there in an iron foundry. It was not until he was eighteen that his musical talent was discovered by Arthur Calhoun, a Negro musician, who gave him his first lessons. A little later he entered Fisk University, where he studied music for a number of years.

Leaving that institution, he went to Louisville, Kentucky, where he served as a waiter; and there an opportunity came for him to sing at the annual banquet of the Pendennis Club by which he was employed. The remarkable beauty of his voice brought him into instant notice; but, although ambitious, he had neither the opportunity nor the necessary funds to undergo vocal training.

Just at this perplexing time, a chance came for him to join the Fisk Jubilee Singers. With them he was heard in Boston, Massachusetts, in Mechanic's Building, and in many concerts elsewhere in the city. Acquaintanceship was renewed with white friends who had heard him sing in an humble capacity in the South, and steps were taken to make it possible for the youth to study in Boston. Light employment was secured for him by which he met his living expenses while arrangements were made for him to study under the late Arthur Hubbard.

ROLAND HAYES

Hayes did not rely on patronage alone. He was a diligent worker, ambitious and farsighted, possessing an attractive personality and determination to succeed. He made influential friends; and by 1916, well equipped musically, he could devote all of his time to concert work.

In the spring of 1917 he organized the Hayes Trio, composed of himself, tenor; William Richardson, baritone; and William Lawrence, pianist. During the summer of the same year the Trio filled Chautauqua engagements throughout New England and New Jersey. Hayes spent the following year in study and travel in the United States with remarkable success in song recitals given from the Atlantic to the Pacific Coast. In 1919, he went abroad with the avowed intention to study African music on its native soil, but after singing in various recitals, the acclaim with which he was greeted showed unmistakably that he was destined for a different career.

In Paris, his first recital was given at the home of Joseph Salmon, the violoncellist, after which he sang in Parisian salons and also gave a recital in the Salle Erard. In London he studied voice and languages under Miss Ira Aldridge from whose studio in Kensington many famous singers have gained a finished artistry. By this time he had been commanded to sing before King George of England, and had had the signal honor of being soloist at a Colonne Orchestra Concert in Paris in 1922. Thus returning to Boston a ripened musician, fresh from many months of vocal schooling and singing, Hayes gave a notable recital in Symphony Hall on January 7, 1923. Regarding his appearances in Cambridge, November 15, and in Boston, November 16-17, 1923, H. T. Parker, writing in the Boston *Evening Transcript*, said, "Child in music of this town is Mr. Hayes, even though it has waited too anxiously and hesitatingly for Europe to applaud him. Here he found his first friends; was schooled; risked himself, gained merit and a following. After our manner, however, too many could not be quite sure of his virtue until London had clapped it; Paris had noted it; German capitals of music joined in the plaudits. By that time, all and sundry in Mr. Hayes' 'home-town' could safely beat their hands together. With a will they did so in Sanders Theatre on Thursday, in Symphony Hall on Friday. Six times was he recalled at Cambridge; almost as many in Boston—and by applause that was general, hearty, significant.''

Of his recital given in Symphony Hall on December 2, 1923, Hale, of the Boston *Herald,* said, ''Dame nature gave Mr. Hayes a beautiful voice. She also gave him singing brains. Not content with nature's gifts, he has studied intelligently. He has learned also by observation, by pondering his art, and by experience. Year by year he has gained in vocal control and in power of interpretation, until now in Great Britain, France, Austria, Hungary, and Czecho-slovakia he is hailed as one of the few concert singers of the world, and his return next year to fulfill many engagements is eagerly awaited.

''Last night he showed beyond doubt and peradventure that he is not a specialist, but a singer well versed in all periods and schools of vocal compositions. The old Italian, the old English, the German classic, the modern French—no one of them is alien to him. His art, his taste, and his soul respond to each demand. It matters not whether he is called on to shine in florid song requiring execution and perfect breath control; to express pathetic sentiment, as in the noble and solemn air from Percell's 'Dodo and Aaeneas' and Schuman's 'Ich habe' in 'Traum geweinet'; or to be lightly gay as in Schubert's 'Forelle' and Quilter's song. If he sang 'Clair de Lune' in a manner to enhance the beauty of Verlaine's verse and Gabriel Faure's music, he comprehended the religious feeling of Franck's 'Procession' and the sadness and dramatic force of Dvorák's 'By the Waters of Babylon.'

"Then there was the group of Negro spirituals which Mr. Hayes sang inimitably, with fervor, exaltation, depth of feeling; without the slightest exaggeration; without any obvious appeal; without thought of audience, but as a revelation of his own soul. Few actors, if any, could gain the dramatic effect he produced with the utmost simplicity by his delivery of 'The Crucifixion,' 'He Never Said a Mumblin' Word,' an interpretation that to applaud seemed almost sacrilegious.

"Seldom is singing of so fine a quality heard in our concert halls. Mr. Lawrence accompanied most sympathetically. His playing of the piano in 'Der Nussbaum' and 'Clair de Lune'' was delightfully poetic, indispensable to the singer.''

In the spring of 1924, after a triumphant tour which included an appearance with the Detroit Symphony Orchestra, Hayes returned to Europe. He has sung in Hungary, Russia and Germany, and according to the Berlin press, judged to be superior to many European singers. He has been heard in Italian cities and appeared with Sir Henry Woods' Orchestra in London at Queen's Hall. During the summer of 1929, the singer had the advantage of coaching under Sir George Hanschel, thus following the artistic line of Miss Ira Aldridge's instruction, since that noted teacher was a pupil of this master.

Hayes was chosen as one of the artists to appear during the series sponsored by the Friends of Music, Incorporated, at the Century of Progress Exposition held at Chicago during the summer and autumn of 1933.[1]

---

[1] His more recent accompanist, Percival Parham of Cambridge, has been praised for his pianistic ability, ease, and sympathetic accompaniments. In 1933, Mr. Parham went to New York to open a studio for the teaching of piano.

For these achievements Hayes has received various honors. On July 1, 1924, the National Association for the Advancement of Colored People awarded him the Spingarn Medal for distinguished achievement. In June, 1932, Fisk University awarded him the honorary degree of Doctor of Music, "to one who has added so much to the happiness of people" and as "one of the greatest interpreters of music."

Marian Anderson, the leading contralto of the Negro race, is endowed by nature with a voice of opulent color, tonal splendor and fine range. She was born and educated in Philadelphia, where she studied voice under Giuseppe Boghetti. She received substantial encouragement from the National Association of Negro Musicians. The singer made her professional début in a recital given in December, 1929; her program included songs by Schubert, Strauss, Schumann and French composers. In Philadelphia she appeared as soloist with the Philharmonic Symphony Orchestra. Of her work, H. F. Peyser, writing in the New York *Telegram* of March 3, 1930, said, "Miss Anderson has one of the rarest voices of the time—a noble contralto, spontaneous in utterance, amazingly rich in timbre, and smooth as satin in texture. There is a welcome absence of coarse exaggerated chest tones, of 'registers,' of perceptible transitions in its ample and remarkably even scale."

With such natural ability she could not but go forward. In New York she was chosen from among 300 competitors to sing with the Philharmonic Orchestra in the New York City College Stadium. Winning still more applause, she evoked expressions of deep interest in her career. In 1930 another opportunity for growth came when she was given a Rosenwald Scholarship for study in Germany. By this she profited immensely. After singing at Hamburg and at Berlin University, she returned to the United States

CHARLOTTE WALLACE MURRAY

LILLIAN EVANTI

MARIAN ANDERSON

FLORENCE COLE-TALBERT

where she appeared in many concerts on tour from the Atlantic to the Pacific Coast.

After being presented by Edith Abercrombie in the second of her mid-winter musicals in the Bancroft Hotel ballroom in New York City, February 1, 1931, the great contralto was booked for a second European tour with William King, who has for long been her excellent and sympathetic accompanist. As a result of advanced vocal studies under Miss Ira Aldridge in London, the singer made noticeable improvement in the freedom and smoothness of her technique. She was engaged for two concerts with the London Symphony Orchestra under the direction of Sir Henry Wood. Following her last appearance in Germany, the *Berliner Morgenpost* declared, "Such caressing timbre is very seldom heard . . . . her singing technically reaches to highest possible degree." Besides having one of the greatest voices of the times, Marian Anderson has a charming stage presence and unstudied poise.

Madame Evanti (Lillian Evans), soprano, a woman of beautiful presence, with a coloratura voice of surprising power, was once a member of the Opera Company at Milan, Italy. Her father was the late W. Bruce Evans, the organizer and first principal of the Armstrong Manual Training High School in Washington, D. C., where she was born and educated. Her mother was a teacher in Washington. After a début recital in Washington, Madame Evanti was in demand for local concerts after which she sang in other cities with marked success. In order to further her studies, she went to Paris and studied voice under Madame Ritter-Ciampi, and took lessons in acting with M. Gaston Dupins. After singing again in the United States, the soprano went to Italy where she devoted her time to her operatic studies. She made her début at Nice in the French opera, *Lakme,* and in 1930 she sang in opera at Turin, Milan, Palermo and other Italian cities.

More recently Madame Evanti has given radio concerts in Paris with Madeline de Valmalette, pianist, and has appeared with the violinist Marquise de Casa Fuerte in Madame Joseph Salmon's salon concerts. From 1932 to 1935 she gave recitals in the United States before capacity audiences that praised the tonal beauty of her voice. In early February, 1934, the singer sang at the White House for Mrs. Roosevelt and her guests.

Eight years ago, Merman Devries, music critic of the Chicago *Evening American,* wrote, *"Julius (Jules) Bledsoe,* Negro baritone, is a sort of baritonal twin to Roland Hayes. His recital program at Kimball Hall last night was in itself a demonstration of superlative musical culture." Glenn Dillard Gunn in the Chicago *Herald and Examiner* stated that "his is the finest Negro voice yet heard in concert halls of America," while the critic of the New York *Sun,* W. J. Henderson, declared that, "neither race nor color were to be considered in any examination of his art."

While it is true that Bledsoe has no superior as a vocal recital artist, he is the most versatile Negro singer on the stage today. Apart from being the leading Negro baritone soloist, and one of the world's best, he has been equally successful in musical comedy, music-drama and in grand opera. He is gifted with a voice of resonant beauty, sings with ease in six languages, and possesses remarkable dramatic ability.

This artist was born in Waco, Texas, December 29, 1899, and is of musical parentage. The family of Bledsoes is a well-known one of successful farmers and educators in Texas. His grandfather, Rev. Stephen H. Cobb, was one of the first Negro ministers ordained in the South after the Civil War, and was noted for his fine voice. His father and mother, Henry B. and Jessie Cobb Bledsoe, were music lovers. Julius began singing when a child and appeared in school and church concerts until his voice changed. He began the study of piano when eight years of age; and during the time his voice was changing, he acted as accompanist for his mother, a soprano singer, and for his aunt, Mrs. Mae Ollie Spiller, who also sang.

Finishing the academic course at Central Texas College, young Bledsoe went to Bishop College, Marshall, Texas, where he was graduated in 1914 with the degree of Bachelor of Arts. In the musical department of this school, Bledsoe continued his studies in piano, harmony and musical history. After taking a post-graduate course in Virginia Union University, he served in the World War Students' Army Training Corps until duly discharged. In 1919 he came to New York for the express purpose of studying medicine, a course urged by the family, and entered the Columbia University Medical School; but at the same time he took voice lessons as a pleasure. While living at the Young Men's Christian Association in Brooklyn, Rufus Maroney, of Texas, who was then the seretary, urged Bledsoe to study for a professional career. At this particular time the author of this volume was visiting New York, and Bledsoe sang for her. She was deeply impressed at the virile quality of his voice and his intelligent interpretation of the fine songs which he rendered. He had then begun his vocal training under Claude Warford. Later he had lessons from Parisolti and Lazar Samoiloff. He and his friends then realized that he was destined for a career other than medicine.

In 1924 Mr. Bledsoe gave a début recital in Aeolian Hall, New York City, under the management of Sol Hurok, after which he was heard in Boston and elsewhere. His particularly fine interpretation of the German lieder was commented upon. At the same time, attention was focused upon his dramatic ability, and he was offered the leading role in *Abraham's Bosom,* a stage play of Negro life by Paul Green. An opportunity to sing in Frank Harling's opera, *Deep River,* the libretto of which gives a romantic southern setting of one phase of Negro life, presented itself in 1926 and gave the artist a chance to display his talent as a singing-actor. According to reviewers, his character in the role of the King was sung "with rich emotional quality."[2] The opera was beautifully mounted and given with a cast drawn from both races including Rose McClendon as Octavia, Charlotte Wallace Murray as the Queen, and Frank Harrison as announcer. The work of the chorus was highly praised, but the critics declared that only the second act could be regarded as pure opera; other acts more operetta than opera. Nevertheless, the work caused a stir in music circles, served to call attention to the possibilities of the Negro artist in serious opera, and added materially to the growing reputation of Julius Bledsoe.

The following year a flattering offer was made for him to take the role of "Jo" in "Show Boat," which ran for two years at Ziegfeld Theatre, New York City, before going on tour. Bledsoe's remarkable singing of the theme solo, "Ole Man River," according to his own interpretation (which he insisted upon), made of the song a tragic scene of the Mississippi River and made a deep impression wherever the music-play was given.

In spite of Jules Bledsoe's success on the dramatic stage in *The Emperor Jones* as well as *Show Boat,* however, he determined to return to concert work, declaring, "I love concert work—for after all, that is my life, the life I love—the dignified, glorious work of the

[2] "Deep River" is the *first opera* to be given with a mixed cast in America.

JULES BLEDSOE

concert stage. It grips one with tendrils lighter than a mist yet drawing and holding as steel talons. That is my life; the life I have trained for.''

In 1931 Bledsoe sang ''The Creation,'' a Negro sermon, for baritone and orchestra, with the Boston Symphony Orchestra, under the direction of Dr. Koussevitzky. The piece is a dramatic poem by James Weldon Johnson, the musical setting by Louis Gruenberg. He then went abroad that year and sang with success in all the large capitals of Europe. Again in the United States on July 11, 1932, Bledsoe received an ovation when he appeared in the role of ''Amonasro'' in Verdi's *Aida* given by the summer grand opera company at the Municipal Stadium in Cleveland, Ohio. He was the first Negro singer to be heard in this role on an accepted American stage, and with only twenty-four hours' notice, he gave a remarkable portrayal of the Ethiopian king in a company that included Eleanora de Cisneros, Paul Althouse and Elsa Olsen.

The fact that the season of 1932-33 was a difficult one for artists and serious music in general, owing to the world-wide financial depression, may account for Bledsoe's appearances in *Hi-De-Ho*, a distinct melange, which in spite of praises by the press is a vehicle unworthy of his great talent. His appearance as ''Amonasro'' in the opera *Aida,* given by the new Chicago Opera Company under the management of Alfred Salmaggi, in July, 1933, was his second engagement in grand opera in the United States. Bledsoe sang in the New York series at the Hippodrome. During February, 1934, he appeared in the European première of Gruenberg's opera abroad, *The Emperor Jones,* which was given in the Municipal Theatre, Amsterdam, with Bledsoe in the title role. Maestro Parenti conducted. Performances followed in Paris, Vienna, Milan, Brussels and London. On

November 24, 1934, the singer attracted a large crowd in a New York production.[5]

Caterina Jarboro, soprano, created a sensation in the musical world in appearing in the title role of *Aida* given on July 22, 1933, by the Chicago Opera Company in the Hippodrome, New York City. She is the first Negro woman singer to have a star role with a white opera company in the United States. So tremendous was the success and so enthusiastic was the welcome of the artists that the schedule of operas was changed in order that the performance might be repeated two days later. The management of the New Chicago Opera Company having proved that the box office receipts as well as the highest artistic ideals have been supported by their innovation, engaged her and Jules Bledsoe in the role of Amonasro for a twenty weeks' season of grand opera in the autumn of 1933.

Speaking of Miss Jarboro's début, the musical editor of the New York *Times* said the next day, "The young soprano brought to its presentation last night some admirable attributes—a vivid dramatic sense that kept her impersonation vital without overacting, an Italian diction remarkably pure and distinct, a musically feeling for phrase and line and a voice whose characteristically racial timbre, husky and darkly rich, endowed the music with an individual effectiveness."

Caterina Jarboro (in private life, Catherine Yarborough) was born in the home of her parents, John Wesley and Elizabeth Harris Yarborough, on Church Street, Wilmington, North Carolina, on July 24, 1903. Her mother, an untrained singer, sang in a local church choir. The

[5] The Cosmopolitan Opera Company gave the "Emperor Jones" at the Hippodrome as a first experiment in American opera. Aldo Franchetti conducted.

daughter's early education was received under the Franciscan Sisters at St. Thomas' Catholic School, Wilmington, and later at the Gregory Normal School. In 1916, she went to Brooklyn, New York, to live with an aunt and to study music. In 1921 she joined the ensemble of the musical comedy, "Shuffle Along," but continued to study voice and piano. She later secured an engagement in "Runnin' Wild" and saved her salary to further her musical education abroad. In 1926 she went to Paris, and while studying there she sang in Latin in the French churches. Ambitious for operatic training, she went to Italy in 1928 and became a pupil of Nino Campinno. In May, 1930, she made her début in the opera *Aida* at the Puccini Theatre in Milan.

Miss Jarboro visited Wilmington, North Carolina, in 1933, when she sang for benefits; and so great was the demand that she be heard in recitals that season, she postponed her return to Paris. Remaining in this country, the opportunity came for her to apply for a hearing as a member of the newly formed grand opera company which in 1933 reaped laurels in out-door performances and in New York at the Hippodrome. A preliminary hearing won for her the distinction of opening the way for future talented and trained Negro women aspirants in grand opera in America.

This "popular price" organization known as "The Chicago Grand Opera Company" presented Miss Jarboro in the role of "Selika" in Meyerbeer's *L'Africaine* as well as in that of *Aida*. In Miss Jarboro's first New York appearance in Alfredo Salmaggi's company, Dreda Aves scored as Amneris, Pasquale Ferrara as Radames and Edward Albano as Amonasro with Graham Harris as conductor. With Jules Bledsoe in the repeated production, Giuseppe Radaelli sang the tenor part. Fulgenzio Guerrieri conducted. On September 7, the Opera Company reopened with *Aïda* in the New York Hippodrome. The cast included Lola Monti-Gorsey in the main role. At an Ebbets Field outdoor performance in Brooklyn on the first of September, Caterina Jarboro sang the principal part, with Arthur Rosenstein, conductor. Her latest success was her appearance as "Aida" before an audience of 6,000 in a performance by the Chicago Opera Company on February 17, 1935, at the Hippodrome, New York City.

William Howard Richardson, baritone, of Boston, Massachusetts, was born in Liverpool, Nova Scotia, the son of Mr. and Mrs. Joseph H. Richardson, who were native Canadians of English, Dutch, and African descent. His paternal grandfather was a professional singer who directed a small concert company composed of his two daughters and three other musicians. The family migrated to Boston when the boy was eleven years of age. It was early seen that he had the gift of an unusually fine natural voice; and, being ambitious to receive proper training, he found ways to take private lessons from George H. Woods under whom he made rapid progress. Upon reaching his majority, he married Minnie A. Williams of Plymouth, Massachusetts.

About this time he became a member of the quartette of Bethany Baptist Church (white), in the Roxbury section of Boston. After four years' service he became baritone soloist of the choir of St. Peter's Church (white) of Cambridge, a position which he has held for over twenty years with the privilege of periods of absence for concert work. For a number of years he was the only Negro member of the Philharmonic Society, a singing organization of Dorchester (Boston), under the direction of Professor Archibald T. Davidson, the well known director of the Harvard Glee Club.

Richardson's first concert appearance of any moment was made on April 20, 1909, at Steinert Hall, Boston.

Following this he was heard in Washington, Nashville, and in other cities as baritone soloist in oratorios and in various productions of Coleridge-Taylor's *Hiawatha* trilogy. In 1913 he appeared on concert tour in leading cities of the north and south as singer in illustration of the author's lecture recital, "The Contribution of the Negro-American to the Art of Music." Visiting Louisiana, he became greatly interested in the folk songs of the Creoles, and gave valuable assistance in Creole and Negro folk song research. Returning to Boston, he continued his studies and welcomed an opportunity for vocal instruction under Arthur Hubbard, the well known Boston teacher of Roland Hayes. He took private lessons in languages and diction and then became a student under the noted vocal instructor, Theodore Schroeder, to whom he is indebted for his most extensive work.

From 1915 to 1917 Richardson made short concert tours both in the South and North, giving recitals of songs in English, French and Italian. After spending the summer of 1917 in Chautauqua work with Roland Hayes, tenor, and William Lawrence, pianist, Richardson ventured his first Jordan Hall recital on January 30, 1919. Maud Cuney-Hare assisted as pianist and Arthur Fiedler as accompanist. Writing of the singer's artistry, Olin Downes, now music editor of the New York *Times*, said, "Mr. Richardson, who was born with a beautiful voice, gave proof of his unremitting industry, his artistic purpose, his consistent growth. He is not merely a maker of musical sounds. He gives these sounds dramatic significance. He sings not merely a melody but a poem, and rightly fits the tone, in its color and inflection, to the text. The quality of his voice remains fundamentally rich and full."

Richardson appeared on the Boston Public Library lecture programs in 1921 and 1931, the first Negro singer who has sung in the educational course arranged by the Library trustees for the city of Boston. In 1923 he was heard in Cuba after a triumphant transcontinental tour that included cities from the Atlantic to the Pacific Coast. In 1926 a three months' tour covered the Virgin Islands and the principal towns in Puerto Rico. In San Juan he appeared as soloist with the San Juan Symphony Orchestra. Under white management, the singer appeared in costume-recitals before leading colleges of the East, and historical and art associations of New England. Dean Butler of the College of Fine Arts, Syracuse University, said of him, "I am sure there are few baritones who can sing such a varied program as delightfully."

From 1930 to 1931 Richardson's recitals embraced classic and modern songs in Italian, French, English and German with the addition of songs in Spanish, and Cuban airs. The reviewer in the Boston *Herald* wrote, "One would have liked to have heard him sing more of the German lieder, for his voice is warm and impassioned, at once lyrical and dramatic." Philip Hale said in an extended review, "Mr. Richardson is blessed by nature; his voice is resonant, firm, commanding, yet smooth and even throughout a liberal compass. He sings fluently and with marked authority."

In a recent song recital given in Boston Mr. Richardson was accompanied by a string quartette from the Boston Symphony Orchestra, with the distinguished conductor, Arthur Fiedler, viola player, and Maud Cuney-Hare, accompanist. "Mr. Richardson has made excellent progress on his concert road," declared the *Christian Science Monitor*, while the Boston *Evening Transcript* stated, "Probably many would call Mr. Richardson's voice a sonorous bass rather than a baritone, though now and again in medium-high range there were tones of rich and even lucious baritone quality. But bass or baritone, Mr. Richardson is endowed with an excellent vocal organ. And training there has been to match in considerable degree the voice itself. One was particularly impressed by the dignity and the sonority and feeling of the stateliness which the singer gave in the 'Invocation of Orpheus' with which the evening began. Similar qualities were discovered in Schubert's huge 'Prometheus'. Equally came a note of lyric melancholy in Mr. Loeffler's 'La Cloche Fêlée' song of wistful memories, of loneliness, of distress.''

The progress of Negro music has been greatly aided by Richardson's efforts, for he has featured new compositions by Samuel Coleridge-Taylor, "Montague Ring" (Miss Ira Aldridge), and Clarence Cameron White; and he has given them their first hearing in America. As an exponent of Creole folk songs in their native patois—French or Spanish—he is the first American singer to present them on the concert stage.

Richardson makes his home in Boston, where he maintains vocal studios in the heart of the musical section and continues to hold the position as soloist at St. Peter's Episcopal Church of which the Rev. Frederick C. Lawrence, the son of Bishop William C. Lawrence, is rector.

William Lawrence, singer and pianist, whose sympathetic and artistic accompaniments played for Roland Hayes, the famous tenor, brought forth highest praise from critics in the United States and abroad, was born September 20, 1897, in Charleston, South Carolina. His father was organist of the Plymouth Congregational Church· of that city. The boy attended Avery Normal Institute and at the same time studied piano with a musically inclined sister and with J. Donovan Moore, a local teacher. Coming to Boston in 1914, he entered the New England Conservatory of Music as a student under Edwin Klahre, a product of the great master Liszt. In 1916 Lawrence was active as an accompanist for Roland Hayes and during the summer of 1917 he was engaged with him and William Howard Richardson by the Swarthmore Chautauqua. As a member of the Hayes Trio, he not only played the accompaniments for the singers, but also gave piano solos. Throughout New England the reviewers commented upon his pianistic talent.

The young musician next became interested in the art of singing. Wishing to devote his time to advanced study, he accepted the post as director of music for one year at the State College at Orangeburg, South Carolina. He returned to Boston and continued his studies with Mrs. Frances L. Grover while taking harmony at Boston University in 1923. At this juncture he was called upon to accompany Roland Hayes and was immediately acclaimed an admirable artist. Later, musical critics named him as one of the world's finest accompanists. Before going abroad with Hayes he gave piano recitals in Boston and elsewhere.

On August 4, 1926, Mr. Lawrence married Miss Lillian Thompson of Columbia, South Carolina, after which he went abroad again where he was engaged in accompanying and in study. In 1929, he discontinued his engagements in order to seek vocal training in Paris where he became a student of voice for over three years. On November 23, 1930, he appeared on the American Students' Atelier Reunion program in Paris as tenor soloist in his own arrangements of Spirituals, accompanied by Madame Boesch, and as composer in "Three Spirituals for String Quartette." Returning to this country in 1932, he gave a number of song recitals on tour. His voice is small but one of beautiful quality, and he sings with finish and style. As pianist-composer, Lawrence has featured his "Rhapsodie Africaine—Bambara."

Florence Cole Talbert, soprano, has brought distinction to her race both in the United States and in Europe. The singer was born in Detroit, Michigan, of musical parentage. Her mother, Sadie Chanler Cole, was a member of the Fisk University Jubilee Singers, and upon her retirement she moved to Los Angeles, California. Florence Talbert received her first musical education at the University of California. She traveled for three seasons after which she entered the Chicago Musical College, and at her graduation was awarded the diamond medal. She was the first Negro woman to take part in the graduating exercises of the vocal department of that college. Her commencement selection, "Care Nome," was sung to an accompaniment by the Chicago Symphony Orchestra.

In 1918, after a short period of travel as soprano with the professional organization known as the Hahn Singers, Madame Talbert gave hundreds of song recitals in principal cities of the United States and in many colleges. After scoring an uncommon success, she decided to continue the study of voice in New York, where she became a student under Oscar Saenger. He said of his gifted pupil, "Her voice is a beautiful soprano, which she uses with consummate skill. This combined with splendid musicianship, places her in the front rank of artists."

In search of operatic training, the singer then went to Italy, where after a period of study under Delia Valeri she sang the title role in the opera *Aïda*. In 1929, she returned to America and resumed concert work. She has an extensive repertoire which includes arias from all of the favorite operas and songs from the French, Italian and English composers. She is of stately presence; her dignity and poise on the concert stage has added to the pleasure given by her admirable singing.[4]

Abbie Mitchell, dramatic soprano, was born in New

[4] In 1930, she married for the second time and as the wife of Dr. Benjamin McCleaves of St. Louis, located first in that city and later in Memphis, Tennessee.

York City and attended the public schools in Baltimore, Maryland. At the early age of fourteen she became the wife of Will Marion Cook. Her first lessons in voice were received from Harry T. Burleigh, who placed her under Mme. Emilia Serrano with whom she studied for four years.

At this period this promising student was gaining stage experience in the music comedies of Will Marion Cook from whom she says she "learned to appreciate the beauty of our own folk-lore, and how to sing the beautiful songs of the black folk." However, in spite of her unquestioned success in this field, the singer retired from musical shows and fitted herself for the concert stage.

She studied musical theory and harmony under Melville Charlton, and then went to Paris where she studied for two years under the great Jean de Reszke. Her first recitals proved her to be an interesting singer of no mean powers, and many return engagements were the rule. As a serious artist of an unusual career, her superb singing of the classics, particularly of the German lieder, is outstanding. Following a New York recital, Charles D. Isaacson of the *Morning Telegraph* said, "Hers is a voice of beauty which is nothing less than remarkable. The use she makes of it, in nearly everything she attempts, sets Abbie Mitchell apart as one worthy of wide attention. She has succeeded in transmitting the timbre of expression to a non-negroid texture. Pure, limpid, graceful is the production of tone, especially delightful in soft passages. Her diction and the handling of the German group of songs was a feat. 'Die Lorelei' of Liszt was memorable. The diction was a model for white rivals. Followed the 'Rittonna Vincintor' from *Aïda*. WHAT AN 'AIDA' THIS WOMAN WOULD MAKE!"

Abbie Mitchell is ambitious to sing in opera and has worked with that end in view. She spent the summer of 1931 in Paris where she studied and sang. Returning to this country that autumn, she went on a concert tour which included a recital at Orchestra Hall, Chicago. The critic of the Chicago *Daily News* said of her efforts, "I have never before heard singing of such sane and beautiful workmanship, or such pure and elaborated vocal style turned with such dignity of purpose and such gratifying effect to the disclosure of how fine a musical instrument the human voice can make." In an extended review of a New York concert, the New York *Evening World* said, "Many vocalists of Nordic persuasion might have been proud of the style and feeling with which she propelled such lyrics as Respighi's 'E So un Giorno Tornasse'." The music editors of the New York *Times,* the *Herald-Tribune,* and other leading journals have accorded her equally high praise. Abbie Mitchell, with *Porgy,* at present is a member of the faculty of Tuskegee Institute School of Music, but continues to devote some time to public performances.

The artistic success of Abbie Mitchell is the more marked in that she overcame a sense of nervous breakdown which was the result of many years' strain of vaudeville and musical comedy singing. Practically losing her singing voice, she turned to the dramatic stage and became one of the leading actresses in the Lafayette Players Stock Company in New York. She was seen in such plays as *Madame X, Help Wanted* and in *Abraham's Bosom.* Recovering her voice, she appeared as "Marguerite" in *Faust,* but continued for some time to appear in both white and Negro dramatic companies before deciding to devote all of her time to the music platform. She is truly an artist of great attainments.

Of all the artists of present acclaim, Paul Robeson stands in the front rank, as a singer-actor. As a musician he is known as a singer of Negro song—pieces in the vernacular; and his artistry as a vocalist must therefore be judged in this restricted field. He himself says, "I sing the Negro songs because they suit my voice and suit me." He is widely heard as an exponent of Negro Spirituals in joint recitals with Lawrence Brown, accompanist-composer, and as such has received enthusiastic praise.

Robeson possesses a beautiful, natural, unforced baritone voice of great volume and his singing of the religious racial song has been marked with sympathetic interpretation. Heywood Broun wrote of him in the New York *World*, "Into his voice there comes every atom of the passionate feeling which inspired the unknown composer of these melodies." In art programs which he has occasionally given, he has not been altogether successful. Robeson has not been so happy in his Symphony Hall concerts given in Boston, for even his deeply resonant, organ-like tones did not make his all-spiritual programs free from monotony to discerning listeners.

Paul Robeson was born in Princeton, New Jersey, and was educated at Rutgers College where he was a member of the football team. Because of the remarkable skill shown in this sport, he was selected as a member of Walter Camp's All-America Football Team. Of more significance was his selection to the Phi Beta Kappa and to the honorary society of Cap and Skull. After being graduated from Rutgers, he entered the Columbia Law School.

While in New York, he embraced an opportunity to take the leading role in the play, *Emperor Jones*, by Eugene O'Neill. His success in the Greenwich Village Theatre production opened the way for his appearance in the play in London in 1925. He devoted a part of the season of 1925-26 to concertizing. He was seen in *All God's Chillun Got Wings* and in *Black Boy* in 1927. His acting created one of the greatest sensations of the present theatrical times. In 1928 he sang in Florenz Ziegfeld's *Show*

PAUL ROBESON

Boat and also replaced Jules Bledsoe in the 1930 revival of this great success which had a run at the Casino Theatre, New York, in the summer of 1932.

The spectacular acclamation of Robeson's dramatic talent made possible an engagement for his appearance in *Othello,* produced in London by an American, Ellen Volkenburg, in 1930. The actor played the part of "Othello" to "Desdemona" acted by Peggy Ashcroft, an English actress, and was hailed as "remarkable, of expressive gesture, superb voice and dignity." The same year, 1931, he was given the title role in O'Neill's *Hairy Ape* produced in London. The popular actor is now rated as one of the leading movie stars of the day. His dramatic portrayal of the *Emperor Jones* in like-named film, completed during the summer of 1933, saves the imperfect succession of the cinema scenes.

The singer-actor's greatest achievement is his playing of the part of the Moor. It would be interesting to compare his interpretation with that of another "Othello," Ira Aldridge, of an earlier day. Of many reviews in London, this one by Ivor Brown in the *Observer,* is significant: "Mr. Robeson's Ebon Othello is as sturdy as an oak, deep-rooted in its elemental passion and many branched in its early tenderness, a superb giant of the woods for the great hurricane of tragedy to whisper through, then rage upon, then break. One thinks of a tree because the greatness is of nature, not of art."

The foremost colored concert pianist of the United States is Hazel Harrison, who was born in La Porte, Indiana. After completing the course at the La Porte high school in 1903, she went to Berlin with her piano teacher, Victor Heinz, accompanied by her mother. At the close of her first year of study under Hugo van Dalen, she was accepted as a pupil of Feruccio Busoni. While in Berlin she played the Chopin E minor and the Grieg A minor concertos with the Berlin Philharmonic Orchestra. After devoting a short time to teaching in New York and Chicago, she made her début as a piano virtuoso under the management of F. Wight Neumann of Chicago. The Kimball Hall recital in Chicago was followed by one given in Aeolian Hall, New York City.

A surprisingly frank review from Henriette Weber, musical editor on the Chicago *Herald-Examiner*, said of her, "Hazel Harrison is a young pianist with a real gift for the keyboard. Her playing is musical, mature and individual. Extremely talented, it seems too bad that the fact she is a Negress may limit her future plans. She is comely, and if a clever press agent could put her forward under a name with a Spanish flair, a big future would be open before her. As it was, she attracted a capacity audience to Kimball Hall." Morris Rosenfeld, Music Editor of the Chicago *Daily News*, stated that "she can well compare her gifts with those of many of her white sisters. Her program was made up of some of the bigger works for the piano and included the Bach-Busoni Chaconne, the B minor sonata by Liszt, two etudes, 'Will o' the Wisp' and 'At the Spring,' the legend 'St. Franciscus Walking on the Waves,' all by the Hungarian composer, some transcriptions by Beethoven-Liszt, and Schubert-Liszt and some Chopin selections. She has a commendable technical facility, a musical taste and a fine grasp of the interpretative contents of the above pieces, and her playing of the Chopin nocturne, and the B minor Scherzo was highly praiseworthy."

In 1921-22 Miss Harrison gave many concerts throughout the South. She studied again in Germany in 1926, after which she continued her lesson in the United States with Percy Grainger. In October, 1930, she was heard in recitals in Town Hall, New York, and in Jordan Hall, Boston, before going on tour. Miss Harrison's recitals in

Boston, in 1930-31, displayed fine technical skill, robust tone and brilliant pianistic interpretation. She is now a teacher of piano at Tuskegee Institute.

Helen E. Hagan who was born at Portsmouth, New Hampshire, in 1893, the daughter of Mr. and Mrs. John A. Hagan, won the Lockwood Scholarship at the Yale University School of Music in 1911. At her graduation she played her original concerto in C minor written for piano and orchestra, with the New Haven Symphony Orchestra. For her "marked ability to conceive and execute musical ideas of much charm and no little originality" she was awarded in 1912 the Samuel Simmons Sanford Fellowship which provided for two years' study abroad. Arriving in Paris, she began her studies at the Schola Cantorum under Mlle. Blanche Selva and the French composer, Vincent d'Indy, and attained a finish and style characteristic of the French school. The unhappy conditions in Europe incident to the World War compelled the young pianist to return to the United States. After the armistice was signed she succeeded in returning to France where her playing gave cheer to the Negro soldiers remaining in the army camps. Her début recital as a concert pianist was given in Aeolian Hall, New York, and she has been widely heard on the concert stage in the West, North and South. Following her first Chicago concert given in Kimball Hall in 1921, the Chicago *Daily News* said, "In the Schumann 'Carnaval' Miss Hagan advanced a fleet and well trained technic, an understanding for the musical readings of the pieces and an unusual fine artistic taste. The 'Carnaval' afforded many chances for tone painting and for poetic fancy, and the recitalist knew how to lure forth the right color for the varying changes of mood."

In 1920 the artist married Dr. John T. Williams of Morristown, New Jersey, where she once maintained a studio as a piano instructor. It is to be regretted that Miss Hagan has not followed her creative gift. She has published none of her writings, but has devoted her time altogether to concert work, and to teaching. She is at present a member of the faculty of the Music Department at Bishop College, Marshall, Texas.

Roy Wilford Tibbs, director of the piano department of the Howard University School of Music, and conductor of the Samuel Coleridge-Taylor Society of Washington, D. C., is a musician whom Director Morrison, of the Oberlin Conservatory, considers "one of the most brilliant pianists we have sent out in many years." Fisk University which started him on his career naturally claims some of this honor. A few years later he spent a short while in study at Paris where he had the opportunity of becoming a student under Isadore Philipp, who regarded Mr. Tibbs as one of the most talented he has had from America. Tibbs, who is also a fine organist, was the first person of any race to be awarded the degree of Master of Music from Oberlin Conservatory for actual work done in that institution on leave of absence from his duties at Howard.

While mainly devoting his time to the work incident to his position, he continues to be heard in public performances both as a pianist and organist. On April 6, 1933, at a notable concert given by the faculty of the School of Music of Howard University, for the benefit of the student scholarship fund, Mr. Tibbs, according to the Washington *Evening Star's* reviewer, "A. E.," gave a "superlative rendition of Liszt's Concerto in E Major in which he was assisted by Charles Cecil Cohen at the second piano." In April, 1934, his public appearances included a guest performance as soloist at a Chamber Music Concert under direction of Dr. Hans Kindler, director of the Washington Symphony Orchestra.

HOWARD UNIVERSITY GLEE CLUB

R. Augustus Lawson, pianist, of southern birth, is one of the finest artists in America. He was graduated from the collegiate and musical departments of Fisk University in Nashville over twenty-eight years ago. Showing exceptional musical talent, he became the protegé of Mrs. Charles Dudley Warner and continued his studies under the direction of Professor Noyes of the Hartford Conservatory of Music. Choosing the profession of a teacher of pianoforte, he maintains a studio in Hartford, where he has long held a fine reputation and has enjoyed a wide following of white citizens.

Lawson, too, has not neglected to develop his interpretative ability. In 1911 he made a short trip abroad in order to widen his experience. The Russian pianist, Ossip Gabrilowitsch, who considered Lawson highly gifted, gave him a letter to the great pedagogue, Leschetizky, at Vienna. The great master afterwards commented upon the artist's "poetic playing and beautiful piano talent." Upon his return home, Lawson appeared South and North in concerts. On January 2 and again on February 5, 1912, he played the "A minor Concerto" for piano by Saint Saens with the Hartford Philharmonic Orchestra, conducted by Robert H. Prutting. On May 26, 1921, he gave a recital at Jordan Hall, Boston, Massachusetts, assisted by William Richardson, baritone. That he is an exceptionally fine pianist who needs make no racial apology may be seen from this important review of this recital. "He has a fluent, even and polished technic, an agreeable touch, and a firm control of dynamic gradations," said Philip Hale in the Boston *Herald.* "His phrasing is that of a well-grounded musician who has individual feeling. In brilliant passages his tone is warm; his strength is sufficient in stormy measures, while the limitations of the piano are recognized and respected. The program was well chosen and served to bring out the finer as well as the more obvious qualities of a thoughtful and serious pianist.''

Flora Thomas, a young pianist from Camden, New Jersey, is at present director of music at the 137th Street Young Women's Christian Association in New York City. She attended the Curtis Institute in Philadelphia, and later studied in Paris where she received the Certificate of Honor from the Schola Cantorum. She gave her debut recital in Steinway Hall, New York.

Jackson Norris, baritone, of Brooklyn, New York, has made his home in Sweden for over thirty years. During 1932 he sang before the King of Sweden and other distinguished persons. He is a church soloist in Stockholm, where he maintains a school of music.

Justin Sandridge, talented and sensitive pianist, was born in Boston, December 16, 1901. He became a student under Mme. Grover and made his début as a concert pianist on November 21, 1926. He appeared later as soloist with the Boston Philharmonic Orchestra, Mme. Leginska, conductor. He has been heard on concert tours and also appeared as soloist on Paul Robeson's program of songs. Mr. Sandridge teaches in Boston.

Charlotte Wallace Murray, mezzo-soprano, was born in Columbia, South Carolina. In Washington, D. C., she became a church singer and a teacher from 1906 to 1915. After studying piano, voice and harmony she appeared in concerts in nearby cities. She married in 1915 and some years later moved with her husband, Dr. Peter M. Murray, to New York City. There she took advantage of musical studies in that city and gave local concerts. Attention was called to her fine voice and presence, and in 1926 she was offered the role of the ''Queen'' in Franke Harling's opera, *Deep River*. She sang opposite Jules Bledsoe during the engagement at Schubert's Theatre. Entering the Institute of Musical Art, she was awarded the Faculty Scholarship for outstanding work as *Katinka* in Gilbert and Sullivan's *Mikado*. After having won a second scholarship, the singer was graduated in the class of 1931. She is now active in concert work.

George Garner, tenor, who was graduated from the Chicago Musical College in 1918, is one of the leading Negro singers of the day. In June, 1926, he finished the course at the American Conservatory of Music with the degree of Bachelor of Music. His wife, Pauline Bell Garner, a product of Northwestern University, is a talented pianist who has appeared as her husband's accompanist. He was the fortunate recipient of $5,000 from private sources, given that he might have the advantage of study abroad under the English musician, Sir Roger Quilter. The tenor's appearance as soloist with the Chicago Symphony Orchestra, was won through competition. Following 1932 concert engagements, he received high critical praise. The Chicago *Herald and Examiner* stated, "The ease, suavity and facility of tone, the warm soft luster of its timbre, the restrained and contemplative delivery brought to these (Italian) old classics, exactly those vocal and musical attributes that best defined their beauties."

Luvena Wallace Dethridge, soprano, who sang on a Negro Day program of the Century of Progress Exposition in Chicago, was born in Richmond, Indiana, where she now makes her home. Her parents were early settlers and of Quaker following. Her education was received in Chattanooga, Tennessee. Later, on the advice of S. B. Garton, a prominent teacher of voice in Richmond, who heard her sing and was impressed with her natural vocal gifts, she studied voice; first with Garton, and later in Italy. After a second period of eight months' study in Rome, she appeared in recitals there and in the United States. Following her return to Rome for continued study in voice and languages, Miss Dethridge gave a recital in the Sala Sgambati. The Italian press commented upon her personality, well-balanced voice and evenness of register. *Il Messaggiero* stated that "she has a gentle, limpid voice, ample in agreeable tones; her intonation and sense of rhythm are, indeed, admirable. In the classical and well-known compositions by Scarlatti, Giordani and Pergolesi she sang with a stylistic correctness worthy of praise."

R. Todd Duncan, baritone, possesses a rich voice and innate dramatic feeling. He is a teacher in the School of Music of Howard University, but finds time for public appearances, the latest of which was at the White House for President and Mrs. Roosevelt. His program given at Secretary of the Treasury and Mrs. Henry Morgenthau's, February 14, 1935, in Washington, D. C., brought him praise. He was chosen to sing the role of "Alfio" in *Cavalliera Rusticana,* given by the Aeolian Negro Opera Company in New York City, under. the direction of Peter Creatore, 1934. At present he is appearing in the title role of *Porgy* in New York City.

Thomas Henry Johnson, born of well-to-do Negro parents of Birmingham, Alabama, was educated at Morehouse College, whence he came to study voice at the New England Conservatory. After giving a début recital at Jordan Hall, he appeared extensively in concerts on tour, in the United States. He is of fine personal bearing, and possessing dramatic ability. He has won critical praise for his stage work in Little Theatre productions. His voice has been described as that of "a light fine-spun tenor of beautiful quality." His programs are those of a sincere, dignified young artist.

An older tenor, Harry Delmore, a singer of thorough technical training, received his musical education in Boston under Arthur Wilson, vocal coach, and private teachers of repute. His début recital in Boston was given in

Jordan Hall, October 18, 1925, after he had sung for some time on southern and northern concert tours. He continued his vocal training and made a study of operatic roles until January, 1932, when he went to Milan, Italy, for more thorough operatic training. Upon his return to Boston, he gave a notable recital in Jordan Hall and also sang arias and appeared in operatic ensemble at the Brookline open air concerts with the People's Symphony Orchestra. Delmore has a dramatic tenor voice of beautiful quality and fine resonance, with surprising power in its upper range. He is at present engaged in private teaching in Boston.

Edward Matthews, a young baritone of musical intelligence and richness of voice, was born at Ossining, New York. He was educated in the public schools of that town and at Fisk University. Coming to Boston, he continued his vocal training under Vincent Hubbard. He toured with the Fisk Singers for one year in Europe where he appeared as soloist. Resuming his studies in Boston, Matthews made his début as a concert singer in 1930 recitals in Jordan Hall, Boston, and in Town Hall, New York. The latter concert was sponsored by Roland Hayes.

At the close of a successful season, he was appointed to direct Negro Folk Music at Fisk University for 1930-31, and was heard on country-wide broadcasts as soloist with the choir. During 1932 and 1933 he gave concerts and fulfilled radio contracts. This sincere artist, Warren Storey Smith, musical editor of the Boston *Post*, says, "is blessed with a voice of singular beauty—and always sings with becoming fervor as well as with taste and understanding." He was acclaimed in 1934 for his beautiful singing in Gertrude Stein's queer opera, *Four Saints*.

Frank Goodall Harrison, baritone, head of the vocal department of Talladega College, Talladega, Alabama, is one of the most refined singers of his race today. He was born in Austin, Texas, the son of Robert and Hattie Harrison. His mother was a woman of deep poetic nature, alive to beauty in all its forms. Young Frank received his education in the public schools of Austin and at Howard University. He then studied at Columbia University and continued vocal training under Oscar Saenger and Myron Whitney in New York. He has also been a student under Frank La Forge; and in spite of his duties as a teacher, he has found time to give concerts in a number of the principal cities and at many colored colleges. Of his beautiful, lyric voice, the Chicago *Tribune* said, "It has a texture of considerably more than common beauty. It is the kind of quality which transfigures any song which he sings." After hearing him sing at Kimball Hall, Chicago, H. Devries said, "Mr. Harrison proved that he not only takes his art seriously but has the zeal and devotion to effect its exploitation."

John Greene, baritone, of Chicago, is rapidly increasing his reputation as a singer of note. In 1933 he was given a Rosenwald Scholarship in order to complete his studies at the Cosmopolitan School of Music and Dramatic Art in Chicago. In the largest audition ever held in Chicago he was given first choice in the baritone class by radio listeners, for the beauty of voice alone, but of greater musical importance was the success of his recitals during 1933 before discerning music-lovers and critics. In Los Angeles, on May 28, he was the soloist at the series of band concerts given in the Greek Theatre in Griffith Park under the direction of Don Philippini.

Aubrey Pankey is a young baritone from Pittsburgh, Pennsylvania, who studied voice at the Hubbard Studios in Boston after having been under the musical guidance of R. Nathaniel Dett at Hampton, who recommended him for having instinctive musical feeling. He studied harmony and languages with private teachers in Boston, and on January 26, 1930, he gave a recital at Jordan Hall, which evoked such critical praise that he was determined to go abroad for further study. His pluck and courage in the face of continued financial obstacles won friendships for him, and in 1931 he was in Vienna studying voice under Theo Lierhaemer. A recital in that city brought his talent to the attention of the Austrian press. During the season of 1932-33, he achieved success in a Berlin, Germany, recital and again in Vienna where he is completing his vocal technique. Josef Reitler wrote of him in the *Neue Freie Presse* of November 23, 1931, "He is the possessor of a musical soul, which in glowing manner is able to approach Schubert and Richard Strauss with a feeling and understanding worthy of a born German. Colorful expression is skillfully combined with a natural mellowness of voice." Robert Konta in the *Weiner Allgemeine Zeitung* of November 26, 1931, designated him "A black man who sings Schubert and Richard Strauss with an overwhelming intensity of feeling and forms them into great unforgettable experiences. He is a boon for our period where one is very easily inclined to see in all Negro musicians mere Jazzband Clowns. There are evidently black men who are messengers of culture at its greatest."

Ralph Banks, baritone, was born and educated in Pittsburgh, Pennsylvania, where he first studied voice. After extensive study in Italy he returned to this country and gave a début recital at Steinway Hall, New York, on November 15, 1929, under the management of Arthur Judson. His program was one of songs of finest content, and he was received as a singer of art songs of the first rank. A reviewer commented on his "refinement of style and repertory" and his command of langauges. Mr. Banks' death occurred shortly thereafter.

Louia Vaughn Jones, one of the foremost violinists of Negro blood, was born in Cleveland, Ohio, where he received his education. As a student under Joseph Balis, he was first violinist of the Central High School Orchestra, violinist with the Treble Clef Singing Society of the high school, and was awarded second prize in a violin contest among public school children. After completing the course at the Central High School in 1913, he entered the New England Conservatory of Music in Boston and was graduated in the class of Felix Winternitz in 1918.

Upon the eve of his graduation he was sent to France with the American Expeditionary Force and became assistant band leader of the 807th Pioneer Infantry during the World War. At the close of the war he returned to Boston and took a post-graduate course at the New England Conservatory. In 1921 he returned to Europe and for two years studied at l'Ecole Normale de Musique in Paris under Lucien Capet and for an extra period with Marcel Darrien and Maurice Hayot. During the seven years he remained abroad, he played in an American jazz orchestra in order to supplement the means expended by his parents for his musical education.

Again returning to the United States, Mr. Jones gave a number of recitals during the season of 1929-30, broadcast as a "W. H. K." artist in Cleveland, and shortly afterwards accepted a position as teacher in the Howard University Conservatory of Music, where he is head of the violin department.

Wesley I. Howard, a violinist of warm and expressive tone, is a graduate of the New England Conservatory, Boston. There he was a pupil of Felix Winternitz under whom he took a post-graduate course in 1916. In France, he studied under Maurice Hayot, professor of violin at l'Ecole Normale de Musique and the Conservatoire National of Paris. His orchestral training was received from Eugene Gruenberg, George Chadwick, Wallace Goodrich and other distinguished American musicians. Howard had five years' experience as violinist of two white symphony orchestras. During the World War, he served as assistant bandmaster in the 809th Infantry Band in France. His first position was that of the head of the violin department and ensemble at Howard University Conservatory. In 1931 he was offered the post of teacher of violin at Hampton Institute, where he has directed the orchestra accompanied by Percy Grainger in a performance of the first movement of Grieg's Pianoforte Concerto.

Etta Moten (Mrs. C. A. Barnett) is a young Texas woman, whose appealing contralto voice, winsome and charming personality, added to her dramatic ability, have brought her success as a screen star. In the films *Gold Diggers of 1933* and in *Flying Down to Rio* she rose to national popularity and was invited to sing at the White House for President and Mrs. Roosevelt. She is now appearing both in the cinema and on the legitimate stage.

Appendix

AFRICAN MUSICAL INSTRUMENTS

A type of lyre was familiar to all who have studied the music of Africa. An interesting little story is told of the origin of this instrument.

Hermes, secretary of Osiris (1800-1500 B. C.), found a tortoise shell on the banks of the Nile; the inner flesh of cartilage had been dried by the sun. Striking the shell it emitted a musical sound and this suggested the Lyre. Bruce, a noted traveller, found the paintings of two harps on the walls of a tomb at Thebes which dated from 1250 B. C. In another tomb was a harp, the catgut strings of which gave forth sounds although the strings had been untouched for 3,000 years. In their form, ornament, and compass, these harps were declared to give proof not only that the mechanical art of the making of musical instruments was at the greatest perfection at the time these harps were made, but that the period from which we date the invention of musical instruments, was only the beginning of the era of their restoration.

German Museums are said to have the finest and most complete collection of African instruments. The most complete collection in America is that of the Metropolitan Museum of Fine Arts in New York City. It embraces the John Crosby Brown and Joseph Drexel collections. In the Brown group, we find specimens from Egypt and the Soudan, Algiers and Morocco, the upper and lower Guinea Coast, and from Central Africa. There are also some rare specimens from the island of Madagascar on the East Coast. Central America and the West Indies have also contributed instruments. The Joseph Drexel is a small, though valuable collection.

The large number of instruments housed at the Smithsonian Institute, the U. S. National Museum at Washington, D. C., are proto-types of those possessed by the Metropolitan Museum. The Commercial Museum at Philadelphia, Pennsylvania, has a large number from Central Africa, the Congo, Senegal and Dahomey and the island of Madagascar. In the latter collection a few particularly unusual instruments are found. The Stearns' Collection of Musical Instruments at the University of Michigan, Ann Arbor, embraces those of various races. It includes a specimen of the kasso that is indigenous to Senegambia. Other collections of African instruments are found at the Hartford Theological Seminary and at the Peabody Museum, Cambridge.

In the catalogue which follows, the classification reads:

Class I. Drums
Class II. Stringed Instruments
    1. Harp type
    2. Psaltery
    3. Lute
    4. Bow played
Class III. Vibrating Sonorous Bodies
    1. Marimba
    2. Flutes
    3. Trumpets and Horns
    4. Lesser Instruments

Owing to the fact that the drum is the most important of all African instruments, they are placed first rather than the stringed instruments. While a great variety of barbarous instruments are found in Africa, a volume might be written on the various drums alone. To this instrument, the natives are so attached that they swear by it with the oath "Tambou."

There seems to be a close affiliation between the drum and the tree. If it is true that the drum was derived from the accidental striking of the hollow trunk of a tree, a living thing in the eyes of primitive man, drum worship would be the natural consequence of the worship of the trees in whose branches was the seat of the gods.

The method of tightening skin drum-heads with cords is of primitive origin and was first made use of by the Africans. An interesting find in a park of monuments, was that of a block of quartz fashioned like a drum which Frobenius thought to be a relic from past ages.

In a book written by Sir Henry Johnston, and published in England, the writer speaks of the commendable part played by the native Africans in the World War, and of the remarkable instances of loyalty to the cause of the Allies. From time to time in the reports concerning these fearless fighters, one finds the statement that it is puzzling to understand how the soldiers so quickly gain a knowledge of the actions of the various companies. This is explained by the use that the African soldier makes of the drum as an instrument of communication. In time of peace or war, the drum is their favorite instrument.

The natives converse by the language of the drum as easily as we do by the English language. The sounds are produced from the drums in such a way as to form words, and the complete measure or rhythmical phrase forms a sentence. "In this way," says Bowditch in *Mission from Cape Coast Castle to Ashanti*, "when company drums are being played at an ehsudu they are made to express and to convey to the bystanders a variety of meanings.

In one measure they abuse the men of another company, stigmatizing them as fools and cowards; then the rhythm changes and the gallant deeds of their own company are extolled." Every Chief has a distinct drum call or motto which is recognizable by the particular beat of his drum. As an example, A. B. Ellis gives the message of the drums of Boakje Tsin-tsin, the Ashanti envoy who came to the Coast during what is termed the Ashanti Scare of 1881—

"Donko — i didi m' ahtum, On esséh?"

The first sentence was produced on a large drum, the second on a smaller one that was pitched a note or two higher,—the rhythm of which is Donkŏ-i|didi mah|tum|-On esséh? The free translation is—"What care I for opinions of the vulgar herd?"

The drums of Amankwa Tia, Ashanti general who fought against England in the war of 1873-4 said

"Pĭrĭ hŭh|Pĭrĭ hŭh|"—"Hasten—Hasten."

A native was asked the drum-call of a chief of an inland town, when he replied, "I do not know, I have never heard his drum. If I could hear it, I could tell you what it said." Regarding this custom of using large drums as a means of communication, Dr. Richard Wallaschek quotes Edward Schauenburg from *Reisen in Central Africa* in which two kinds of drum languages are described, "At Kujar he saw a native beating the drum with the right hand and varying the tone by pressing his left on the skin, so as to imitate the sound of the Mandingo words. During the wrestling match it sounded like 'Amuta, Amuta' (attack) during the dance 'ali bae si' and all the participants understand it."

Another instance is related by Dr. S. C. Fuller, a prominent physician in Massachusetts, whose father was the owner of a plantation about fifteen miles from Monrovia, Liberia. It was a nightly occurrence for the farm hands to communicate from their thatched houses to friends at a great distance, by means of drum signals.

Often they would hear bursts of laughter following the answering drum-taps, that bespoke a joke or an amusing rejoinder.

Travellers have told of their surprise in learning of the use of the drum for the carrying of messages. Decima Moore, traveling with her husband who was making astronomical observations in Africa for the English Government, writes, "In the evening the tom-toms began, not in any grand musical carouse but just in fitful tappings, and listening intently in the intervals we could hear faint and far away an answering tap-tap, tap-tap, tap-tap, from the next village. It was the bush telegraph by means of which news of our arrival in Ojeso was being drummed on to the villages along our route."

The large signal drums of the Niam Niam are found in every Monbuttoo village. Akin to drums of the West Coast, known South of the Bongo, a small variety is made semi-circular in shape, compressed and fitted with a top handle; the sound opening is below. Schweinfurth, *The Heart of Africa*, p. 113.

In speaking of an elephant hunt, Schweinfurth says, "In close proximity to each separate group of hamlets and more frequently than not at the threshold of the abodes of the local chieftains known as the 'borrumbanga' or Chief Court, there is always a huge wooden kettle-drum, made of a hollow stem mounted upon four feet. The sides of this are of unequal thickness, so that when the drum is struck it is capable of giving two perfectly distinct sounds. According to the mode or time in which these sounds are rendered, three different signals are denoted, the first being the signal for war, another that for hunting and the third a summons to a festival. Sounded originally in the mbanga of the chief, these signals are in a few minutes repeated on the kettle-drums of the 'borrumbanges' of the district and in an incredibly short space of time, thousands of men, armed if need be, are gathered together." Schweinfurth, *The Heart of Africa*, p. 24.

Alexander Dumas in "l'Homme a queue" states that the "Niam-Niam" are known among themselves as "Zanzey," cannibals.

Ogidigbo—A drum of different sizes, which preserves the name, "Ajagbo," of the first king of the Yorubans, who reigned about 1780.

Each drum has its own measure or rhythm and in order to preserve this rhythm, sentences are invented to call it to mind.

Gbo|Ajagbo|-|Gbo-oba gbo|-|ki emi ki osi|gbo. "Grow old, Ajagbo, grow old king, grow old, may I also grow old." Ellis, A. B., *The Yoruba Speaking People*, p. 9.

Mombasa—Made of pottery and supposed to be covered with

human skin. Rudely painted in red and blue colors. Height 6 inches; depth of large head 7 in., of small head, 4 inches.

Mombasa—of wood, hollowed and open at bottom. Head of snake-skin. Height 11 inches; depth 7 inches.

Mombasa—a drum of wood covered with skin, height 9½ inches; depth 5 inches.

Daff—In Algiers, known as a Deff and in Arabia, as Daff, a hand drum with square frame of wood and two heads of skin. The daff is struck with the hands.

Mbe—French Congo. A long cylindrical body of wood, one end covered with skin.

N' Dungo—A drum made with a long wooden body tapering slightly near the ends. The center of one side is a handle. Ends are made of sheepskin laced together with strips of hide or of fiber cord.

The instrument is carried on the shoulder of one man while a second walks behind beating it. It is often ornamented with skulls.

Ngoma—A large kettle-drum, native to East Africa; receives its name from the dance performed by the Kafirs.

Nkonjo—Used by the Mpongwe, Gaboon and French Congo tribes to accompany like-named dance. The drum-heads are of skin and are beaten alternately by fingers and palms. Drum-sticks are rarely used.

Drum—From the Congo district, about the top is a beautifully designed head band of rose, white, blue and yellow beads. Some of the bodies are ornately carved. (See specimens in Metropolitan Museum of N. Y.)

Ochingufu—A peculiar type of drum suspended from a pole and struck with wooden beaters tipped with rubber. About 4 feet long, 2 feet at the bottom. Larger drums are 10 feet long, carried on the shoulders.

Drum—From Central Africa of the kettle-drum type made of wood. Specimens in American Museums.

M'kul—A drum of the Fan tribe, French Congo, height 2 feet 1 inch; depth 1 foot 2 inches. Cut from a block of wood, the center hollowed out. When used in war, this drum is beaten in the middle. In times of peace, it is used to accompany the Mbe in song and dance and it is then struck in the center or on the side.

In West Africa, these drums are used to carry messages. Rev. A. W. Halsey of New York, tells of a certain missionary who, finding himself in need of an umbrella, spoke to the man in the palaver house. The drum was struck several times. From a considerable

AFRICAN MUSICAL INSTRUMENTS 391

distance a boy came running with the article. The drum had said:
"Missionary in palavèr house—Caught in rain—needs umbrella."
The drum is known by different names in various sections of the
country. There is the native instrument of West Africa that is
known as the Tom-Tom all over Africa.

The *Sangbois* is the name by which the tom-tom is best known
in various sections.

Ngoma Ku (East Portuguese—Africa), is the largest of the African drums. It is described as a hollowed hole of a mkenga, or
other soft tree, with a cylindrical solid projection from the bottom,
which holds it upright when planted in the ground: length 3 to 5
feet; diameter 1 to 2 feet; the outside is protected with a network
of strong cord.

Over the head is stretched a rough parchment made of calf's skin
and a cap of green hide, mounted when loose, and afterwards
shrunken by exposure to fire, protects the bottom. Mary E. and
Wm. A. Brown, *Musical Instruments and their Homes,* p. 262.

Ngoma—Drums of various sizes played singly or in groups, music
both rhythmic and tonal.

Muntshintshi—(The Big Drum), South Africa, said to be made of
a hollowed stem, like ordinary mortar or it may be rounded and
provided with 3 legs. A piece of skin is stretched over the opening.

This may be the skin of an elephant's ear, or of a buffalo, of an
ox or of an antelope (Mangulive). The tones are low. It is found
in all of the Capitol Cities and is supposed to be an instrument of
mystery.

It is prohibited to look inside the drum when the skin cracks.
The instrument is repaired by a special person. Its use is as
follows:

To announce a calamity, the warning of a flood, the death of a
chief or when fire in the bush threatens the Capitol. (The Nkomati
river rises in January and February.) In event of war, the Muntshintshi is used to summon the soldiers to town. It is also used to
lead the Nkino (dance) which is held at the Capitol during the
winter when the harvest is over.

Shikolombane—A smaller drum of piercing high tone; accompanies the Muntshintshi.

DRUMS USED IN RAIN CEREMONIES

Ngo'ma hulu—Big round drum.

Mboikula—Middle-sized round drums of different pitch whose
names mean "changing." Used when tone is changed between the
big and little drums.

Mtiumba (singular, *Mutuimba*)—Name of two small drums, made of hollowed wood, slightly narrowed and rounded at the bottom, where there is a hole to let out the air. The skin of a calf or antelope is stripped across the open mouth of the upper section. Natalie Curtis Burlin, *Songs and Tales from the Dark Continent*, p. 119.

Tama—An hour-glass drum, in like shape, from Senegal and Congo regions. It is held under the left arm and the sounds are varied by pressure of the arm upon the strings.

Pwi'ta (E. Portuguese)—Name of a drum used in like named dance. ''A long hollow log with an antelope skin or cow-skin stretched across one end. The other end is open to receive the right hand of the player which is thrust into the log. The fingers of a player are wet in a bowl of water and when pulling on the reed, the moist fingers are slipped up and down. The fingers stick to the reed just enough to cause the vibrations which he makes at will, according to the pitch or sound desired. The skin of the drum resounds and the sides reverberate.

''Two tones may be made on the *Pwi'ta* about a fourth apart. The high tone is produced by pressing the fingers of the left hand on the skin of the drum, thus shortening the vibrations; the lower tone is obtained when the left hand is lifted so that the whole surface of the drum-skin is free to resound.'' Natalie Curtis Burlin, *Songs and Tales from the Dark Continent*, p. 119.

Tabala (Interior of Africa)—From Senegal. A widely-known war-drum found among the Moors as well as the Fulani of Senegal. Among the Fulani, it is considered a mark of authority and is kept in the hut of chiefs. Also used at weddings to announce the ceremony and beaten all night when used to spread alarm through the country. A fine specimen can be seen at the Commercial Museum, Philadelphia, Pa.

War Drum (Ivory Coast)—Long and narrow and ornamented with human skulls.

Gangan—A war drum mentioned in old folk tales. The king called all the birds to come to clear a piece of ground—''Come let us go to the house—Kini-kini, and there we can dance the *bata*. If the bata will not sound we can dance the dun-dun. If the dun-dun will not sound we will dance the Gangan.'' A. B. Ellis, *The Yoruba Speaking People*, p. 254.

Daluka (from the Soudan)—Identical with Egyptian drum.

Addugha (Dahomey)—War drums, the largest of which is ''*He-is-able-to-do-any-thing.*'' Often rudely carved with native figures.

At the "Grand Customs," the great war drums are carried in front of the procession.

Gbedu (Yoruba)—A tall drum usually carved with figures representing animals and birds. The Gbedu is only beaten at religious fetes and at public ceremonies. At the sacrifices, a portion of the blood of the victims is always sprinkled upon the symbolic carvings. A. B. Ellis, *The Yoruba Speaking People*, p. 100.

Gumbia—Name of the drum of the Maroons of Sierra Leone—it is also known in Jamaica from which Maroons were taken to Nova Scotia and thence to Sierra Leone.

The *Bamboula and Ka* are the two African drums known in the West Indies. The name of the former survives in the folk-songs of Creole Louisiana in America.

The *Bamboula* is made from the joints of two very large bamboo from which it is said to derive its name. Another explanation is given that "oula" is the termination of many Congo verbs and "boula" means to beat.

Lafcadio Hearn describes the last two as follows:

"The larger of the two was the 'ka,' so-called because made out of a quarter barrel or quart (patois 'ka'). Both ends of the barrel are removed, a wet hide, well wrapped about a couple of hoops is driven on and in drying, the stretched skin obtains still further tension. The other end of the ka is always left open. Across the face of the skin a string is tightly stretched to which are attached, at intervals of about an inch apart, very short thin fragments of bamboo or cut feather stems. These lend a certain vibration to the tones.

"The smaller drum was called 'bamboula.' It was 3 to 4 feet long and 8 or 9 inches in diameter. A skilful player (bel tambouyé) straddles his "ka" stripped to the waist, and plays upon it with the finger tips of both hands simultaneously. Occasionally the heel of the naked foot is pressed lightly or vigorously against the skin so as to produce changes of tone. This is called 'giving heel' to the drum—*bailly talon*. Meanwhile, a boy keeps striking the drum at the uncovered end with a stick so as to produce a dry, clattering accompaniment." He adds that its tapping can be heard at surprising distances and that "experienced players often play for hours at a time without exhibiting wearisomeness or in the least diminishing the volume of sound produced.

"The sound of the drum itself, well played, has a wild power that makes and masters all the excitement of the dance—a complicated double roll with a peculiar billowy rising and falling." Often contests were held between celebrated *tambouyé*. Lafcadio Hearn, *Two Years in the French West Indies*.

The drums commonly used on the Gold Coast are made of hollowed sections of trunks of trees, with a goat's or sheep's skin stretched over one end. They are from one to four feet high and vary in diameter from about six to fourteen inches. Two or three drums are usually used together, each drum producing a different note, and they are played either with the fingers or with two sticks. Those looking on, beat time by clapping the hands.

In his travels in South Africa, Livingstone describes drums of that section which he heard played around the "kotla" (audience place): "Their drums are neatly carved from the trunk of a tree, and have a small hole on the side covered with a bit of spider's web; the ends are covered with the skin of an antelope pegged on, and when they wish to tighten it they hold it to the fire. The instruments are beaten with the hands." In the Kru country tiny little hand drums are made in varying shapes and sizes—sometimes the instrument is slung around the body. The exterior strings are painted red and blue. A more pronounced decoration is found on the drum of the "Yassi" (Society of Spots) of Sierra Leone. Some of the instruments are spotted with various colors.

Mary Kingsley tells of a drum from West Africa which is made from an old powder keg, a piece of raw hide tied tightly over it and it over a bung-hole. A piece of wood with a bit of rubber is passed through the hole. The drummer with wet hands grasps the inserted stick and works it up and down. A double sound ensues, the knob beats the drum skin while the stick gives a screech. Mary Kingsley, *West African Studies*.

Various musical instruments peculiar to themselves are invented by the Joloffs. They possess the native drum, the tom-tom, but also have a kettle-drum in which the skin is stretched across one half an enormous calabash highly polished and sometimes elaborately carved. The Bushmen, whose instruments are very crude, possess a drum which they make by stretching a dried antelope skin over any hollow article.

A. B. Ellis in *The Land of Fetish*, describes an amusing happening at Camp Prahsu. From four different parts of the camp, he heard a reveille played by four separate bugles. Knowing that there were not four corps in encampment, he thought troops had arrived unexpectedly, but it was not true. One bugler was blowing on behalf of the Home Constabulary, another for a half dozen Sierra Leone policemen whom the Governor had brought with him, a third for the three or four Fanti police who were at Prahsu, and a fourth for the Kru laborers. As the camps were circumscribed, one bugle would have been quite sufficient, but then "how much glowing military ardour would have been lost!"

Algernon Rose describes the "food-beat" as consisting of three triplets immediately followed by two notes somewhat slower. In the interior of Africa, the beating of the *tabala* announces a wedding. To its rhythm the women sing all night. The natives believe that in time of war the spirits themselves are interested in the result of the battle, and the people believe that the gods favor their own particular cause. The forming of companies by the brave women of Russia was a repetition of the old custom of forming Amazon corps among the Ewe-speaking people of Africa. As early as 1729, Amazon corps among the Dahomans were divided into three bodies. Each corps of these female soldiers had its own band consisting of horns, drums and the chinfugu, a native cymbal. The standing army among the people was in the form of town companies and each military organization had its own deity. The deity which is the special protector of the company during war is supposed to inspire the men with courage, and a tree is selected to protect it with its shade.

The African is not without an appreciation of the art of camouflage, as noted by the following incident which Newlands describes in his story of Sierra Leone, "Airkarlie, Momba Kinda (son of one of the principal kings), of a town on the Sierra Leone River was commissioned by Bai Foki, king of the country, to drive the Susus (said to have descended from the Hyksos or Shepherd Kings of Egypt) Mohammedans from Mellacouri, out of the land. Airkarlie had a drum called *tablay* made, which was to be in possession of none but the king or chief in authority. Plans were made to attack the Susus by the Temnes, and the Airkarlie ordered the drum to be beaten. Hearing the drum for the first time, the Susu Almami at Sain dugu sent to see if his own tablay was in its place. Being told that it was, he ordered 150 armed men to proceed to Ro Marung and bring the offending tablay, the person who was beating it and the person who ordered it to be beaten. The Susus proceeded unaware that more than 500 Temnes were in ambush in a thicket. They were all captured, their arms seized without a gun being fired and they themselves taken as prisoners."

Mr. Bowditch in service of the Royal African Company, writes of a reception given in 1817, the gathering of thousands of persons of whom the greater part were warriors. The guests were met with bursts of martial music and as they arrived before the King— "More than 100 bands burst at once on our arrival, with the peculiar airs of their several chiefs; the horns flourished their defiances, with the beating of innumerable drums and metal instruments, and then yielded for a while to the soft breathings of their long flutes, which were truly harmonious; and a pleasing instrument like a bag-pipe without the drone, was happily blended.

"It is a gorgeous spectacle, the captains and attendants gowned in Ashanti cloths of extravagant price, costly silks, gold ornaments. Wolves and rams' heads as large as life, cast in gold, were suspended from their gold-handled swords which were held around them like round bills and rusted in blood; the sheaths were of leopard skin, or the shell of a fish-like shagreen. The large drums supported on the head of one man and beaten by others were braced around with the thigh-bones of their enemies, and ornamented with their skulls. The kettle-drums resting on the ground were scraped with wet fingers and covered with leopard skin. The wrists of the drummers were hung with bells and curiously shaped pieces of iron which jingled loudly as they were beating. The smaller drums were suspended from the neck by scarves of red cloth; the horns (teeth of young elephants) were ornamented at the mouth-piece with gold and the jaw-bones of human victims— the royal stool, said to be about 400 years old, entirely cased in gold, was displayed under a splendid umberella, with drums, sankos (sehnku, a native stringed instrument), horns and various musical instruments cased in gold, about the thickness of cartridge paper. The swell of the bands gradually strengthened on our ears, the peal of the war-like instruments bursting upon the short but sweet responses of the flutes; the gaudy canopies seemed to dance in the distant view and floated broadly as they were springing up and down."

In contrast to this moving barbaric spectacle, is the following odd mixture of an old and new civilization: At a big palaver held on the banks of the Subin river, the subject of which was the Ashanti boundary, the visitors were greeted by the Omankin of Bompata, his state umberellas, court and full band. The band consisted of a large English drum, two kettle-drums and several fifes. Immediately they struck up "God Save the King"—Scarcely had the echoes died away in the forest before the Omankin and his retinue started for the town followed by the band playing "Way Down Upon the Swanee River."

The spectator asks us to imagine this incongruous picture:—

"The drummer beating the big drum for all he was worth and the conductor wildly waving his wee bit of stick—a sudden apparition of a half-naked band, playing the familiar tune with furious joy, right away in a remote, wild corner of the Ashanti forest."

Linga—The *banda-linga*, the largest of tom-toms used among the Banda-Linda of Ouaka (Oibanguichari), is described by Mme. Grall in an article on "The Tom-Tom Language of the Africans" in *La Revue du Monde Noir*, Paris, France, April, 1932. It is made of two sound-boxes, one being smaller than the other, hollowed out of a tree trunk. A rubber mallet is used to strike each side of the slit which cuts the upper middle part. Eguiri-linga— A smaller male tom-tom. Kossi-linga—Also called kolinga, is the smallest on which the highest notes are produced.

Kuitra, North Africa—A lyre species sounded by plucking the strings.

Zither, Zoloffs—A species of Zither having 10 strings and made of a vegetable fibre.

Kinandi-kinubi—British West Africa. "Devils Harp," a variety of ancient Greek lyre of 5 strings. A fine example is said to be housed in the Imperial Museum at Berlin.

Colangee—Sudan. Similar to the Wambee. The strings are plucked.

Samiurius—Kafir. The body is a flat and narrow strip of wood. Short distance from one end occurs a small hole, and a metal string or a cord is stretched from one end to the other of the wood. The performer places his mouth against the back of the bow over the hole and by varying the tension of his lips, five notes can be produced. The Kafirs use the *Samiurius* in the war-songs and love-songs. The instrumental music alternates with the voice.

Harp-Mandolin—A favorite instrument of the Niam-Niam (Zandey), a heathen people. "It resembles the harp in the vertical arrangement of its strings, whilst in common with the mandolin, it has a sounding-board, a neck, and screws for tightening the strings. The sounding-board is constructed on strict acoustic principles. It has two apertures; it is carved out of wood and on the upper side is covered by a piece of skin; the strings are tightly stretched by means of pegs and are sometimes made of fine threads of bast, and sometimes of the wiry hairs from the tail of a giraffe.

"The music is very monotonous and it is very difficult to distinguish any actual melody in it. It invariably is an accompaniment to a moaning kind of recitative, which is rendered with a decided nasal intonation. I have not infrequently seen friends marching about arm-in-arm, wrapt in the mutual enjoyment of their performances and beating time to every note by nodding their heads." Schweinfurth, *The Heart of Africa*, Vol. II, p. 30.

²²*Maraca*—An instrument of Puerto Rico imported by enslaved Africans, and used with the "aguinaldos"—songs of Christmas and New Year's.

Bomba—A large drum used in Puerto Rico and Haiti. It is used alone and also with other crude instruments of Negro origin, many of which are made of hollowed wood and gourds, skilfully fashioned.

In the English colony of Jamaica, West Indies, Negro instruments include various drums: the "*Gumbie*," 6 feet long, the "*Goombah*," a hollow block of wood played by two persons; the "*Cotter*" which is made of rough wood, and the "*Dundo*" and the "*Gumbay*." The *Bangil*—A crude kind of guitar made by the natives. *Banjour*—A stringed instrument quite unlike the American banjo. *Bender*—An instrument which sounds like a jews' harp. *Banja*—A rustic instrument akin or similar to the guitar. *Flutes*—Made of hollow parts of the bamboo.

But few instruments of the Psaltery type are known among the Africans and those are found in the Kongo districts of former German East Africa and in the Mahomedan provinces on the North Coast.

Marouvane or *Valiha*—From the Island of Madagascar. Sometimes called *Valiha*. Made of Bamboo with 16 fibre strings raised from the back by 2 small pegs.

One specimen has the palm-leaf hood that serves as a resonator and is mounted with wire strings. Both of these instruments which the author has seen in the New York Museum are of considerable beauty.

Another form from the Kongo district consists of a wooden tray, mounted with a single string passed back and forth through holes at the ends, while a similar specimen from Central Africa is made from the tail of a Crocodile, forming an inverted shell with a skin stretched over the top and strings supported by a wooden bridge. Length 4 feet 1 inch; diameter 3 inch. (No. 553 in New York Museum.) (1489.)

Marouvane or *Valiha*—Sometimes Vahila.

The *Sousounon* and the *Gendang boeloe* of the Battaho, Sumatra, are similar to the Marouvane, as is also an instrument found in the Philippines and among the Dyaks of Borneo. *Engel Catalogue*, p. 306. Mahillon, vol. I, p. 419.

Valea or *Valiha*—This is made from a joint of bamboo by cutting several V shaped grooves lengthwise of the bamboo. The string so loosened, remains attached a little above the surface and tightened by small wedges. The specimen which the author saw in the Philadelphia Museum, is a duplicate of a *Valiha* in the New York Museum. The reed of which the *Valea* is made, is of beautiful biscuit-color as is the palm-hood. The tone it gives forth is guitarlike, the sound being augmented by length and hollowness of the bamboo.

Valia or *Vali*—The national instrument of the Malagash race.

ZeZe—From Lake Panalomba in Blantyre district to the south of Nyasa. A variation of the *Schumgha*. Usually a single string, a bow-shaft and a resonator, but the shaft has three crude stopping places for different sounds and the gourd which comes from a plant called Cheepende is much larger than the little bread-fruit shell. At end of the shaft, the string passes over a bridge of quill to impart a jarring.

The *ZeZe* has a prominent place when the Blantyre tribe are en fête; used as an accompaniment to the singing.

Zaze also *Tzetze*—Found among the stringed instruments in Madagascar. The specimens to be seen in the Philadelphia and New York museums consist of two pieces of gourd, one fastened on top of the other to give resonance, with an arm fastened on the convex side of the upper gourd.

This arm carries two strings made of twisted raphia fiber.

Schumgha—There are many varieties. It is formed of an ordinary bow-shaft tied back at the middle. The instrument is held horizontally, supported on the right in the hollow of the player's right thumb, while it is gripped on the left by his teeth. The disengaged fingers of the right hand twang the strings while the left hand stops the notes.

Lestendall—The name given the Schumgha in Swaziland.—The specimen found at Barberton is said to be an improvement on the one known in Mozambique.

Pungwee, N. E. Rhodesia.—The name comes from the river in Portuguese East Africa. The shape denotes that it was suggested by the Kafir Canoe. The instrument, boat-shaped with a long prow, is hollowed out of one piece of wood. The prow furnished a handle similar to that by which the ancient, square shaped psaltery was held.

The *Pungwee* has 5 strings. It is used by the witch doctors, who place the Pungwee on a calabash in order to increase the tone.

Algernon Rose, "Private Collection of African Instruments," *Monthly Journal International Mus. Society*, 1904.

Banjo—Strictly an American instrument said to have been invented by a Negro who made the first banjo from a cheese-box. It has been conjectured that the name may be a variant of the African term "bania." According to Thomas Jefferson, the instrument which the Negro brought from Africa, is the original of the Guitar.

Dr. Wilhelm Heintz, writing in the *Frankfurter Zeitung*, Germany, says of the hand-harp—"In the Cameroons there is a species of hand-harp which has its counterpart in the ancient Egyptian harps dug from thousand year old graves."

A HARP TYPE—Since to the African the drum is a far more important instrument than any of the stringed variety, the author's order of cataloguing is the reverse of the usually accepted one.

However, almost all African tribes possess some form of stringed instrument which shows that their appreciation of musical tones was far above that of mere savages. Various stringed instruments differing in form according to the locality are found under the same name.

Henry Balfour in his work on the musical bow, states that the bow is the simplest form of the harp type. Closely allied to the musical bow, as in the viol type of instruments, is the

Muet—Made from the stalk of the building palm with strings of fibre raised from the surface by a high notched bridge; a large gourd which is placed beneath the bridge serves as a resonator. In some types, the single central gourd is supplemented by one at each end, a form suggestive of the Vina of India. *Mahillon Catalogue*, Vol. II, P. 100; *Ankerman Ethnologischa*, P. 24, abt. 33; *Ratzel History*, Vol. II, P. 330.

Tzetze—Found as far west as the Congo. Akin to the *Janter* of India.

Hova Guitar—Madagascar. The same as the Tzetze on the continent.

Obah—West Coast, popular among the Kroo and well-known in Sierra Leone.

Kanih—Harp type, similar.

Gambareh—Used by the Sarracolets. A triangular frame of wood with one corner inserted in a gourd. Seven fibre strings; when played, the gourd is held against the body; length 1 foot 8 in.; diameter of gourd, 5 in. *Engel Catalogue*, P. 308; *Mahillon Catalogue*, Vol. I, P. 420.

Kasso—Senegambia, resembles closely the harp of Burmah, has arched shaped body and arched neck suggestive of the beautiful forms found in the tombs of ancient Egypt. (See No. 498 in New York Museum.)

Kasso—Dahomey, West Coast and in the Bissoga Islands.

Kove—Found on borders of the Senegal.

Sarong—A similar instrument found in Sierra Leone. A section of a large gourd closed by a membrane of sheep-skin and pierced by a long straight stick. Beneath the membrane and protruding at points near the edge of the gourd are four sticks—two parallel with the neck and two at right angles. A high notched bridge in the center of the membrane rests on a cushion, the strings passing from a ring in the lower edge of the gourd to the neck, where they are fastened by loops instead of pegs. Henry Balfour, *Natural History of the Bow.*

Wambee or *Valga*—West Africa, found in the area lying between the Niger and the Kongo; although found in widely separated localities—the Colangee of the Baganda Tribe on the northwest shores of Lake Victoria and Valga the specimens are identical. An example of this instrument from Assaba on Western edge of the Sahara is pictured by Ankerman. (Ethnol. P. 23, Abt. 30.)

Gaboon—French Kongo, same as Valga. Body an oblong box of wood, the soundboard attached thereto with brass tacks. Five rods at the back lashed together with strips of bark or fibre to within a foot of the upper end. Fibre strings. Originally a small bridge fastened to the center of the soundboard. Length 3 feet 5½ inches; width 5½ inches.

Valaza, Bayanza tribe—A tribal spelling for *Valga.*

Ubo—Lagos.

Kissumba, Benguela, Portuguese W. Africa.

Sancho—Northern Guinea. Also used by Negro tribes inhabiting west of the Bahr-el-Abiad. A species of the Wambee or Kissumba.

Ombi—Bakalai, also West Coast. Native harp—plucked strings. Body made box-like and over its open side is stretched a piece of skin, sometimes an elephant's ear, sometimes a snake skin. Long curved neck of small circumference extends from one end of the body outward and upward. Fibre strings are stretched from neck to bridge, generally located in sound-box.

Ombi—Fan tribe, French Kongo. An oblong body hollowed out of wood, one end elongated and finished in a rude scroll surmounted by a carved head.

Korro—Large harp with 18 strings.

Simbing—Small harp with 7 strings.

Nanga—In the lute type, a stringed instrument, pear-shaped in body, the strings of which are plucked with the fingers, is found the popular Guenbii—also *Ganibry—Gunibre* and *Gimbrede* of the North Coast. It is a simple pear-shaped instrument with a straight wooden neck, the body formed from the shell of a turtle or a gourd and often decorated in rich colors.

Tambour and

Kiutra—A highly developed form of the *Guenbii*, found where the native has come into contact with Persian, Arabian, and Moor.

Tamboura—North Africa. Like the Tambour, a narrow deep body of wood, the neck inlaid with pearl. There are 8 tuning pegs, 4 in front and 4 on the side. There are steel strings, and 14 movable gut frets; length 2 feet 6½ inches, width 6 inches.

The Tambour or Tamboura was in use in Egypt and Assyria 3,000 years ago. It is to be seen in the carvings and wall paintings of ancient Egyptians and was known by the name of *Nofre,* meaning beauty and goodness.

Kara—Sudan. A pear-shaped *Guenbii* of simple form.

Cambrah—West Coast. An elongated body hollowed out of a block of wood, the opening being covered with membrane and the strings fastened to strips of leather wound around the neck, the usual string-pegs being omitted.

Kakoshi—Masango tribe. This instrument which can be seen in the National Museum in Washington, the outlines of which resemble a violin, consists of hollow body, sometimes with, and sometimes without a sounding-board. Midway in its length is a cross-bar from which are stretched strings to the pegs, placed in a long neck. The cross-bar held in place by cords.

Kinandi—A "Devil's Harp," considered by some tribes to have magical power. No white man is allowed to approach it without uncovered feet.

Sanku—Gold Coast. A hollow wooden box, resembling a violin, the body of which is perforated with holes and covered with a skin to which is attached a long stick or neck. It has 8 strings, in 2 rows, supported perpendicularly by a bridge. Played with the fingers like a guitar and produces a soft and soothing tone. (Ashantee and the Gold Coast, by J. Beecham, 1841.)

Sehnku—Species of guitar. See above.

Sistrum—Abyssinia. An instrument of the guitar type found only in Abyssinia. "It evidences a stage of musical program (in Egypt) which some nations at present have not yet attained." Carl Engel, *Music of the Most Ancient Nations,* p. 243.

Koonting—Sort of guitar with 3 strings.

Gubo—Zulu. An instrument common throughout the tribes of South Africa. "It consists of a bow of bamboo, the string tightly stretched across it and this struck by a slender strip of split bamboo. The mouth of the player performs the office of sounding-board, one end of instrument being held to the lips with one hand, while the other manages the string. Performers can be seen sitting for an hour together with an instrument of this sort. They stick one end of the bow into the ground and fasten the string over a cavity covered with bark, which opens with an aperture for the escape of the sound. They pass one hand from one part of the bow to the other and with the other they play upon the string with the bamboo twig and produce a considerable variety of buzzing and humming airs which are really rather pretty.

"This is quite a common pastime with the lads who are put in charge of the goats. I have seen them apply themselves very earnestly and with obvious interest to their musical practice, and the ingenious use to which they apply the simplest means for obtaining harmonious tones testifies to their penetration into the secrets of the theory of sound." Schweinfurth, *The Heart of Africa*, Pg. 287-8.

Banjo—West Africa. A 6-string native banjo possessed by the Joloffs, who are said by A. B. Ellis (in the *Land of Fetish*, p. 10) to be the only real black people found in West Africa. They are natives of the country north of Gambia, dress in Arabian costume and claim the Arabians as their ancestors. A type most frequently met in the Sudan.

It is said that the earliest lyre of which we have any example is the 3-stringed lyre which has existed from time immemorial. Such a lyre was hung on the mast of Queen Hatasu's ship that she sent to the Coast of Arabia. The boated lyre always has the hollow shape and form of half a boat, built up in ribs and strings strung from point to point. The Greek lyre was evolved from this instrument.

Kisirka—Nubia. Boat-shaped lyre with slanted bow.

Robaba—Nubian. Another lyre akin to the robaba, is known to the Mittoo people. Schweinfurth in "The Heart of Africa," (p. 413), says that it *constitutes one of the evidences* that the *inhabitants* of the *Nile valley have real affinity with* the *tribes* of *Central Africa.*

The robaba is a cross between a lyre and a mandolin. It is formed from the large shell of the Annondout mussel and has 5 strings with a quadrangular sounding board, covered with skin with a circular sounding hole at each corner.

"*Chadangá li,*"—A one-stringed bow played horizontally like a flute; one end is held in the mouth and the other in one hand. Small snail-shells are attached to it. A simple bow-string gives forth a sylvan sound when struck with a quill plectrum and the shells rattle. The hand steadying the bow pinches the string at different points with various degrees of pressure and this produces a buzzing melody.

Maza'mbe—A variation of the Changali; 2 feet long, thicker at the middle than at the ends.

Kissar from Nubia, West Africa—Made of wood and leather; its body consists of wood hollowed in the form of a bowl and covered with sheepskin. The 5 strings are made of the intestines of the camel and are vibrated with the fingers by means of a plectrum made of a piece of horn or leather and fastened with a cord to the instrument. The fingers of the performer are used alternately with the plectrum.

It is tuned according to the pentatonic scale. Length 2 feet diameter 10½ inches. The Kissar is used in a worship dance ("Zar") in the Nile district. The instrument is known in Egypt. Specimen in New York Museum.

In the instrument found in the Kensington Museum and presented by the late Viceroy of Egypt, is a plectrum made of horn.

Angra Ockwena—British East Africa, Baganda tribe. A quadrangle body cut from a solid block of wood in form resembling an arm chair with a high back; 5 rods at the back and 5 fibre strings. The sounding board is bound to the body with strips of bark or fibre, the surface rudely ornamented with dots and lines of black paint. The specimen in the New York Museum is that of a very pretty instrument, the body decoration giving an impression of burnt wood. Length 3 feet 8 inches, width 4½ inches, depth 5 inches.

Magadis—Egypt. Small sounding-board over which are drawn strings to a cross piece.

Gubo—Kafirs and Zulus. Plucked or bowed strings. A narrow strip of wood between the ends of which are stretched strings of fibre. A section of the shell or gourd is attached to one end for a resonator, which is held against the body of the performer when the instrument is played. The tension of strings is regulated by twisting them to form a loop instead of winding about the pegs.

It is rarely sounded by means of a bow, but more often with the fingers or a plectrum.

Rabab—Kafir.

Rebec—More like a double-bass than a violin. The name came from Arabic term for "unbeliever." The name may also have come from Egypt and Persia. A like instrument was introduced into Spain by the Saracens and Moors. The rabab rested on the ground and was bowed like a 'cello.

A specimen is housed in the Museum at South Kensington, England. Its outline is similar to the mandolin, beautifully fretted with sound-holes and has 4 double strings which are tuned in pairs in fifths.

Zeze (*Tzete*)—Mombasa, East Africa—made of a handle of wood to which is attached a large gourd. It has a single string of vegetable fibre, length 4 inches, diameter 8 inches.

Another variety in Mombasa, differs from the *Zeze* in that it has two strings, one in front and one on the side. They pass over a bridge of hard quill. Length 2 feet 2 inches, diameter 7 inches.

Koundyeh or *Ngiemeh*—Sierra Leone.

A rude fiddle made from a cocoanut shell, its opening being covered with a membrane having a sound-hole. One string and long neck.

Goye—South Africa.

"Who on hearing of the Bori Goye-playing can fail to be reminded of the story of King Saul, who was also possessed by a dark spirit bound by the sweet music of the harp which David played?" Frobenius, "The Life of a South African Tribe," Vol. II, P. 571.

Igubu—Kafir.

The chief instrument of the Kafirs. It is made from a long stick which is bent like a bow by a string; the stick is fastened to a round gourd and the gourd placed on the breast which acts as a sounding board. When the string is struck with a piece of reed the instrument gives out a sort of monotonous tone. The natives play it for hours as they walk over the country. Dudley Kidd—"The Essential Kafir."

Marimba—

Mahambi or *Mihambi;* also known as Timbali and Valapo. The Marimba is known by various names according to the part of the country in which it is found. It is one of the commonest of African instruments and is very popular. It is a native piano. It is also called the xylophone by foreigners.

The West African variety has wooden keys, while iron-keyed marimbas are found in the East.

This African "piano" consists of two bars of wood placed side by side; in the south straight bars are used while in the northerly districts the bars are bent round. Across the bars are placed 15 to 20 pieces of hard wood of different lengths with a calabash hung underneath each. The pieces of wood that form the keyboard are graduated in length. It is played either resting upon the ground or suspended from the performer's neck by a cord and is beaten by two rubber-tipped sticks. In many instances the chamber below is ornamented.

The illustration given is the picture of a Marimba in the New York Museum.

SCALE OF 16-BAR MARIMBA WHICH I INSPECTED IN THE COMMERCIAL MUSEUM OF PHILADELPHIA

[From South Africa]

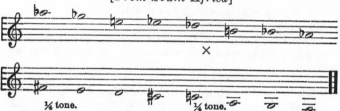

¼ tone.　　　　　　　　　　¼ tone.

A scale almost identical is voted from an African lyophone by Stephen Chauvet in "La Musique Negre."

The tone-color of the Marimba is sweet and clear and pleasant to the ear. In Sierra Leone it is known as the "Kalange." It is used in Argola, by the Portuguese in their dances; and it is also found in Central America. It was doubtless brought to that country by the slaves from Africa.

In certain districts in Africa its use is confined to princes of royal blood—this is true in the Kwango district of the Congo. Friedenthal in "*Musik, Tanz and Dichtung beiden Kreolen Amerikas,*" says that it is noticeable and worthy to note that the Marimba is used less by Africans and their descendants than by the civilized Indians or natives of Central America.

It is also interesting to note that when Percy Grainger introduced the Marimba in his orchestra work "In a Nutshell" (1917) played by the New York Philharmonic Orchestra, the press referred to it as a new instrument. The Marimba is often accompanied by rattles and drums.

Balfo—Belongs to harmonicon class, consists of metallic bars and wooden slabs.

Eleke—Mpongwe tribe, Gaboon, French Congo—akin to the Zanze.

Zanze or *Sansa*, Guinea, Central and South Africa.

Found in the upper and lower Guinea and similar to an instrument found at Delagoa Bay in neighboring South East Africa.

The natives hold the instrument in both hands and pluck vibrating tongues with the thumbs. The tone is regulated by lengthening or shortening the tongues which are adjustable. Krebiel says that it is an instrument so strongly built that it is likely to stand for centuries.

Oonpoochawa—The Zanze of Ashantee.

Ochingufu—It has a wooden body in form of a deep box with an open top. Struck by two beaters.

Mbi'la (or *Zanza*)—East Africa. A resonating box over which are clamped two banks of metal teeth or keys of different lengths which are snapped downward by the fingers emitting a hum of gentle sound.

A specimen seen from the Zambesi district, Central Africa, has an ornamented bottom of cut-shells and stone-beads.

Hearing the Mbi'la played by Mr. C. Kamba Simango (Ndau tribe, East Africa) one is delighted with the Aeolian like tone of the instrument accompanying the words of the singer.

Kisanjii—A Zanze of Angola—so called on the West Coast.

Vissandschi—A Zanze of the Bateka tribe.

Ganze—West Africa.

A box of light wood furnished with 23 iron keys and surrounded at the base with a leather band. The body is decorated with rude carving. It is held with the fingers of both hands, the keys being set in motion by the thumbs. Length, 1 foot; width, 8 inches; (smaller specimen, length, 6½ inches; width, 3½ inches).—*Musical Instruments and their Homes*, by Mrs. J. C. Brown and William A. Brown, p. 231.

Balangi—Sierra Leone.

Usually made from the wood of a dead rosewood tree cut to the proper size and then laid in the ground to season. After six months, it is taken out, cleaned, and after having been thoroughly oiled, it is placed, during the dry season, in the sun. After a few weeks, it is ready for use and the strings are fitted.

A similar instrument is made from a gourd, partly covered with goat skins and a narrow cross-piece of bamboo nailed over it. Tones are produced by striking the bamboo pieces with sticks.

Tapaka—A circular tambourine from North Coast.

T'Gutha—An instrument of the Hottentots, similar to *Kemangeh.*

Marcello—Consists of a series of slabs of hard wood strung together by means of twisted guts. The number of the notes vary from 8 to 10 or 12 bars. The tuning is not unlike our own diatonic scale from C to F, ½ tone lower.

It is said that certain Kafirs exhibit even more dexterity in execution than the best Hungarian cembalo players. The Kafir pieces start with weird phrase, the theme succeeded by remarkable variations, which are composed of rapid runs. These are not taken "glissando" but are actual runs made with incredible activity.—Algernon Roses' Private Collection.

In East Africa, the Thorbecke Expedition discovered a double marimba or xlophone, which was an unusual one.

Solomon Plaatje of Kimberly, South Africa, a native writer who died in 1932, told the author that the playing of the boys at Johannesburg on the timbila (Bantu xylophone), was indeed worth hearing. The singing of the primitive tribes and the playing of other instruments were equally marvelous.

The flute is well liked by the Africans, and they converse by it as they do with the drum. Among the Bongo, even the small boys make little flutes while their elders make instruments out of the most meagre materials.

"The flute of Heaven" is an instrument possessed by the Thonga Makakane of South Africa. They believe the flute to be enchanted and that its music forces Heaven to spare them.

A flute used by the natives on the Gold Coast is much larger than the European instrument. One variety is blown obliquely over the end which is half shut by a thin piece of wood. The holes on the side are governed with the fingers.

The Madi are expert flute players, and they spend much time in learning certain pieces. The Mandingo, the Buzi and the Temne and Mende of Sierra Leone are among the tribes that are fond of flute music.

The flute of the Kafir is often a length of bamboo cut off above the joint. When playing, the Kafir blows from right to left and hums while he plays, which produces the much-liked buzzing tone.

Mundo'le—Zulu, East Africa.

A flute made of bamboo, a straight piece having been cut between the knots of the stem. It has one hole through which the player blows and three or four holes near the bottom of the flute which are stopped with the fingers for differences of pitch. Its length is 2 feet.

As it is too loud for indoor use, it is used by the shepherds and cowherds.

Pwete—A corruption of the Fanti wood *keti*. A reed open at both ends with a little notch in the mouth-piece, which is scraped thin to divide the wind.

"Mr. Dalzel remarks that the King's women understand and practice the combination of the perfect concords, thirds and fifths and their little airs, played upon the flute and other instruments, are not inelegant." Sir Richard Burton—A Mission to Gele, King of Dahomey—Vol. 2, p. 115.

DAHOMEY AIR OF THE FLAGEOLETS

Quoted from Dr. M'Leod by Sir Richard Burton, "A Mission to Gelele," Vol. 2, page 115.

Gheteh—North Africa and Egypt. A single-beating reed. A tube of bamboo terminates in the metal bell and is fitted with a mouth-piece containing a single-beating reed.

E'raqyeh—A double beating reed found in Egypt. A cylindrical tube of wood with small air chamber situated just beneath the mouthpiece.

Duduben—Gold Coast North Africa. Long wooden instrument played like a clarinet.

Mam—"Lady Maket" pipes, considered the ancestor of the Egyptian pipes.

Zummarah—And the Arabian *Arghoul*, double pipes played with a single beating reed mouthpiece.

Zourna and *Zamr*—Found in North Africa and Egypt and are considered the earliest specimens of the conical tube fitted with a double beating reed.

Goura—An instrument peculiar to the Hottentots. It is made from a flexible rod of bamboo, a short distance from the end of which is inserted a peg and a bit of flattened quill. From the latter is drawn a string to the opposite end of the bamboo, where it is fastened.

When played, the quill is placed before or between the lightly-closed lips and the performer directs his breath so that the string vibrates like that of an Aeolian harp. *Chambers Journal*, September 7, 1872.

Whistle—Central Africa.

Open at both ends, and ornamented with silver wire. It is used to call the cattle at milking time and when not in use is worn as an ornament for the ear.

The African trumpets are made from horns of the Bongotragelaph (Boocercus) elephant tusks, and from great tree stems. When the trumpets are made of wood they are in imitation of ivory ones, both in shape and size.

Dongorah—A slim trumpet peculiar to the Mittoo. It is 18 inches long and resembles the "Mburah" of the Bongo.

The Mittoo trumpet is made of long gourd flasks with holes in the side. The musical performances of these people are said to be superior to the Bongo.

A trumpet known on the West Coast is in length, 1 foot 8 inches, the end broken.

Shipalapala—South Africa. A horn from the phifa antelope. When the chief wishes his men to assemble quickly and the distance is too great for the sound of the big drum to be heard, the courier blowing the Shipalapala runs to the capital of a sub-chief; there he transmits his message to another runner who starts at once with the trumpet to another district. This is repeated until the whole tribe is notified. At the sound of the trumpet, the warriors cry "a hi hlomen!" (to arms). The Shipalapala is also used to call the natives for dances and for feasts.

Manyinyee—Central Africa. Huge wooden trumpets varying from 4 to 5 feet in length. They are closed at the far end and ornamented with carvings representing a man's head. The other end is open and in an upper apartment is the opening into which the performer blows.

Another Manyinyee is made like a huge wine bottle. The performer takes it between his knees like a violoncello.

Tamboor—A trumpet, not to be confounded with the drum of similar name.

The African horn is usually made of ivory and blown from a hole in the side. Mary H. Kingsley, in *West African Studies*, writes that "It is a fine instrument and should be introduced into European orchestras, for it is full of colour."

The signal horns are to found in nearly every part of the continent and vary in size from the small signal whistle of the cattle herders of South Africa to the ivory horns of the native chiefs of the central portion of the country.

Ratzell (*History*, vol. 3, p. 39) says, "The greatest industry is expended in the manufacture of signal horns for use in war and witchcraft." Among the Madis these are straight in shape, made of wood and covered with lizard skin or leather, while the Latukas made them horn-shaped of ivory with a polished mouthpiece and most carefully protected by a cover.

Mangoal—Signal-horns of different antelopes. The tones are not unlike that of fifes. Has 3 holes like small flutes.

Mburrah—Long narrow pipe cut out of wood and which has a widened air-chamber close to the mountpiece very similar to the ivory signal-horn frequently seen in all Negro countries.

Mphalapa'la—Zulu. A horn of the sable antelope. It is used to summon the people to their chief and is also blown by heralds of marriage ceremonies.

King's War Horn—Blown from a side aperture. (Seen in the Commercial Museum, in Philadelphia.) Large carved tusk used to call tribes to war.

The Africans possess a goodly number of lesser instruments such as Rattles, Gongs, and Cymbals.

Nthamba—Zulu. Is a rattle made of the fruit of the Mutamba tree, which when dried is full of loose seeds.

Nthuzwa—A rattle deftly fashioned of a box made of woven reeds filled with pebbles. Square and flat.

Ngonge—A wooden bell cut from solid block of wood. Sometimes globular, sometimes irregular. They are worn, strung on the back of the women mourners, at funeral dances.

Cymbal—Soudan—Of iron and beaten in accompaniment to their drum. Length, 11½ inches.

The "Bull-roarer" (Yoruba)—A thin strip of wood 2½ inches broad, 12 inches long, tapering at both ends, which is fastened to a stick by a long string. It produces a strange roaring noise. Andrew Lang shows that it has been used in the mysteries of Ancient Greece, Australia, New Mexico, New Zealand and South Africa. It is an instrument of the forest god "Oro."

Sheré-Shango—Holy rattle.

Osé-Shango and *Oshé Shango*—Dance clubs, the upper portion decorated with heads and thunderbolts in combination. There are Edju dancing clubs of wood and ivory.

In Central South Africa, oblong boxes made of maize are filled with peas or stones and take the place of castanets, in Central South Africa.

Sistrum—Said by Carl Engel to be found only in Abyssinia; at the present day is known also in Nubia. It consists of a thin metal frame through which passes a number of metal rods. It is shaken by a handle and made to jingle. It was used by the Egyptians in the worship of Isis.

A few instruments known in Latin America are known as Creole instruments, the most important being the Marimba which was introduced into Guatemala by the Africans.

Cocha—Cuba. A kind of rattle made from Castilla Cane with hard seeds inside. They are used by the people of color and shaken in accompaniment to the guitar. Height 14 inches, width 6 inches.

Maruga—A tin rattle with shot inside. Length 11 inches.

Guiro—A long thin gourd with notches cut on the back. It is scraped by a thin stick. Length 16 inches; a longer one 18 inches.

Excellent illustrations of these instruments can be seen in *Musical Instruments and their Homes*, by Mrs. J. Crosby Brown and William Adams Brown.

NEGRO FOLK SONGS

These songs have an interesting history. "My Lord Delivered Daniel," a Negro Spiritual in major key of G, was noted in *Slave Songs of the United States*, 1867; *Jubilee Songs*, 1872, and *Hampton Plantation Songs*. Two variants are found—one in Florida, "O Daniel"; another from Kentucky, "My God Delivered Daniel." Apart from solo arrangements for voice, S. Coleridge-Taylor wrote a piano transcription, and a trio for violin, cello, and piano.

"Didn't my Lord Deliver Daniel," is noted in G minor in *Jubilee Songs*, 1872; *Slave Songs of the United States*, 1874; and *Story of the Jubilee Singers*, 1875. A variant from Kentucky is called "Didn't Old Pharaoh get Lost."

"Wrestling Jacob," is a spiritual found in four variants, of which Col. Higginson wrote in 1867, "It is one of the wildest and most striking of the series. There is mystical effect and passionate striving throughout the whole." While a paraphrase on the biblical text, the words had a special appeal to the Negro for Africans are very fond of stories of wrestling. Many interesting ones are found in the Bula Tales from Tamerun.

"Wrastling Jacob," a variant in A flat, is found in the *Calhoun Plantation Songs*.

"My Lord What a Morning," a Spiritual from the Southeastern Slave States noted in *Jubilee Songs*, 1872. A variant, "Stars begin to fall," noted in Slave Songs of the United States, 1867, comes from Edisto Island and a version, "My Lord what a Morning," is found in *Cabin* and *Plantation Songs*, Hampton, 1890-1901. "My Lord, what a Mourning," is a variant found in *Jubilee* and *Plantation Songs*, 1887. The theme of this Spiritual was used in "A New Hiding Place," written for piano by H. T. Burleigh.

"I Want To Be Ready," in E flat major, a religious song from Kentucky. Other variants are—"Walk Jerusalem Jes' like John"; Barton's *Recent Negro Melodies*, 1899; "When I came t'die," *Hampton Cabin and Plantation Songs*, 1901; and "Walk Jerusalem Jes like Job."

"Old Ship of Zion," a Spiritual from Maryland and Virginia is known in many variants. It was heard in Maryland in 1842, twenty-five years before it was noted in *Slave Songs of the United*

States, 1867. Possible variants are "Old Ship of Zion" heard sung by "Aunt Dinah" in Kentucky and noted by Rev. Barton, and "Don't you see that Ship a sailing," from North Carolina. A song almost identical, "In the old Ship of Zion, don't you weep after me," comes from Bahama Islands. According to Mr. Newman I. White, the song was mentioned in a book published in 1853. (Sarah Josepha Hale's *Liberia,* or *Mr. Peyton's Experiment.* New York, 1853, pp. 36, 41.)

Col. Higginson, in his essays in the *Atlantic Monthly* gives three versions of the song. It is composed of thirty or forty stanzas. The theme was used for the fugue in Henry F. Gilbert's Symphonic sketch, "Overture on Negro Themes."

"Inching Along," a song of assured faith, is unique in that only three notes of the scale are used in the scope of the melody. The song comes from Alabama and was noted in *Jubilee Songs,* 1872, and in *Story of the Jubilee Singers,* by Marsh, 1875. Possible variants are, "Keep a inchin' along," in *Calhoun Plantation Songs,* and an interesting version arranged by William Arms Fisher who secured the melody from Harvey B. Gaul of Pittsburgh.

"Great Campmeeting in the Promised Land," a spiritual in F major from South Carolina to Florida. Noted in *Slave Songs of the United States,* and in the *Hampton Collection,* 1901.

A variant, "O Brother, Don't Get Weary," is noted in 1867 from Florida. The scale is that of the flat seventh. The story is told that the hymn was made by a number of slaves who were not allowed to sing and pray, but at the death of the master this privilege was given them and in their joy they sang this Spiritual.

Julien Tiersot who visited America some years ago speaks of "A great Camp-meeting in the promised Land" as characteristic of the religious music of the Negro and finds it an "interesting and noteworthy similarity" that at the dictation of Taiti Negroes who visited France a few years ago, he had written down a song, equally religious, which closely resembled the American song in melodic and rhythmical structure.

To the student of the ethogeny of the South Sea Island natives, this would not be surprising.

"Go Down Moses," a song of slavery noted in *Jubilee Songs,* Part 1, 1872; *Story of the Jubilee Singers,* 1874; *Slave Songs of the Fisk Jubilee Singers,* 1874; and variant in *Hampton Series Negro Folk Songs, Book 1,* Natalie Curtis Burlin. Other variants are "Let God's Saints Come In" from Virginia, and "Go Down Moses" from Bahama Island.

This remarkably moving racial cry for delivery is a paraphrase on the Biblical text found in the first chapter of Exodus. The influence on the mind of the oppressed Negro, of the story of Moses who was divinely appointed to deliver the Israelites out of Egypt is perceptible. A Hebraic song of like sentiment is known. The Jews early settled in Egypt while many of them found refuge in Abyssinia. The Abyssinian language attests to this fact.

The subject of Moses appealed strongly to the Negro and he made use of it in many forms such as, ''Did not Old Pharaoh get lost?'' ''When Moses Smote the Water,'' and ''Turn Back Pharaoh's Army.'' ''When the Lord called Moses'' is a song from the middle southern states sung in the minor key with a flat seventh. Of the dramatic original ''Go Down Moses,'' Dvorák said the theme ''is as great as the motif in Siegfried.'' The song has no less than twenty-four verses.

''Nobody Knows de Trouble I've Seen,'' is a Spiritual of slavery, noted in *Slave Songs of the United States*, 1865, and in *Jubilee and Plantation Songs* as ''Nobody Knows the Trouble I See.'' Versions are found as ''Nobody Knows de Trouble I See, Lord'' from Florida, arranged for solo voice by James Weldon Johnson; and ''Nobody knows de trouble I've had,'' noted in *Slave Songs of the United States*, 1867. The early song comes from the Sea Islands and was heard sung in Charleston, South Carolina, before 1865. It is written in the pentatonic scale, and was heard in the Sea Islands when the Government had failed to carry out its promise in regard to the allotment of land to the freedmen. Gen. Howard, called to address the gathering of colored people, asked them to sing. The sad strains of the old song as it broke forth from the throat of an old woman, deeply affected the speaker. Mr. Krehbiel declares that the two emotional poles, despair and hopefulness, are touched in this song. A similar song, ''I'm a rolling,'' is found in the *Story of the Jubilee Singers* with their songs, by J. B. T. Marsh, 1875; in *Slave Songs of Fisk*, 1874, and in the Oliver Ditson *Collection*.

The original version has been arranged for solo voice by H. T. Burleigh, and Clarence Cameron White, while ''Nobody knows de trouble I see, Lord,'' has been arranged as a solo by H. E. Krehbiel, and a chorus for men's voices by Arthur Mees.

''Sometimes I Feel Like a Mother-less Child,'' a slave song from Mississippi, in the minor key, noted in *Cabin and Plantation Songs*, Hampton, 1874 and 1901; in *Negro Spirituals by Barton*, 1898; *Religious Folk songs of the Negro*, 1901 (third edition). Alice

Haskell quotes a variant known as "Moanin' Dove" heard in Beaufort County, South Carolina. "Sometimes I feel like I wanna go home, sometimes I feel like a motherless child, as I kneel by de roadside an' pray" was sung in Kentucky in triple time. There are many arrangements for solo voice, and a piano transcription, as well as a trio for violin, 'cello and piano by S. Coleridge-Taylor.

"I'm Troubled in Mind," a slave song noted with the flat seventh, and found in *Slave Songs of the United States*, 1867. A similar melody with different words, "O my Body Racked wid de Fever," comes from Georgia. "I'm-a Trouble in de Mind" is a version from Port Royal Islands. A Tennessee song is noted in *Story of the Jubilee Songs*, 1875. Piano transcription by S. Coleridge-Taylor.

"Don't Be Weary, Traveler," a slave song from Virginia in minor key, noted in "*Slave Songs of the United States*," 1867, and in *Cabin and Plantation Songs of Hampton*, 1874 and 1901. Solo arrangements and piano transcription by S. Coleridge-Taylor.

"Let Us Cheer the Weary Traveler," a slave song of hope found in Kentucky in the major mode. Noted in *Slave Songs of the United States*, 1867.

"I Long To See that Day," a slave song in major mode, known in the Bahama Islands, may be the original of several versions well known in America as "There's a Meeting Here Tonight." It is noted from Port Royal Islands in Slave Songs, 1867, and in Jubilee Songs in 1872. A variant, "My Way's Cloudy," is found in *Cabin and Plantation Songs of Hampton*.

Two distinct types of slave songs are familiar throughout the southern states. There are but few songs using the practice of slavery as a theme in the text.

"*Many Thousand Gone*," is found in Jubilee Songs, 1872, and in *Story of the Jubilee Singers, by Marsh*, 1875. The song originated during the war of the rebellion and was first secretly sung. Afterwards, when Beauregard took the slaves of the island to build fortifications at Hilton Head and Bay Point, they sang—

> "No more auction block for me,
>   No more, no more;
> No more peck o' corn for me,
>   Many thousand gone."

The peck of corn and pint of salt were rations doled out to the slaves.

"Is Master Goin' To Sell Us Tomorrow" is another slave song

depicting the heart-break and tragedy of the helpless enslaved. It appears in *Cabin and Plantation Songs*, Hampton, 1874 and 1901. *Jubilee and Plantation Songs*, 1887.

"O'er the Crossing," a Spiritual thought to be of African origin. Noted in *Slave Songs* of the United States, 1867, as a Virginia song, though it is known in many Southern States. A number of variants are found such as "My Body Racked 'Long Fever" from Port Royal Islands; "O Yonder's My Ole Mother," and "My Lord Called Daniel." Col. Higginson speaks of the song as "an infinitely quaint description of the heavenly road" while H. E. Krehbiel writes of the words—"Despite its rudeness, this song, because of its vivid imagery, comes pretty near to being poetry of the genuine type."

"The Gospel Train," a revival song, pentatonic, noted in Jubilee Songs, 1872, and in *Jubilee and Plantation Songs*, 1887. A variant is found in the Bahama Islands, "Get on Board," noted in Edward's *Songs and Stories*, 1895. Other variations are, "From Every Graveyard" and "Git on Board Little Children." *Hampton Cabin and Plantation Songs*, 1901.

Brown in *Lippincott's Magazine*, Dec. 1868, mentions in "Song of the Slave" a "Gospel Train" song conceived by Oscar Buckner, a Negro Slave, who visioned the conductor and brakeman as biblical characters.

"Roll Jordan Roll," a Spiritual in E major which shows the use of the flat seventh. It is a variant of the Bahama Island Song, "I Long To See The Day," noted by Charles Edwards in 1895, (*Bahama Songs and Stories*), and "Roll, Jordan, Roll" which was heard in South Carolina and noted in Slave Songs of the United States. The version as given in story of the *Jubilee Singers*, 1875, has been arranged for men's voices by Arthur Mees. The popular song of Jordan, sung before 1860, was parodied by a Negro soldier nicknamed "Elephant Iron," when on the road to St. Etienne in France. Music and words are given by Lieut. John J. Niles in *Singing Soldiers*.

"Somebody Knocking At Yo' Do'," a Spiritual in pentatonic scale noted in the Calhoun collection. A version, "O Sinner You'd Better Get Ready," is found in the Hampton collection, *Cabin and Plantation Songs*. A version which the author collected in Texas is, "Just Well Get Ready, You Got To Die."

An example of songs used as Burial Hymns is, "These Are My Father's Children." It is noted in *Jubilee Songs*, 1872, and in Marsh's *Story of the Jubilee Singers*, 1875.

The Rev. Mr. Barton, with whom the author had correspondence, quotes a variant, "Sooner in de Morning," while two other variants, "These Are All My Father's Children," from North Carolina, and "The Trouble of the World," from Royal Islands are noted in *Slave Songs of the United States*, 1861.

The editors of the latter collection say of the customs of sitting up and singing over the dead, a practice of native tribes in Africa, that it existed in the early days in South Carolina. When an elder member of the family died, the family assembled in the room in which was the coffin, and singing and marching around the casket, the children were passed first over and under the coffin according to age, after which those delegated to perform the duties of pallbearers, raised it on their shoulders and marched with it to the grave.

BIBLIOGRAPHY

American Composers on American Music, by Henry Cowell and others. Stanford University Press, Stanford University, California.

Africa, a journal published by the International Institute of African Languages and Culture. London, England.

Anglo-African Magazine, August, 1859.

Autographs of Freedom. Rochester, New York, 1853.

Ankerman, "Ethnologischa" Abt. 33.

Atlantic Monthly, February, 1862; May, 1864.

BALFOUR, HENRY, *Natural History of the Musical Bow.* Oxford, 1899.

BALLANTA-TAYLOR (Nicholas George Julius)—*Journal of West Africa,* July 14, 1930. *Saint Helena Island Spirituals.* Foreword. 1925.

BARNES, JAMES, "An interview" in *Musical America,* March 6, 1915.

BASSETT, RENE, *Revue des Traditions Populaires*—"Les Chants et les Contes des Ba Ronga." June, 1918.

BLEEK, DR., *Folk-Lore,* June 30, 1919.

Blackwood's Magaine, Discussions on "Barbadoes." October, 1833. London.

BURTON, SIR RICHARD, *A Mission to Glele, King of Dahomey. Lake Regions of Central Africa.* London, 1702.

BROWN, MARY E. and WILLIAM A., *Musical Instruments and Their Homes.* New York, 1908.

Boston Symphony Program Books—Philip Hale, historian-critic.

BOWDITCH, *Mission from Cape Gold Coast Castle to Ashantee.* London, 1902.

BURLIN, NATALIE CURTIS, *Songs and Tales from a Dark Continent.* New York, 1908.

CHRISTIANOWITSCH, *Esquisse Historique de la Musique Arabe aux temps anciens.* Cologne, 1863.

CHAPMAN, M. J., "Barbadoes," *A Poem of the West Indies.* London, 1833.

COLCORD, JOANNA, "Roll and Go" *Songs of American Sailormen.* Indianapolis, 1924.

COLERIDGE-TAYLOR, SAMUEL, *Twenty-four Negro Melodies Transcribed for Piano.* Boston, 1902.

Century Magazine, February, 1895.

CHAUVET, STEPHEN, *La Musique Nègre*. Paris, 1929.

CHILD'S "English Country Songs." *Ballads*, volume 2. Number 95. *Chamber's Journal*, September 7, 1872.

DALCROZE, *Eurhythmics, Art and Education*. New York, 1920.

DE BEAUVOIR, ROGER, *Le Chevalier de Saint-Georges*, Calmann Lévy, Editor. Paris, 1838.

DESDUNES, R. L., *Nos Hommes et Notre Histoire*. Montreal, 1911.

DE VAISSIERE, P., *Saint-Domingue*, 1629-1789.

DOUGLASS, FREDERICK, *Life and Times of Frederick Douglass*. Boston, 1883.

DUBOIS, W. E. B., *The Souls of Black Folk*. Chicago, 1909.

DUBOIS, FELIX, *Timbuctoo, the Mysterious*. Paris, 1907.

DUPONT, PAUL, *Biography of José White*. Paris, 1874.

EBOUE, M. FELIX, "The Banda, Their Music and Language" in *Revue du Monde Noir*, April, 1932. Paris. Mlle. P. Nardal, Sec. Gén.

ELLIS, A. B., *The Yoruba Speaking Peoples*. London, 1894.

ELLIS, GEORGE W., *Negro Culture in West Africa*. New York, 1914.

ENGEL, CARL, *Music of the Most Ancient Nations*. London, 1893.

FAUSET ARTHUR HUFF, "Folklore from Nova Scotia," *American Folk-Lore Society. Stories from Colored Canadians*.

FERRIS, WILLIAM H., *The African Abroad*. Vols. I and II. New Haven, 1913.

FISHER, WILLIAM ARMS, *Seventy Negro Spirituals*. Boston, 1926.

FROBENIUS, LEO, *The Voice of Africa*. Vols. I and II. London, 1913.

GREGOIRE, ABBE, *An Enquiry concerning the Intellectual and Moral Faculties of the Negro*. Paris, 1808.

GROUT, LEWIS, REV., *Zulu-Land and Life among the Zulu-Kafirs of Natal and Zulu-Land*. Philadelphia, 1864.

HALE, SARAH JOSEPHA, "Liberia or Mr. Peyton's Experiment," New York, 1853. Quoted by Newman I. White in *American Negro Folk Songs*.

HANDY, WILLIAM C., *The Folk-Blues as Music, An Anthology*. Introduction by Abbé Niles. New York, 1926.

HEARN, LAFCADIO, "Lafcadic Hearn and Congo Music" in *The Musician*. Boston, 1906. *Two Years in the French West Indies*.

HIGGINSON, THOMAS WENTWORTH, *Army Life in a Black Regiment*. Boston, 1870.

IDELSOHN, A. Z., Jewish Music *In Elements of Jewish Song*. New York, 1902.

JAHANGIR, *Memoirs*—1605-1627.

JOHNSON, JAMES WELDON, ''O Black and Unknown Bards'' in *Fifty Years and Other Poems*. Boston, 1918.

JOHNSON, GEORGIA DOUGLASS, *The Heart of a Woman*. Boston, 1918.

Journal of American Folk-Lore, vol. XXV.

Journal of Race Development, "Negro Social Life in West Africa,'' vol. IV.

JOUNOD, HENRI A., *Life of a South African Tribe*. Vols. I and II. New York, 1927.

KIDD, DUDLEY, *The Essential Kafir*. London, 1904.

KINGSLEY, MARY, *West African Studies*. London, 1901.

KING, GRACE, *New Orleans; The Place and People*. New York, 1899.

KREHBIEL, H. E., *Afro-American Folk Songs*. New York, 1899.

KING, STANTON C., *King's Book of Shanties*. Boston, 1893.

KRAPPE, ALEXANDER HAGGERTY, *Folk Song*.

LOTI, PIERRE, *Le Roman d'un Spahi*. Paris, 1881.

Lippincott's Magazine, December, 1868.

LOCKE, ALAIN (editor), *The New Negro*. New York, 1925.

MONTGOMERY, JAMES, *The West Indies and Other Poems*. London, 1814.

MURPHY, JEANETTE ROBINSON, ''The Survival of African Music in America,'' *Popular Science Monthly*, 1899, vol. IV, pp. 660-672.

Music and Drama, June 3, 1882.

Musical America, ''Gathering Folk-tunes in the African Country.'' September 25, 1926.

MOLONEY, SIR ALFRED, Gov. of Lagos, *Proceedings of Royal Geographical Society*, 1890.

WORK, MONROE, editor, *Negro Year Book*, Tuskeegee, Alabama. 1931-32.

NEWLAND, H. O., *Canoeing on the Rokelle; Sierra Leone*. London, 1916.

NILES, JOHN· J., *Singing Soldiers*. New York, 1927.

NERY, DE SANTA-ANNA, F. J., *Folk-Lore Brésilien*. Paris, 1889.

ODUM, HOWARD W., and GUY B. JOHNSON, *The Negro and His Songs*. Chapel Hill, 1925.

ORPEN, J. M., *Cape Monthly Magazine*, vol. IX, July, 1874.

OSGOOD, HENRY O., *So This is Jazz*. Boston, 1926.

PARK, MUNGO, *Travels in the Interior Districts of Africa*. London, 1800.

PARKMAN, DAILEY, and SIGMUND SPAETH. *Gentlemen be Seated, A Parade of Old-Time Minstrels*. Foreword by Daniel Frohman.

PLAATJE, SOLOMON T., *Sechuana (Bechuana) Proverbs with Literal Translations and Their European Equivalents*. London, 1906.

PIKE, G. D., *The Jubilee Singers of Fisk University*. Boston, 1872.

POUSHKIN, ALEXANDER, *Poems*, Translated from the Russian by Ivan Panin. Boston, 1888.

RATZEL, FRIEDRICH, *Volkerkunde, Die Naturvolker Afrikas*, Leipzig, 1895.

REISNER, GEORGE, *Lectures; and Bulletins of Boston Museum of Fine Arts and Harvard University Expedition in Egypt.*

RIBERA, JULIAN, *Cantigas de Santa Maria*, pp. 23-31; 43-57.

ROSE, ALGERNON, "Private Collection of African Instruments," *Monthly Journal International Music Society*, 1904.

ROSE, COWPER, *Four Years in Southern Africa*. London, 1905.

ROSENFELD, PAUL, *An Hour with American Music*. New York, 1907.

RUSSELL, J. H., *The Free Negro in Virginia*, 1619-1863. Baltimore, 1913.

Strad, The, "José White." July, 1909.

SCHOMBURG, ARTHUR, *Racial Integrity*. New York, 1913.

SCHWEINFURTH, H., *The Heart of Africa*, vols. I and II. New York, 1874.

SMITH, C. A., "Ballad Survival in the United States, *The Musical Quarterly*, January, February, 1916.

STANLEY, HENRY M., *In Darkest Africa*, vols. I and II. New York, 1891.

TAPPAN, LEWIS, "Disfellowshipping the Slave-holder," *Autographs of Freedom*, Rochester, 1854.

THEAL, G. McCALL, *Yellow and Dark Skinned People of South Africa*. London, 1910.

Theatre, The Arts, Monthly, "The Grand Old Days," June, 1931. *The Theatre Arts Monthly.*

Times, London Musical, "Haydn in London." May 1, 1909.

TROTTER, JAMES M., *Music and Some Highly Musical People*. Boston, 1878.

VUILLERMOZ, *Musiques d'Aujourd hui*, Paris. Freely Translated by Cm. S. C., October 13, 1923.

WALLASCHEK. R., *Vier Jahre im Africa*, vol. I.

COLLECTIONS

The Evert J. Wendell Collection of Sheet Music of the "Forties"— housed at Harvard University.

The "Maud Cuney-Hare Private Collection of Negro-American Music"—Sheet music, pictures and clippings.

Calhoun Collection—*Plantation Songs*, 2nd edition.

Calhoun—*Picture and Song*, 1909.

Allen, W. F., and others, *Slave Songs of the United States*. New York, 1867, 1874.

Hampton Series, *Negro Folk Songs, Book I. Cabin and Plantation Songs*. 1874, 1901.

Johnson, J. Rosamond, *The Book of American Negro Spirituals*. New York, 1925. An introduction by James Weldon Johnson.

White, Newman I., *American Negro Folk Songs*. Harvard University Press, 1928.

Krehbiel, H. E., *Afro-American Folk Songs*. G. Schirmer, New York and London, 1914.

Barton, Wm. E., *Negro Spirituals*. Boston, 1898.

Saint Helena Island Spirituals, Recorded and Transcribed at Penn Normal, Industrial and Agricultural School, Beaufort County, South Carolina, by Nicholas George Julius Ballanta-(Taylor). G. Schirmer, Inc. New York, 1925.

Johnson, J. Rosamond, *Utica Jubilee Singers Spirituals*. Oliver Ditson Co., Boston. An Introduction by C. W. Hyne.

Johnson, Hall, *The Green Pastures Spirituals*. New York, 1932.

INDEX

ABOUT THE EDITORS

Henry Louis Gates, Jr., is the W. E. B. Du Bois Professor of the Humanities, Chair of the Afro-American Studies Department, and Director of the W. E. B. Du Bois Institute for Afro-American Research at Harvard University. One of the leading scholars of African-American literature and culture, he is the author of *Figures in Black: Words, Signs, and the Racial Self* (1987), *The Signifying Monkey: A Theory of Afro-American Literary Criticism* (1988), *Loose Canons: Notes on the Culture Wars* (1992), and the memoir *Colored People* (1994).

Jennifer Burton is in the Ph.D. program in English Language and Literature at Harvard University. She is the volume editor of *The Prize Plays and Other One-Acts* in this series. She is a contributor to *The Oxford Companion to African-American Literature* and to *Great Lives From History: American Women*. With her mother and sister, she coauthored two one-act plays, *Rita's Haircut* and *Litany of the Clothes*. Her fiction and personal essays have appeared in *Sun Dog, There and Back*, and *Buffalo*, the Sunday magazine of the *Buffalo News*.

Josephine Harreld Love, pianist, music scholar, and arts administrator, is currently director of Your Heritage House, Detroit, Michigan, the fine arts museum for young people that she established in 1969. She has served on the music faculties of Oakland and Wayne State Universities and the University of Michigan. She developed the musicological research specialties of African-American music history and children's music in French-speaking parts of the world.